Labour Law in Great Britain

Labour Law in Great Britain

Seventh Edition

Mark Butler

This book was originally published as a monograph in the International Encyclopaedia of Laws/Labour Law and Industrial Relations.

Founding Editor: Roger Blanpain
General Editor: Frank Hendrickx
Volume Editor: Frank Hendrickx

Wolters Kluwer

Published by:
Kluwer Law International B.V.
PO Box 316
2400 AH Alphen aan den Rijn
The Netherlands
E-mail: international-sales@wolterskluwer.com
Website: lrus.wolterskluwer.com

Sold and distributed in North, Central and South America by:
Wolters Kluwer Legal & Regulatory U.S.
7201 McKinney Circle
Frederick, MD 21704
United States of America
Email: customer.service@wolterskluwer.com

Sold and distributed in all other countries by:
Air Business Subscriptions
Rockwood House
Haywards Heath
West Sussex
RH16 3DH
United Kingdom
Email: international-customerservice@wolterskluwer.com

ISBN 978-90-411-9963-8

e-Book: ISBN 978-90-411-9964-5
web-PDF: ISBN 978-90-411-9965-2

The Author

Mark Butler LL.B. LL.M. Ph.D. is a non-practising barrister and a Lecturer in Law at Lancaster University, specializing in employment law.

He is a graduate of the University of Manchester, where he completed all of his academic studies, including an LL.M. in International Business Law and a Ph.D.

He holds a Doctorate of Philosophy following the completion of a thesis that evaluated age discrimination protections across the then EU-25. He has been involved in European projects with the Council of Europe, the Fundamental Rights Agency and the European Commission. Since 2014, he has been the Deputy General Editor of Sweet & Maxwell's *Encyclopaedia of Employment Law*, as well as authoring several articles and books on labour law.

The Author

For wise and guiding friends in labour law everywhere.

Preface

I am grateful to the Kluwer team, in particular to Joeri Lauwers for kindly inviting me to continue the hard work of previous scholars and to contribute to the *International Encyclopaedia* with reference to Great Britain. To that end, this revised edition takes account of changes that have been brought in through a change in the UK government. However, as did my predecessor, I have largely retained the approach of its original authors and my learned predecessors, Professors Hardy, Fredman and Hepple.

However, over the last few years since the last British edition, British employment law has seen a change in direction, generally underpinned by the political ideology of the current Conservative government. This edition therefore concentrates on such changes. Of further interest, which is refernenced, is that since the previous edition was published the UK has voted to leave the European Union. Although it is unclear what this means from a labour law perspective, discussion on this has been added where it was considered necessary.

Can I especially express my sincere gratitude to: the UK's Equality and Human Rights Commission, Professor Catherine Barnard, David Cabrelli, Daniel Barnett, Professor Simon Deakin, John Hendy QC, Professor Sir Bob Hepple QC, Dr Virginia Mantouvalou, the late HHJ Jeremy McMullen QC, Rt. Hon. Lord Justice Ryder PC, Advocate-General Eleanor Sharpston QC, and Professor Robert Upex amongt other key labour law scholars, as well as colleagues at the Universitiy of Lancaster. A special thanks goes to Professor Stephen Hardy who continues to provide invaluable support in my academic endeavours, and who introduced me to this text.

As ever, my heartfelt thanks to my family whom have been ever supportive in allowing me to complete this edition.

Finally, the dedication and hard work of the publishing team have made this edition once more possible. All credit to them. The errors are mine with the usual disclaimers.

Preface

Table of Contents

List of Abbreviations

ACAS	Advisory, Conciliation and Arbitration Service
All ER	All England Law Reports
BERR	Department of Business, Employment and Regulatory Reform
BIS	Department of Business Innovation and Skills
CA	Court of Appeal
CAC	Central Arbitration Committee
CBI	Confederation of British Industry
CO	Certification Officer
CRE	Commission for Racial Equality
DDA	Disability Discrimination Acts 1995 and 2005
DRC	Disability Rights Commission
DTI	Department for Trade and Industry
DWP	Department for Work and Pensions
EA	Employment Act 2008
EAT	Employment Appeal Tribunal
ECtHR	European Court of Human Rights
ECHR	European Convention on Human Rights 1950
ECJ	European Court of Justice
ECR	European Court Reports
EC	European Community
EES	European Employment Strategy
EHRC	Equality Human Rights Commission
EOC	Equal Opportunities Commission
EqPA	Equal Pay Act 1970
EqA	Equality Act 2010
ERA	Employment Rights Act 1996
ERelA	Employment Relation Acts 1999 and 2004

List of Abbreviations

ESM	European Social Model
ET	Employment Tribunal
EU	European Union
HRA	Human Rights Act 1998
HL	House of Lords
ICR	Industrial Cases Reports (formerly Industrial Court Reports)
ILJ	*Industrial Law Journal*
ILO	International Labour Organization
IRLR	Industrial Relations Law Reports
JES	Job Evaluation Study
KIR	Knight's Industrial Reports
MLR	*Modern Law Review*
OJLS	*Oxford Journal of Legal Studies*
OMC	Open Method of Coordination
QBD	Queen's Bench Division of the High Court
RRA	Race Relations Act 1976
SC	Supreme Court of the UK
SDA	Sex Discrimination Act 1975
TLR	Times Law Reports
TUC	Trades Union Congress
TULRCA	Trade Union and Labour Relations (Consolidation) Act 1992

Introduction

Chapter 1. General Features

§1. A Comparative Perspective

1. In his celebrated, seminal book *The Worker and the Law* the late Lord Wedderburn's controversial opening: 'Most workers want nothing more of the law than that it should leave them alone', still bears testament today to the disdain for overlegalism in labour law.

Moreover, as the founding author of this monograph, Professor Sir Bob Hepple QC FBA, records:

> Industrial relations make the case for Great Britain to be regarded as the innovating state of labour law. Consequently, Great Britain was for a time not only the 'workshop' of the world, it was also an exporter of labour law. The 21 million British citizens who emigrated during the 19th and early 20th centuries, to the United States, the British colonies and overseas dominions, took with them not only the attitudes and behaviour they had learnt in the industries of the mother country.

Which places Great Britain's labour law into its true context where its construction was built on the pretext of age-old English common law which, ideologically, epitomizes the *laissez-faire* liberal capitalism which became ascendant in Great Britain between 1820 and 1850. Consequently, its legacy is that Great Britain stands apart, as a comparative neighbour of the Roman-Germanic civil law systems, prevalent elsewhere in Europe.

2. However, from these humble and restrictive beginnings, Britain was the first country (1824) to legalize trade unions, and the liberal and utilitarian beliefs behind this era of toleration, in which collective bargaining could begin to develop, spread over the next decades to other parts of Europe. French and German workers, sponsored by their governments, came to Britain at the time of the Great Exhibition to study how the new reformist British trade unions worked. The 19th-century British factories and workmen's compensation legislation served as a model in many parts of the world, as far apart as France and Japan. As Hepple[1] notes, it was the pioneer

1. B. Hepple, in *The Making of Labour Law in Europe: A Comparative Study of Nine Countries to 1945* (London, 1986), p. 2.

of British socialism, Robert Owen, who can be regarded as the 'father' of international labour law because as early as 1818 he carried on his campaign to end the exploitation of human resources into Europe and presented a petition to the Five Powers then meeting at Aix-la-Chapelle, appealing to them to regulate working hours throughout the continent. His petition was dismissed, but when at the end of the century the movement was revived Britain played a leading role in the various conferences which culminated in the founding of the ILO in 1919. Successive British governments promoted international standards not infrequently based on British practice.

3. By comparison with civil law countries, the British trade union organization in its early years seemed archaic, the structure of industrial relations appears to be chaotic, labour law is uncodified, the common law contract of service is still the cornerstone of legal thinking, and there is an absence of positive legal rights to organize and to strike. In 1954, Otto Kahn-Freund could write that 'there is, perhaps, no major country in the world in which the law has played a less significant role in the shaping of [labour–management] relations than in Great Britain, and in which today the legal professions have less to do with labour relations',[2] and in 1959 he again remarked on the British 'policy of abstention on the part of the law and the reluctance to apply legal sanctions'.[3] In some senses, this reference to 'abstention' of the law was misleading.

For one thing, it was wrong to imply that the State was an essentially neutral party to industrial conflict. For another thing, there *was* a great deal of regulatory legislation on subjects such as health and safety in factories, mines and some other workplaces, minimum wages in 'sweated' trades, workmen's compensation for accidents, and the law of social insurance, the latter inspired by Bismarck's Prussian/Germanic welfare system. Moreover, Kahn-Freund's description of British voluntarism could be regarded as an accurate one right up to the 1960s and, in some respects, even later. In the field of collective labour relations, British labour law, unlike that in most comparable countries, conferred no positive rights to organize and to strike, despite the growing political power which the unions could have used, but did not, to secure these rights. Legal intervention was largely limited to a series of negative immunities from the judge-made common law, which was hostile to collective action, and to some relatively weak supports for collective bargaining.

4. Between 1963 and 1979 it seemed that Britain was feeling its way towards a more legally regulated system of industrial relations. In 1963 Britain became the last country in Europe (apart from Ireland) to introduce statutory minimum periods of notice to terminate employment, and this was followed by a whole series of new rights, especially on unfair dismissal, for individual employees. The US model of anti-discrimination legislation was transplanted into the different social and legal climate of Britain, and membership of the EEC (from 1973) brought with it a new

2. O. Kahn-Freund, Chap. 11, 'The Legal Framework' in A. Flanders and H.A. Clegg (eds.), *The System of Industrial Relations in Great Britain* (Oxford, 1954), p. 44.
3. O. Kahn-Freund, 'Labour Law' in M. Ginsberg (ed.), *Law and Opinion in England in the 20th Century* (London, 1959), p. 238.

range of social legislation on matters such as collective redundancies, acquired rights on the transfer of undertakings and equal pay. For a time, between 1971 and 1974, it seemed that US Taft–Hartley style laws would serve as the main instrument for the restructuring of collective labour relations in Britain, but the Industrial Relations Act 1971 failed, not least because it was based on the mistaken assumption that employers would use the law and that trade union leaders would cooperate with it. It was followed by a 'social contract' between the Labour government (1974–1979) and the Trades Union Congress (reminiscent of such other famous accords as the Danish September 1899 agreement, the French Matignon Agreement (1936) and Grenelle *constat* (1968) and the German Margaretenhof agreement (1954)). This produced a great volume of new legislation and enhanced the role of the employment tribunals (established in 1964), which, like labour courts in other countries, are composed of employer and worker members alongside a legally qualified chairman. However, this period was marked by a growing conflict between incomes policies, which interfered with collective bargaining, and reformist legislation, which aimed to support and encourage the development of collective bargaining.

5. A radical change in direction was signalled by the election in May 1979 of a right-wing Conservative government which abandoned both direct incomes policies and support for collectivism. Instead, it implemented a consistent strategy of legal restrictions on trade unions and the restoration of market regulation. The preoccupation of state policies with the power of trade unions distinguished the response of Britain to the economic crisis from that of other Western European countries. In many countries the inflexibility of labour markets was seen as a major cause of the crisis, and measures were adopted to reduce labour costs and to deregulate employment protection laws. The British government during this period also resorted to measures of this kind, which involved the denunciation of no fewer than five ILO conventions (on public contracts, minimum wage-fixing machinery, the protection of wages, night work and underground work for women). In developments of this kind Britain moved earlier and further than other Western European governments. The trend to deregulation was not unique, but in those other countries the systems of labour law have generally retained the values of democratic pluralism.

Unions were still seen as the 'social partners' of the employers; collective bargaining remained at the centre of labour relations. In Britain, by contrast, the main thrust of the government's strategy was built around attempts to weaken trade unions, through measures such as the privatization of heavily unionized public corporations, the devolution of industrial relations to the workplace where unions were relatively weak in a time of high unemployment, and legislation which severely restricted the freedom to organize, to bargain and to strike. These policies were put dramatically to the test, notably in a series of conflicts between the unions and the law in the miners' strike (1984–5) and in the disputes in the printing industry (1983–6). In this period the British government was willing to defy international standards, such as in its refusal to accept the findings of the ILO Committee on Freedom of Association in 1984 that the withdrawal of trade union rights for some civil servants constituted a violation of ILO conventions. Britain vigorously opposed attempts by the EU to extend its activities into the social sphere. Thus in December

1989, the UK government stood alone in refusing to support the Community's Charter of Fundamental Social Rights of Workers, and opposed several of the draft directives which emerged under the EU Commission's Action Programme to implement the Charter. In December 1991, the UK objected to a new 'Social Chapter' in the Maastricht Treaty on European Union, leaving the then other 11 Member States to reach their own agreement on social policy.

6. Hepple's observation in the original editions of this title, that 'The winds of labour law [had] changed again since the election to power in 1997 of a new Labour government' was further reinforced in the sequel of two general elections in 2001 and 2005, where the then Labour government retained power. In 1997 the new Labour government moved quickly to reverse the ban on trade unions at GCHQ, to incorporate the European Convention on Human Rights, and to 'sign up' to the Social Policy Agreement, which is now incorporated into the Treaty of Amsterdam (see paras. 18–20 below). Simultaneously, from 1997–2006, New Labour deliberately distanced itself from the traditional socialist policies of its predecessors, instead seeking to take the countries approach to employment relations and associated protections in an entirely new direction. Central to its policies was the view that conflict in industrial relations should be replaced by cooperation, and that the key to successful industrial relations is a combination of both efficiency and fairness.

This New Labour philosophy was set out in the policy White Paper *Fairness at Work*, published in 1998, and enacted in its Employment Relations Acts of 1999 and 2004. Here it was stressed that while the proposals for a labour law framework were based on the rights of the individual, whether exercised on their own or with others, the government's aim was to replace the notion of conflict with the promotion of partnership. The then government, while offering new rights, demanded that employees in return accepted their responsibilities to cooperate with employers. Such an approach can be quite neatly summed up: 'The days of strikes without ballots, mass picketing, closed shops and secondary action [were] over.'

Instead, the aim of the government at that time was to achieve the 'most lightly regulated labour market of any leading economy in the world' while at the same time, affording British workers 'basic canons of fairness'. So far as the creation of new rights was concerned, arguably the most radical was the provision of a new procedure for statutory recognition of unions for bargaining purposes. This statutory process was supplemented by an individual right to be accompanied by a trade union official or co-worker in disciplinary or grievance procedures. This enhanced the role that trade unions could and ought to have played in resolving disputes. Also important was the introduction of a national minimum wage. Other significant developments included the introduction of a qualified right not to be dismissed while taking industrial action, and a reduction in the qualifying period that applied when accruing the right not to be unfairly dismissed. The commitment to implement the Social Policy Agreement at Maastricht, now incorporated into the Treaty of Amsterdam, led to the promise to provide a range of 'family friendly' rights, including the right to a period of unpaid parental leave, and to equality between part-time and full-time workers. On the other side of the ledger, the government committed itself to maintaining the key elements of the employment legislation introduced by the Conservative government during the 1980s, including a continuance of restrictive laws on picketing and the prohibition of the closed shop. From 2001–6, the British government has sought to attain its outstanding goals, by way of introducing statutory procedures for dismissals, parity for part-, full-time and fixed-term workers, as well as introducing enhanced maternity and paid paternity leave. Since 2007, under the Brown premiership, new Labour sought to consolidate its reforms and even repeal some of its changes. Most notably, its Employment Act 2008 which repealed the statutory procedures enforced since 2004 and the then pending Equality Bill 2009, marking out the electoral banner for the forthcoming General Election in 2010.

Yet, following the 2010 General Election and the emergence of Coalition Government, given the major parties' inability to form a majority Government for the first time in post-war Britain, the Conservative-Liberal Democrat Government set about with zeal to reduce red-tape and remove employment laws. To that end, the Equality Act 2010 was a diluted version of that originally proposed by the outgoing Labour Government. Further, the Coalition Government immediately sought to increase the qualifying period for employment protection from dismissal up to a two-year qualifying period. Moreover, as Hepple observed ('Back to the Future: Employment Law under the Coalition Government'[2013] ILJ Vol. 42 pp. 203-223) their 'pushmi-pullyu' approach challenged the neo-liberal hegemony in terms of reforming the Tribunal Rules and the introduction of fees as a pre-requisite gateway to access to the employment litigation landscape.[4] This period can be categorized as employment laws being ruled by market forces.

Since May 2015 the Conservative Government has formed a majority Government in Britain. And although there was some tinkering of employment laws, much of the political period since 2015 has been dominated by the topic of Brexit. The Conservative manifesto that resulted in the party returning to sole power including a promise to hold a referendum on membership to the EU. This was duly held on 23 June 2016. Against many predictions of experts, the British public voted to trigger Article 50 of the Treaty of the European Union and leave the Union. As a result of this referendum decision, then leader leader of the Conservative Party, and Prime Minister, David Cameron opted to resign from post. In a party leadership challenge, Theresa May was selected to replace David Cameron as party leader, and thus was appointed the new Prime Minister. Quite significantly going forward, Theresa May sits more to the right wing of politics than David Cameron, and appears to very much reflect the neo-liberal ideology at the centre of the Conservative Party. This may have consequences for employment laws in the future. However, in a miscalculation and with a view to strengthening her political position, Theresa May held a further general election on 8 June 2017. The result was that the Government's majority was significantly reduced. This makes it much more difficult for the Government to push through any contentious reforms.

The UK is set to leave the EU by April 2019. At present negotiations are ongoing. It remains unclear what implications there will be for employment rights on Brexit. The current government is making promises that workers' rights will be

4. These fees have recently been struck down as unlawful by the Supreme Court, resulting in a fee no longer being payable for access to the employment tribunals.

retained and not watered down. However, it remains to be seen whether this will be the case. In the background is the neo-liberalist ideaology on which the party is founded, and on which the current Prime Minister subscribes to. There is also the euroscepticism that is prevalent on the Government backbenches. And that the Conservative Party was opposed to the decision of the 1997 Labour Government to sign up to the EU's Social Policy Agreement, from which many employment rights have derived. It is a period of uncertainty in Britain as to what direction employment rights will go in next.

§2. Geography and Population

I. The Countries

7. The island of Great Britain comprises England (total area including inland water 130,410 square kilometres), Wales (20,758 square kilometres) and Scotland (including its many inhabited islands 78,789 square kilometres). Separated from north-western Europe by the natural 'moat' of the English Channel, the island has avoided foreign invasion since 1066. To the west, across the Irish Sea, lies Ireland which the British colonized from early times until 1922.

8. England was united as a kingdom over a thousand years ago and Wales became part of this kingdom during the Middle Ages. The thrones of England and Scotland were dynastically united in 1603 and in 1707 a single Parliament was established for the whole of Great Britain. In 1800 the United Kingdom was completed by a union joining the Irish Parliament and that of Great Britain. In 1922 southern Ireland (now the Republic of Ireland) became a self-governing country. The six counties of Northern Ireland had in 1920 been given their own subordinate Parliament and they have remained within the United Kingdom. As noted earlier, this monograph is concerned only with Great Britain. Northern Ireland and the Republic of Ireland are the subject of separate monographs in this series. Scotland did hold a rReferendum on Independence in 2014. However, the decision of the Scottish people was to remain part of the United Kingdom. The current majority party of the Scottish Parliament, the Scottish National Party, have mooted the possibility of a second referendum on the matter of independence. However, support for this appears to have waned.

9. When studying British statistics it is important to note whether they refer to England alone, to England and Wales, to England, Wales and Scotland (i.e. Great Britain) or to the United Kingdom as a whole. United Kingdom statistics and other data sometimes include the Isle of Man (558 square kilometres) and the Channel Islands (194 square kilometres), which strictly are not part of the United Kingdom but are dependencies of the Crown.

II. The People[5]

10. According to the 2011 Census in the UK, the estimated population was 63.7 million (of which 2 million lived in Northern Ireland). This can be further contrasted with the figure of 38.2 million in the UK in 1906. The majority (about 50 million) reside in England (see http://www.ons.gov.uk/ons/taxonomy/index.html?nscl=Population, for details).

11. The people of Great Britain were traditionally relatively homogeneous, with none of the linguistic, cultural or religious divisions which characterize either Northern Ireland or parts of continental Europe. Living in a unitary state, whose boundaries have remained stable for centuries, most of the inhabitants share the English language (although in Wales there has been a revival in recent years of Welsh which now enjoys the status of an official language under the Welsh Language Act) and there is a fairly uniform system of free secular popular education up to the age of 16. The Anglican church has been a state church since the 16th century (as is the Presbyterian church in Scotland), subordinate to the ruling political class; dissenting minorities secured rights to equal treatment during the 19th century and non-conformism has had an important influence on sectors of the working class, particularly in Wales. The British traditions of religious and cultural tolerance have meant that groups of political refugees, such as the Huguenots in the 17th century, the East European Jews in the late 19th century and the post-war Polish and Hungarian exiles, have been readily integrated. So Britain has escaped the phenomenon of religious, linguistic or racial divisions in the trade union and labour movements.

12. Race relations have, however, become an important factor in social and industrial life as a result of the influx, since the late 1950s, of economic migrants from the New Commonwealth countries such as the West Indies, India and Pakistan.

At the census held in 2011, one in eight UK citizens were born abroad. Nevertheless, racism remains a serious problem in Britain, manifesting itself in a variety of ways, including open hostility, discrimination in education and employment, disadvantage and exclusion from access to material benefits and decision-making. There have been suggestions across the media that incidents involving open hostility on racial grounds have increased dramatically following the Brexit referendum.

§3. Political and Legal System

I. Constitution

13. The British constitution is not to be found in a basic document or set of documents. It has evolved over the centuries and consists of Acts of Parliament and

5. These and other demographic statistics are derived from the Office of National Statistics website, www.statistics.gov.uk, in *Population and People Trends* (London, National Statistics, 2009).

other legislation, judge-made common law and precepts and practices known as constitutional conventions. These conventions are political usages, not directly enforceable in courts of law. The most important feature of the constitution is parliamentary sovereignty. Parliament (which means effectively the democratically elected House of Commons because the House of Lords has only a delaying power) can enact any law on any subject; even the rules and conventions of constitutional law can be changed by ordinary legislation. This means that there are not the formal restraints against encroachment on individual liberties which exist in other liberal democracies. The United Kingdom government is a party to the European Convention on Human Rights, but, until 1998, the terms of the Convention were not enacted as part of domestic law (in force since 2000). Concern over issues such as the denial of the right to belong to trade unions at the government Communications Headquarters (GCHQ) by the Conservative government in 1984, and earlier legislation by a Labour government permitting compulsory trade union membership (the closed shop) has led in recent times to pressures for the incorporation of a Bill of Rights.

Indeed, this was a central manifesto commitment of the Labour Party when it was elected to power in 1997. The newly elected Labour government moved swiftly to honour its commitment, and enacted the Human Rights Act 1998, which incorporated the European Convention of Human Rights into domestic law. However, there remain at least three fundamental limitations on the effectiveness of the Human Rights Act. First and most important, the statute was deliberately framed in such a way as to preserve parliamentary sovereignty. British courts are not empowered to strike down legislation passed by Parliament even if it is held to conflict with a Convention right. Instead, they have only the power to declare that such a breach has occurred, in the hope that Parliament will move to correct the defect. Second, the Act simply transposed Convention rights as a whole, without adapting or updating them. Thus, although the Convention includes the freedom to associate in trade unions, it does not provide for a right to strike or to bargain collectively. Finally, the Act specifically binds only public bodies or bodies carrying out private functions, and can only be invoked by victims of the breach. Thus most private employers acting in their capacity as employers (which has been held to be a private function) will not be bound directly by the Act. It should also be noted that although the Act was passed in 1998, it did not come into effect until October 2000.

14. Parliamentary government does not, however, mean government by Parliament. The public or civil service is non-partisan and serves the government in office; its members enjoy security of employment irrespective of the political complexion of the party in power. The government consists of members of both Houses of Parliament (mostly drawn from the Commons). The Cabinet is collectively responsible to the Commons; a government that lost the support of a majority in the Commons would have to resign or call an election. The government is not, however, the delegate of Parliament. Because of the way in which the two-party system operates, the government is generally able to command Parliamentary support for the implementation of its policy. Those who are baffled by the apparently sudden reversals of legislative policy should remember that apart from times of war or national emergency (as in 1931) there has never been a coalition government in Britain. Where major policy differences exist between the Conservative and Labour Parties, it can be expected that the party with a parliamentary majority will be able to reverse the legislation initiated by its predecessor. At various times, however, the largest party in the Commons has had to rely on the parliamentary support of the small Liberal Party and the Scottish and Welsh Nationalists. For example, the minority Labour government's labour relations legislation introduced in March 1974 could not be carried in full because of the absence of support from these smaller parties, and also because of the use of their delaying powers by the House of Lords in which there was, until the reforms at the very end of the 20th century, a majority of hereditary Conservative peers. The emergence in 1980 of a Social Democratic Party (SDP) in alliance with the Liberal Party signalled the possibility that future governments might consist of a coalition of more than one political party. This possibility, however, remained faint so long as the electoral system continued to be based on a constituency based 'first-past-the-post' system which can produce far larger majorities in Parliament than the proportion of electoral support enjoyed by a particular party. Thus after the 1987 election, it seemed clear that the two main parties would continue to dominate the electoral scene. In fact, the years between 1979 and 1997 were characterized by the overwhelming predominance of the Conservative Party in Parliament, followed by an even greater dominance of the Labour Party between the years 1997 and 2010. This pattern could well change if proportional representation is introduced. An electoral system based on proportional representation has already produced coalition government in the devolved Scottish legislative assembly. As recent as January 2010, Parliament held a free vote to consider whether an alternative vote system could be used for future General Elections. The vote resulted in maintenance of the status quo. Electoral change looks unlikely to happen anytime in the foreseeable future.

II. Trade Unions and the Political System

15. An understanding of the relationship between collective bargaining and legislation enacted by Parliament is impossible unless two vital facts are borne in mind. First, which as Professor Sir Otto Kahn-Freund has emphasized,[6] is that British trade unions won minimum labour standards, without the aid of legislation, before the franchise was extended to the town artisan in 1867 and to the country operative and miner in 1885. The suffrage never assumed the same importance in the formative period of the British unions as it did elsewhere in Europe. The British unions came to rely on their industrial strength rather than the parliamentary struggle. Secondly, the trade unions had given birth to their own leaders and their own pragmatic, reformist organizations, long before the socialist movement assumed importance. The socialists who formed the Marxist Social Democratic Federation (SDF) in 1884 and the less orthodox Independent Labour Party (ILP) in 1893, faced an already established trade union leadership, predominantly liberal in outlook. In 1900 a number of unions affiliated to the Trades Union Congress (TUC) combined

6. O. Kahn-Freund, in M. Ginsberg (ed.), *Law and Opinion in the Twentieth Century* (London, 1959); *Selected Writings*, London, 1978.

with the SDF, ILP and Fabian Society to establish the Labour Representation Committee from which emerged the Labour Party. British trade unions are the products of the practical organization of wage earners and are not the creation of political parties; nor are they the outcome of a socialist critique of society as they are in some other European countries.

16. There is no organizational link between the TUC and the Labour Party, although there is a regular liaison. Individual trade unions, representing about half the total affiliated membership of the TUC, are affiliated to the Labour Party. Trade union block votes traditionally exercised a decisive influence on Labour Party conferences and shifts in the political balance between right and left in unions were therefore be reflected in shifts in Labour Party policy. However, after successive electoral defeats during the 1980s and early 1990s, reforming party leaders were determined to end the union block vote and replace it with one member, one vote.

This was gradually achieved during the 1990s and unions no longer have direct representation on parliamentary selection. However, they continue to play an active part in labour party policy making. There are 22 trade unions currently affiliated to the Labour Party at national level.

III. Legal Systems

17. England and Wales, on the one hand, and Scotland, on the other, have different systems of law, different legal professions and a different judiciary as well as different education systems and different local government organization. In order to extend this devolution of decision-making from London, a Scottish Parliament and Welsh Assembly, with limited law-making powers, were set up in 1999.[7] At present, Acts of Parliament do not extend to Scotland and Wales, unless they are expressly stated to do so. In practice nearly all labour legislation does expressly extend to the whole of Great Britain and it is only a few old Acts which are peculiar to a single law district. Moreover, employment and industrial relations are a reserved matter and therefore not devolved to the Scottish Parliament. The English common law, by which is meant here all the law that is not the result of legislation, differs in some important respects from Scots law. Scots law today is a hybrid system with roots in the Roman (civil) law as well as being under the living influence of the English common law.

IV. European Union (EU)

18. The United Kingdom became a member of the European Economic Community on 1 January 1973. Since then, both the powers and the size of the Community have expanded considerably. The Treaty on European Union (the Maastricht Treaty), which came into force in 1993, added two new 'pillars' to European Community law, to form an overarching European Union. The 1993 Treaty was again

7. Scotland Act 1998, Schedule 5, Part II, H1.

amended by the Treaty of Amsterdam, which came into force in 1999. During this period, the commitment of the European Community to social law has gathered pace. The founders of the Community considered that social and employment law was an area which should remain in the jurisdiction of Member States, and that the establishment of a common market would be sufficient on its own to bring about increasing standards. Thus, although the Treaty of Rome declared that the Community was committed to promoting better working conditions for workers, legislation to achieve this was not considered necessary. There were only two important exceptions to this, namely free movement of labour and equal pay for men and women. During the 1970s it became clear that the establishment of a common market was not sufficient and in 1972 the heads of government committed themselves to a Community which gave equal priority to social policy as to the realization of economic union. However, in the absence of a Treaty amendment, there was still no secure basis for Community legislation in the social field. Only legislation which could be shown to be necessary to attain one of the objectives of the Community, or to remove an obstacle which directly affected the functioning of the common market was permitted under the Treaty of Rome. The result was that, outside of the area of equal pay (see below) and of health and safety, only three major directives emerged during the 1970s. The Collective Redundancies Directive (75/129) provided for consultation of workers in cases of mass redundancy; the Insolvency Directive (80/987) protected workers in cases of insolvency; and the Acquired Rights Directive (77/187) protecting workers in cases of transfers of undertakings. Following a decade of near stagnation of social policy, the drafters of the Maastricht Treaty hoped to put social policy on an entirely new footing, to reflect a positive commitment on the part of the Union to social as well as economic aims. The Social Chapter was intended to give clear powers to implement social policy law. However, because of unyielding opposition by the UK government, still at that stage dominated by the Conservative Party, the Social Chapter was annexed to the Treaty as an Agreement binding only on 11 of the then 12 members of the Union, excluding the UK. The electoral success of the Labour Party in Britain in 1997 removed this obstacle, and the Treaty of Amsterdam incorporated an amended version of the Agreement into Articles 136–143 EC (now Articles 252–259 of the Treaty of Lisbon). Legislative powers are divided into three categories:

(a) legislation on the working environment; working conditions; information and consultation of workers; integration of excluded persons; and equality at work. Such legislation may be adopted by the Council by qualified majority under the co-decision procedure (which gives significant weight to the views of the European Parliament);
(b) legislation on the social security and social protection of workers, termination of employment; representation and collective defence of the interests of workers and employers (including co-determination); and conditions of employment for third country nationals. Such legislation can only be passed by the Council acting unanimously, after consulting the European Parliament;
(c) pay, the right of association, the right to strike or to impose lock-outs remain outside of the legislative competence of the EU.

Also crucial to the new social provisions is the central role afforded to 'Social Dialogue', which gives management and labour a pivotal role in the process of law-making in the social field. Indeed, the social partners are involved throughout the legislative process, playing a substantial role both in drafting and implementing new measures.

19. The result of the accumulation of new powers since the Single European Act 1986 has been an acceleration of social policy directives. For example, the Working Time Directive (93/104), adopted in 1993, sets maximum limits on working time and provides for a minimum period of paid holiday throughout the Union; the Works Council Directive (94/45) provides for European Works Councils; the Pregnant Workers' Directive (92/85) provides for protection of pregnant workers against dismissal and a period of maternity leave; the Parental Leave Directive (96/34) provides for parental and family leave; and the Part-Time Workers Directive (97/81) and the Workers on Fixed Term Contracts Directive provide safeguards for flexible workers.

20. Following on from the Nice Summit in 2000, a new Charter of Fundamental Rights was agreed, modernizing the 1989 Charter. However, it remains the Treaty of Amsterdam which moved to create the European Social Model (ESM). The ESM's strategic objectives included[8] promotion of:

- new forms of European governance (meaning co-decision making and the promotion of open methods of policy coordination);
- a new economic and social agenda; and
- and a better quality of life.

Subsequently, from 2005 the ESM with its European Employment Strategy (EES) emerged as the new policy agenda setter. More significantly, since the Lisbon Summit, an open method of coordination (OMC) in terms of social policy agenda emerges. Such examples of social dialogue at work, as Hepple argues,[9] have been enhanced more recently by the advent of the OMC. OMC was implemented post-Lisbon Summit to further the 'coherent and systematic approaches' to policy and law-making achieved at the Luxembourg, Cardiff and Cologne Council meetings. OMC is designed to assist Member States in developing their own policies. Part of the OMC model is to instigate a 'high level forum' which would bring together the EU institutions, the social partners and other bodies to consider progress of policies to date. OMC provides for:

- the fixing of timetables for achieving prescribed and agreed EU policy goals, whether short, medium and long term;
- the establishment of benchmarking against global indicators, as a means of comparing best practice;

---

8. Shaping the New Europe, COM (2000) 154.
9. B. Hepple, 'New Methods of Integration in the EU', Ch. 9, in *Labour Laws and Global Trade* (Hart Publishing, Oxford, 2005), Ch. 9, at p. 231.

- the translation of EU guidelines into national and regional policies, accepting differences; and
- the monitoring and evaluation of such policy development, by way of peer review.

The Treaty of Nice 2003 presented an opportunity for OMC to expand its remit. The enlargement of social Europe in 2004, and again in 2008 presented new challenges to the ESM. In terms of enlargement, in 2004, Cyprus, Malta, as well as the Czech and Slovak Republics, Estonia, Hungary, Poland Lithuania, Latvia and Slovenia joined to create and extend EU15 into the new EU-25. In 2008, Bulgaria and Romania became EU Members with Croatia joining in 2013. The final frontier, being Turkey's accession, with accession talks having reopened in 2014.

21. The effect of EU membership on the British Constitution and the legal systems of England and Scotland is profound. The supremacy of European Community law over the laws of Member States was quickly asserted by the European Court of Justice;[10] but because treaties are not automatically binding in British law, domestic legislation was needed in order to ensure that British law reflected the obligations undertaken by the UK within the European Union. This was done by the European Communities Act 1972, which crucially provides, in Section 2(4), that any enactment passed or to be passed in the UK must be construed so as to be consistent with Community law. In addition, Section 2(1) provides that directly effective or directly applicable Community law is binding in the UK. This includes secondary Community law and future Community law. Given the potential conflict between supremacy of EU law, and the central constitutional principle of sovereignty of the legislature, it is not surprising that it took some time for the British courts to recognize the supremacy of EU law. In recent cases, this conundrum has been dealt with by asserting that the supremacy of EU law is no more than an implementation of Parliament's intention as expressed in the European Communities Act, albeit with the unusual effect of requiring legislation subsequent to that Act to be read subject to it. Finally, Section 2(2) enables the government to implement Community obligations which are not directly effective by means of subordinate legislation made by Ministers of the Crown subject to parliamentary approval. This procedure was used to give effect to Directive 77/187 on safeguarding employees' rights in the event of transfers of undertakings; and to remedy the infringement by the UK of ex Article 119 (was Article 141, now Article 157 TFEU) in respect of equal pay for work of equal value. The use of this procedure, rather than legislation by Parliament itself, has been severely criticized because it allows only for short debates and the ministerial order has to be accepted or rejected *in toto* without the possibility of amendment. Where EU law is not clear, the court or tribunal may refer questions of law for preliminary ruling by the ECJ under Article 267 TFEU (ex Article 177 and ex Article 234) of the Treaty. After some controversy, it has been decided that employment tribunals have jurisdiction to deal with claims under directly applicable EU law where this is related to their other statutory jurisdictions, for example in respect of equal treatment.

10. Case 26/62 *Van Gend en Loos* [1963] ECR 1.

22. The European Court of Justice has devised several powerful means of ensuring compliance with EU law. Although the main method for implementation should be by means of domestic legislation, Member States have frequently been recalcitrant in enacting legislation, or have passed provisions which do not fully implement their obligations. The Treaty of Rome envisaged that such breaches would be dealt with by enforcement proceedings initiated by the European Commission.

But it soon became clear that such proceedings would not be sufficient to ensure compliance, in part at least because such proceedings were beyond the control of aggrieved individuals. To fill the lacuna, the Court developed the doctrine of 'direct effect', according to which a citizen of any Member State can enforce his or her rights under EC law in the courts of that Member State even if there is no legislation implementing EU law, or if existing legislation is defective in its implementation. Not all EU legislation is, however, directly effective: a provision must be clear and unconditional and not dependent on a national implementing measure. Under this test, the Court has held that the provisions on freedom of movement and equal pay are directly effective.

However, in the case of directives, the ECJ has held that, since a directive is only binding on the Member State and not on private individuals, it can only be directly enforced against the state (vertical direct effect) and not against private employers (horizontal direct effect).[11] The result is that crucial employment rights, such as those available under the Equal Treatment Directive, are only enforceable by public employees against their employers and not by those in private employment. This anomaly has been corrected to some extent by a wide definition of the 'state'. In *Foster* v. *British Gas plc*[12] the European Court of Justice held that an 'organ of the state' includes a body 'whatever its legal form, which has been made responsible pursuant to a measure adopted by the State, for providing a public service under the control of the State and has for that purpose special powers beyond those which result from the normal rules applicable in relations between individuals'. Following this guidance, the House of Lords held that the British Gas Corporation, prior to its privatization, was an 'organ of the State', the fact that the government did not possess executive or day-to-day control being irrelevant. The absence of horizontal direct effect has also been corrected to some extent by the doctrine of state liability, under which a state may be held liable to compensate a person who has lost his or her rights because a directive has not been properly implemented.[13]

Recent developments have seen the ECJ effectively sidestep this limitation of directive rights in limited circumstances, where it can be stated that the directive is simply a manifestation of a 'general principle' of EU law.[14] In such circumstances the general principle is given both horizontal and vertical direct effect, with the directive providing an indication of the operation of that principle. This opens up an interesting question in relation to the status of the Charter of the Fundamental

11. Case 152/84 *Marshall* v. *Southampton and SW Hampshire AHA (Teaching)* [1986] ECR 723.
12. Case C-188/89 *Foster* v. *British Gas* [1990] ECR I-3313.
13. Cases C-6/90 and C-9/90 *Francovich* [1991] ECR I-5357.
14. See Case C-144/04 *Mangold* v. *Helm* [2005] ECR I-9981and *Kücükdeveci* v. *Swedex GmbH & Co KG* [2010] IRLR 346.

Rights of the European Union, which was given legal status under the Treaty of Lisbon. The ECJ has to ultimately decide whether the Charter is simply a reflection of 'general principles' or not. If the answer is in the affirmative then directives that contain rights reflected in the Charter will potentially not be hindered by the horizontal/vertical direct effect distinction.

Finally, the Court has facilitated the proper implementation of directives by the principle of 'indirect effect', which requires courts in Member States to interpret existing legislation so far as possible to give effect to EU law.[15] This is so even if the legislation was not passed with the purpose of implementing relevant EU law.[16]

Membership of the EU (and formerly the EC and EEC) has clearly played a pivotal role in developing labour and employment law in the UK. However, following the referendum decision on 23 June 2016 to withdraw the UK from the EU the status of these development and current European rights as implemented in the UK is uncertain. Once the UK has finalized its departure from the Union, there will no longer be an obligation to retain and maintain the rights derived from it. However, the current Conservative Government is in the process of introducing legislation that will fill the gap left behind by withdrawing from the EU. This is in the form of the European Communities (Repeal) Bill 2017. The Bill, if passed will come into effect on the day that the UK formally withdraws from the EU. This Bill, in its present form, seeks to do three key things. First, it repeals the European Communities Act 1972, which is the Act that gives European law precedence over UK law. Secondly, it will end the jurisdiction of the Court of Justice of the European Union. Thirdly, it will copy across all existing EU legislation in to domestic UK law. The intention behind the Bill is that it removes the supremacy of the EU, while ensuring that stability and consistency for business and citizens are maintained. The intention appears to be to give the UK greater time to scrutinize the current European laws when deciding which to repeal, amend or keep. This is rather than trying to unravel 40 years of laws during the two-year negotiation period that has been triggered.

V. Human Rights (HRA)

23. The objective of the member governments of the Council of Europe, under whose auspices the text of the European Convention of Human Rights (ECHR) was concluded in November 1950, was to secure the universal and effective recognition and observance of rights that had been proclaimed in the Universal Declaration of Human Rights on 10 December 1948 by the General Assembly of the United Nations. The 1950 European Convention on Human Rights (ECHR) established protection for basic human rights to: life, non-degrading treatment and slavery, liberty, punishment in accordance with law, fair hearing, privacy, freedom of conscience and expression, association and non-discrimination. The European Convention on Human Rights ('the Convention') was drafted by the Member States

15. Case 14/83 *Von Colson and Kamann* v. *Land Nordrhein-Westfalen* [1984] ECR 1891.
16. Case C-106/89 *Marleasing SA* v. *La Comercial Internacional de Alimentacion SA* [1990] 1 ECR 4135.

of the Council of Europe, and signed in Rome on 4 November 1950, entering into force on 3 September 1953. It has now been ratified by 41 Member States of the Council of Europe (Albania, Andorra, Austria, Belgium, Bulgaria, Croatia, Cyprus, the Czech Republic, Denmark, Estonia, the Federal Yugoslav Republic of Macedonia, Finland, France, Germany, Georgia, Greece, Hungary, Iceland, Ireland, Italy, Latvia, Liechtenstein, Lithuania, Luxembourg, Macedonia, Malta, Moldova, Netherlands, Norway, Poland, Portugal, Romania, San Marino, the Slovak Republic, Slovenia, Spain, Sweden, Switzerland, Turkey, Ukraine and the United Kingdom).

24. The Human Rights Act 1998 in effect incorporates Convention rights further into UK law, from October 2000. The White Paper, *Rights Brought Home: the Human Rights Bill* (October 1997), gave as the primary aims of this incorporation:

- to enable Convention rights to be enforced in the UK; and
- to enable alleged breaches of rights in the UK to be decided by the UK courts and tribunals.

Consequently, under Sections 6–8, HRA 1998, all public authorities must act in compliance with the Convention. Indeed, 'It is unlawful for a public authority to act in a way which is incompatible with a Convention right' (Section 6(1)). Therefore, if a public authority acts in a way which is inconsistent with Convention rights then a claim for a declaration, damages, or an injunction will lie against it. The articles of the European Convention of Human Rights which need to be considered in relation to employment law are:

- the right not to be subjected to inhuman or degrading treatment (Article 3);
- the right not to be required to perform forced or compulsory labour (Article 4);
- the right to a fair trial (Article 6);
- the right to respect for private life (Article 8);
- the right to freedom of thought (Article 9);
- the right to freedom of expression (Article 10);
- the right to freedom of peaceful assembly and to freedom of association with others, including the right to form and to join trade unions (Article 11);
- the right to enjoy to the substantive rights and freedoms set forth in the Convention without discrimination (Article 14).[17]

25. The ECHR has already had one major impact on employment law in the UK in that it was responsible for the end of the closed shop, whereby a trade union could enter into an agreement with an employer requiring the employer to employ only those who were already, or were willing to become, members of the trade union (see *Young, James and Webster* v. *UK* (1982) para. 442 below).

---

17. R. Allen, R. Crasnow, and A. Beale, *Employment Law and Human Rights*, 2nd edn (2007, Oxford). For a useful guide on the non-discrimination right and its similarities with the EU non-discrimination rights see the Fundamental Rights Agency's *Handbook on Non-Discrimination Law*.

§4. THE ECONOMY

I. General

26. The outstanding feature of the British economy over the last hundred years has been its decline from the manufacturing workshop of the world to the status of a thoroughly second-rank economic power. Output per head is the most basic indicator of a country's productive power. A recent authoritative account of the pattern of productivity explains that 'the UK appears as the leader at the beginning of the period [1870], but is overtaken by the United States in the next decade, by Sweden between the wars, by France and Germany around 1960, by Italy around 1970 and Japan probably in the late 1970s'.[18]

27. More recently, the global downturn and the collapse of major banking institutions has caused the UK economy to fall into recession and a 'double dip' recession. Looking for causes of the UK's economic failures has been a major preoccupation of UK economists.[19] It would be generally agreed that the low level of UK investment has been of crucial importance. For it is investment in new machinery and factories which increases the productivity of labour by incorporating new technology.

During the 1950s and 1960s the stock of capital in UK manufacturing grew at around 3.5 per cent per year, only two-thirds of the rate in Europe and one-third of that in Japan. But this immediately invites the question: why was UK investment so much lower? One answer might be low profits, and indeed by the early 1970s the profit rate in British manufacturing, around 10 per cent, was less than that in Europe and far below that of Japan. But this cannot be the fundamental explanation, for in the early 1950s the profit rate in Britain was around 20 per cent and the investment rate was even lower then. Indeed, the decline in profitability over the period has been attributed to low investment and the declining competitiveness which it brought. The involvement of the City in overseas investment has often been blamed for starving British industry of finance. But there is little evidence that it has been shortage of finance which has constrained British firms until 2008. What does seem to be clear is that British industry, early in the post-war period, became locked into a low investment pattern from which it has been unable to break out. This is despite the greatly increased competition it has faced, both at home and from imports and in its export markets. Much energy has been dissipated on mergers, whose benefits in increased efficiency have been severely limited. The banks have never taken it upon themselves to develop and implement strategic plans for individual industrial sectors and government efforts have been limited to a few general investment incentives.

28. Not only has investment been low in total, but its effectiveness has not been up to international standards. The amount of output derived from each unit of

18. R.C.O. Matthews, C.H. Feinstein, and J.C. Oddling-Smee, *British Economic Growth 1856–1973* (Oxford, 1982), p. 33.
19. R. Peston, *Who Runs Britain? And Who's to Blame for the Mess We're in?* (Hodder, 2008).

investment has been as much as one-third below that of France and Germany. Studies of the motor industry in particular have suggested much lower productivity in British plants of identical design to those in Europe. Bad organization and management, poor training and bad industrial relations are favourite explanations. The latter finds some support in the fact that some large UK plants have been abnormally strike prone by international standards. The fact that British unions entered the 1950s in an entrenched position (unlike those in most of Europe and Japan), but without a strong modernizing ethos, may have reinforced the negative effects of sluggish and complacent management. However, surveys into the implementation of new technology have found workforce opposition to be a factor of negligible importance in comparison with factors such as low expected profitability, doubts as to whether the equipment would be fully used and lack of technical expertise. Most recently, attention has been focused on lack of training as a key factor in explaining manufacturing weakness in the UK.

29. The recent history of the British economy has to be viewed in this context. The successive Conservative governments pursued the opposite policy of attempting to force rationalization of industry by more deflation, high interest rates and a rise in the pound. Productivity grew rapidly in 1981–2 as unemployment rose by about 2 million. There has been fierce rationalization in the public sector, especially in the steel and the coal industries where bitter strikes ended in defeat for the trade unions and sweeping job losses. In the 1980s manufacturing industry achieved rapid productivity growth (more than 4 per cent per year). But this was achieved by closing plants and reducing manning levels rather than by sustained investment in new products and processes. The investment expansion which occurred at the end of the 1980s was concentrated in those areas of the service sector most closely tied to the consumption boom (retail trade and the financial sector). This consumer boom was based on cuts in tax for the better off and an explosion of consumer credit, sparked off by the deregulation of the financial sector. The mounting balance of payments deficit, which preceded the recession of 1990–2, demonstrated how narrow this boom really was and that the 'Thatcher miracle' had utterly failed to revitalize manufacturing industry. The economy, however, began to show healthier signs during the 1990s, with unemployment beginning to drop from 1993.[20] Looking backwards from 2000, it was notable that the UK had experienced 30 quarters of uninterrupted growth with low inflation and a trend of falling unemployment.

Unemployment was down to lower levels than at any time during the past two decades, at less than 6 per cent of the labour force. Inflation remained low and stable, with consumer prices rising at the lowest pace since the 1960s. In fact, inflation in the UK has recently been the lowest among EU countries. In addition, and significantly, business investment boomed in the late 1990s, reaching the highest ratio to GDP since 1965. At the same time, parts of the economy have suffered from the continuing increase in the value of the pound, an increase which the OECD refers to as both unexpected and puzzling. This has been particularly problematic in manufacturing: employment in manufacturing was reduced by 3 per cent in 1999, and there was little investment in this sector. Nevertheless, the OECD predicted

20. This section is based on OECD *Economic Surveys: United Kingdom* (OECD, 2005).

continuing good macroeconomic performance. An important factor has been the granting of independence to the Bank of England, which sets interest rates free of political pressures. This has allowed the monetary policy framework to become, in the words of the OECD, 'remarkably transparent'. This has been augmented by greater transparency, stability and accountability of fiscal policy, with the government aiming to reduce public sector net debt to below 40 per cent of GDP. However, all is not entirely rosy. Productivity in the UK continues to lag well behind other advanced economies.[21] This is attributable to various factors, including relatively ineffective competition policy, less entrepreneurial dynamism than other countries and uneven educational achievement. Business spending on research and development is low by international standards. Most seriously, poverty, especially among children, is unacceptably high. The then Labour government attempted to rectify this situation by putting in place an active labour market policy, called the 'welfare to work' programme, to facilitate the integration into the labour market of young people, long-term unemployed, disabled people and lone parents. Furthermore, there is greater emphasis on in-work benefits, such as a working families tax credit and the introduction of a minimum wage.

The economic policy of the Conservative Government since 2010, which includes the years when they formed a coalition government with the Liberal Democrats, has been characterized by austerity measures. Central to their manifestos has been to balance the books, and to deal with public debt. This has included introducing wide-ranging reform to the welfare system. Unemployment rates have been falling at a steady rate while the Conservative Government has been in power, and stood at a 42-year low of 4.4 per cent for the three months to June 2017. However, despite positive unemployment rates, the opposition parties point to the fact that much of the positive advancement in the unemployment rate has been made up of individuals in precarious and part-time employment.

II. The Changing Structure of the Labour Force

30. The most prominent characteristic of the early 1980s was the accelerated increase in unemployment figures, partly as a result of the strict monetary policies of the incumbent Conservative government. Unemployment reached a peak of 3.78 million in January 1986 (over 12.3 per cent of the working population) and remained at relatively high levels throughout the rest of the 1980s and early 1990s. This contrasts with the pattern in previous decades. In the twenty years prior to 1967, the general unemployment level in Britain was among the lowest in the Western world – usually between 1 and 2 per cent. The peak figure in the 1970s was only 1.47 million (excluding students). The period since 1993, however, has seen decreasing rates of unemployment, with the ILO putting the unemployment rates in Great Britain at 6.4 per cent in 1998, down from 8.9 per cent in 1995. This downward trend was aided by the change in government policy, with the then Labour government, which was in power 1997-2010, publicly committed to prioritizing the reduction in unemployment.

21. V. Cable, *The Storm: The World Economic Crisis* (Hodder: London, 2008).

By the end of 2000, unemployment rates were at their lowest since 1975, reaching 1.616 million or 5.5 per cent of the working population in November 2000 (using ILO measures). Inflation was also low, at about 3.1 per cent.[22] However, pockets of the economy still demonstrated intractably high rates of unemployment, and large scale redundancies were on-going, even in the new service sector. By 2013, the unemployment rate remained at 7.7 per cent. Since 2013 the unemployment rate has decreased steadily. For the three months up to June 2017 the unemployment rate was recorded at 4.4 per cent.

31. For those in work there have been several significant changes in the structure of employment. Of particular importance has been the shift of the working population away from production industries to service industries. Employment in the manufacturing sector fell from 7.28 million in 1976 to 5.38 million in 1991. By spring 2005, this had dipped even further, to 4.5 million. Almost 75 per cent of total employment is now in the service sector. These trends are reflected in the changing occupational structure of employment, which displays a marked shift away from manual towards non-manual occupations. By 2001 more than 61 per cent of the workforce was employed in non-manual occupations.

32. A second important change in the structure of the workforce has been the increase in the number of women workers. The female workforce has grown rapidly since 1959, reaching 11.54 million in 1998, and accounting for 44.1 per cent of those in employment in the UK. By 2000, there were 12.46 million women in employment, bringing the number of women in employment and the employment rate for women to their highest recorded levels. The UK has the third highest women's employment rate in all EU countries. Women are, however, concentrated in service industries and non-manual occupations. The increase in working women has been paralleled by an increase in part-time work. There were nearly 7 million part-time workers in Great Britain in 2000 as against about 3.2 million in 1971.

This represents the highest proportion of part-time workers in the EU, apart from Denmark and the Netherlands. The part-time workforce is predominantly female with women accounting for over 79 per cent of all part-time employees (as against about 33 per cent of full-timers).

33. Another feature of the labour force is the relatively disadvantaged position of the ethnic minority population. Most serious is the fact that unemployment among ethnic minority groups is higher than that among whites. Thus in 1997, the unemployment rate for Black African men was more than three times (25 per cent) that for white men. Pakistani/Bangladeshi men also have high rates. The position of black African and Pakistani women is even more serious: their unemployment rates were four times those of white women in 1997. There was some improvement in

22. All figures in this section are taken from statistics published in the *UK Labour Force Survey Spring Quarters Historical Supplement* 2008, the Employment Gazette and in Labour Research (Labour Research Department, London).

the late 1990s, with unemployment in all groups falling. However, the unemployment rates for Pakistani/Bangladeshi groups were still 17 per cent in 2005, and 15 per cent for black groups.[23]

34. Employment in the public sector, which traditionally constituted an important portion of the workforce, diminished significantly during the 1980s due to privatization of nationalized industries and the government policy of 'slimming down' the public services. Between mid-1983 and mid-1989, the public sector share of the total workforce in employment fell from 29.4 per cent to 23.1 per cent.[24]

In 1998, about 5.96 million people were employed in the public sector, down from 6.1 million people mid-1989, and representing approximately 22.2 per cent of all persons in employment. Since then, these numbers have increased marginally, reflecting the general increase in employment. Thus in spring 2000, about 6.35 people were employed in the public sector, representing about 22.9 per cent of all in employment.

23. The information in this paragraph is derived from *UK Labour Force Survey Spring Quarters Historical Supplement* 2000.
24. *UK Labour Force Survey Spring Quarters Historical Supplement* 2000, Central Statistical Office, Economic Trends, December 1989; *The Bulletin*, February 1990, p. 21.

Chapter 2. Definitions and Notions

§1. Employment (Industrial) Relations

35. The reader who seeks any clear or explicit definition in Britain of basic notions, such as industrial relations and labour law, will be disappointed. The subject of industrial relations (since 1999, renamed employment relations throughout the UK) has become an accepted area of academic study. But the scope of the subject has been determined empirically with attention being concentrated on the collective bargaining activities of trade unions.[25] Allan Flanders, elaborating Dunlop's analysis,[26] has defined industrial relations as a system of rules which appear 'in different guises in legislation and in statutory orders; in trade union regulations; in collective agreements and arbitration awards; in social conventions; in managerial decisions; and in "accepted custom and practice". In other words, the subject deals with certain regulated or institutionalized relationships in industry.'[27] Flanders's emphasis was on the institutions of job regulation excluding 'personal' and 'unstructured' relationships from the system of industrial relations. Since the 1960s, however, the prevailing conception of industrial relations has broadened to include the informal, largely unstructured relationships on the factory or shop floor which modify or even contradict the official institutions. The emphasis has increasingly been on the impact of informal work group relations, and unofficial 'custom and practice' as means of controlling jobs. An important landmark in this new approach was the Report of the Royal Commission on Trade Unions and Employers' Associations (1968)[28] which distinguished the formal system of industrial relations embodied in official institutions, from the informal system 'created by the actual behaviour of the trade unions and employers' associations, of managers, shop stewards and workers'.

§2. Labour Law

36. This changing emphasis has also had an influence on the study of the law relating to industrial relations. Right down to 1939, legal studies were almost exclusively concerned with the common law of 'master and servant' (the earliest book on this subject by Matthew Dutton was published in Ireland in 1723),[29] and with legislation on safety and welfare and workmen's compensation for accidents. This law of master and servant, concerned exclusively with common law and, less often, legislation affecting the individual employment relationship has developed into what is today generally called 'employment law'. This includes the rights and duties of individual employer and employee and is sometimes extended to such matters as the

25. Notably in H.A. Clegg, *The Changing System of Industrial Relations in Great Britain* (Oxford, 1979).
26. J.T. Dunlop, *Industrial Relations Systems* (New York, 1958).
27. A. Flanders, *Industrial Relations: What is Wrong with the System?* (London, 1965).
28. Cmnd 3623, 1968.
29. Matthew Dutton, *The Law of Masters and Servants in Ireland* (Dublin, 1723).

employer's vicarious responsibility to third parties for the torts (delict) of his employees.

37. The legal aspects of relations between trade unions and employers and internal trade union matters were, however, little studied before 1939 and then only concerning specific legislation or case law. Books on trade union law usually focused on the judicial interpretation of Acts of Parliament defining the legal status of trade unions and the protection of acts in so-called 'trade disputes'. There were also a few studies of the practice of conciliation and arbitration. This particularly narrow focus and the neglect of collective labour law can only be understood in the light of two factors. First, the pragmatic case by case orientation of English lawyers, who generally eschew the broader conceptual and doctrinal study of the subject; and secondly, the neglect of the sociology of law by English academic writers.

38. It was in this situation that Otto Kahn-Freund, the great German exponent of industrial relations 'pluralism', arrived in England in 1933. He found in the London School of Economics the intellectual environment in which he was able to combine his experience as a judge of the Berlin Labour Court, his wide understanding of the sociology of Marx, Weber and others, with his study of English law and the British practice of collective bargaining. It is to him that the scientific study of collective labour law in Britain, a study filled with valuable comparative insights, owes its origin. Where English lawyers thought collective agreements not worth studying because they were never directly enforced in courts, Kahn-Freund found them a fascinating subject precisely because of the apparent 'abstention' by the law. He was able to generalize this into a theory of the absence of an intention to create legal relations (itself a continental rather than English notion) in collective bargaining. In studying the legal support given to collective bargaining he expounded general principles such as that of 'voluntarism'– the aim of the law is to help the parties reach a settlement not to impose it – and that of the 'priority of autonomous institutions' – the law intervenes only if the parties' own machinery has failed to produce a result.[30]

39. The elaboration of general principles such as these, and the continental and the United States influences, have resulted in a change of scope and emphasis of legally based studies. The scope of labour law is now defined in terms of the law

30. A bibliography of the writings of the late Professor Sir Otto Kahn-Freund (1900–1979) will be found in his *Selected Writings* (London, 1978). Many of his most important ideas are crystallized in his *Labour and the Law* (2nd edn, London, 1977) (also available in German and Italian translations), and *Labour Relations: Heritage and Adjustment* (London, 1979). A third edition of *Labour and the Law*, ed. by P.L. Davies and M.R. Freedland, was published in 1983. Appraisals of his work will be found in F. Gamillscheg *et al.* (eds.), *In Memoriam Sir Otto Kahn-Freund* (Munich, 1980), and Lord Wedderburn, Roy Lewis and (the late) Jon Clark (eds.), *Labour Law and Industrial Relations: Building on Kahn-Freund* (Oxford, 1983). For his earlier period in Germany, see Roy Lewis and (the late) Jon Clark (eds. and Introduction), *Labour Law and Politics in the Weimar Republic: Selected German Writings of O. Kahn-Freund* (translated by J. Clark) (Oxford, 1981).

which is used 'to regulate, to support and to restrain the power of management and the power of organized labour'.[31]

40. Labour law may now be understood in this way in academic studies, but legislation still uses a bewildering variety of descriptions of the same subject matter. Thus labour courts were known as 'industrial tribunals' until as recently as 1998, when their name was changed to the more appropriate title of employment tribunals. Even more confusingly, successive statutes dealing with aspects of labour law have been given a variety of different titles, such as the Industrial Relations Act of 1971, the Trade Union and Labour Relations Act 1974, the Employment Protection Act 1975, consolidated in the Employment Protection (Consolidation) Act 1978), followed by Employment Acts of 1980, 1982, 1988, 1989, 1990 and a Trade Union Act of 1984. Much of the legislation was consolidated towards the end of the Conservative period, with the Trade Union and Labour Relations Consolidation Act 1992 dealing mainly with collective issues, and the Employment Rights Act 1996 covering largely individual labour law. However, the Labour government which came to power in 1997 chose to call its amending legislation the Employment Relations Acts of 1999 and 2004.

§3. Social Law

41. This lack of uniformity is also reflected in the absence of any clear dividing line between labour law and social law. The latter concept has not until recently been recognized in academic studies in the UK, but at the level of the European Union it is widely used, often interchangeably with the notion of social policy law. There is still, however, little agreement on the exact scope of social law and the extent to which it overlaps with or even subsumes labour law. In a wide sense social law includes all studies of the operation of law in society, although at EU level, it is usually used to denote law which is not directly concerned with the operation of the common market but instead with social or individual rights. More narrowly, it is often used to cover only social security law, that is the law relating to the administration of contributory and non-contributory state benefits for income maintenance. The term welfare law usually covers both social security and the law relating to personal welfare services. Legislation on contributory state benefits was originally dealt with by National Insurance Acts, but in 1975 these were consolidated in the Social Security Act and amended in subsequent three decades under the Social Security Acts (1998, 2000, 2005).

§4. Collective Bargaining

42. The absence of agreed or statutory definition of the scope of study is matched by the lack of any precise definition of some of the main subjects of study. For example, the term 'collective bargaining' (which is said to have been invented

31. O. Kahn-Freund, *Labour and the Law*, 3rd edn, p. 15.

by Beatrice Webb in 1891)[32] was for many years regarded as the collective equivalent of industrial bargaining in the labour market: 'Instead of the employer making a series of separate contracts with isolated individuals he meets with a collective will, and settles, in a single agreement, the principles upon which, for the time being, all workmen of a particular group, or class, or grade, will be engaged.'[33]

43. This analysis was criticized by Allan Flanders[34] as being inadequate because it suggests that collective agreements commit someone to buy and sell labour, whereas in fact, collective agreements simply lay down the terms upon which individual workers sell their ability to work. This led Flanders to develop the alternative theory of collective bargaining as an 'institution for the joint regulation of labour management and labour markets'.[35] Against this view Alan Fox has argued that in collective bargaining there is:

(1) a bargaining process during which the parties deploy arguments, present evidence and issue threats; this may or may not end in
(2) an agreement which adjusts the antithetical interests of buyer and seller. This may or may not be embodied in
(3) a contract into which both parties decide to enter ... In practice these elements often appear to be fixed in a single process ... But it is important to distinguish them for analytic purposes.[36]

Whatever the relative merits of these theories for understanding the phenomenon of collective bargaining, it has to be stressed that for certain legal purposes (such as trade union recognition) 'collective bargaining' has a much more limited definition excluding certain subjects such as bargaining about investment plans (see below Part II, Ch. 4).

44. The voluntary nature of much of the dispute settlement machinery in Great Britain is often cited as a distinctive feature of British industrial relations. The extent to which this reflects reality is discussed in the section on historical background (see below Ch. 3). At this point it is necessary to analyse what 'voluntary' and 'compulsory' mean. At one end of a spectrum the word 'voluntary' suggests that disputes are resolved entirely by the parties themselves, using agreed procedures or industrial action without any third party intervention; at the other end of the 'voluntary' spectrum are negotiated settlements reached after third parties have assisted the employer and unions, with their consent, through means such as conciliation or mediation.

---

32. In *The Cooperative Movement in Britain* (London, 1891) and subsequently developed by her and Sidney Webb, *Industrial Democracy* (London, 1898).
33. Sidney and Beatrice Webb, *Industrial Democracy*, p. 173.
34. *British Journal of Industrial Relations*, 6 (1968), p. 1.
35. *British Journal of Industrial Relations*, 6 (1968), p. 1; for a defence of this definition against a Marxist criticism, see Clegg, *The Changing System of Industrial Relations in Great Britain*, Ch. 11.
36. *British Journal of Industrial Relations*, 13 (1975), p. 151.

45. The antonym of 'voluntary' is 'compulsory' but, as Kahn-Freund explained,[37] 'compulsory' is used in at least four different senses in Britain. (1) The parties must use a particular procedure prescribed by law, such as compulsory arbitration. In the 20th century this has applied only in time of war. (2) One of the parties may invoke a particular procedure without the consent of the other side. The most prominent example is unilateral arbitration. From 1940 to 1980, in various forms, it was possible for representative trade unions or employers' organizations to invoke arbitration to oblige employers in otherwise well-organized industries to observe employment terms established by collective bargaining in that industry. The Employment Protection Act 1975 utilized unilateral arbitration of terms of employment as the final sanction against employers who failed to recognize independent trade unions or to disclose information to unions, once recognized, for purposes of collective bargaining. With the repeal of the extension and recognition provisions by the Employment Act 1980 all that remained of unilateral arbitration until the new Labour government legislation came into effect was the almost unused provision relating to disclosure of information. However, the Employment Relations Act 1999 introduced a species of binding unilateral arbitration by permitting the union, in cases of employers who refuse to observe a CAC recognition declaration, to request the CAC to impose a legally binding collective bargaining procedure on both parties (see para. 525). (3) The results of a process (e.g. a collective agreement or arbitration award) are binding on one or both parties. As will be seen later, collective agreements are presumed not to be intended to be legally enforceable between the collective parties, but some of their provisions may take effect as binding obligations in individual contracts of employment (see Part I, Ch. 2). Only to this extent are they 'compulsory', and in this connection it should be remembered that it is possible (in theory, at least) for the individual employee and employer to opt out of the terms of the collective agreement. The awards of arbitrators are not legally enforceable, unless they take effect through individual contracts of employment. This is expressly provided for in the case of unilateral arbitration, but may occur by implication in other cases. (4) No industrial sanctions may be used by either side during a defined period. This was the case under the Industrial Relations Act 1971 when a 'cooling-off ' period could be imposed in certain emergency disputes but this was repealed in 1974.

The legislation since 1980 has achieved a similar objective by requiring pre-strike ballots in respect of virtually all strikes whether 'official' (i.e. union-backed) or unofficial (wildcat); the effect of this is a compulsory delay until a ballot has been held. In a wider sense, the removal of immunities from many traditional forms of industrial action since 1980 has removed the key element of freedom to impose social sanctions, which underpinned the so-called 'voluntary' system. Although these provisions were introduced by the neo-liberal Conservative governments under Thatcher and Major, they have largely been maintained by the Labour governments led by Tony Blair.

---

37. Kahn-Freund, *Labour and the Law*, 3rd edn, p. 147.

§5. Dispute Resolution

46. Conciliation and arbitration are not defined by law in Britain, although machinery is provided by statute to implement these methods of dispute settlement. However, these terms are a well-known part of industrial relations vocabulary. Conciliation is a voluntary, informal process of dispute resolution, whereby an independent third party assists the parties to a dispute to clarify the points of disagreement and attempts to promote a settlement. No binding award is made and any agreement reached is the responsibility of the parties. Arbitration differs from conciliation in that reference is made to an independent third party to adjudicate on the dispute and come to a decision. In voluntary arbitration, the decision is not legally binding, but the parties have nevertheless embarked on the procedure on the understanding that they will abide by whatever decision is reached. In the case of compulsory arbitration (see above), the award is usually legally enforceable as an implied term in the contract of employment. Mediation, on the other hand, leads to a recommendation by the third party which the parties to the dispute are free to reject. In Britain, arbitration and mediation may involve the settlement of both conflicts of interest and conflicts of right, a distinction which, as we have seen, is in any event difficult to make in a British context.

Chapter 3. The Historical Background

§1. The Traditional Voluntary System until the 1960s

47. In order to understand modern British labour law and employment (formerly industrial) relations it is necessary to appreciate three features of the legal framework of industrial relations as it developed until the 1960s. The first is the tradition of individualism; the second is the tradition of support for voluntary collective bargaining and abstention of the law from industrial action; and the third is the selective nature of regulatory or 'protective' legislation.

I. Individualism[38]

48. As Hepple previously described it:

> The notion of the individual contract of employment is central to the legal analysis of industrial relations. This fragmentation of industrial relations into millions of individual relationships is not an accidental or modern phenomenon. It is deeply rooted in social and legal tradition. The conception of the reciprocal rights and duties of the parties flowing from their free exchange of promises arrived relatively late on the legal scene in Britain in comparison with the continental countries influenced by Roman law.

The reason was the tradition of the Statute of Labourers passed by Edward III in 1351, following an Ordinance of 1349, later reinforced by the Elizabethan Statute of Artificers of 1563, and the tradition of the Poor Law Act 1601. Under these laws the 'servant's' status determined the obligation to work at wages arbitrarily fixed by justices of the peace, usually themselves masters. Servants were liable to punishment for not accepting the work, for not doing it according to directions, or for deserting the master. As late as 1850 Blackstone's definition of the master–servant relationship was still in vogue among lawyers and, according to that definition, the relationship need not be based on contract. For example, a labourer could be compelled to serve by justices of the peace; a parish apprentice indentured under the Poor Law had to serve a master with whom he had no contract; and the mere condition of 'having no visible effects' could give rise to a direction to compulsory work.[39] The sanctions were criminal. When the Elizabethan statute fell into disuse, the legal basis for prosecutions against workers were the 19th-century Master and Servants Acts. It was the trade unions which were largely responsible for the modification and repeal of these penal laws by the Master and Servant Act 1867 and the Conspiracy and Protection of Property Act 1875 respectively. Trade union agitation arose primarily because of the effect of the laws on the freedom to strike:

---

38. This section draws extensively on B. Hepple, in G.S. Bain (ed.), *Industrial Relations in Britain* (Oxford, 1983), Ch. 16.
39. P.S. Bagwell, *Industrial Relations in 19th Century Britain* (Dublin, 1974), p. 30.

> it was a recognized tactic of the employers, particularly in dealing with smaller strikes, to cause all the strikers to be arrested for breach of contract and then to confront them with the alternatives of returning to work on the employer's terms or suffering up to 3 months' imprisonment. Furthermore, as the law stood, a troublemaker might be silenced not just once but repeatedly.[40]

Between 1858 and 1875 an average of 10,000 prosecutions of workmen for breach of contract took place each year in England and Wales.

49. The repeal of the Master and Servant Acts removed a major impediment to the development of the notion of freedom of contract between equal contracting parties by civil sanctions alone. However, the intellectual backwardness of the legal analysis of 'master and servant' relationships has had a lasting impact on the modern law. One consequence has been the patchy and inadequate coverage of labour law. Another has been the inordinate complexity of labour law. The bulk of labour legislation in the 19th century developed outside the framework of the contract of employment. This 'atrophy' of the contract of employment, as Kahn- Freund called it,[41] is largely attributable to the absence of an explicit and flexible contract model in the formative period of labour law. The most important consequences of the heritage of ideas evolved over centuries under the influence of the Statute of Labourers, the Statute of Artificers, and the Poor Law is that the form of contract which emerged in the 19th century effectively guaranteed the rule-making powers of the employer. When the worker at the factory gate accepts an offer of employment, neither he or she nor the employer may be conscious that they have concluded a binding contract of service. In law they have done so although nothing was said about wages or hours of work, let alone such matters as holidays, sick pay, pensions or what is to happen if there is a stoppage of work due to a power failure. If there is no legislation in point, and no express agreement, it is left to the courts and tribunals to make sense of the contract by implying terms as to these matters.

Evidently, where there is collective bargaining the courts may be prepared to fill in the gaps by incorporating the relevant terms of the collective agreements as implied terms of the individual contract. The great success of collective bargaining in many industries has meant that the courts have rarely been called upon to imply terms. In reality, where there is no collective agreement or arbitration award or legislation, the superior economic power of employers enables them to dictate terms of the contract which the individual employees are in no position to contest through the courts, least of all when they are still working for the employer. The law of contract was developed by the courts, and the principal conceptual instrument they use to fill the gaps left by the parties is the implied intention of the parties. In a few extreme cases (such as contracts in restraint of trade) public policy is used to nullify a contract, but never to mould it. This means that the idea of positive legal regulation of the contract by imperative norms is alien to the common law approach:

40. D. Simon, 'Master and Servant': in: *Democracy and the Labour Movement* (London, 1954), p. 160.
41. O. Kahn-Freund, 'Blackstone's neglected child: the contract of employment', *Law Quarterly Review* 93 (1977) 508 at p. 524.

parties are even free to 'contract out' of protective legislation unless and until Parliament says they cannot do so. This is quite different from the continental legal systems which for two centuries have applied general imperative norms to all contracts and special norms to the contract of employment. Moreover, when British judges have sought to imply terms they have relied heavily on custom and practice. The task of discovering the custom is greatly simplified, as indicated below, when there is a collective agreement. Where none exists everyday obligations, such as the speed of work, the conditions of labour and the subjection to discipline, are implied from what the parties do in practice, and that means in effect what the employer has laid down and applied in works rules, even informally. Some obligations, such as fidelity, the maintenance of mutual trust and confidence, and obedience to the employer's reasonable commands, are regarded as fundamental. They are implied as a matter of law from judicial precedents which have been influenced from the traditions of the law of 'master and servant'. The judicial perspective, even in recent times, has been unitary rather than pluralist, although under the impact of modern legislation there are some signs of change.

II. Voluntary Collective Bargaining

50. The traditional British system of industrial relations until the 1960s rested on a social consensus that the state's role should be minimal. Trade unions and strikes emerged from illegality at criminal law in a series of statutes from 1824 to 1875. However, the courts almost immediately began to develop a series of common law liabilities, with the effect that most industrial action, while not unlawful at criminal law, was likely to give rise to civil liability. Parliament responded, not by creating statutory rights to strike or organize, but by enacting immunities to specific common law torts if committed in the course of a trade dispute. Hence the law of industrial action until the 1970s consisted largely of legislative responses to judicial creativity. In the late Lord Wedderburn's words: 'This period saw the pendulum swing regularly back and forth between judge-made liabilities and cautious parliamentary protection.'[42] Thus, although the Conspiracy and Protection of Property Act 1875 stated that simple conspiracy was not a crime if done in the context of a trade dispute, the courts held that this did not prevent liability for the civil tort of conspiracy in taking industrial action.[43] In the same year, the *Taff Vale*[44] case made it possible to sue a trade union in respect of this tort. In addition, the tort of inducing breach of contract of employment made most organized action tortious.[45] The legislature responded with the Trade Disputes Act 1906, which gave immunity to any person acting in contemplation or furtherance of a trade dispute in respect of the torts of conspiracy, inducing breach of contract of employment or (for the avoidance of doubt) interfering with business. It also gave immunity for peaceful picketing if carried out in contemplation or furtherance of a trade dispute; and,

---

42. Lord Wedderburn, *The Worker and The Law* (3rd edn, Harmondsworth, 1986), p. 17.
43. *Quinn* v. *Leathem* [1901] A.C. 495.
44. *Taff Vale Railway Company* v. *The Amalgamated Society of Railway Servants* [1901] A.C. 426.
45. *South Wales Miners' Federation* v. *Glamorgan Coal Company Ltd* [1905] A.C. 239.

significantly, a blanket immunity to trade unions from actions in tort. The limitations on political activities by unions established in the *Osborne*[46] case were countered by the Trade Union Act 1913. After the controversial case of *Rookes* v. *Barnard*[47] resuscitated the obsolete tort of intimidation, the Trade Disputes Act 1965 was passed to reverse its effect and to give immunity for intimidation in contemplation or furtherance of a trade dispute. This pattern led Kahn-Freund to describe the British system of labour law as 'abstentionist'. Similarly, the law gave support for voluntary collective bargaining without enacting specific legal rights.

The recognition of trade unions for collective bargaining was achieved without the aid of legislation or any significant demand for such legislation. Robson noted,[48] in 1935, that 'England is the home of trade unionism; it was on her soil that the practice of combined bargaining first arose; yet here alone is the collective contract still denied the elementary right of legal enforcement in the courts of law despite the fact that it is the recognized method of determining the conditions of employment of the vast majority of wage earners'. However, there was a certain amount of 'auxiliary' legislation designed to promote and support voluntary collective bargaining. This included (i) the minimum wage-fixing machinery established in selected 'sweated' trades where collective bargaining was non-existent, originating with the Trade Boards Act 1909; (ii) the successive Fair Wages Resolutions of the House of Commons, from 1891, which imposed obligations on government contractors to pay 'fair' wages, of which collectively agreed terms were a primary guide; and (iii) the machinery established in 1896 and 1919 to encourage the use of voluntary conciliation and arbitration.

51. It is a striking feature of Britain's war-time legislation, and of the policy of the first twenty years after the Second World War, that this served to consolidate the traditional voluntary system. The Conditions of Employment and National Arbitration Order No. 1305 severely restricted strikes and lock-outs and made it compulsory to submit disputes to arbitration. In practice, however, the peacetime system of voluntary collective bargaining remained intact. Moreover, the unions were deeply involved in carrying out wartime measures such as the allocation of labour and paying out unemployment benefits for the Ministry of Labour. At plant level, joint production committees distributed work and administered discipline. Labour benefited from this policy of 'tripartite corporatism'. Average earnings in real terms were 24 per cent higher in 1944 than in 1938 (due to extra overtime and bonuses) and membership of trade unions rose by about one-third during the war to bring it up to 8 million (45 per cent of the workforce). When a Labour government was elected with a massive majority in 1945, the unions did not seek any major changes in the traditional system. The only immediate measure was the repeal of the Trade Disputes and Trade Union Act 1927, which a Conservative government had imposed in the aftermath of the 1926 General Strike to outlaw 'political' sympathy strikes, to restrict financial support by union members for the Labour Party, and to forbid civil servant unions from affiliating to outside bodies such as the Trades Union Congress

46. [1910] A.C. 87.
47. [1964] A.C. 1129.
48. W. Robson, 'Industrial law', *Law Quarterly Review*, 51 (1935), p. 204.

(TUC). The war-time Order 1305 remained in force, with union consent, until 1951 when it was repealed as the result of withdrawal of trade union support following the prosecution of some strikers. It was replaced by Order 1376 of 1951 which restored the freedom to strike and lock out and allowed representative organizations to invoke unilateral arbitration in order to extend collective agreements. When the Order was replaced by permanent legislation in 1959 (under a Conservative administration) a modified form of such extension remained a feature of the law until 1980. Other legislative changes in the immediate post-war period also aimed to improve support for the traditional voluntary system. These included a new and amended Fair Wages Resolution of 1946, and a Wages Councils Act of 1945. The latter replaced the earlier trade boards legislation and enabled the renamed 'wages councils' to recommend that the Minister made a wages order not only where there was no collective bargaining machinery but also where such machinery was inadequate, as, for example, where it had collapsed leaving workers unprotected in times of depression. Trade union acquiescence in the consolidation of the voluntary system was closely linked to the implementation of Beveridge's proposals for a reformed comprehensive system of social security.

52. The welfare state, together with the voluntarist system of industrial relations, was part of the policy not only of the post-war Labour government but also was accepted by the Conservative administrations from 1951 to 1964. In retrospect, it is possible to see that this 'rested upon a middle-class acquiescence in the current balance of industrial power'.[49] There was a stable economic basis for the social consensus. In the 1930s, despite high levels of unemployment, wage and salary earners in employment enjoyed relative prosperity, and Britain was cushioned from the economic crisis by its foreign assets. During the war Britain lost £7,000 million, a quarter of its national wealth, but the sporadic post-war economic crises were held in check by loans from the United States. Britain had not suffered military occupation or physical destruction as other European countries had, and there was no significant pressure for the renewal of industry and the 'modernization' of industrial relations. In that climate it is not surprising that there were no moves towards restructuring labour law, for example by introducing forms of co-determination of the kind which the British occupation forces, with British trade union advice, fostered in Germany. Even in the industries which the Labour government nationalized (civil aviation, cable and wireless, coal, railways, long-distance road transport, electricity, gas, iron and steel and the Bank of England), the legislation went no further than to require the boards of the new public corporations to 'consult' with 'appropriate organizations' with a view to establishing and maintaining negotiation and arbitration procedures, provisions which have proved to be largely symbolic. Co-partnership or even more radical notions of workers' control formed no part of the traditional consensus.

---

49. Lord Wedderburn, 'Labour Law and Labour Relations in Britain', *British Journal of Industrial Relations* 10 (1972), p. 270 at p. 275.

III. Regulatory Legislation

53. The primacy of voluntary collective bargaining meant that regulatory legislation, directly laying down rules of employment on matters such as wages, hours, health and safety, has tended to take second place. The policy of the law has been not to regulate by statute the terms of employment of those who are considered capable of protecting themselves. Legislation applied primarily to children and women and not to adult men. In the 20th century, the principle has been to cover by direct regulation only those who are not protected by collective bargaining and to deal only with those subjects which do not appear to lend themselves to collective bargaining. Even where there is regulatory legislation, it has often been designed to allow for its replacement by approved collective agreements, which are at least as good in content as regulatory legislation. In any event, legislation can always be supplemented by collective bargaining on the same subject. The most important consequence of the approach has been the absence of the kind of comprehensive regulation that is to be found in other industrial countries of such matters as hours and holidays for all employees. Significantly, apart from the mining industry, the eight-hour day in Britain was achieved by collective bargaining rather than legislation. There was specific regulation of the hours of women and young persons in certain activities but these were repealed in 1986 and 1989 respectively. Thus until the change wrought by the decisive influence of EU law, the hours of adult men were always regulated by collective bargaining. Membership of the European Union (EU) has, however, made it inevitable that British traditions should be affected by the continental pattern of regulation. As will be seen below, the implementation of the Working Time Directive, regulating hours of work and periods of paid holiday, will be subject to more direct legal regulation than ever before.

54. The reason for the tradition of selective use of statutory norms as a means of worker protection is to be found in the ebb and flow of struggle of unions and reform groups inside and outside Parliament, and the resistance by powerful groups of employers and intellectual supporters of *laissez-faire*. The earliest legislation, including the Regulation of Chimney Sweepers Act 1788 and the Health and Morals of Apprentices Act 1802, was concerned with child labour. The initial aim of the short-time committees from 1831 onwards was the 10-hour day for all employees, regardless of sex and age, but when the political reality of the time made this unattainable, the committees modified their aims to concentrate on the hours of work of women. The first major victory for the short-time committees was the Factories Act 1844 which equated women with young persons, restricted their hours, and required dangerous parts of machinery to be fenced, as well as strengthening the powers of the inspectorate which had been established by the Factories Act 1833. The opportunities for evasion were many and some loopholes were closed in seven Acts passed between 1844 and 1856. Most important of all was the Ten Hours Act of 1847 which conceded the main demand of the short-time committees. In the second half of the 19th century this legislation, which applied only to textile factories, was gradually extended to cover factories and workshops over a wide range of old and new manufacturing industries. At different times activities outside these industries were also regulated: mines from 1842 (but with effective inspection only from

1860), shops from 1886 (although the health and safety aspects of shop work were not covered until 1963), and standards comparable to factory legislation were not extended to agriculture until 1956.

Surveying the scene in 1972, an official committee of inquiry, under the chairmanship of Lord Robens, found that there were nine main groups of statutes supported by over 500 subordinate statutory instruments. These contained a mass of intricate and ill-assorted detail. Some 5 million workers worked in premises not covered by any occupational health or safety legislation. A result of the recommendations of the committee was the comprehensive Health and Safety at Work etc. Act 1974. The existing legislation relating to health, safety and welfare is very slowly being replaced by this new comprehensive system, which is based on the philosophy of self-regulation. This does not, however, mean that there has been a significant shift to collective bargaining over these matters in place of statutory regulation. The legislation is based on the concept of 'consultation' with safety representatives and safety committees rather than bargaining (see para. 508).

55. There were already signs in the late 1950s and early 1960s that the social consensus which had sustained the traditional voluntarist framework was under strain. The pressure of full employment had contributed to a shift of power to the workplace: employers anxious to retain and recruit labour did not need much prompting to accede to demands for pay increases made by shop stewards on behalf of workgroups. Shop stewards were increasingly identified by politicians and the media as the main cause of 'wages drift', increases in earnings not accounted for by central industry-wide negotiations, and so a serious impediment to the control of inflation which, together with the maintenance of full employment, was a major goal of successive governments from 1945. Trade unions were also blamed for their failure to control the relatively large number of unofficial ('wildcat') strikes in breach of agreed procedures, and for the inefficient use of manpower through the imposition of restrictive 'custom and practice' over-manning. The more deep-seated causes of Britain's post-war economic problems, such as the high levels of military spending and the insistence of the multinational enterprises on keeping Britain as an international financial centre and open economy with a high level of capital export and relatively little domestic investment, received much less attention in the public debate. Trade unions were unable to influence factors such as these, but they came to be seen as a major cause of Britain's relative economic failure. The preoccupation of successive governments was with the exchange rate and the balance of payments, and wage-induced inflation could be readily identified as a source of economic instability.

56. Two broad strategies were adopted to control this phenomenon. One was a succession of incomes policies, the other was the use of the law in order to influence the conduct of industrial relations. These strategies were not consistently applied, and, indeed, they were not infrequently discordant. The political parties, the trade unions and the employers were locked in ceaseless battle over these questions. In the period 1948 to 1979 there were no fewer than six different incomes policies: voluntary wage restraint under the Labour administration (1948–50); a freeze on prices under the Conservatives (1956–7); a 'pay pause' under the Conservatives (1961–2); the Labour government's voluntary (1965) and later (1966–7) compulsory incomes policy; the Conservative's Counter-Inflation Acts (1972–4); and Labour's 'social contract' with the TUC (1974–6), followed by a unilateral policy (1977–9) and a 'concordat' with the TUC (February–May 1979). Each of these policies had distinctive features and used different institutional devices. Some were voluntary and some of them had statutory support. All of them ended in failure. However, it is important to note that, while 'encroaching very directly upon the autonomy of collective bargaining',[50] these policies did not reshape labour law itself.[51] The Prices and Incomes Acts of 1966 and 1967 and the Counter-Inflation Acts of 1972 and 1973 nominally rested upon criminal sanctions, but these were never enforced; the traditional 'immunities' in respect of industrial action were not removed and, indeed, the Act of 1966 actually widened them. Moreover, the policies exempted either wholly or in part the machinery designed to help the low paid and to achieve equal pay for men and women. The negative restraints on the results of collective bargaining were accompanied by a series of positive measures to encourage or promote trade union growth and recognition: in the period from 1948 to 1979 union density among manual workers grew from 50.3 per cent to 63.0 per cent, and among white-collar workers from 33.0 per cent to 44.0 per cent.

57. Indirectly, however, incomes policies did have a major impact on the conceptual framework of labour law. Successive governments always tried to secure trade union consent to their incomes policies. This 'corporate bargaining' recognized the trade union interest in a wide range of policy issues outside the traditional 'economic' questions of terms and conditions of employment. In return for this political influence the unions were ready to accept periods of pay restraint and more state interference in 'free' collective bargaining. For example, during discussions with Prime Minister Heath in 1972 the unions demanded the repeal of the Industrial Relations Act (*below*) and some other legislation in return for agreement on pay restraint. The Heath Government regarded this as too high a price, but the subsequent Labour government entered into a 'social contract' with the TUC. In return for a programme of social and legal reforms, the TUC agreed a policy of temporary pay restraint. The first stage of the reforms was the repeal of the Industrial Relations Act; the second was the enactment of a wide range of new legal rights for trade unions and workers in the Employment Protection Act 1975; the third stage was to have been an extension of workers' participation in the enterprise, but this did not get beyond the government policy statement on industrial democracy (1978) in response to the Report of a Committee of Inquiry under the chairmanship of Lord Bullock (1977). The government's attempts to continue some form of pay restraint after the social contract had collapsed led to a high level of industrial unrest in the winter of 1978–9, widely regarded as a major reason for Labour's defeat in the 1979

50. P. Davies and M. Freedland, 'Editors' Introduction' to Kahn-Freund's *Labour and the Law*, 3rd edn, p. 7.
51. Lord Wedderburn, 'Labour Law Now: a Nudge and a Hold', ILJ 13 (1984), p. 73.

elections. The most significant result of the incomes policies was the 'politicization' of industrial relations, the complete blurring of the distinction between economics and politics on which the traditional system was based. Government attempts to impose wage restraints and to restructure collective bargaining (below) forced the trade unions directly into the political arena. The traditional consensus that the state was essentially 'neutral' or 'abstentionism' could not survive. The boundaries between 'legitimate' economic 'trade disputes' and political action came under stress in a way which had not occurred since the abortive General Strike of 1926.

58. The second strategy which signaled the breakdown of the traditional voluntary system was that of direct legal intervention. Here policies both of reform and of the restriction of collective bargaining have been adopted and these have not always been consistent. On the side of reform, the first legislation on the contract of employment since 1875 had been introduced by a Conservative administration in 1963 and received 'without enthusiasm' by the unions. The Contracts of Employment Act 1963 laid down minimum periods of notice to terminate employment (these have been progressively increased since then but are still low by European standards), and to require employers to provide employees with written statements of their main terms of employment, largely in the hope that this would remove the causes of some disputes. The Redundancy Payments Act 1965, introduced by a Labour government, provided for lump sum payments based on age and length of service for those dismissed on grounds of redundancy after a minimum of two years' employment. The Conservative's Industrial Relations Act 1971 implemented the recommendation of the Royal Commission on Trade Unions and Employers' Associations (1965–8) (chaired by Lord Donovan) that there should be a statutory right for employees not to be unfairly dismissed. This was re-enacted, with improvements, in Labour's Trade Union and Labour Relations Act 1974, and, as already mentioned, the Employment Protection Act 1975, as part of the 'social contract', created a number of other rights for individual employees, such as maternity pay and the right to return to work after pregnancy and confinement, guarantee payments by the employer when work is not available, and protection of wages on the insolvency of the employer. As already mentioned, a comprehensive Health and Safety at Work etc. Act was enacted in 1974. Starting with the Equal Pay Act 1970 and complemented by the Sex Discrimination Act 1975, action has been taken against discrimination on grounds of sex and marital status, and the Race Relations Act 1976 (replacing the earlier Act of 1968) deals with discrimination on racial grounds. With a number of other statutory interjections on the way, the current non-discrimination protections can be found in the Equality Act 2010, which provides protection from discrimination across nine protected characteristics. The growing volume of legislation can be seen from the fact that compared with some five general Acts of Parliament regulating employment passed between 1950 and 1959, and 16 from 1960 to 1969, there were 30 such Acts from 1970 to 1979. Most of the new individual rights were enforced through the industrial tribunals (since 1996 called employment tribunals), established in 1964 (see below, Ch. 5). The case law has spawned several specialist law reports and journals devoted to labour law.

59. The policy of reform has also been evident in the legislation on collective labour relations. The Donovan Commission wanted to introduce 'order' into the largely informal system of plant bargaining, in order to reduce wages drift, restrictive practices and strikes. They hoped that reform could be achieved 'if possible, without destroying the British tradition of keeping industrial relations out of the courts'.[52] However, the Conservative government, elected in 1970, saw legislation as the 'main instrument' in bringing about reform. The Industrial Relations Act 1971 contained a series of provisions designed to reform bargaining structures, to secure recognition of unions by employers, to encourage legally enforceable collective agreements and to reform union rules, in particular so as to make governing bodies responsible for controlling and disciplining their members. The immediate cause of the failure of the 1971 Act was the defeat of the Heath government in the February 1974 election which arose from the confrontation with the miners' union over incomes policy. However, the TUC's policy of non-cooperation with the Act had rendered it largely inoperable: the Act tried to bring about too drastic a change in existing institutions and behaviour by means of law, it was based on the mistaken assumption that employers would use the law, and the transplantation of legal institutions from the United States (e.g. bargaining units, cooling-off periods, etc.) took insufficient account of the different economic and political climate in Britain.

60. The Labour government's 'social contract' legislation (1974–6) returned to the path of reform by restoring the presumption that collective agreements were presumed not to be intended as legally enforceable contracts, and recreating extended immunities from legal action in respect of acts 'in contemplation or furtherance of a trade dispute'. An Advisory, Conciliation and Arbitration Service (ACAS) and a Central Arbitration Committee (CAC) were created and novel collective rights to trade union recognition and the disclosure of information for collective bargaining, as well as improved provisions for the extension of collective agreements to non-organized workers, were granted. Consultation rights were enacted in respect of collective redundancies (this in response to a European directive), health and safety and occupational pension schemes. The wages councils system (*above*) was strengthened and provision was made for encouraging collective bargaining in industries covered by those councils. Some 'individual' rights, such as those to time off work for trade union duties and activities and protection against victimization for trade union membership and activities, underpinned this reassertion, by legal means, of the primacy of the collective bargaining system.

61. Labour law policies, however, contained a strand of restriction of trade union power and collective bargaining. In 1969 Mr Wilson's Labour government had unsuccessfully proposed penal sanctions against unconstitutional strikers who failed to observe a 28-day 'conciliation pause' as well as ballot requirements for certain official strikes and a power to control inter-union disputes over recognition. The Conservatives' Industrial Relations Act, somewhat inconsistently with its support

52. Report of the Royal Commission on Trade Unions and Employers' Associations, Cmnd 3623 (1968), para. 190.

for collective bargaining (*above*), contained a strong element of individualist philosophy in its ban on the closed shop, with some limited exceptions, and the positive right not to belong to any trade union or to a particular union. This was an individual right capable of undermining the organizational strength and representativeness of trade unions. The Act also contained many restrictions on the right to strike, and civil liabilities for so-called 'unfair industrial practices'. These led to several confrontations between unions and the courts. The 'social contract' legislation was reformist in character, but some parts of it were restrictively interpreted by the courts and tribunals. For example, dislike of the consequences of the widening of the statutory immunities by Parliament led the Court of Appeal between 1977 and 1979 to impose novel limitations on these immunities, the statutory recognition provisions became largely inoperable because of restrictive judicial interpretations; and the protection for trade union activities proved to be very limited. For their part, employers were increasingly complaining that the new laws imposed undue burdens on them. The language and philosophy of individual rights, which had become increasingly pervasive, was also criticized from the Left on the grounds that this had strengthened managerial control over jobs giving an enormous impetus to unilateral rule-making by management, in particular through the formalization of disciplinary procedures. The factors which most severely undermined the reformist legislation were economic and political. By 1979, unemployment was mounting, inflation remained at high levels, public expenditure was being cut, and there was acute discontent with the government's policies. In May 1979, the Conservatives led by Mrs Thatcher were elected to power.

§2. The 1980s and Early 1990s

62. The policies and legislation of Mrs Thatcher's administration fundamentally shifted the parameters of labour law. The solution to the major problems of the 1970s – inflation and the politicization of the unions – was sought in the restoration of 'free' markets. The argument was that trade union 'coercion' had caused inflation and unemployment and fluctuating living standards. The unions' 'coercive powers' were said to rest upon their legal 'privileges'. Therefore, in the words of Professor Hayek, whose ideas have been extremely influential, 'there can be no salvation for Britain until the special privileges granted to trade unions three quarters of a century ago are revoked'.[53] Trade unions and labour legislation were seen as a distortion of market relations between employer and employee. In order to make 'free' markets work, it was necessary to 'get the state off people's backs' and to 'deregulate'. It was also necessary to curb effective demand, so as to reduce inflation, and this involved weakening trade union power, and also severely reducing public expenditure. This ideology was reflected in the seven main pieces of legislation introduced by the Conservative government: the Employment Acts 1980, 1982, 1988, 1989 and 1990, the Trade Union Act 1984 and the Trade Union Reform and Employment Rights Act 1993. The legislation concerned with collective matters up

53. F.A. Hayek, *1980s Unemployment and the Unions* (London, 1980), p. 58, and see generally Lord Wedderburn 'Freedom of Association and Philosophies of Labour law', ILJ 18 (1989), p. 1.

to 1992 was consolidated by Trade Union and Labour Relations (Consolidation) Act 1992, and individual employment legislation by the Employment Rights Act 1996. This legislation pursued four specific policies.[54]

63. First, workers' rights of self-help through collective organization and industrial action were effectively restricted to their own employment units. For example, workers were now allowed to picket only outside their own place of work, and the immunity from civil action in 'trade disputes' was narrowed to disputes between workers and their own employer. Secondary action, or solidarity action by workers in one enterprise to support fellow-workers at a different enterprise, was progressively restricted, until the Employment Act 1990 finally made it unlawful. This prevents unions from using traditional methods of preventing the supply of goods to an employer in dispute or banning the sending of work to nonunion shops. Secondly, trade union funds have been placed at the mercy of the law. Previously only union officials could be sued for acts which fell outside the boundaries of permissible 'trade disputes'. Since 1982, union funds themselves have been at risk even if the action is unofficial. The increasing likelihood of confrontation with the courts has exposed the unions to the additional dangers of heavy fines for contempt of court and the sequestration of all or a substantial part of their assets to pay the fines and damages (see paras. 481 and 570 below). Thirdly, contrary to the public policy of the previous hundred years, in the new structure of labour law there was a clear commitment to restrict collective bargaining. The government itself gave a lead by banning membership of trade unions at the Government Communications Headquarters (GCHQ) in January 1984 (see para. 431 below) and, in 1987, by suspending the collective bargaining rights of teachers. Statutory provisions for the recognition of trade unions by employers were repealed in 1980. The legislation since 1980 was also calculated to weaken trade union organization. This was done in part by the incentive of large penal awards against employers and trade unions in favour of those who leave a trade union and are then dismissed by the employer. Unions were required to have secret ballots before industrial action. The 1984 Act limited this duty to action which had received official sanction; but because this appeared to give union executives an incentive to disown local action, the Employment Act 1990 extended the requirement more widely unless union officials repudiated the action. The repudiation provisions were, however, so stringent as to compel union leaders, in effect, to police their members. The law also gave a remedy to individuals who were refused work on the ground of non-membership of a union (for example, where a pre-entry closed shop was in operation). It was likewise unlawful to put pressure on an employer to engage only unionists and to negotiate and consult with trade unions, while at the same time it was lawful to induce an employer not to negotiate with a trade union.

64. Fourthly, central to the whole strategy was the control of labour through the market. The most striking feature of the years since 1979 has been the decline in union membership. The spectre of unemployment had a depressing effect on the labour market in general and this was accentuated by official policies. Traditional

54. A. Pollert, 'The unorganized worker: the decline of collectivism', ILJ 34 (2005), pp. 217–238.

supports for the low-paid were removed; in 1983 the government secured the repeal of the Fair Wages Resolution (above); and the provisions for extending collective agreements to unorganized sectors of a trade or industry were repealed in 1980. In 1986 the functions of wages councils were severely restricted; followed, in 1993, by the complete abolition of all minimum wage-fixing machinery. Indeed, under the Youth Training Scheme, employers were financially penalized if they paid workers above certain low levels. Similarly, traditional tripartite bodies were abolished or transformed, giving employers a majority vote. For example, the tripartite Manpower Services Commission was abolished in favour of decentralized administration by employer-dominated Training Enterprise Councils. Job security was diminished by Orders which first (from July 1980) increased the qualifying period for unfair dismissal rights from six months to one year, and then (from June 1986) to two years. Welfare rights were dismantled, for example abolishing earnings related benefits for unemployment and sickness payments in 1982, reducing many other benefits in real value, replacing sickness benefit by an inferior system of statutory sick pay from the employer for the first 28 weeks' absence and imposing charges for a number of formerly free services. These cuts not only served to reduce public expenditure but they also acted as a powerful discipline on workers to hold down their jobs.

65. Measures such as these had the effect of widening the gulf between an elite of relatively well-paid secure workers who had the good fortune to remain in full-time employment, and a growing 'reserve army of labour' on the fringes of the 'core' labour market. Many of these fringe workers were women, young persons and members of ethnic minorities. The trend since the 1970s has been for inequality to grow between those in full-time secure employment and the various types of marginal workers such as outworkers, part-time workers, casual workers and temporary workers, most of whom fall outside the protection of the employment legislation. In such a climate, labour law was transformed. On the one hand, the trade unions weakened by unemployment and the movement towards the privatization of heavily unionized public corporations were now exposed to a wider range of common law liabilities than at any time since 1906 and they had lost most of the traditional 'auxiliary' legislation which supported collective bargaining. On the other hand, the individual employment protection legislation applied to a diminishing 'core' of the labour market, with workers fearful of unemployment.

§3. 'New Labour's' Policies, 1997–2001

66. The Labour government, elected in 1997, consciously set about forging a 'Third Way' in employment law and employment relations, distinct both from that of its Tory predecessors, and from the corporatist policies of previous Labour Administrations. Central to this vision was the belief that industrial relations should be based on partnership rather than conflict and should contribute to a labour market which is both efficient and fair.[55] This entails both rights and responsibilities. Thus the government enacted or proposed to enact a series of rights, to be exercised both individually and collectively, while at the same time retaining some of the key legal provisions enacted by the Conservatives to restrict industrial action. So far as individual rights were concerned, one of the first measures to be enacted was the National Minimum Wage Act 1998, which broke new ground in providing for a national minimum wage covering all regions of the UK and all sectors of the economy. In departing from the previous strategy of creating minimum wage setting mechanisms only in those areas in which collective bargaining had not taken root, with the partial aim of encouraging collective bargaining, the new measure acknowledged the need for state regulation as a primary mechanism for setting minimum wages, rather than just as a prop to collective bargaining. According to the Low Pay Commission, the Act, which came into effect on 1 April 1999, directly affected then around 1.3 million workers.[56] The move towards a universal basic threshold of individual rights established by law rather than collective bargaining was given added momentum by the incorporation of the European Convention on Human Rights (ECHR), enacted in the Human Rights Act 1998; and the accession to the EU Social Policy Agreement, facilitating its inclusion in the body of the Treaty of Amsterdam. This in turn committed the government to implementing the growing body of regulatory legislation at EU level setting a framework of individual rights. Thus the Working Time Regulations 1998[57] putting into effect the EU Working Time Directive and parts of the Young Workers' Directive, entailed a dramatic departure from the previous reliance on collective bargaining as the primary means for regulating working time and holidays. The Data Protection Act 1998 implemented the EU Data Protection Directive, giving employees the right to know what personal information about them is being held, and to whom it may be disclosed, as well as a right to receive a copy of their personal files on request and to demand that any inaccuracies be corrected or removed. Basic rights for parents are enacted in the Employment Relations Act 1999. The structure of individual rights were further strengthened by the widening of rights not to be unfairly dismissed to include workers employed for more than one year (rather than two years, as previously) and the increase in levels of compensation for unfair dismissal to a maximum of £58,400.

In addition, the government enacted legislation, the Public Interest Disclosure Act 1998, to protect 'whistle-blowers' or individuals who raise genuine concerns at work about criminal acts, miscarriages of justice, illegality or danger to health and safety or the environment. Finally, significant advances in race discrimination legislation were enacted in the form of the Race Relations (Amendment) Act 2000.

55. C. Kilpatrick, 'Has New Labour reconfigured employment legislation?', ILJ 32 (2003), pp. 135–163.
56. Low Pay Commission, 'The National Minimum Wage: Making a Difference', Third Report, Vol. 1, Cm 5075, London, 2001, p. 22.
57. SI 1998/1833.

§4. 'New Labour's Third Way' 2001–2007

67. The second and third term Labour governments, elected since 2001 (2001 and 2005) up to 2007 adopted a 'third way'[58] approach toward labour law, culminating in a minimum rights approach while balancing that with the vast and pervasive Europeanization of the British workplace. This underlying theory sought to remove employment law disputes from the litigation model and move them towards in house solutions and/or towards arbitral mechanisms. Moreover, key EU directives on maternity, parental, paternity rights emphasizing flexibility at work maintained basic labour standards and the UK's traditional individualistic model established during the 1980s, while EU directives on employee consultation and information sought to challenge such individualism in the employment relationship.

68. However, the Labour government's incorporation of the ECHR has since 2000 affected British employment law, generally in terms of its processes, procedures, fairness and inclusions. Consequently, British labour lawyers have witnessed an increase in statutory procedures governing workplace rules. Furthermore, an increase in the remit, often also influenced by EU developments, has taken place with the inclusion of transsexuals, sexuality, religion and age (since 1 October 2006).

§5. 'Brownite' Social Justice 2007–2010

69. During Gordon Brown's premiership, the lacklustre Labour government sought to rekindle its zeal for social reform. To that end, the EU's Charter of Fundamental Rights was adopted in the UK, gaining the equivalence to the effect of Treaty rights. Accordingly, an enhancement of the human rights sphere marked the commencement of an era of consolidation. Most significantly, the Labour government led by Gordon Brown sought to introduce a long-awaited Equality Bill which brought all the former ant-discriminatory Acts under one over-arching, umbrella Statute. More pragmatically, it enacted the Work and Families Act which updated the maternity//parental leave entitlements.

§6. Coalition Government 2010–2015

70. The 2010 General Election returned, for the second time since the Second World War, a coalition government in the UK. To that end, the partnership between the Conservatives under the premiership of David Cameron, and the Liberal Democrats immediately caused a compromise: the 'coalition government agreement' which was to be the basis/agreed terms of reference, for their joint governance. Consequently, a radical reform of Employment Tribunals was undertaken. Its Employment Reform and Regulatory Act 2012, its flagship of reformist zeal, introduced

58. A. Giddens, *The Third Way and its Critics* (Cambridge: Polity Press, 2000).

measures to limit employment hearings and reduce the caseload, while promoting compromise.

Welfare reforms were also central to the coalition government agreement. This was greatly influenced by the economic downturn which continued to have impact. At this time unemployment was around the 2.61 million mark.

In terms of employment laws the Coalition government ought to introduce 'no fault' dismissal for micro firms with fewer than 10 employees (which was unsuccessful); looked to simplify dismissal processes; introduced employment tribunal fees (which was successfully challenged and struck down before the Supreme Court: *UNISON* v. *MOJ* (2017); revised the Transfer of Undertakings (Protection of Employment) Regulations 2006 (from January 2014 amended TUPE Regulations 2013); consolidated 17 national minimum wage regulations; and created a universally portable CRB check that can be viewed online.

§7. Conservative Government 2015: the Brexit Years

71. The years since the Conservative Party was returned as the sole governing party have been dominated by Brexit, and the implications that this will have on citizens' rights, including those within the workplace. As a result there have been few major developments (although some are noted below) in the field of employment law in Britain, outside of the usual annual refinements to matters such as levels of maximum compensation awards, and minimum wage rates.

As noted Brexit has been dominant over the past couple of years. However, outside of this debate one of the key changes in the field of labour law has been through the Trade Union Act 2016, and associated secondary legislation. This tightened up the rules on industrial action by raising the thresholds that have to be achieved in order for the action to be deemed lawful and thus protected. The Act removed the legal protection for industrial action if the ballot turnout of those eligible to vote was below 50 per cent. It also introduced tougher thresholds where the vote for industrial action involved public services, including in the health, education, transport, border security and fire sectors. In these circumstances there is a need for at least 40 per cent of those eligible to vote (not those that did vote) to have voted in favour of the industrial action for it to be legal. This makes it much tougher for lawful industrial action to take place.

72. Other notable developments during this period have included the introduction of the National Living Wage, and the Gender Pay Gap Regulations 2017. The National Living Wage was introduced on 1 April 2016. This works in much the same way as the national minimum wage by guaranteeing a minimum wage rate, and applies to workers aged 25 and over. The Gender Pay Gap Regulations 2017 will require employers employing over 250 workers to publish their average pay according to gender. This will, to an extent, enhance transparency on pay.

Chapter 4. The Role of Government Institutions in the Shaping and Administration of Labour Law and Industrial Relations Policy

73. The growth of legal regulation has been accompanied by the development of regulatory government agencies, which are funded by government but operate independently. During the 'social contract' era of the 1970s, the guiding principle was the establishment of tripartite bodies, whose aim was to facilitate the operation and spread of collective bargaining. The two most important of these institutions were the Advisory, Conciliation and Arbitration Service (ACAS) and the Central Arbitration Committee (CAC). A different model was followed in the fields of sex and race discrimination legislation, where, following the US model of the EEOC, two commissions were established with the duty of promoting equality of opportunity.

During the 1980s and 1990s, the Conservative government policies were opposed to tripartism and aimed at constraining collective bargaining. Thus although ACAS and the CAC survived, they were stripped of some of their central powers.

In particular, ACAS's statutory duties in respects of the extension, development and reform of collective bargaining machinery were abolished and most of the CAC's unilateral arbitration jurisdiction removed. Instead, the conservative government established two new bodies, the Commissioner for the Rights of Trade Union Members and the Commissioner for Protection Against Unlawful Industrial Action, to provide assistance (including the payment of legal costs) to individuals wishing to bring proceedings against their unions or in relation to unlawful industrial action. However, the demand for these bodies was clearly overestimated: the Commissioner for the Rights of Trade Union Members had only nine applicants each year on average; and the Commissioner for Protection Against Unlawful Industrial Action assisted only one applicant in its entire lifetime. Not surprisingly, the new Labour government under its Employment Relations Act 1999, provided for the abolition of these two institutions. At the same time, the new legislation includes important reforms of ACAS and the CAC, particularly in the administration of the statutory recognition procedure. The main institutions are surveyed in this section.

74. Despite the growth of these institutions, it remains true to say that most disputes are not processed through machinery provided by the state. They are settled informally through workplace procedures and joint industrial bodies; and voluntary procedures are generally encouraged by legislation. For example, employers are obliged to give every employee a note specifying the disciplinary and grievance procedures applicable to each employee.[59] Another example is that statutory rights of employees in respect of unfair dismissal[60] and redundancy payments[61] and

59. Employment Rights Act 1996, s. 3. Since 1989 employers with fewer than 20 employees have been exempted: Employment Rights Act 1996, s. 3(3).
60. Employment Rights Act 1996, s. 110: only one agreement has been approved.
61. Employment Rights Act 1996, s. 157.

guarantee payments[62] may be replaced by procedures voluntarily agreed by the collective parties with the approval of the Secretary of State. (In practice, however, few parties have attempted to obtain approval and rigorous criteria are applied before approval is given.) In addition, officers of the Advisory, Conciliation and Arbitration Service must have regard to the desirability of using voluntary procedures before intervening in individual or collective disputes. Since 1998, an employment tribunal is required to reduce a compensatory award in an successful unfair dismissal case if the complainant was given notice that the employer had a procedure for appealing against dismissal and the complainant chose not to use it.[63]

In 2001, an arbitration scheme was introduced as an alternative to employment tribunals in unfair dismissal cases. But this project failed to attract sufficient usage to be a successful alternative to proceedings before the tribunal.

§1. Advisory, Conciliation and Arbitration Service (ACAS)

75. This service was established from 2 September 1974[64] as an essential element in the Social Contract package of statutory aids to collective bargaining.[65]

It was charged with the general duty of promoting the improvement of industrial relations, and it took over from the Department of Employment the functions of conciliation, arbitration and mediation. As mentioned above, its remit originally included the extension, development and, where necessary, reform of collective bargaining machinery; but these functions were removed in 1993. ACAS has three key characteristics. First and foremost is its stress on the value of voluntary dispute settlement. It therefore has no powers of compulsion – it seeks to discharge its responsibilities through the voluntary cooperation of the parties concerned. In addition, it must have regard to the desirability of using voluntary procedures before intervening in individual or collective disputes.[66] The second characteristic is its impartiality and independence from government. Although it is required to report annually to the Secretary of State, it is independent of government and is not subject to the direction of ministers. Thus during the period of operation of incomes policies, the service made it clear that it did 'not act as an interpreter or an enforcement agency' for government incomes policies. The third is continuing tri-partism.

ACAS has a tripartite council consisting of a part-time independent chair, and 12 members: 4 representatives for employees, including 3 appointed in consultation with the TUC), 4 representatives for employers (including 3 appointed in consultation with the CBI), and 3 independent members. Council members are appointed by the Secretary of State for Trade and Industry and the Council provides overall guidance on the running of the service. Day to day management, under the control of the chair and a chief executive, is carried out through an Executive Board.

62. Employment Rights Act 1996, s. 35.
63. Employment Rights (Dispute Resolution) Act 1998, s. 13.
64. It replaced the former Commission on Industrial Relations which had somewhat different functions and structure.
65. It was placed on a statutory basis from 1976 by EPA 1975, Part I, now TULRCA 1992, Part IV, Ch. 4.
66. ACAS *Annual Report*, 1976.

76. In carrying out its general duty to promote the improvement of industrial relations, ACAS operates in three key areas: (i) preventing and resolving disputes; (ii) conciliating in actual and potential complaints to employment tribunals; (iii) providing information and advice; and promoting good practice. Since 1983, ACAS has had the responsibility of designating a list of independent experts to be available in case a tribunal may need to appoint an independent expert in a case in which a job evaluation is needed for the purpose of a claim for equal pay for work of equal value. ACAS also performs a major new function of alternative dispute resolution in individual unfair dismissal cases. Finally, ACAS has several important functions under the new statutory recognition procedures, such as assisting in negotiations to determine the bargaining unit, and helping the parties to draw up a procedure agreement.

77. The role of ACAS was enhanced in 2014, making it a mandatory part of a dispute before a claim could be launched in tribunal. Whereas previously ACAS only needed to be notified once a claim had been submitted, as from 6 May 2014, it became a compulsory requirement in advance of lodging a complaint with tribunal. This notification starts an early conciliation process through ACAS, with a view to keeping the dispute out of tribunal. However, where early conciliation is not engaged with by either the employee or the employer then an early conciliation certificate is issued. This certification enables a claim to be lodged with tribunal. In appreciation of the tight deadlines for issuing a claim then engaging with the conciliation process will pause the time limit. The underlying purpose of this mechanism is to reduce the burden on tribunals and seek to resolve disputes outside the court room.

I. Preventing and Resolving Disputes

78. ACAS's role in preventing and resolving disputes falls into two main categories. The first comprises collective conciliation and is supported by arbitration or dispute mediation where necessary. It is usually the most appropriate when resolving adversarial disputes. The conciliation approach is essentially voluntary, with no pre-conditions requiring the parties to accept any particular outcome. Instead it aims to assist the parties to identify their own ways of settling their differences.

The second, which it calls advisory mediation, is used to facilitate a cooperative and joint problem-solving approach. It is used in preventing disputes from arising or tackling underlying problems beyond the scope of immediate dispute resolution.

ACAS continues to play an active role in preventing disputes through conciliation. Advisory mediation is regarded by ACAS as a 'practical expression of partnership in the workplace' aiming at a cooperative problem-solving approach in order to prevent disputes, address underlying issues and achieve an overall improvement in working relationships.

II. Conciliating in Actual and Potential Complaints to Employment Tribunals

79. ACAS conciliators have a statutory duty to promote settlements of a wide range of employment rights disputes, including unfair dismissal, protection of wages, race and sex discrimination, equal pay and disability discrimination, which have been or could be made to an employment tribunal. All such complaints are directed initially to ACAS. Since 2009, judicial mediation has been introduced in the employment tribunals, so as to enable the staying of proceedings while mediation is attempted so as to resolve the employment dispute.

III. Providing Information and Advice and Promoting Good Practice

80. ACAS provides free advice to employers, employers' associations, individual workers and trade unions on a variety of subjects. It regards its advisory function as the principal means of fulfilling its statutory duty to promote the improvement of industrial relations and devotes a considerable proportion of its resources for this purpose. Advice includes both short-term assistance on specific matters and long term, in-depth assistance which the service considers to be more likely to lead to lasting improvements in industrial relations. ACAS also encourages the adoption of good practice in working relationships through providing training seminars and workshops; and through a wide range of publications. Finally, ACAS has general power to issue codes of practice containing practical guidance to promote the improvement of industrial relations. Under this power, a Code of Practice on Disciplinary Practice and Procedures has been issued. ACAS has also issued two further Codes of Practice, as it is obliged to do, one in respect of the disclosure of information for purposes of collective bargaining, and one concerned with time off for trade union officials and members. These three Codes were revised in 1997 and 2004. Under the Employment Relations Act 1999, ACAS has revised the Time-off Code with effect from 2010.

IV. Alternative Dispute Resolution

81. ACAS has been given a central role in establishing the voluntary dispute resolution mechanism set up by the Employment Rights (Dispute Resolution) Act 1998 as an alternative to employment tribunal hearings. The aim of the scheme is to reduce the case-load of employment tribunals, by offering the parties a more informal, speedier, more private and less costly alternative to a tribunal case. Under the Act, parties may agree in writing to submit their dispute to arbitration, in which case, the jurisdiction of employment tribunals will be ousted. ACAS has been given the power to prepare and operate an such an arbitration scheme, thereby extending its arbitration role beyond its traditional function of arbitrating collective disputes between employers and trade unions. Most significantly, whereas ACAS arbitration has never been legally binding, the new powers of arbitration in unfair dismissal cases require a mechanism by which arbitrators' awards can, if necessary, be enforced in the same way as employment tribunal decisions. This is particularly true if the award includes a re-employment order.[67]

§2. Central Arbitration Committee (CAC)

82. The Central Arbitration Committee was established in 1975 as a permanent tripartite arbitration committee maintained at state expense, and reconstituted in 2000.[68] It consists of a chairman and members with experience as employers and workers' representatives respectively. For hearings, the chairman (or deputy) sits with two other members, one drawn from each side. It is independent of ACAS and is not subject to government direction of any kind. The powers of the CAC have waxed and waned under successive governments. It played a vigorous role during the 1970s in enforcing many of the 'statutory props' introduced as part of the Social Contract legislation, including providing unilateral arbitration in respect of claims for the extension of terms of employment and the observance of fair wages by government contractors; claims arising from failure to comply with ACAS recommendations for union recognition or to disclose information for collective bargaining; disputes on statutory joint industrial councils and claims in respect of equal pay under collective agreements.

With the repeal by the Conservative government of the 1980s and 1990s of most of these statutory powers, the Compulsory jurisdiction of the CAC was narrowed, to cover only disclosure of information for collective bargaining purposes. Until the new powers granted it by the 1999 legislation came on stream, the CAC's only major activity was complaints of an employer's failure to disclose information for collective bargaining purposes, as required by the statute. However, even in this area, activity was minimal: the CAC received 11 complaints between January 1999 and March 2000, and most of these were resolved by voluntary agreement rather than by CAC decision. The CAC has always played a vigorous role in voluntary arbitration. These facilities were widely used in the first years of the existence of the CAC, primarily because they provided a means to correct anomalies created by the operation of incomes policies. However, the voluntary arbitration function slowed to a trickle and has now all but dried up.

Thus from a peak 1,030 references in 1977 and 1,065 in 1978, there were only 15 in 1989, and none at all in 1999/2000. Nevertheless, through all these changes, the CAC maintained its basic philosophy of informal dispute resolution. As its long-standing chairman Sir John Woods said:

> The Committee is not a court in the traditional sense. Its procedures and hearings are structured so as to achieve complete informality. The aim is to encourage the approach by way of problem solving rather than by emphasising the aspects of conflict and verdict. Above all there is a commitment to the principles of sound industrial relations and workable solutions.[69]

---

67. All statistics are derived from ACAS *Annual Report* 2008–9.
68. TULRCA 1992, s. 5, 259–265.
69. CAC *Annual Report* 2008–09.

83. Under the 1999 legislation of the New Labour government, the CAC once again plays a central role. There are two primary areas of jurisdiction. First, powers are given to the CAC by the Transnational Information and Consultation of Employees Regulations 1999, which put into effect the European Works Council Directive of 1994. The Regulations provide for the CAC to decide such issues as whether employees are given sufficient information to ascertain the number and location of staff in the undertaking, whether a valid request has been made for the establishment of a works council, and the structure of the body that negotiates the establishment of the works council (the special negotiating body). The preferred method of approaching such issues is to propose an informal meeting, with the parties being given the option of utilizing ACAS's conciliation services. This is without prejudice to the parties' right to proceed to a formal hearing where necessary.

84. The second, and probably the most far-reaching of the new powers, is concerned with the novel statutory recognition procedures introduced by the Employment Relations Act 1999. The new provisions provide that in certain circumstances an independent trade union may apply to the CAC for a declaration that it should be recognized to conduct collective bargaining regarding pay, hours and holidays on behalf of a group or groups of workers in a particular bargaining group. When an application is submitted, the CAC must first decide whether it is admissible, using such factors as to whether or not the trade union has 10 per cent of workers in its proposed bargaining unit in membership and whether or not a majority of workers in the unit would be likely to favour recognition. Once the application is accepted, the CAC must decide, unless the parties have agreed voluntarily, whether the proposed bargaining unit is the appropriate one. At the next stage, the CAC must decide whether or not a ballot should be held: if more than 50 per cent of workers in the unit are already members of the trade union, the CAC may grant recognition with a ballot. If a ballot is held, a majority of those voting must be in favour, and this must constitute at least 40 per cent of workers in bargaining unit.

Once recognition has been granted, the parties must agree a bargaining procedure: if no agreement can be reached the CAC must determine the procedure. Unusually, this amounts to a legally enforceable contract, and if one party does not abide by the procedure the other may seem an Order for specific performance from the court. The CAC also has the power to declare a union to be derecognized.[70]

§3. Equality and Human Rights Commission

85. The Equality Act 2006 established an Equality and Human Rights Commission (EHRC).[71]

Fundamentally, this legislation merged the previous, long-standing anti-discrimination agencies in the UK – the EOC, CRE and DRC. This new body

70. TULRCA 1992 Sched. A1 Part 1, as inserted by ERA 1999, Sched. 1.
71. C. O'Cinneide, 'The Commission for Equality and Human Rights – a new institution' [2007] ILJ vol. 36, pp. 141–162; and C. McCrudden, 'Equality legislation and reflexive regulation' [2007] ILJ vol. 36, pp. 255–266.

became operative from 2007, and seeks to promote human rights. It also has responsibility for the operation of the current discrimination statutes and the plethora of equality regulations, including religion or belief, sexual orientation and age. The EHRC has improved powers (when compared with the three commissions it replaced) to promote equality and deal with discrimination. There is also pressure on the government to create a single discrimination statute, to replace the three main discrimination statutes.

86. Historically, the EOC and CRE followed the same model and so can conveniently be dealt with together. Consisting of 8 to 15 members appointed by the Secretary of State, each Commission is charged with the general duty to work towards the elimination of discrimination, to promote equality of opportunity between men and women (EOC) or persons of different racial groups (CRE) and to review the operation of the anti-discrimination legislation.[72] The Commissions function as an important supplement to the individual right of recourse to an employment tribunal on a discrimination complaint. Many cases of unlawful discrimination may not reach a tribunal: an individual may lack the resources or courage to initiate an action: evidence of individual detriment may be difficult to amass; or an individual remedy may be of little assistance to others affected by discriminatory practices (there are no class actions). To remedy some of these weaknesses, each Commission had the power to assist an individual complainant and to institute its own proceedings in relation to discriminatory advertisements, instructions or pressure to discriminate, and discriminatory practices, as does the EHRC today.

87. More significantly, the EHRC has the additional power to initiate and conduct a 'formal investigation' into cases of suspected unlawful discrimination. This power, which combines investigative and judicial functions, carries with it the ability to demand written or oral evidence and the production of documents.

The aim of the investigation is to secure a change in the discriminatory practices, and to this end the EHRC may make recommendations for changes in policy or practice, either during or after the completion of the formal investigation. Moreover, if unlawful discrimination is revealed, the EHRC has its own sanction, in the form of a 'non-discrimination notice', which (subject to the right of appeal to an employment tribunal) may require the respondent not to commit any further unlawful discrimination and to keep the EHRC informed of any changes instituted to do so. Recourse to judicial sanctions is envisaged only as a last resort – if the notice is not overturned on appeal and there is persistent discrimination within five years, the EHRC can take the respondent to the County Court and obtain an injunction. The most recent example being the EHRC's action in 2009 against the British National Party forcing it to change its Constitution, so as to be inclusive rather than discriminatory. Formal investigations have not had the impact that might have been expected, partly because the procedures are cumbersome and the courts have implied procedural requirements which have enabled some respondents to avoid or

72. SDA 1975, Part VI; RRA 1976, Part VII.

seriously delay investigation.[73] The EHRC also has powers to undertake and assist research or educational activities and to issue Codes of Practice.

88. The two well established commissions were joined by the Disability Rights Commission (DRC), which operated from 2000 to 2007. Established by the Disability Rights Commission Act 1999, the commission had the duty to work towards the elimination of discrimination against disabled persons, to promote the equalization of opportunities for disabled persons, and to encourage good practice in the treatment of disabled persons. Its powers include proposing changes in the law, advising public agencies on the practical application of the law, undertaking research and giving legal support or advice in cases which raise questions of principle or where it is unreasonable to expect the individual complainant to deal with the case unaided. EHRC retained the DRC's power to enter into a legally binding written agreement with a person if it has reason to believe he or she has been conducted an unlawful act. The agreement is enforceable through the County Court. Its first annual budget of £11 million was nearly twice as much as that of the EOC (£5.8 million) and three-quarters of that of the CRE (£14.5 million). In its legal strategy plan for 2001–3, the DRC has stated its intention to spend about a quarter of its annual legal budget of £1.25 million on supporting individual test cases in order to clarify the law, and signal good practice to agencies. It has also announced its intention to conduct at least one formal investigation during this period.[74]

§4. Certification Officer (CO)

89. The CO is an independent statutory officer, established in 1975, who is responsible for supervising several aspects of the internal affairs of trade unions. The CO was originally established with the primary function of scrutinizing trade unions to decide whether they were truly independent of employers and issuing certificates of independence as well as monitoring the annual returns and accounts of unions and employers' associations, and supervising political funds and mergers between unions. However, these powers were progressively augmented by the legislation of the 1980s. Thus it has the power to deal with complaints by members that a union has failed to maintain an accurate register of members; and that a union has failed to comply with the statutory provisions for secret postal ballots for electing members of its executive committee, president and general secretary; It is also responsible for ensuring the observance of statutory procedures governing the setting up, operation and review of political funds; and for ensuring that statutory requirements concerning the actuarial examination of members' superannuation schemes are observed. These powers have been further augmented by the Employment Relations Act 1999, to include, most importantly, complaints by union members that there has been a breach of the rules of the union relating to appointments or elections; disciplinary proceedings, balloting on any issue other than industrial

73. See C. McCrudden *et al.*, *Racial Justice at Work: Enforcement of the Race Relations Act 1976 in Employment* (London, Policy Studies Institute, 1991), pp. 48–120.

74. *Equal Opportunities Review*, 83 (1999) p. 2; 96 (2001), p. 9.

action and the constitution or proceedings of any executive committee, conference or other body of the union. In addition, the CO's enforcement powers are to be strengthened to include an enforcement order which may be enforced in the same way as an order of the court.[75]

§5. Relevant Government Departments

90. Employment-related functions have, under successive governments, been exercised by various government departments and independent or semi-independent government agencies. The Labour Department of the Board of Trade was set up in 1886 mainly to collect information on trade unions, strikes and other matters.

During World War I, a separate Ministry of Labour was established, exercising various functions in relation to conciliation and arbitration, functions which were retained by its successors, the Department of Employment and Productivity and finally the Department of Employment, until they were transferred to ACAS in September 1974. During the 1980s the Department of Employment was once again given responsibility for training functions and gained responsibility for government policy on deregulation. The Department of Employment has always played a central role in the coordination and formulation of policy, research and consultation with employers' associations and trade unions, as well as having specific functions such as the promotion of equal opportunities, and the collection of labour statistics.

It was also responsible for wages councils, Employment Tribunals, the Employment Appeal Tribunal and Courts of Inquiry. However, in 1995 the functions of the Department of Employment were split between two different departments, the Department for Education and Employment (DfEE) and the Department of Trade and Industry (DTI). In June 2001 the then Prime Minister, Tony Blair, carried out an extensive reorganization. This retained the key role of the Department of Trade and Industry which has an employment relations directorate, whose functions include the development of legislation on terms and conditions of employment, such as hours of work, pay, individual employment rights, employee consultation and trade unions and collective rights; the negotiation and implementation of European employment directives; and promotion of workplace partnership. It is also responsible for employment tribunals, ACAS and the Low Pay Commission which advises on the national minimum wage. From 2007 the DTI became BERR (Business, Employment & Regulatory Reform)and from 2009, BIS (Business, Innovations and Science) emerged.

The new Department for Work and Pensions has taken over some responsibilities from the old DfEE and Department of Social Security. Its responsibilities include the New Deal at work and its successor – the Work Programme, the former Labour government's and now, Coalition Government's main strategy for combating unemployment, welfare benefits and matters relating to disability.

---

75. Employment Relations Act 1999, Sched. 4.

The Home Office remains responsible for race equality, work permits and immigration matters. Also, the Cabinet Office is responsible for coordination of equality issues across government, and for the implementation of the anti-discrimination directives under Article 13 of the EC Treaty (now Article 18 of the Treaty on the Functioning of the European Union).

Chapter 5. Employment Tribunals and Courts

§1. Jurisdiction of Employment Tribunals (ETs)

91. A specialized system of labour courts, now known as employment (formerly industrial, until 1996) tribunals, has only existed in the UK since 1964. Known for many years as industrial tribunals, they were first created, under the Industrial Training Act 1964, to deal with the relatively minor question of appeals by employers against levies imposed on them by industrial training boards. Since then, the jurisdiction has been expanded enormously, to cover almost all the statutory individual employment rights. Thus, tribunals have jurisdiction in respect of complaints of unfair dismissal, redundancy payment, failure to consult over proposed redundancies or transfer of undertakings, equal pay, breach of the employment provisions of the sex, race and disability discrimination legislation, unlawful deductions from wages, unjustifiable discipline, exclusion or expulsion from a trade union; Sunday working, working time and the national minimum wage. They also have jurisdiction over specific issues in respect of health and safety at work, training and compensation.

The Donovan Commission suggested that industrial tribunals should be concerned with individual rights only, and not in collective matters, 'since these are matters which must be settled by procedures of, or agreed through, collective bargaining'.

While this is broadly the case, the distinction has not always proved easy to draw, as with the right not to be dismissed for trade union activities, and the right to have one's trade union consulted about impending redundancies. The newly introduced right to claim for unfair dismissal during industrial action is a particularly important breach of the divide between collective and individual jurisdiction. The jurisdiction of employment tribunals has recently been extended to include claims for breach of contract of employment and other related contractual claims arising or outstanding on the termination of employment, thus remedying the awkward separation of jurisdictions between tribunals and the ordinary civil courts which previously existed.

However, collective disputes, insofar as they give rise to civil action, are dealt with by the ordinary courts.

§2. Jurisdiction of Courts

92. The ordinary courts have exclusive jurisdiction in respect (1) actions in tort (delict), the most important of which are for injunctions and damages in connection with industrial action; (2) actions for damages for personal injuries and in respect of a person's death. They also have jurisdiction over contractual claims, but, as has been seen above, employment related contractual claims can now be brought before tribunals. In England and Wales these actions may be brought in either the county court or the High Court, depending on the value of the claim, its importance, complexity and need for speed. In Scotland, the action may be brought in either the Sheriff Court or in the Court of Session. There are special speedy and relatively cheap procedures for small claims in the County Court and Sheriff Court. There is an appeal to the Court of Appeal (Civil Division) in England and Wales, or to the Sheriff Principal and then to the Inner House of the Court of Session in Scotland. Other cases, in particular those for injunctions arising out of industrial action, are brought before a single judge in the High Court in England and Wales (in either the Queen's Bench or Chancery Division) and the Court of Session (Outer House) in Scotland. There is an appeal to the Court of Appeal and the Inner House of the Court of Session respectively. The House of Lords is the final appellate court for both England and Wales and Scotland; appeals to this body require either leave of itself or of the court below. The High Court and the Court of Session also have a general supervisory jurisdiction over inferior tribunals. In addition, the High Court has an inherent jurisdiction to review certain decisions and actions of public employers.

§3. Composition of Tribunals

93. The President of the Employment Tribunals (a judicial officer appointed by the Secretary of State for Justice) is responsible for their running (with a President of Employment Tribunals for Scotland). The system is divided into regions, with a number of Regional Offices of Employment Tribunals (ROETs), each with a regional chairman, and ETs sit at these regional centres and at a number of permanent centres. Applications are lodged at the appropriate local ET. The Employment Tribunal Service (ETS), which is now part of the Tribunals Service, an agency within the Ministry of Justice, has responsibility for the overall administration of ETs. It has a Director appointed by, and who reports to, the Secretary of State for Business (BIS). ETs have a tripartite structure, consisting of a legal chairman, known since 2006 as an Employment Judge (application for such post are open to solicitors, barristers, advocates or fellows of the Chartered Institute of Legal Executives with at least seven years' post-qualifying experience, or persons who have gained experience in law which, in the opinion of the Senior President of Tribunals, makes them suitable for appointment. Appointment is by the Judicial Appointments Commission)[76] and two lay members with employment/industrial experience, historically drawn from panels appointed by the Secretary of State for Business, one after consultation with the trades unions, the other after consultation with employers' organizations. Yet, since 2000, the trades unions and employers panels' input has lessened to allow for wider and more representative panel members to be recruited from the British general public. This structure made ETs more acceptable to trade unions than the ordinary courts, which, as we have seen, had frequently been hostile to trade union interests. Further, since 2010 Employment Judges sit alone, save for equality claims or where the parties request a Full Tribunal.

The lay members have full voting rights and it is not unknown for them to outvote the lawyer chairman/Employment Judge, although they are generally reluctant to do so on points of law. The lay members are not intended to act as representatives of trade unions or employers' associations. Instead, they are expected to act as neutral arbiters, drawing on their experience of industrial relations to enhance the

76. Secretary of State for Scotland in Scottish tribunals.

quality of their decision making. Indeed, the overwhelming majority of decisions are unanimous.

§4. PROCEDURE

94. Despite their structure, ETs retain many of the characteristics of ordinary courts. The adversarial system prevails. Each party is responsible for presenting and proving its case. And the tribunal has no investigative powers of its own. Furthermore, the tribunal itself has no power to promote or order a compromise, the function of conciliation being given instead to ACAS at the pre-hearing stage. On the other hand, their enforcement powers are not as strong as those of ordinary courts. The ultimate sanction for breach of an order made by an ET is payment of a sum of money; it has no power to issue injunctions or to fine or imprison for contempt of court. Instead, the County Courts in England and Wales and the Sheriff Court in Scotland have jurisdiction to enforce tribunal orders in the same way as other Orders. The procedures of tribunals were streamlined by both legislation in 1998, 2004 and 2012.[77] Since 2009 judicial mediation has been introduced in ETs. This opens the possibility of a different approach from that which ETs adopt in unfair dismissal cases.[78]

95. Tribunals have several advantages over the ordinary courts. For instance, they are much quicker, most cases reaching a first hearing in under 26 weeks, whereas a case in the civil courts can take years rather than months. Furthermore, tribunals are more accessible, sitting, as we have seen, all over the country. Although the basic adversarial procedure remains, tribunals are more informal than courts: there are no complicated pleadings and tribunals are not bound by the strict rules of evidence. It was initially envisaged that legal representation would normally be avoided in tribunals. A party can choose any representative or be unrepresented. State-funded legal aid is not available for representation before tribunals, although some funding is available for legal assistance in preparation of a case. Legal representation is in practice relatively common, particularly on the parts of employers.

However, despite this, the proportion of parties represented by legal representatives at hearings has declined in recent years. This is with many applicants (from the employee side) electing to represent themselves due to the cost of legal representation. The Annual Report of the Employment Tribunals Service (the ETS Report) provides useful statistics on employment claims. For example, it was reported that in the year 2010–11 there were approximately 122,800 applications to the ET. Of these applications, approximately 47,900 were unfair dismissal claims. However, since July 2013, when employment tribunal fees (noted below) were introduced, these numbers have reduced dramatically. In the first quarter following the introduction of fees (October–December 2013) it was noted that there were 79

77. Employment Rights (Dispute Resolution) Act 1998.

78. The ACAS Arbitration Scheme for the Resolution of Unfair Dismissal Disputes is available on the ACAS website www.acas.org.uk.

per cent fewer applications than compared to the same period in 2012. For comparison purposes thr total number of cases in the year to June 2013 was around 196,000, while in the year to September 2014 this reduced around 44,000 claims. The most recent statistics released (1 April 2015 – 31 March 2016) indicate that there was a total of 83,031 applications.

96. Successive governments have been concerned to create procedures to deal efficiently with the case-load and weed out unmeritorious cases. Since 1989, there have been provisions for a pre-hearing review, at which a party to the proceedings may be required to pay a deposit of up to £1000 if he or she wishes to continue to participate in the proceedings. This has been criticized as an unprecedented obstacle to the pursuance of a legal claim by the poorest applicants. Similarly, costs awards are aimed at deterring unreasonable and misconceived cases. The basic principle is that each party bears his or her own costs; but an award of costs must be considered in cases in which proceedings which have no reasonable prospect of success have been pursued. In this respect, the unreasonable behaviour of a party's representative may be taken into account. The amount which a tribunal may award without an assessment of the costs up to £20,000 in 2012. This too has been criticized, in that it might act as a deterrent to applicants and also because it might encourage employers to use lawyers if they think they could recoup their costs. This would detrimentally affect the non-legalistic aims of tribunals. Additionally there is concern about the ability of a tribunal judge to undertake the necessary detailed assessment of costs, given that this is not a task that they historically have often undertake.

Although costs are not normally awarded by the ET, it does have power to make costs orders against a party (or a party's representative). There are three forms of costs orders available: (i) a costs order; (ii) a preparation time order; and (iii) a wasted costs order. A costs order will only be made if a party is legally represented, after taking into account the ability of the party to pay. A costs order is normally limited to a maximum of £20,000. It may be made in a number of circumstances, e.g. where in bringing the proceedings the party or the representative has 'acted vexatiously, abusively, disruptively or otherwise unreasonably, or the bringing or conducting of the proceedings by a party has been misconceived' (rule 40(3), Rules of Procedure).[79]

97. On 27 January 2011, the government announced its consultation on Tribunal reform: *Resolving workplace disputes*.

Subsequently, in November 2011 the government published its response, proposing:

- wider usage of mediation;
- modernizing Tribunals: Underhill Review – new ET Rules (April 2012);
- revising the law on compromise ('settlement') agreements;
- the RAPID Resolution Scheme (e.g. holiday pay claims);

79. Employment Tribunals (Constitution and Rules of Procedure) Regulations 2004 SI 2001, 1861; Employment Tribunals (Constitution and Rules of Procedure) (Scotland) Regulations 2001 SI 2001, 1170.

- that all Tribunal claims to be lodged with ACAS in first instance – early conciliation;
- fraising the unfair dismissal qualifying period from one year to two years (effective from April 2012);
- employer penalties (fines);
- the introduction of claim fees (£250 claim fee/£1,000 hearing fee/£1,500 appeal fee) (effective from July 2013).

Subsequently, its Enterprise and Regulatory Reform Act 2013 enacted the government's aim to cut the costs of doing business and attempted to remove regulatory burdens that were inhibiting innovation. The relevant employment law provisions include:

- ACAS pre-claim conciliation: prospective claimants being required to contact ACAS before they can begin certain types of employment tribunal proceedings, so that parties can be offered conciliation to attempt to resolve their dispute within a prescribed period without it reaching the tribunal system.
- Certain decisions without a need for a hearing: a 'rapid resolution' scheme for certain simple or low value tribunal claims, where the parties consent in writing to the determination of their claim by a 'legal officer' will be introduced so that these can be determined without the need for a hearing.
- EAT hearings by a single judge: cases in the Employment Appeal Tribunal (EAT) will be able to be heard by a judge sitting alone. However, a judge may direct that proceedings are to be heard by a judge and two or four appointed members. The Secretary of State may specify that particular proceedings must be heard by a judge and a certain number of appointed members.
- Additional financial penalties for employers who breach employment laws: tribunals will be given a discretionary power to impose financial penalties (subject to a minimum of £100 and a maximum of £10,000) on employers where they are found to have breached a claimant's employment rights and the tribunal considers that the employer's behaviour had one or more 'aggravating features' e.g. where the action was deliberate or committed with malice. Where compensation is awarded to the claimant, the penalty must be set at 50 percent of that amount. However, if the employer pays the penalty within 21 days, it will be reduced by 50 percent.
- Settlement (formerly 'Compromise') agreements: references to 'compromise' agreements in employment legislation such as the Employment Rights Act will be replaced with 'settlement' agreement as the Government believes this better reflects the purpose and intent of such agreements.
- Changes to the Equality and Human Rights Commission: changes will be made to the Commission's remit by removing some of its powers and duties and by reducing the frequency with which it is required to report on progress in society (to every five years from every three years).

These changes were embedded during 2014.

98. The most contentious reform that was implemented was the introduction of fees to the employment tribunal system. Fees were brought in through the 2013 Employment Tribunals and the Employment Appeal Tribunal Fees Order (the Fees Order), which came into effect on 29 July 2013. The Order required the person bringing a complaint to pay a fee, otherwise the Tribunal would refuse jurisdiction over the dispute. A two tier structure was introduced. For simpler claims, which were primarily simple monetary claims such as unauthorized deductions from wages, the application fee was £160 and hearing fee £230. These increased to £250 and £950 where the matter was more complex (which included unfair dismissal and discrimination claims). EAT fees were set at an application fee of £400 and a hearing fee of £1200. The fees (noted briefly above) had a significant impact upon the number of claims being brought before Tribunal, which led to a challenge of the fees before the courts.[80] The challenge was primarily based on submissions that the fee structure was unlawfully impeding access to justice, although other submissions including that they indirectly discriminated against female applicants were also made. Up to, and including in, the Court of Appeal the fees system was declared lawful. However, the Supreme Court, handing down its judgment on 26 July 2017, decided otherwise and found the system to be unlawful. Lord Reid giving the lead judgment stating that the fall of around 70% in the number of claims since the introduction of the fees had been 'so sharp, so substantial, and so sustained as to warrant the conclusion that a significant number of people who would otherwise have brought claims have found the fees to be unaffordable'. Lord Reid continued, and when considering claims that attracted no financial recompense, stated that even in cases where the fees were not unaffordable, they could still be preventing access to justice by 'render[ing] it futile or irrational to bring a claim'. This formed the basis against which the Supreme Court held that the ET fee system was unlawful. This has returned the ET system to a fee-free system. At present there does not be any intention on the part of the Government to re-introduce fees to the ET system in a modified manner.

§5. Employment Appeal Tribunal (EAT)

99. The EAT was established by the Employment Protection Act 1975. It is a superior court of record dealing with appeals from the decisions of employment tribunals and the Certification Officer.[81] The constitution of the EAT is laid down in the Employment Tribunals Act 1996, which expressly give it the powers of the High Court. The jurisdiction of the EAT extends to England, Wales and Scotland. It has up to five courts in London and one court in Edinburgh, the Scottish Division. Appeals to the EAT are generally on a point of law only, although on certain appeals from decisions of the Certification Officer, an appeal may be on law or fact. The EAT frequently sees its role as to establish guidelines and standard criteria for application by tribunals, although it has at times preferred to refuse appellate jurisdiction

80. *R (on the application of Unison) v Lord Chancellor* [2017] UKSC 51 SC.
81. See http://www.employmentappeals.gov.uk.

by classifying issues as questions of fact in order to discourage legalism and technicality, retaining the tribunals' character as quick, cheap and accessible means of resolving disputes. Its functions are laid out in the Employment Appeal Tribunal (Amendment) Rules 2004.[82]

100. There is a further appeal on questions of law from the EAT to the Court of Appeal (CA) in England and Wales and to the Court of Session (Inner House) in Scotland, but the leave of either the EAT or the higher court must first be obtained. From these courts, there is a final appeal, with leave, on questions of law to the House of Lords, the highest court. In practice, most appeals do not go beyond the EAT.

101. The EAT has up until recently mirrored the employment tribunal in having a tripartite composition, which is unusual for an appellate body, consisting of a judge, drawn from a panel of High Court and Court of Session judges, and either two or four lay members, drawn from a panel of persons appointed because of their special knowledge and experience of industrial relations. However, since 25 June 2013 all hearings in the EAT will be heard by a judge sitting alone, unless the judge directs otherwise and requires wing members to also sit.

As in the case of ET proceedings, in any case there is an equal number of persons with experience as representatives of employers and workers respectively, again the aim being to draw on industrial relations expertise, rather than to adopt a partisan approach. A majority of these appeals were lodged by employees.

102. The doctrine of precedent, by which lower courts and tribunals are bound by the *ratio decidendi* (or grounds) of decisions of higher courts, applies equally to the ETs and the EAT. Thus, ETs are bound by the decisions of the EAT and of all the higher courts. The EAT is in turn bound by decisions of the Court of Appeal and the Court of Session (Inner House), and, at the top of the pyramid, the Supreme Court (formerly the House of Lords). The EAT is considered to be of equal jurisdiction to the Queen's Bench Division of the High Court and the Court of Session (Outer House); therefore decisions of these latter courts will have persuasive but not binding force in the EAT. This system of precedent means that law reporting is a matter of some importance. Since tribunal decisions are binding only on the parties, reports of these decisions are of interest only as illustrations of the practice of tribunals. Reports of decisions of the EAT and superior courts are, however, potential precedents.

103. As noted above, the EAT, up until the decision of the Supreme Court in *R (on the application of Unison)* v. *Lord Chancellor* was subject to a fee system (£400 application fee/£1200 hearing fee). However, since this decision, handed down on 26 July 2017, fees are not applicable to applications to the EAT.

---

82. SI 2004/2526.

Chapter 6. Sources of Labour Law

104. Legal norms regulating employment relationships are derived from a variety of sources, including common law, legislation, codes of practice and voluntary or autonomous sources.

§1. Common Law

105. At common law, the focus of legal analysis is the relationship between the employer and each individual employee. This relationship is characterized as a contract, the assumption being, as in other contractual relationships, that there is a personal and voluntary exchange of freely bargained promises between two parties (employer and employee) equally protected by the civil law alone. In practice, however, the terms and conditions of employment of most employees are not negotiated individually and on an equal basis with the employer. In the vast majority of cases, terms and conditions are either unilaterally imposed by the employer, or are laid down in a collective agreement between the employer or employers' organization and the relevant trade unions. Nevertheless, industrial relations continues to be characterized by lawyers as a mass of individual contracts of employment and it is through the mechanism of contract that most rights and obligations take effect. For example, terms and conditions laid down in a collective agreement are only given legal effect if they can be shown to be incorporated into an individual contract.

106. The common law has also been a source of legal norms regulating collective relationships. A series of civil wrongs regulating industrial action was developed by the courts (for example, the tort of inducing breach of contract) and although these have been overlaid by a complex system of statutory immunities, the foundation remains the common law. The relationship between trade unions and their members is construed as one of contract.

§2. Legislation

107. In the absence of a written constitution, the major legislative impetus comes from Parliament. Although voluntary collective bargaining was the primary source of protection for employees until the 1960s, certain aspects of industrial relations have been regulated by the state since the 19th century. This included legislation protecting children and women, regulating some aspects of health and safety and establishing mechanisms for setting minimum wages in certain industries. More recently, there has been a rapid increase in employment legislation. To these must be added numerous statutes applying to specific sectors of employment.

108. In addition to Parliament, other bodies such as Ministers, Departments of State, public corporations and local authorities have limited law-making powers, subject to repeal or alteration by Parliament. There are several hundred pieces of subordinate legislation of this kind, covering matters as diverse as the employment of children, levies for industrial training, minimum wages orders, the licensing of employment agencies and the procedure of ETs. There is also a large number of regulations applying to specific employment. A peculiar feature of law-making in the UK is that regulations governing the terms and conditions of employment of civil servants (in central government) are made by the Minister for the Civil Service under the ancient prerogative powers of the Crown. It was only in 1984 that it was established, for the first time, that the exercise of these powers is subject to judicial review on grounds of illegality, irrationality or procedural impropriety.[83]

§3. Relation between Legislation and Common Law

109. Because legislative intervention developed in parallel and often independently of the common law concept of the contract of employment, the relationship between statutes and the contract is complex:

(1) Some statutory rights operate wholly outside of the contract of employment. For example, a breach of an employer's statutory safety duties may be the subject of criminal prosecution or administrative enforcement under the Health and Safety at Work Act 1974 or, in some cases, a civil action for damages by an injured employee in tort.
(2) In some cases, both statutory and contractual rights exist, as in the case of statutory rights to guarantee payments for employees who are laid off work, maternity pay and payment for time-off (see Part I, Chs. 4 and 5). In such cases, overlap is avoided by express provision in the statute either for the setoff of sums of money awarded under the statute against amounts due under the contract, or vice versa, or by the creation of 'composite' rights enabling the employee to claim those features of the contractual and statutory rights which are most favourable.
(3) Some legislation expressly provides that the duties they impose are to take effect as terms of the individual contract. An example is the Equal Pay Act 1970 which provides that an 'equality clause' is deemed to be included in the contract of every man and woman employed at an establishment in Great Britain.
(4) Other statutes are silent on this point, leaving the courts and tribunals free to decide whether or not rights arise under the contract. This has on occasion led to the employee being deprived of statutory protection (e.g. protection against unfair dismissal is lost if the contract is illegal because of an agreement to defraud the Revenue of PAYE tax).
(5) Arbitration awards made by the CAC under its statutory jurisdiction take effect as compulsory terms of the contracts of employment of the employees concerned (see Part II, Ch. 4).

83. *Council of Civil Service Unions* v. *Minister of the Civil Service* [1984] 3 All ER 935 HL; see Part II, Ch. 1.

§4. CODES OF PRACTICE

110. Codes of Practice are issued under statutory powers to provide guidance to industrial relations practitioners on the application of various statutory provisions. The Codes do not have the same status as statute or subordinate legislation: failure to observe the provisions of a Code does not of itself render a person liable to legal proceedings. But a Code is admissible in evidence in proceedings before an ET or the CAC or court and any provision of the Code which appears to be relevant to any question arising in the proceedings must be taken into account by the tribunal or CAC or court in determining that question.[84] Several bodies now have powers to issue Codes which have to be approved by both Houses of Parliament.

111. Several agencies have duties to produce codes of practice, subject to the approval of the Secretary of State and Parliament. Thus ACAS has a general power to issue codes of practice to promote the improvement of industrial relations.[85]

ACAS has issued three such codes, which it revises regularly. The Codes of Practice on disclosure of information for collective bargaining in effect since 1977 and was last revised in 1997 and 2009; and the same is true for the Code on time off for trade union duties and activities. The Code on disciplinary practice and procedures which has been in force since 1977, was initially replaced by 2010 ACAS Code of Practice on Discipline and Grievance Procedures. This has since been updated by a new version of the Code of Practice, which came into effect in March 2015.

84. TULRCA 1992, s. 207.
85. TULRCA 1992, ss. 199–202.

Chapter 7. International Labour Law

§1. Scope and Sources

112. The increasing international migration of labour gives rise to three distinct problems. (1) The limits of the jurisdiction (i.e. the power to hear and determine issues) of national courts and tribunals. (2) The choice of the system of law to be applied in determining cases with a foreign element. (3) The law as to nationality and the minimum standards to be applied to workers of foreign nationality. In England and Scotland the terms 'private international law' and 'conflict of laws' are synonymously applied to the first two of these problems. Rules as to nationality and the treatment of foreign workers are considered as part of constitutional and administrative law.

Since England and Wales, Scotland, and Northern Ireland have separate legal systems, it follows that English private international law rules are distinct from those of each of the other law-countries within the United Kingdom: thus Scots law and the law of Northern Ireland are as 'foreign' in England as the law of Italy or France. Scottish private international law rules are markedly similar to those of the English and Northern Irish legal systems, and the following brief account of the English rules may be taken to be generally similar to the Scottish and Northern Irish rules.

113. Judge-made case law has been an important source of the law in this field. The rules have been developed piecemeal by the judges on the basis of principles of justice, comity and convenience. The 'choice of jurisdiction' question is treated entirely as a question of procedure. Whether or not a court or tribunal is competent to try an issue depends solely upon procedure, and not upon nationality, domicile or residence. So far as proceedings in the High Court are concerned so long as a claim form has been served upon a person, who is present within the jurisdiction, in accordance with the rules of procedure he or she is subject to the power of the court even though he or she is a foreigner and the cause of action has no factual connection with England. This basic common law rule has been modified by Acts of Parliament and rules of court, which give a discretionary power to a judge to authorize service of legal process upon a defendant abroad in a limited number of cases. For example, where a contract was made within the jurisdiction or a breach of contract was committed within the jurisdiction it may be possible to obtain leave to serve process abroad in an action affecting that contract and by so doing create an 'assumed jurisdiction'. The details fall outside the scope of this monograph. The scope of the jurisdiction of the employment tribunals, which deal with various statutory employment rights has already been discussed.

114. The problem as to which national labour law to apply depends upon (1) the English and Scottish private international law rules, as developed by the judges, which determine whether a contract or tort (delict) is governed by a particular system, and (2) the express or implied territorial scope of Acts of the United Kingdom Parliament and of subordinate legislation. These are matters which have received little attention from the courts and legal writers.[86] These problems are particularly important in the context of the freedom of movement guaranteed by Ex Article 48 (Now Article 45 of the Treaty on the Functioning of the European Union) and the freedom of establishment guaranteed by ex Article 51 of the foundational Treaty of Rome (now found at Article 54 of the Treaty on the Functioning of the European Union). The EC Convention on the Law Applicable to Contractual Obligations (1980), together with Protocols, which seeks to harmonize the rules applying to all cases having a foreign element, whether or not they have any connection with the EC, makes special provisions in Article 6 for the choice of law in the case of employment contracts. This has been implemented in the UK by the Contracts (Applicable Law) Act 1990.

§2. Choice of Law Rules

115. One must distinguish three questions: (1) which is the law that applies to the contract or tort (delict)? (2) If English (or Scottish) law is the applicable law, is there a statute which, within that law, restricts its application in space, i.e. is there a self-limiting statute such as a statute restricted to the contracts of employees who ordinarily work under the contract in Great Britain, or excluding those who under an English or Scottish contract ordinarily work abroad? (3) Is there a statute which by its terms applies irrespective of what is the law applicable to the contract or tort in question, for example on the ground that the employee ordinarily works under the contract in Great Britain, thus including those who do so under a contract governed by foreign law i.e. 'is there a true *loi d'application immédiate* which, on proper analysis, is a crystallized rule of *ordre public*'?[87] In regard to question (1), before the Rome Convention was implemented, the English and Scottish courts applied the 'proper law of the contract', by which is meant the law that the parties intended to govern the contract. Where their intention has not been expressed and cannot be implied from the circumstances, the 'proper law' is the legal system with which the contract is most closely connected. In this latter case the judge put himself in the position of the 'reasonable person' in order to discover the law with which the contract has the 'closest and most real connection'. The Rome Convention on the law applicable to contractual obligations (implemented since 1 April 1991 by the Contracts (Applicable Law) Act 1990) permits free choice of law as a general rule, and where there has been no such choice the contract is governed by the law of the country with which it is most closely connected.[88] Article 6(1) of the Convention, by way of derogation from this general principle, provides that in the case of individual employment contracts a choice of law made by the parties 'shall not have the result of depriving the employee of the protection afforded by the mandatory rules of the law that would be applicable under para. 2 [of Article 6] in the

86. For a more detailed treatment than is possible here see Dicey and Morris on *The Conflict of Laws* (13th edn, London, 2000), Part II, Ch. 33.
87. O. Kahn-Freund, *Selected Writings* (London, 1978), p. 271.
88. See generally, C.J.G. Morse, in Dicey and Morris, Part II, Ch. 33, above, and in *Contract Conflicts* (ed. P.M. North) (London, 1982 *et seq*), pp. 143–173, and in (1982) 2 *Yearbook of European Law* 107.

absence of choice.' These mandatory rules would include not only those relating to the contract itself but also other legal rules such as those on health and safety. Article 6(2) says that where there has been no valid choice contracts of employment shall be governed by the law of the country in which the employee habitually carried out his work even if he is temporarily employed in another country, or if he does not habitually work in any one country by the law of the country in which the place of business through which he is engaged is situated. To this there is a proviso allowing the application of some other country's law if it appears from the circumstances as a whole that the contract as a whole is more closely connected with that country. The concept of 'habitual' place of work appears to be similar to that of 'ordinary place of work' under British employment legislation.

§3. Application of Statutes

116. An important feature of judicial interpretation of statutes in Britain is that the courts have refused to apply to statutes the ordinary criteria of private international law. In other words, instead of regarding the territorial scope of statutes as being co-terminous with the proper law of the contract, labour legislation has generally been confined in its operation to work done within the territorial boundaries of Great Britain. For the purposes of employment rights legislation, it is immaterial whether the law which governs any person's employment is the law of the United Kingdom or a part of the United Kingdom, or not.[89] (It is to be noted that most labour legislation extends to the whole of Great Britain, including Scotland; in a few exceptional cases, such as agricultural wages and teachers' remuneration, there is separate Scottish legislation.) For example, the Factories Acts have been judicially interpreted as applying only to work within Great Britain,[90] and most modern employment protection legislation has been expressed to apply only to those employees who under their contracts of employment 'ordinarily work' within Great Britain.[91] This is the case, for example, with the right to complain of unfair dismissal, various other rights arising in the course of employment, maternity rights, rights upon the insolvency of the employer, and the protection of wages. The criteria for applying the former: Equal Pay Act 1970, the Sex Discrimination Act 1975 and the Race Relations Act 1976 are that the work must be 'at an establishment' in Great Britain and, subject to a number of exceptions, this covers all those who are not proved to do their work 'wholly or mainly' outside Great Britain.[92] With regard to redundancy payments, an employee who ordinarily works outside Great Britain is not entitled to a redundancy payment unless on the 'relevant date' (i.e. the date

---

89. ERA 1996, s. 204(1).
90. *Yorke* v. *British & Continental Steamship Co.* (1945) 78 LILR 181 (accident in Gibraltar to employee under contract governed by English law: held dock regulations made under Factories Act 1937 did not apply), *Tomalin* v. *S. Pearson Ltd* [1909] 2 KB 61 (Workmen's Compensation Acts applied only to accidents arising out of and in the course of employment in Great Britain); *see* now Social Security Act 1975, s. 131 and regulations thereunder.
91. ERA 1996, s. 196. This was repealed by the ERA 1999, ss. 32(3), 44, Sched. 9(1) from a date to be appointed.
92. Equal Pay Act 1970, s. 1(1); SDA, ss. 6, 10; RRA, ss. 4, 6, 8, 9, 37.

when the dismissal takes effect) he is in Great Britain in accordance with instructions given to him by his employer. An employee who is outside Great Britain on the 'relevant date' is entitled to a redundancy payment only if he ordinarily works inside Great Britain.[93]

117. The criterion used to determine the territorial application of legislation is usually whether the employee 'ordinarily works' outside Great Britain. The Court of Appeal has held[94] that the correct approach is to examine the relevant terms of the contract of employment, express or implied, over the whole period of the contract.

If the contract expressly or impliedly requires the work to be wholly or substantially done outside Great Britain, no problem arises. Similarly, there is no problem if the contract expressly or impliedly requires the work to be wholly or substantially done inside Great Britain. The difficulty arises where the contract leaves it to the employer's discretion where the work shall be carried out. In such a case, the Court of Appeal has said[95] that it must be asked where the employee's base was to be, and in the absence of special factors leading to the contrary conclusion the country where his base was to be is likely to be the place where he is to be treated as 'ordinarily' working. This is so, even if he spends a considerable amount of time working abroad. In ascertaining the 'base' all the relevant express and implied terms of the contract must be considered, including those which define where the employee's headquarters were to be, indicating where his travels would begin and end, where his orders came from, where his residence was and in what currency he was to be paid. It seems that an employee cannot have a 'moving' base and cannot during the whole period of his contract be ordinarily working both inside and outside Great Britain.[96] However, the House of Lords in *Lawson* v. *Serco*[97] held that it would be unusual for an employee who worked and was based abroad, including British posted workers, to be afforded the statutory protections of employment law given to other, resident British workers.

118. Generally, British labour legislation affords an example of *loi d'application immédiate*, or crystallized *ordre public*. For example, the Trade Union and Labour Relations (Consolidation) Act 1992, the Employment Rights Act 1996 and the Equal Pay Act 1970, apply irrespective of the proper law of the contract.[98] A similar result has been achieved by judicial interpretation in respect of the Truck Acts which

93. ERA 1996, s. 196(6), repealed from a date to be appointed by the ERA 1999. Generally speaking, for the purposes of calculating a person's period of continuous employment (upon which eligibility and the amount of payment depends) no account may be taken of weeks during which he was employed outside Great Britain and no social security contributions were being made.
94. *Wilson* v. *Maynard Shipbuilding Consultants A.B.* [1978] ICR 376; *Todd* v. *British Midland Airways Ltd* [1978] ICR 959; *Janata Bank* v. *Ahmed* [1981] ICR 791, CA.
95. *Wilson's* case at p. 387, *Todd's* case at pp. 964, 967.
96. *Wilson's* case at p. 384, overruling *Portect (UK) Ltd* v. *Mogensen* [1976] ICR 396.
97. *Lawson* v. *Serco* (2006) UKHL 3, [2006] ICR 250 HL.
98. TULRCA 1992, s. 289; ERA 1996, s. 204(1); Equal Pay Act 1970, s. 1(11).

regulate deductions from wages of manual employees.[99] An English or Scottish court will, in these cases, apply the British statute, insofar as the statute has territorial application (e.g. to a person ordinarily working inside Great Britain), to a person working under a contract governed by foreign law. This approach may be justified on the ground that labour legislation is part of the public policy of the *lex fori* (Great Britain), and employers should be prevented from abusing their superior bargaining power by obtaining the employee's agreement to apply a less socially advanced system of law.

§4. Collective Labour Relations

119. Article 6 of the Rome Convention does not apply to collective agreements. Instead, the law applicable to a collective agreement must be identified by the general rules of the Rome Convention, Articles 3 and 4. However, the law applicable by virtue of Article 6 will determine whether a term from a collective agreement has been incorporated into an individual contract of employment. Furthermore, if the law applicable under Article 6(2) makes the collective agreement legally binding on the employer, the employee will not be deprived of the protection afforded by the collective agreement by the choice of the law of another Member State in the individual contract.[100] In Britain, a collective agreement is conclusively presumed by Section 179 of the Trade Union and Labour Relations (Consolidation) Act 1992 not to have been intended by the parties to be a legally enforceable contract unless the parties expressly agree in writing that it shall be enforceable.

The Court of Appeal has held that this provision is not a material consideration in determining the proper law of the collective agreement. This was in the context of a case in which Maltese ship-owners claimed damages from the International Transport Workers' Federation (ITF), based in London, on grounds *inter alia* of their failure to issue a certificate, that the crew of a ship flying a Maltese flag and manned by a Spanish crew were engaged on terms acceptable to the ITF.

The undertaking to issue the certificate was contained in a 'special agreement' on a printed form issued by ITF in London, but executed in Bilbao, Spain. It contained no statement of enforceability under Section 18 of the British Act. On a preliminary point, it was held that the proper law of the 'special agreement' was Spanish law and not English law. This was because the agreement, intended to be used worldwide, had been entered into in Spain and affected the recruitment of Spanish crews and so had its 'closest and most real connection' with Spanish law. Section 18 of the British Act was treated as substantive and not merely procedural in effect: hence it was the proper law, rather than the *lex fori* which should govern the issue.[101]

99. *Duncan* v. *Motherwell Bridge & Engineering Co. Ltd* 1952 SC 131 (held by Inner House of Court of Session that Truck Act 1831 applied if deductions made from wages paid in Scotland irrespective of proper law).
100. Dicey and Morris, *op. cit.*, para. 33-052.
101. *Monterosso Shipping Co. Ltd* v. *ITF* [1982] ICR 675, CA. No reference was made in *Monterosso* to TULRA 1974, s. 30(6) (now TULRCA 1992, s. 289) which provides that for purposes of the Act

120. So far as industrial action is concerned, trade unions and others who take international solidarity action with workers in other countries risk legal liability in tort (delict) in British courts. There have been several instances of such action leading to the grant of injunctions. This has been because the statutory immunity afforded to any person who commits certain torts 'in contemplation or furtherance of a trade dispute' (Part IV, Ch. 5), has been held not to apply.[102] The re-definition of a 'trade dispute' in the Employment Acts 1980 and 1982 and the illegality of secondary action now make it likely that most types of action will fall foul of the law (Part II, Ch. 5). Moreover, the territorial scope of the immunity was specifically narrowed by the Employment Act 1982. There is a 'trade dispute' only so long as the person whose actions in the UK are said to be in contemplation or furtherance of a trade dispute relating to matters occurring outside the UK are likely to be affected in respect of one or more of a list of specified subjects by the outcome of the dispute.[103] Even where the industrial action is lawful where committed, the courts have allowed the recovery of money paid as a result of that action on grounds of economic duress because the relevant contracts were governed by English law.[104]

'it is immaterial whether the law which (apart from this Act) governs any person's employment is the law of the United Kingdom, or of a part of the United Kingdom, or not'.

102. In particular on a variety of grounds in a series of cases involving action by the ITF against 'flags of convenience', and also solidarity action by communications workers against apartheid in South Africa.
103. TULRCA 1992, s. 244(3). The subjects are those which fall within the permitted scope of a 'trade dispute' so presumably excluding a strike over the investment plans of a multinational enterprise.
104. *Dimskal Shipping Co. SA* v. *ITWF* [1992] IRLR 78, HL.

Part I. The Individual Employment Relationship

Chapter 1. Formation of the Relationship

§1. Categories of Workers

I. Introduction

121. The coverage *ratione personae* of British labour law is not consistent. As we have seen the contract of 'service' was slow in overtaking the pre-industrial characterization of the employment relationship according to status and the nature of the employment (e.g. 'servant in husbandry', 'artificer', 'labourer'). In the 19th century the law struggled to develop a general notion of a contract of service regardless of the type of work. Unlike the civil law systems of continental Europe which moved from a general theory of contract towards a specific concept of an autonomous contract of employment, British labour law only slowly conceptualized the contract of employment on a case by case basis utilizing pre-industrial conceptions of 'service'. The common law developed a distinction between those under a contract for services (self-employed workers) and those under a contract of service (employees), which does not correspond exactly to the civil law distinction between *locatio conductio operis* and *locatio conductio operarum*. The English common law category of 'employee' is frequently narrower than the range of persons under a contract of employment in a civil law system. Scots law, despite its civil law roots, has broadly speaking adopted the English approach. Statute law, since the 19th century, has usually been limited in coverage to those under contracts of service, but the tests for determining whether the contract is one of service has been left to the common law. By 1951, Kahn-Freund could say that the common law had 'fallen into a maze of casuistry'.[105] This tendency has become even more pronounced in the past 50 years. The changes in the labour force,[106] from the pattern of full-time employment in the core of the labour market, towards part-time, temporary and homework (including the expanding 'cottage' technological industry), and the expansion of self-employment and of employment in the twilight area between employment and self-employment, have highlighted the uncertain inconsistent and

105. (1951) 14 *Modern Law Review* 504.
106. See generally S. Fredman, 'Labour Law in flux: the changing composition of the workforce' ILJ 26 (1997), p. 337.

inadequate coverage of the common law concepts. There are many workers who in reality fall within the category of dependent labour, such as those on the 'lump' in the building industry, who are not always regarded as working under contracts of service. There is ample scope for the avoidance of labour legislation.

Quite apart from the inadequacies of the common law tests of the contract of employment, legislation is sometimes confined to employees in specific employments (e.g.) merchant seamen, teachers, agricultural workers or to certain types of contract of service, with complex exclusions in particular statutes of different categories such as part-time workers, casuals and domestic servants in private households.

II. Contract of Service or Contract for Services

122. The criteria for distinguishing between a contract of service and a contract for services have been developed by the courts on a casuistic basis. For this purpose, several tests have been expounded. The early cases, emphasizing the elements of command and subordination inherent in the employment relationship, established a test based on the employer's power to control the manner in which the work is done.[107] A contract of service, on this test, is one under which an employer 'can not only order or require what is to be done, but how it shall be done'.[108] The test yields straightforward answers in some cases, but is difficult to apply where the employee's skills surpass those of the employer and the employer is a corporate entity. Thus more recent cases have held that control cannot be the determining test when dealing with a professional person or a person with skill and experience.[109] The greater the skill, the less significant is control in determining whether the employee is under a contract of service.[110] Yet, even recently, the Court of Appeal has continued to regard the test in determining whether a person is an employee as being 'who lays down what is to be done, the way in which it is to be done, and the means by which it is done'.[111]

123. A second test, which has been applied in only a few situations, is whether the person forms part of the employer's organization. Denning LJ (as he then was) explained this as follows:

> Under a contract of service, a man is employed as part of the business, and his work is done as an integral part of the business; whereas under a contract for services, his work, although done for the business, is not integrated into it but is only accessory to it.[112]

107. *Performing Rights Society Ltd* v. *Mitchell and Baker Ltd* [1925] 1 KB 762, *Mersey Docks and Harbour Board* v. *Coggins and Griffiths Ltd* [1947] AC 1.
108. *Collins* v. *Hertfordshire County Council* [1947] KB 598 at 615, *per* Hilberry J.
109. *Cassidy* v. *Ministry of Health* [1951] 2 KB 343 at 579; *Morren* v. *Swinton and Pendlebury Borough Council* [1965] 2 All ER 349; *Market Investigations* v. *Minister of Social Security* [1969] 2 QB 173.
110. *Beloff* v. *Pressdram Ltd* [1973] 1 All ER 241 at 250.
111. *Lane* v. *Shire Roofing* [1995] IRLR 493 at 495.
112. *Stevenson, Jordan & Harrison Ltd* v. *Macdonald & Evans* (1925) 1 TLR 101.

This test has been applied, for example, to determine whether a regular contributor to a newspaper is an employee,[113] but it has failed to provide a comprehensive test, particularly in cases where the worker provides some equipment or is paid on a piece-rate basis.

124. The courts have therefore moved to a more complex test, the so-called multiple or mixed test, in which a multiplicity of factors are considered, none of which is necessarily determinative. The starting point of this approach is to ask whether there is a sufficient degree of control to make the worker an employee, and then to ask whether the provisions of the contract are consistent with its being a contract of service.[114] This is a somewhat question-begging approach, because if it were asked whether the contract was consistent with a contract for services, precisely the opposite result could be achieved. Moreover, everything depends upon the weight which is given to a particular 'inconsistency'. A number of cases have emphasized, as the most significant 'inconsistency' with a contract of employment, the entrepreneurial character of self-employment, asking the question: Is the person in business on his or her own behalf?[115] Factors to be considered in this context include the extent to which the person takes the chance of profit or risk of loss by investing money or equipment in the business,[116] and the extent to which the individual is dependent or independent of a particular paymaster for the financial exploitation of his or her talent.[117] This test has been referred to as the 'fundamental test',[118] but the Court of Appeal has rejected the notion that any single test is fundamental. Thus, in any case, consideration should be given to all the factors, including degree of control, the risk of loss and the chance of profit, the provision of equipment, the methods of tax and national insurance payment, and the parties' intentions. The ET should 'consider all aspects of the relationship, no single feature being in itself decisive and each of which may vary in weight and direction'.[119] In *MacFarlane* v. *Glasgow City Council* (2001),[120] on the other hand, the EAT distinguished *Tanton's* case. The case involved qualified gymnastic instructors working at sports centres operated by the Council. If an instructor could not take a class, she would arrange for a replacement from a register of coaches maintained by the council. The replacements were paid by the Council and not by the applicant. Lindsay J, the then President of the EAT, said that *Tanton* was distinguishable on the grounds, amongst others, that the applicant could not simply choose not to work in person and that she was not free to provide any substitute, but only someone from the Council's own register.

---

113. *Beloff* v. *Pressdram Ltd* [1973] 1 All ER 241.
114. *Express and Echo Publications Ltd Taunton* [1999] IRLR 367, CA.
115. *Ready-Mixed Concrete (SE) Ltd* v. *Minister of Pensions* [1968] 2 QB 497; *Lane* v. *Shire Roofing* [1995] IRLR 493 at 496.
116. *Market Investigations Ltd* v. *Minister of Social Security* [1968] 3 All ER 732.
117. *Per* Cook, J. in *Market Investigations Ltd* v. *Minister for Social Security* [1969] 2 QB 173 approved in *Ferguson* v. *John Dawson* [1976] 1 WLR 1213, *Young & Woods* v. *West* [1980] IRLR 201; and *Lee* v. *Chung* [1990] IRLR 236.
118. *Addison* v. *London Philharmonic Orchestra Ltd* [1981] ICR 261; *Midland Sinfonia Concert Society Ltd* v. *Secretary of State for Social Services* [1981] ICR 454; *Warner Holidays Ltd* v. *Secretary of State for Social Services* [1983] ICR 440.
119. *O'Kelly* v. *Trusthouse Forte (plc)* [1983] ICR 728 at 743.
120. *MacFarlane* v. *Glasgow City Council* (2001) IRLR 7 Scot EAT.

125. There has been much debate as to whether the classification of a contract is a question of fact or law, appeals to the higher courts only being available on points of law. The House of Lords has now made it clear that only when the parties intend all the terms of the contract to be contained in a document or documents is the question of interpretation of those documents a matter of law.[121] Where the intention of the parties, objectively ascertained, has to be gathered partly from documents but also from oral exchanges and conduct, the terms of the contract are a question of fact. The question whether the parties intended a document to be the exclusive record of the terms of their agreement is also a question of fact. The issue of casual staff was again considered by the House of Lords, in *Carmichael* v. *National Power plc* (1999). The case involved tour guides who were taken on by means of an exchange of letters on a 'casual as required basis' to act as guides taking parties on tours of power stations operated by the predecessor of the respondent company. As in the *Clark* case, they were not obliged to take work and the company did not guarantee that work would be available. They were paid only for the hours they worked. The ET and the EAT held that they were not employees but the Court of Appeal allowed their appeal on the ground that the exchange of letters gave rise to a contract of employment. The majority of the Court of Appeal avoided that issue of absence of mutuality by implying terms relating to the performance of the guides' duties. The then House of Lords rejected this approach and allowed the company's appeal. Lord Irvine of Lairg LC said that had the appeal turned exclusively on the construction of the exchange of letters he would have had no hesitation in holding as a matter of construction that there was no obligation on the company to provide work or the guides to accept it. He said that it was clear that the parties did not intend the letters to 'constitute an exclusive memorial of their relationship' and that, in looking at the documents, the surrounding circumstances and how the parties conducted themselves, the tribunal was correct to conclude that they did not intend that their relationship should be regulated by contract. A similar approach can be seen by the Court of Appeal in *Troutbeck SA* v. *White and Todd.*[122] The case primarily concerned the low level of actual day-to-day control that Troutbeck retained over the workers. Although acknowledging the requirement of control as a factor to be considered, this had to be viewed in the overall context of the relationship. In finding the individuals to have contracts of services, the Court of Appeal placed particular weight on the signed document between the parties, which referred to "this employment agreement", and that the expressed intentions of the parties and the surrounding circumstances supported that this document was a true representation of the relationship. See also *Stevedoring & Haulage Services Ltd* v. *Fuller* (2001) and *Wilson* v. *Circular Distributors Ltd* (2006).[123]

126. One of the major sources of difficulty concerns marginal workers, such as homeworkers, casual workers and agency workers. None of these could be said to be entrepreneurs and yet they do not fit comfortably in the traditional categories of

121. *Carmichael* v. *National Power Co.* [2000] IRLR 43.
122. *Troutbeck SA* v. *White and Todd* [2013] EWCA Civ 1171.
123. *Stevedoring & Haulage Services Ltd* v. *Fuller* (2001) and *Wilson* v. *Circular Distributors Ltd* (2006).

workers employed under a contract of service. In this connection it is important to determine not only the nature of the contract, but whether or not there is a contract at all. Almost all employment, however transient, constitutes a simple wage-work bargain; but where there is a series of such contracts over time between the same parties, the question arises whether there is a continuing overriding or 'global' contract which governs the whole of the relationship. Recent case-law has used the concept of 'mutuality of obligation' to determine whether a global contract exists; indeed, such mutuality, whereby an employee is obliged to work and an employer to continue to provide work or remuneration, has been held to be the 'irreducible minimum' of a contract of service. Where the worker has the option of declining to work on any specific occasion, then he or she cannot be said to be employed under a contract of service. This is so even if, in practice, economic need obliges the worker to accept the work. Thus it has been held that 'regular casuals',[124] and trawler-men engaged to work for the duration of a specific voyage,[125] were not employed under a global contract because they were not contractually obliged to work between specific engagements. Since many employment protection rights depend on being employed under a contract of service, the consequence is that some of the most vulnerable workers remain unprotected. However, in one important case, the Appeal Court was willing to imply the existence of such a contractual obligation on the basis of a course of dealing, so that a homeworker who had regularly worked for an employer was held to be working under a contract of service.[126]

127. An innovative approach to mutuality was adopted by the Court of Appeal in *Cornwall CC* v. *Prater*,[127] where it was asked to decide on whether mutuality can exist for individual assignments within a working relationship, rather than only across the global contract. In considering this matter, the Court of Appeal held that if an individual on agreeing to an assignment is obliged to carry out that work and complete it, and the purported employer is obliged to continue to send work for the duration of the assignment and pay for it, then mutuality can be found to exist for the duration of the assignment. This could mean that homeworkers for the duration of assignments they agee to, casual workers for the duration of the task they have agreed to, and agency workers for the duration of their placing with a client company, could be found to have mutuality. However, this does not necessarily mean that the employment rights of such workers are enhanced, as the periods in between assignments, when no work is being offered or completed, will break the period of continuous service. The impact of this is that the individual, although perhaps having employee status for limited periods, will not meet the threshold working periods needed to qualify for rights such as unfair dismissal protection and/or rights to redundancy payments.

---

124. *Carmichael* v. *National Power plc.* [2000] IRLR 43; *O'Kelly* v. *Trusthouse Forte plc* [1983] IRLR 369.
125. *McCleod* v. *Hellyer Brothers Ltd* [1987] IRLR 232. See generally B. Hepple (1986) 15 ILJ at 75.
126. *Nethermere (St. Neots) Ltd* v. *Gardiner* [1984] ICR 612 (CA); see also *Airfix Footwear (Ltd)* v. *Cope* [1978] ICR 1210.
127. *Cornwall CC* v. *Prater* [2006] EWCA Civ 102.

128. Another area of difficulty concerns cases where one or both parties to the employment relationship choose to place themselves in one category rather than another in order to reap the benefits of a particular tax or social security regime. In strict contract theory, the parties' agreement should be conclusive. However, the courts have been willing to look beyond the label given by the parties to the substance of the relationship. For example, an employer could not escape liability for breach of a statutory safety duty owed to a building worker by pleading that the worker had agreed to be self-employed simply in order to mislead the Inland Revenue.[128] But where there is a detailed written contract which explicitly carries out the genuine intentions of the parties to create a status of self-employment, that contract has been regarded as 'the best material from which to gather the true relationship between them'.[129] Thus the contract of employment has become a personal work contract.[130]

III. Specific Categories of Worker

A. *Employees*

129. The statutory definition of employee is based on the common law contract of service. Thus an employee is defined as 'an individual who has entered into or works under (or where the employment has ceased, worked under) a contract of employment, otherwise than in the police service'. A contract of employment, in turn, means 'a contract of service or apprenticeship, whether it is express or implied and (if it is express) whether it is oral or in writing'.[131]

130. Most employment rights are limited to employees. For example, rights to complain of unfair dismissal,[132] to claim compensation for redundancy,[133] to be given a written statement of employment terms,[134] and a variety of other individual employment protection measures are confined to employees. Similarly, some collective rights, such as legally binding recommendations by ACAS for disclosure of information to trade unions, may be enforced only through the contracts of employment of employees.[135] The Employment Relations Act 1999, s. 23, has given a power to the Secretary of State to confer employment rights, either as 'workers' or 'employees' on individuals of a specific description. This is an important recognition of the inadequacies of the common law definitions, and may lead to the widening of employment protection.

---

128. *Ferguson* v. *John Dawson & Partners (Contracts) Ltd* [1976] 1 WLR 1213.
129. *Massey* v. *Crown Life Insurance Co.* [1978] ICR 590 at p. 594.
130. M. Freedland, 'From the contract of employment to the personal work nexus', ILJ 35 (2006), pp. 1–29.
131. ERA 1996, s. 230(1); see below for apprenticeship; TULRCA 1992, s. 295(1), subject to s. 235 which gives a wider definition in relation to ballots before industrial action.
132. ERA 1996, s. 94(1).
133. ERA 1996, s. 135.
134. ERA 1996, s. 1.
135. TULRCA 1992, s. 185.

B. Workers

131. Some statutes extend beyond employees to those who work under contracts personally to execute work or labour. In the Employment Rights Act 1996 a 'worker' is defined as 'an individual who has entered into or works under (a) a contract of employment, or (b) any other contract, whether express or implied and (if it is express) whether oral or in writing, whereby the individual undertakes to do or perform personally any work or services for another party to the contract who is not a professional client or customer of the individual's profession or business'.[136]

There is a similar definition in the Trade Union and Labour Relations (Consolidation) Act 1992. These definitions are wide enough to cover all employees, those who are temporarily unemployed and work-seekers, as well as those under contracts of services to personally perform work. They exclude those who do not personally render services but engage others to do so,[137] and also exclude the contract for the sale of a completed work (e.g. by an author)[138] and those such as solicitors who work for a 'professional client'.[139] Parliament has, however, expressly provided that individuals providing general medical, pharmaceutical, dental or ophthalmic services under the National Health Services are to be treated as workers for some purposes.[140] Inclusion in the category of 'workers' is important to secure certain collective rights, such as listing as a trade union (which must consist of workers).

Similarly, the Equality Act 2010 (formerly Race Relations[141] and Sex Discrimination Acts,[142] etc.) apply to those employed under a contract of service or apprenticeship as well as those employed under a contract personally to execute any work or labour. A contract which entitles a person to delegate all the contractual duties to others to perform does not qualify as a contract personally to execute work.[143]

C. Public Employees

132. Although this monograph is primarily concerned with workers in the private sector, it is important to give a brief account of their legal status, particularly since the contracting-out of many public services has led to transfers of workers from the public to the private sector.[144] Public sector employment includes: (i) those who are employed by public corporations; (ii) those employed by local authorities,

136. ERA 1996, s. 230(3); TULRCA 1992, s. 296.
137. *Express and Echo Publications Ltd* v. *Taunton* [1999] IRLR 367.
138. *Writers' Guild of Great Britain* v. *BBC* [1974] ICR 234.
139. *Carter* v. *Law Society* [1973] ICR 113.
140. TULRCA 1992, s. 279.
141. RRA 1976, s. 78(1).
142. SDA 1975, s. 82(1).
143. *Mirror Group Newspapers Ltd* v. *Gunning* [1986] IRLR 27; *Tanna* v. *Post Office* [1981] ICR 374; cf. *Hitchcock* v. *Post Office* [1980] ICR 100.
144. See generally S. Fredman and G. Morris, *The State as Employer* (London, Mansell 1989); and (up to 1970) Hepple and O'Higgins, *Public Employee Trade Unionism in the UK* (Ann Arbor, Michigan, 1971).

including education, the social services, and fire services; and (iii) central government employees, including the National Health Service and the armed forces. In some respects, public employees are treated in the same way as their private sector counterparts. In particular, employees in local government, the National Health Service and public corporations are all employed under contracts of employment and fall within the scope of most employment protection rights. However, the availability of public law remedies to employees in these sectors is controversial and a complex case-law exists.[145] Two sectors, the police and the civil service, are subject to different treatment from private sector employees. Police are not employed under contracts of employment but are considered to be 'independent' officers, exercising 'original authority' derived directly from the legal powers inherent in their office.[146]

Police officers are paid by local police authorities and are under the 'direction and control' of the chief constable.[147] In the important area of natural justice, police constables have been held to be 'office-holders'. Basic terms and conditions are specified in statutory regulations and they are subject to statutory disciplinary codes.

The police are excluded from most individual employment rights,[148] other than statutes relating to sex and race discrimination,[149] and also from collective rights.[150] Prison officers may claim employment protection rights, but have no right to take part in industrial action.[151]

133. The most important distinct group of public sector employees is civil servants, or 'Crown servants'. The legal framework governing Crown servants harks back to the personal retinue of the monarch rather than the complex bureaucratic structure of the modern civil service. Crown servants may be dismissed at will, and it is debatable whether they have contracts of employment. The source of the power of the state as employer is the Royal Prerogative, 'the residue of the discretionary power left at any moment in the hands of the Crown'.[152] This power has been delegated by the sovereign on the advice of ministers by successive Orders in Council, by virtue of which the Minister for the Civil Service may determine the terms and conditions of employment of civil servants. However, the effect of these archaic common law rules has been largely mitigated by the extension to the civil service of most statutory employment rights, rights against discrimination, and also collective rights.[153]

---

145. Fredman and Morris, *The State as Employer*, pp. 251–275; Deakin and Morris, *Labour Law* (2nd edn), pp. 182–184.
146. *Fisher* v. *Oldham Corporation* [1930] 2 KB 364; *Attorney-General for New South Wales* v. *Perpetual Trustee Co.* [1955] AC 477.
147. Police Act 1996, as amended.
148. ERA 1996, s. 200.
149. SDA 1975, s. 17(1); RRA 1976, s. 16(1).
150. TULRCA 1992, s. 280(1).
151. Criminal Justice and Public Order Act 1994, ss. 127(1)–(2).
152. Dicey, *Law of the Constitution* (8th edn), p. 421.
153. ERA 1996, ss. 191–193 (the main exceptions are the right to a written statement of employment terms, to minimum notice period and to redundancy payments, but in respect of the latter there are more favourable rights in the Civil Service Compensation Scheme); SDA 1975, s. 85; RRA 1976, s. 75; DDA 1995, s. 64 (but members of the armed forces are not covered by the DDA 1995); TULRCA 1992, ss. 273–276 (but members of the armed forces do not enjoy collective rights).

D. Office-holders

134. The concept of an 'office' is sometimes applied to those in positions of authority in various public and private institutions. For example, there are the fellows of Oxford and Cambridge colleges and the steward and bailiff appointed by the lord of a manor. Historically, offices such as these were distinguished from the 'contract of service', and the proprietary interests attaching to these offices were specially protected by the common law. In modern times tax legislation specifically applies to 'office-holders'. In other cases the mere fact that an individual holds an 'office' does not preclude him or her from belonging to the category of workers or that of employees.[154] The traditional approach is that in these cases it all depends on factors such as whether he or she is a member of the corporate body in question, whether the office is a permanent one created by an enactment, whether the office continues to exist whether or not it is occupied at any particular time, and how the office-holder can be removed. However, there does appear to have been a shift in the judicial thinking with regards office holders, with the question of employment status no longer being determined solely by reference to the contract classifying the occupation by type: office or employment, spiritual or secular. Nor will there exist a presumption against a contract of service. Instead, such positions will undergo the same objective analysis of the intentions of the parties set against the factual background.[155]

The most important example of an office-holder in modern law is the director of a limited liability company. If he or she is also a working (i.e. executive) director then he or she will have a service contract with the company.[156] There is also an important category of elective and other offices, such as those in a trade union, where special protection (e.g. in respect of natural justice) is granted by the courts.[157]

E. Manual Workers

135. In general labour legislation applies equally to manual (or 'blue-collar')workers and non-manual (or 'white-collar') employees. However, some 19th-century legislation was limited in coverage to those engaged in manual labour. The last of this legislation, the Truck Acts was repealed by the Wages Act 1986.

F. Domestic Servants

136. In the 19th century special rules applied to those 'whose main or general function is to be about their employer's person, or establishments, residential or quasi-residential, for the purposes of ministering to their employer's needs or wants,

154. *Miles* v. *Wakefield* [1987] IRLR 193 at p. 197.
155. *The President of the Methodist Conference (Appellant)* v. *Preston (Respondent)* [2013] UKSC 29.
156. E.g. *Secretary of State for Trade and Industry* v. *Bottrill* [1999] IRLR 326.
157. E.g. *Taylor* v. *NUS* [1967] 1 WLR 532; *Ridge* v. *Baldwin* [1964] AC 40.

or to the needs or wants of those who are members of such establishments or those resorting to such establishments'.[158] The Truck Acts excluded such employees from their coverage. This pattern has been continued by some modern legislation, despite the fact that such employees tend to be particularly vulnerable. The most important example is the Equality Act 2010 (Race Relations Act 1976) which does not apply to employment in a private household except where the discrimination is by way of victimization.[159] The previous Sex Discrimination Act 1975 contained a similar exclusion, but after the European Court held that this constituted a breach by the UK government of its obligations under the EC Treaty,[160] the Act was amended. The Equality Act 2010 now includes domestic and other workers in a private household, unless objection is likely to be taken to a worker of a particular sex because the job involves a degree of social or physical contact with the employer or a knowledge of intimate details of the employers life.[161]

G. Specific Employments

137. Among the groups of workers to whom specific legislation applies are: agricultural workers, bakers and confectioners, building and engineering workers, hotels and catering workers, civil aviation employees, docks and harbours employees, drivers, teachers, electricity and gas workers, firemen, hairdressers, laundry workers, court officials, local government officers, merchant seamen, national health service employees, oil-rig workers, shop and office workers, postal workers, railway workers, share fishermen and some transport workers.[162]

H. Apprentices/Trainees

138. Many of the cases and legal rules on apprenticeship were decided in different social conditions, and appear anachronistic in modern conditions. A contract of apprenticeship is one under which the employer agrees to instruct and teach the apprentice his or her trade, profession or business and to maintain him or her during the existence of that relationship. The apprentice in turn agrees to serve and to learn from the employer. The apprentice may leave only if the employer's conduct indicates that the employer is unwilling to teach the apprentice and the employer may only dismiss the apprentice if the latter's conduct makes it impossible to instruct him or her. A wrongfully dismissed apprentice may claim damages not only in respect of loss of earnings but also for the value of lost future prospects. Employment protection legislation usually applies to apprentices,[163] but an apprentice who

158. *Junior Carlton Club* [1922] 1 KB 166.
159. RRA, s. 4(3).
160. *Commission of the European Communities* v. *UK* [1984] IRLR 29 ECJ.
161. SDA 1975, s. 7(2)(*6a*) as inserted by SDA 1986, s. 1.
162. For further details see *Sweet and Maxwell's Encyclopedia of Employment Law*.
163. For example, ERA 1996, s. 230(2).

comes to the end of a fixed term apprenticeship cannot claim a redundancy payment or complain of unfair dismissal if he or she is not kept on as a journeyman.[164]

A far more important source of employment-related training is found in government-sponsored schemes. These date back to the Industrial Training Act 1964 but proliferated during the 1980s and 1990s. Since 1998, the New Deal has provided state subsidies or allowances for the employment of trainees. In some cases these trainees are expressly taken on as 'employees', but in other cases, although working under the control of an employer, they are simply in receipt of training allowances and are not treated as employees.[165] A pupil-barrister is neither an apprentice nor an employee and so is excluded from rights such as the national minimum wage.[166] The Secretary of State has the power to specify whether or not trainees are to be treated as 'employees' for specific purposes, and designation orders have been made under anti-discrimination[167] and health and safety legislation. Notably, the Court of Appeal, reaffirmed the obligations placed on the employer taking on apprentices, namely to provide work and granting job security throughout the period of the contract of apprenticeship.[168]

I. Casual and Fixed-term Workers

139. There is no separate legal category of casual workers. Until 1979 there was important progress towards the decasualization of labour, notably through a special regime of job and income security for registered dockworkers.[169] However during the 1980s, this policy was reversed, as illustrated by the repeal of the dockworkers' scheme in 1989. Until 1977 there was a significant part of the workforce, particularly in seasonal trades and services, work for relatively short periods of time, or with frequent breaks in continuity of service, for a particular employer. The effect of this is usually to deprive them of employment protection rights. First, their freedom to choose whether or not to work on a particular occasion, and the employer's freedom to deny them work may lead to a finding that there is insufficient 'mutuality of obligation' to constitute a contract of employment.[170] Secondly, even if they are employees, they may have insufficient continuity of employment to qualify for particular statutory rights.[171] The UK is in the process in 2001 of implementing EC Directive 99/70/EC which gives effect to the framework agreement on fixed-term work. This agreement deals with one type of temporary work only, covering those workers who have an employment contract or relationship entered into directly between an employer and a worker where the end of the contract or relationship is

164. *Northeast Coast Shiprepairers Ltd* v. *Secretary of State for Employment* [1975] ICR 755.
165. See Art. 2, SI 1998, 1425. For a case decided under an earlier work experience programmes, see *Daley* v. *Allied Suppliers Ltd* [1980] ICR 649.
166. *Edmonds* v. *Lawson QC* [2000] IRLR 391.
167. SDA 1975, s. 14; RRA 1976, s. 13.
168. *Flett* v. *Matheson* [2006] ICR 673 CA, *per* Pill LJ.
169. Under the Dock Workers Employment Scheme 1967 (SI 1967, 1252) repealed by the Dockworkers Act 1989.
170. *O'Kelly* v. *Trusthouse Forte plc*, above.
171. For a critique of the framework agreement see Jill Murray, (1999) 28 ILJ 269 para. 89, note 6.

determined by objective conditions such as reaching a specified date, completing a specific task, or the occurrence of a specific event. The agreement applies the principle of non-discrimination requiring that fixed-term workers shall not be treated in a less favourable manner than comparable permanent workers solely because they have a fixed-term contract or relation unless justified on objective grounds. Where appropriate the principle of *pro rata temporis* is to apply.

Fixed-term workers must be informed of vacancies for permanent positions, and employers must facilitate appropriate training opportunities to enhance their skills, career development and occupational mobility. The agreement requires Member States to place some general limits on the use of this kind of temporary work. At the time of writing, British regulations setting these standards are still awaited.

J. Temporary and Agency Workers

140. Distinct from casual workers of the kind just described are those commonly known as 'temporary' workers because their services are supplied by an intermediary (the employment agency or business) for the benefit of a third party (the hirer) for a limited period of time. The activities of fee-charging employment agencies and businesses are regulated under the Employment Agencies Act 1973 as amended. A distinction is drawn between the 'employment agency' which supplies workers for placement with employers, and the 'employment business' which supplies the services of workers it itself employs. The system of regulation applies to both, and is not limited to those supplied on short-term assignments, although in practice this is a major part of their activities. Detailed regulations[172] lay down standards for the conduct of employment businesses and agencies. ETs may, on the application of the Secretary of State, prohibit a person from carrying on or being concerned with the carrying on of an agency or business which has been improperly conducted. Workers may not be charged fees by an employment business or agency, save in exceptional circumstances, but there is no regulation of the fees charged to hirers. The workers supplied by an employment business or agency have relationships with both supplier and hirer. The legal nature of these relationships is ambiguous. It has been held that 'where A contracts with B to render services exclusively to C, the contract is not a contract for services (or of service) but a contract *sui generis*, a different type of contract from either of the familiar two'.[173]

The absence of an obligation on the part of the worker to accept any particular assignment has been held to indicate the absence of a contract of service between the supplier and the worker.[174] Even if there is sufficient mutuality of obligation, there may be insufficient control to render the worker an employee of the the agency or business.[175] Whether or not the temporary worker has a contract of service with

172. Conduct of Employment Agencies and Employment Businesses Regulations 1976 (SI 1976 715), as amended 1993, 2003 and 2009.

173. *Construction Industry Training Board* v. *Labour Force Ltd* [1970] 3 All ER 220, *per* Cooke J; *Ironmonger* v. *Movefield* [1988] IRLR 461.

174. *Wickens* v. *Champion Employment* [1984] ICR 365.

175. *Montgomery* v. *Johnson Underwood Ltd* [2001] IRLR 269.

the hirer, seems to depend on the degree of control which the hirer exercises,[176] but there have been cases in which the court has found that there is no contract of any kind with the hirer.[177] The relationship between the worker and the supplier is to a limited extent governed by the regulations (e.g. the employment business must supply a written statement of employment terms to the worker, and the supplier is responsible for deducting social security contributions). The hirer may be responsible, under health and safety legislation, for work accidents to the worker. These cases should be contrasted with the decision in *Motorola Ltd* v. *Davidson and Melville Craig Group Ltd* (2001), a case where the worker was held to have become an employee of the end user.

141. In the present context, the significance of the Court of Appeal decision in *Dacas* v. *Brook Street Bureau (UK) Ltd* (2004)[178] should not be overlooked. Although that case was confined to a consideration of the relationship between the worker and the agency (simply because she had not appealed against that part of the tribunal's decision relating to her relationship with the end user), the observations of the Court of Appeal make it clear that in dealing with these kinds of cases tribunals should examine the facts very carefully to ascertain whether an employment relationship between the worker and the end user can be inferred. It is clear, at least from the judgment of Mummery LJ, that he regarded it as likely that there might have been an implied contract between Mrs Dacas and the authority, but that the case would have had to be remitted to the tribunal for it to determine the issue.

Cases subsequently decided by the EAT suggest that there is a tendency to hold that the agency worker is an employee of the end user. The two most recent decisions of the EAT – in *Cable and Wireless plc* v. *Muscat* (2005)[179] and *Royal National Lifeboat Institution* v. *Bushaway* (2005) – both upheld the tribunal's decisions that the agency workers concerned were employees of the end user. In *Muscat* v. *Cable & Wireless plc* (2006), its most recent decision on this issue, the Court of Appeal has said that the view of the majority in *Dacas* was correct. Smith LJ said that it was right for tribunals to follow the guidance given in that case, but pointed out that the guidance does not direct tribunals to reach any particular conclusion, only to consider the possibility that an implied contract may exist between the person performing the work and the end user.

This area has received the attention of the Court of Appeal, as already observed in *Dacas* v. *Brook Street Bureau (UK) Ltd* (2004). However in *Bunce* v. *Postworth Ltd t/a Skyblue* (2005) and *James* v. *London Borough of Greenwich* (2008), the Appellate courts furthered its reasoning in relation to agency workers. For instance in *Bunce*, the Court of Appeal had to deal with a very similar situation to that confronting it in the *Dacas* case. The worker concerned brought unfair dismissal proceedings against both the agency and the client but only appealed to the EAT against that part of the tribunal's decision dealing with his relationship with the agency. The agreement in question provided that its terms were not to give rise to a contract of

176. *Motorola Ltd* v. *Davidson* [2001] IRLR 4.
177. E.g. *O'Sullivan* v. *Thompson-Croom* (1973) 14 KIR 108.
178. *Dacas* v. *Brook Street* [2004] IRLR 358 CA.
179. *Cable & Wireless plc* v. *Muscat* [2006] ICR 97 SCA; *RNLI* v. *Bushaway* [2005] IRLR 674.

employment. It made clear that there might be intervals between assignments when no work would be available and stated that there was no obligation on the worker to accept any assignment which was offered. The Court of Appeal upheld the decision of both the tribunal and the EAT that the claimant was not an employee of the agency. This was on the basis, as in the *Dacas* case, that there was no mutuality of obligation and an insufficient degree of control to establish a contract of employment. In this case the CA expressed the view that in order to question whether a contract of employment can be implied it must first be questioned whether the arrangement in question is a genuine agency arrangement or whether it is only consistent with an implied contract between the worker and the end user and would be inconsistent with there being no such contract. It is only where the arrangement is not genuine that one can question whether a contract can be implied.

142. It is clear that the same requirements of mutuality of obligation and a sufficient degree of control apply in the case of the relationship between the worker and the hirer or 'end user', as this person has come to be called; however, it is now equally clear in the light of *James* v. *London Borough of Greenwich* (2008) that one must first determine whether a genuine agency arrangement is in place. In *Stephenson* v. *Delphi Diesel Systems Ltd* (2003) Elias J said:

The significance of mutuality is that it determines whether there is a contract in existence at all. The significance of control is that it determines whether, if there is a contract in place, it can properly be classified as a contract of service, rather than some other kind of contract.

In general, in view of these requirements, it is unlikely that a worker placed by an agency will become an employee of the hirer, although application of the tests already considered may lead to the conclusion that an employment relationship has arisen. In this context, as in the other considered, it is important to emphasize that each case depends on its own facts.

In the present context, the significance of the Court of Appeal decision in *Dacas* v. *Brook Street Bureau (UK) Ltd* (2004) should not be overlooked. Although that case was confined to a consideration of the relationship between the worker and the agency (simply because she had not appealed against that part of the tribunal's decision relating to her relationship with the end user), the observations of the Court of Appeal make it clear that in dealing with these kinds of cases tribunals should examine the facts very carefully to ascertain whether an employment relationship between the worker and the end user can be inferred. It is clear, at least from the judgment of Mummery LJ, that he regarded it as likely that there might have been an implied contract between Mrs Dacas and the authority, but that the case would have had to be remitted to the tribunal for it to determine the issue. Cases subsequently decided by the EAT suggest that there is a tendency to hold that the agency worker is an employee of the end user. Two recent decisions of the EAT – in *Cable and Wireless plc* v. *Muscat* (2005) and *Royal National Lifeboat Institution* v. *Bushaway* (2005) – both upheld the tribunal's decisions that the agency workers concerned were employees of the end user. In *Muscat* v. *Cable & Wireless plc* (2006), its most recent decision on this issue, the Court of Appeal has said that the view of the majority in *Dacas* was correct. Smith LJ said that it was right for tribunals to follow the guidance given in that case, but pointed out that the guidance does not direct tribunals to reach any particular conclusion, only to consider the possibility that an implied contract may exist between the person performing the work and the end user.

143. Several cases have concerned the reasonableness of an order that the employee transfer to a new place of work. Where there is no express obligation to transfer, the courts have been willing to imply a reasonable term, taking into account such factors as the nature of the employer's business and whether the employee had been moved before.[180] Even where there is an express mobility clause which requires the employee to transfer to another location, an ET may imply a term that reasonable notice will be given to the employee when the employer decides to exercise its powers to require the employee to move.[181] Although the Court of Appeal has refused to imply a term that the employer's exercise of an express or implied right to require mobility should be exercised only for 'genuine operational reasons' (such a term being too uncertain in scope),[182] the EAT has utilized the implied term that the employer must not behave in a manner calculated to undermine the relationship of trust and confidence when exercising an express power to require mobility.[183] A requirement that an employee must move may in some circumstances amount to indirect sex discrimination where this has a disproportionate adverse impact on women, unless it can be objectively justified.[184]

144. The Agency Worker Regulations 2010, which came into force on 1 October 2011, provide that agency workers (i.e. temps) will have the same rights to pay, benefits, rest periods and holidays a someone recruited directly by the hirer (including the hirer's own directly recruited temp workers and employees). There is a 12 week qualifying period, so genuine short-term agency temps will not qualify for this right. The 12 weeks do not have to be continuous; there can be breaks between assignments and absences on grounds of e.g. sickness or jury service.

Agency workers are classed as 'workers' rather than as employees. All workers, including agency workers, are entitled to certain rights which include:

- paid annual leave;
- rest breaks and limits on working time;
- the National Minimum Wage;
- no unlawful deductions from wages;
- discrimination rights under the Equality Act 2010;
- health and safety at work.

The Regulations grant agency workers the entitlement to the same or no less favourable treatment as comparable employees with respect to basic employment

180. *Jones* v. *Associated Tunnelling Co. Ltd* [1981] IRLR 477 (EAT).
181. *Prestwick Circuits Ltd* v. *McAndrew* [1990] IRLR 191, Ct of Session; *United Bank Ltd* v. *Akhtar* [1989] IRLR 507, EAT.
182. *Murco Petroleum Ltd* v. *Forge* [1987] ICR 282.
183. *United Bank Ltd* v. *Akhtiar* [1989] IRLR 507, EAT.
184. *Meade Hill* v. *British Council* [1995] IRLR 478 (see Part I, Ch. 8, below).

and working conditions, if and when they complete a qualifying period of 12 weeks in a particular job.

If an agency worker is working on more than one assignment the agency worker will have two or more assignments that need to accrue separately. In other words, if an agency worker has assignment A and assignment B, they would need to work for 12 weeks on assignment A before their rights apply to assignment A and 12 weeks on assignment B before their rights apply to assignment B. The 2010 Regulations aim to ensure an agency worker is engaged on the same relevant terms and conditions as a 'comparable employee'. In other words, 'what terms and conditions would the agency worker have got if they had been directly recruited into the role?' An employee is a 'comparable employee' if at the time of an alleged breach of the regulations:

- both employee and agency worker are working for and under the supervision and direction of the hirer;
- both employee and agency worker are engaged in the same or broadly similar work (this could include an examination of qualification and skills)
- the employee works or is based at the same establishment as the agency worker (the employee can work or be based at a different establishment but only where such an employee cannot be found working or based at the same establishment).

145. The Agency Workers Regulations apply to:

- individuals who work as temporary agency workers;
- individuals or companies (private, public and third sector e.g. charities, social enterprises) involved in the supply of temporary agency workers, either directly or indirectly to work temporarily for and under the direction and supervision of a hirer;
- and hirers (private, public and third sector).

A temporary work agency (TWA) supplies agency workers to work temporarily for a third party (the hirer). The agency worker works temporarily under the supervision and direction of the hirer but only has a contract) an employment contract or a contract to perform work or services (personally) with the TWA. Under the Regulations a TWA is a person (individual or company) in business, whether operating for profit or not and including both public and private sector bodies, involved in the supply of temporary agency workers. This could be a 'high street' agency, but also an intermediary such as an umbrella company or a master or neutral vendor if they are involved in the supply of the agency worker.

An agency worker (often referred to as a 'temp') is someone who has a contract with the TWA (an employment contract or a contract to perform work personally) but works temporarily for and under the direction and supervision of a hirer.

The hirer (end-user) is a 'person'– e.g. company, partnership, sole trade, public body – which is engaged in economic activity (whether or not for profit) and which books agency workers via a TWA. The hirer is responsible for supervising and directing the agency worker while they undertake the assignment. A hirer will have its own legal identity – so a division within a company will not be a separate hirer if it does not have its own legal identity.

The definition of an agency worker excludes those who are in business on their own account where the status of the hirer is that of a client or customer of a 'profession or business undertaking' (i.e. a genuine business to business relationship). Individuals may choose to do this for the sake of flexibility or for tax reasons. However, this is the only element of these Regulations where there can be 'objective justification' for less favourable treatment. Essentially, hirers have to ask themselves 'is there a good reason for treating the agency worker less favourably?' Cost may be one factor to take into account but hirers are unlikely to be able to rely on cost alone to justify different treatment. Practical and organizational considerations could also be a factor. Even if there is objective justification, hirers may want to consider whether it is possible or feasible to offer agency workers certain access to facilities on a partial basis, as an alternative to excluding them altogether.

146. However, equal treatment is not required in respect of all the terms and conditions that the person would have received had they been recruited directly. It covers basic working and employment conditions. They are those which are ordinarily included in relevant contracts (or associated documents such as pay scales, collective agreements) of direct recruits. This means terms and conditions normally set out in:

- standard contracts;
- a pay scale or pay structure;
- a relevant collective agreement;
- a company handbook or similar.

K. Homeworkers

147. A further important category of workers is that of outworkers, usually working at home rather than at the employer's establishment, or working from home as a base (e.g. market research). These are well established working practices, dating back to the times of 'sweated labour' in the early 20th century. Recent estimates suggest that in the 21st century the number of home-based workers is increasing to as many as 350,00 people in the UK work at home and a further 500,000 work from home as a base, together accounting for 4 per cent of the workforce.[185] Homeworking has traditionally been common in the manual trades, such as sewing, and it is popularly considered to consist largely of manufacturing done at home. In fact, white-collar and service work now form the predominant type of home-based work, with further additions in the areas of new technology, such as punch card operation and word processing.

Homeworkers tend to fare less well than their counterparts working at the workplace. Even if the rate paid for the job is similar, allowances for overheads are the

185. All figures in this paragraph are to be found in C. Hakim, *Home-Based work in Britain*, DE Research Paper No. 60 (1987) and (1987) 95 *Employment Gazette*, 92–104 and 221–225.

exception rather than the rule and holiday pay is a rarity.[186] The vast majority are employed by non-unionized establishments. Despite their vulnerability, homeworkers do not form a separate legal category. There are some statutory protective measures applicable to homeworking, such as the requirement that the employer observes minimum safety requirements,[187] and the national minimum wage.[188] However, these regulations are inadequate and often unenforced. Furthermore, employment protection rights, as we have seen, depend on being able to establish both a contract of service and the necessary continuity of service. The employment status of homeworkers is ambiguous: some recent cases have held that homeworkers may be employed under a contract of service[189] but these are confined to their own facts. A recent survey found that while 57 per cent of home-based workers believed themselves to be self-employed, as many as 20 per cent had doubts about their correct employment status.[190]

L. Part-time Workers

148. Part-time workers form an increasingly important sector of the workforce, making up almost 30 per cent of the UK workforce, with almost 75 per cent of part-time workers being women.[191] The concept of indirect sex discrimination has been important in removing obstacles to their employment (see Part I, Ch. 8 below). The limitations of this approach are that a male comparator has to be found (and there may be none, e.g. in an all-female workforce), proof of significant adverse impact on women may be difficulty, and the defence of objective justification may include the very market forces which cause discrimination. ILO Convention No. 175 of 1994 and the accompanying Recommendation No. 182 contemplates specific rights for all part-time workers.

The significantly weaker Agreement between the EC Social Partners, implemented by Council Directive 97/81/EC relies on a general principle of non-discrimination between part-time and full-time workers which is subject to a defence of objective justification. In addition, the Agreement encourages improvements in the quality and availability of part-time work.

The Part-Time Work directive has been implemented in the UK by the Part-Time Work (Prevention of Less Favourable Treatment) Regulations 2000. The Regulations create the right for a part-time worker to be no less favourably treated than a full-time worker.

---

186. C. Hakim, 'Employers' Use of Homework and Outwork and Freelances' (1984) 92 *Employment Gazette* 146.
187. Factories Act 1961, s. 133.
188. National Minimum Wage Act 1998, s. 35.
189. *Airfix Footwear Ltd* v. *Cope* [1978] ICR 1210; *Nethermere (St. Neots) Ltd* v. *Gardiner* [1984] ICR 365.
190. Hakim, *op. cit.*
191. These statistics relate to the employment figures for September 2013: *Office of National Statistics, Statistical Bulletin: Labour Market Statistics*, November 2013.

§2. WRITTEN STATEMENT OF EMPLOYMENT TERMS

149. The employer is obliged to provide every employee (with some exceptions) with a written statement reflecting the main terms of employment.[192] The aim of this provision is to 'ensure for the benefit of an employee that the terms of his (or her) contract of employment are set out in writing so that the employee knows his legal rights in terms of the contract and can, if need be, insist upon them by legal action against the employer'.[193]

150. The statement must be given to the employee not later than two months after the beginning of his or her employment with the employer. The statement should identify the parties, specify the date on which the employment began and state the date on which the employee's period of continuous employment began (taking into account any employment with a previous employer which counts towards that period). It should also give particulars of the following terms of employment which were in effect on a specified date not more than seven days before the date on which the statement was issued:

- the scale or rate of remuneration, or the method of calculating remuneration (including for example, any terms on piece-rates, or overtime pay);
- the intervals at which remuneration is paid (that is, whether weekly or monthly or other specified intervals);
- any terms and conditions relating to hours of work (including any terms and conditions relating to normal working hours);
- any terms and conditions relating to:
  (a) entitlement to holidays, including public holidays, and holiday pay (sufficient to enable the employee's entitlement, including any entitlement to accrued holiday pay on the termination of employment, to be precisely calculated);
  (b) incapacity for work due to sickness or injury, including any provision for sick pay;
  (c) pensions and pension schemes (employees who are covered by special statutory pensions schemes and whose employers are already obliged by law to provide information about them are excepted);
- the length of notice of termination which the employee is obliged to give and entitled to receive to terminate the contract of employment;
- the title of the job which the employee is to do or a brief description of the work for which the employee is employed;
- where the employment is not intended to be permanent, the period for which it is expected to continue or, if it is for a fixed term, the date when it is to end;
- either the place of work or where the employee is required or permitted to work at various places, and indication of that and of the address of the employer;

192. ERA 1996, ss. 1–7. Similar provisions were first introduced in 1963, and were revised in 1993 following the Council Directive 91/533/EEC and, as finally amended by Employment Act 2002.
193. *Owens* v. *Multilux Ltd* [1974] IRLR 113 at p. 114.

- any collective agreements which directly affect the terms and conditions of the employment including, where the employer is not a party, the persons by whom they were made; and
- where the employee is required to work outside the United Kingdom, for a period of more than one month, the period for which he or she is to work outside the UK, the currency in which remuneration is to be paid while working outside the UK, any additional remuneration payable to the employee, and any benefits to be provided to or in respect of the employee, by reason of being required to work outside the UK, and any terms and conditions relating to the employee's return to the UK.

Most of the particulars must be in a single document, but the employee may be referred to another document setting out sick pay and pension arrangements. The employee may be referred to the law or to a collective agreement relating to notice provisions. Where before the end of the period of two months after the beginning of the employment the employee is to begin work outside the UK for a period of more than one month, the statement must be given to the employee not later than the time he or she leaves the UK to begin the work.

151. In addition the Employment Relations Act 1996 requires the statement given to the employee to include a note which must:

- specify any disciplinary rules (other than those relating to health and safety at work) which apply to the employee or refer to a document, reasonably accessible to the employee, which specifies the rules;
- specify by description or name the person to whom the employee can apply and the manner in which such applications should be made:
  (a) if he is dissatisfied with any disciplinary decision relating to him; or
  (b) for the purposes of seeking redress of any grievance relating to his employment; and
  (c) where there are further steps which follow from an application under (ii)(a) or (ii)(b), explain those steps or refer to a document which explains them and is reasonably accessible to the employee;
- whether the employer has an occupational pension scheme which has a certificate that it is 'contracted-out' of the state pension scheme under the Pension Schemes Act 1993.

The obligation to provide a written statement under the 1996 Act does not apply to certain categories of employees, such as seamen on ships registered in the UK under an approved crew agreement and Crown servants. The note specifying disciplinary rules need not be given if the number of employees employed by the employer and any associated employer was less than twenty on the day when the employment began.[194]

194. ERA 1996, s. 3(3).

152. It is essential to note that the statement is not the contract itself, and may be an inaccurate reflection of the terms to which the parties actually agreed. 'The document is a unilateral one merely stating the employer's view of what those terms are ... In the absence of an acknowledgement by the parties that the statement is itself a contract and that the terms are correct, the statutory statement does not itself constitute a contract in writing.'[195] While the statement is strong *prima facie* evidence of the terms of the contract, it is by no means conclusive.[196] Nor does the fact that an employee has signed acknowledgement of receipt necessarily mean that she or he has signed a contract or accepted the accuracy of the terms in it. It is only a contract if the parties acknowledge it as such.[197]

153. Any changes in the listed particulars must be given to the employee 'at the earliest opportunity' and in any event not later than one month after the change. Where the change results from the employee being required to work outside the UK for a period of more than one month, the change must be notified not later than the time when he or she leaves the UK to start the work if that is earlier. A statement of change does not in itself vary the terms of the contract; at most, it may provide evidence of an agreed variation. Nor does the fact that an employee continues working without objection mean that he or she has impliedly agreed to the change, especially where the variation relates to a matter which has no immediate practical application.[198]

154. Where no statement has been given, or a statement is incomplete or its accuracy is in doubt, the employee may complain to an ET, which will determine any missing particulars or confirm, amend or substitute for inaccurate particulars.[199] The tribunal should attempt to discover what the parties have in fact agreed, 'taking into account all the circumstances, including the parties' subsequent conduct. In this exercise, the tribunal is not confined to the tests applicable in deciding the terms to be implied in a commercial contract. If the tribunal cannot ascertain the agreed terms, it may imply a reasonable term. 'Section 11 would seem to impose upon the tribunals a statutory duty to find the specified terms and in the last resort to invent them for the purpose of literally writing them into the contract.'[200] Although this appears to be an important departure from the traditional means of discovering contractual terms, recent cases have stressed that the function of the tribunal is to establish the accuracy of the statutory statement, not to recast the contract, nor to adjudicate on the fairness or unfairness of the employment relationship[201] (see Part I, Ch. 2 below). The effect of this determination is that the employer is deemed to have supplied a statement in the corrected form. However, the tribunal cannot

195. *System Floors Ltd* v. *Daniel* [1982] ICR 54 at 58.
196. *Ibid.*, approved in *Robertson* v. *British Gas Corporation* [1983] ICR 351. This also reflects Directive 91/5333: Joined Cases C-253/96 to C-258/96, *Kampelmann* v. *Landschaftsverband Westfalen-Lippe* [1998] IRLR 333 at 342.
197. *Gascol Conversions Ltd* v. *Mercer* [1974] ICR 420.
198. *Jones* v. *Associated Tunnelling Company Ltd* [1981] IRLR 477.
199. ERA 1996, s. 11.
200. *Mears* v. *Safecar Security Ltd* [1982] ICR 626 CA.
201. *England* v. *British Telecommunications* [1990] IRLR 330 at 331.

enforce the terms of the contract; the employee's remedy for breach of contract is in the County Court or High Court.

§3. Capacity to Contract and Restrictions on Employment

I. Young People

155. Persons under the age of 18 have limited capacity to contract, as now governed by the Young Worker Regulations 1996. A minor may obtain benefits under an employment contract, but the general rule is that he or she is bound only if the obligations are on the whole beneficial to him or her. It seems that simple financial advantages are enough to make the contract 'beneficial'.[202]

156. There are statutory restrictions on the employment of children under the school-leaving age of 16. The minimum age at which a child may be employed is 13. Between the ages of 13 and 16 children may not be employed at all in any factory, mine, transport undertakings or United Kingdom registered ship. They may be employed in industrial undertakings only if members of the same family are employed there. Previously, local authorities had the power to regulate the employment of children under 16, but this was replaced in 1973 by an enlarged power for the Secretary of State to restrict their employment. There is specific control over the employment of children during the last year of compulsory schooling in work experience schemes and special regulations apply to the employment of children in the entertainment industry. Until 1989, a wide variety of legislation regulated the employment of 'young persons', i.e. persons over 16 but under 18 years of age. However, such regulations were repealed by the Employment Act 1989, on the grounds that they imposed an 'administrative burden' on employers, and that long hours did not have a different effect on young persons from those on adults. However, the UK was forced to re-regulate in this area by virtue of the Council Directive 94/33/EC on the Protection of Young Persons (implemented under the Young Worker Regulations 1996). The Working Time Regulations 1998 now contain specific provisions on the length of the working week, night work and rest periods relating to young workers (see Part I, Ch. 4 below). The National Minimum Wage Act 1998 does not apply to 16- and 17-year-olds and a lower rate than that for adults has been set for those aged 18–21 (*see* Part I, Ch. 5 *below*).

II. Women

157. Both single and married women have the same capacity to contract as men, and sex discrimination on grounds of marriage has been outlawed since 1975 (below, Ch. 8). Protective legislation, restricting women's employment on night and shift work, and prescribing other differential treatment, has been repealed.[203]

202. *Chaplin* v. *Leslie Frewin (Publishers) Ltd* [1966] Ch. 71.
203. SDA 1986, s. 7; EA 1989, s. 9.

III. Foreign Workers

158. Successive UK governments have imposed increasingly stringent limitations on the rights of workers from outside the European Economic Area (EEA) to work in the United Kingdom. Discrimination against EU citizens is prohibited by Article 17 of the EC Treaty, and freedom of movement of workers entails the abolition of discrimination based on nationality (i.e. of EU Member States) in respect of employment, remuneration and other terms and conditions of employment. There are detailed EU regulations which are directly applicable in the United Kingdom.[204] The EU's *acquis* has been extended to citizens of the EEA countries (Norway, Iceland, Liechtenstein). Discrimination against any person on grounds of race, colour, ethnic or national origins or nationality is prohibited by the Equality Act 2010 (see Part I, Ch. 8 below). This section is concerned only with so-called 'third country nationals' (TCNs). Immigration controls and work permits are for the most part prescribed in a complex set of non-statutory regulations administered with a large measure of discretion. Only a very brief description is possible here.

159. Non-EEA nationals may be admitted for work in the UK in a number of circumstances. The principal categories are: (1) seasonal work for full-time students for up to three months, provided they can maintain themselves without recourse to public funds; (2) teachers and language assistants for up to two years on exchange schemes; (3) Commonwealth citizens, one of whose grandparents was born in the UK, for up to four years; (4) trainees who come to the UK specifically for training or work experience; (5) overseas journalists and broadcasters, sales representatives, private servants in diplomatic households, ministers of religion, operational ground staff for overseas airlines; (6) employees in certain other forms of approved employment. Anyone outside these categories requires a work permit which is given for a specific job where no suitable British or EEA national is available. *150.* There are some further restrictions including the prohibition on employment of non-British subjects in the civil service without a certificate1 and as regards military employment.[205] The recruitment of workers from outside the United Kingdom by private employment agencies and businesses is regulated, for example to ensure that the worker obtains full written details of the employment in a language he or she can understand.[206]

204. See C. Barnard, *EC Employment Law* (4th edn, London, 2012), pp. 111–154.
205. Aliens Employment Act 1955.
206. Conduct of Employment Agencies and Employment Businesses Regulations 1976, SI 1976 715, reg. 6, as amended.

Chapter 2. The Sources of Terms of the Contract of Employment

§1. Express and Implied Terms

160. The reciprocal rights and duties of employer and employee depend upon the express and implied terms of the contract of employment. Where the parties have not expressly dealt with any matter, the courts are willing to imply terms in order to make the contract a workable one. These terms are sometimes treated as resting upon the presumed intentions of the parties (terms implied in fact), sometimes as based on custom and practice and sometimes as a legal incident of the relationship or status of employer and employee (terms implied in law). Two particular approaches from the law of commercial contracts have traditionally been adopted by the courts in deciding whether to imply terms in accordance with the presumed intentions of the parties. The first is 'to give such business efficacy to the transaction as must have been intended'.[207] The second is to imply 'something so obvious that it goes without saying; so that if, while the parties were making their bargain, an officious bystander were to suggest some express provision for it in their agreement they would testily suppress him with a cry of "Oh, of course!"'.[208]

More recently, the courts have acknowledged that implied terms may involve judicial norm-making rather than reflecting the actual intentions of the parties. According to this approach, the relationship of employer and employee requires that there should be some kind of agreed term on certain matters, such as sick pay or the place of employment. Where that term has not been agreed and the parties would not have agreed had they been asked at the time of contracting what that term should be, the court has to imply the term.[209] In this type of case, all the facts and circumstances of the relationship, including the way in which the parties have worked the contract since it was made, must be considered. Recent decisions differ as to whether such a term should be upheld as a legal incident only if 'necessary' to the relationship,[210] or whether the more flexible 'reasonableness' test is appropriate.[211] The most important terms which have been implied in law as 'necessary' incidents of the relationship are (1) the reciprocal duty of cooperation; (2) the employee's duty of faithful service; and (3) the employer's duty to take reasonable care for the health and safety of his employees, and the employee's duty to take reasonable care about his employer's business. These are discussed in Chapter 3 below.

161. The scope of implied terms is important for several reasons. Many of them were developed in the context of the employer's right at common law to dismiss an employee without notice. Where the breach of the term is sufficiently serious, the employee may be said to have repudiated the contract, so entitling the employer to

207. *The Moorcock* (1889) 14 PD 64 at 68.
208. *Shirlaw* v. *Southern Foundries Ltd* [1939] 2 KB 206 at p. 227.
209. *Lister* v. *Romford Ice and Cold Storage Co. Ltd* [1957] AC 555 (House of Lords); *Mears* v. *Safecar Security Ltd* [1982] ICR 626 (Court of Appeal).
210. *Mears* v. *Safecar Security Ltd* at pp. 650–651 per Stephenson LJ; *Courtaulds Northern Spinning* v. *Gibson* [1988] IRLR 305 at p. 309.
211. *Howman & Son* v. *Blyth* [1983] ICR 416 (EAT) at p. 420; *Jones* v. *Associated Tunnelling Co. Ltd* [1981] IRLR 477 (EAT).

dismiss him or her without notice. Conversely, the employee may be able to claim damages for breach of contract where the employer repudiates a contractual obligation. Legislation on redundancy payments and on unfair dismissal has incorporated the contractual notions into the statutory definition of 'dismissal'. This is particularly important in the context of 'constructive dismissal' where the employer's repudiation may entitle the employee to terminate the contract without notice. Moreover, in determining the reasonableness of an employer's actions, tribunals are strongly influenced by the express and implied contractual obligations of the parties. The legislation has therefore spawned an important body of case law on implied terms, particularly those implied in law. We must next examine the judicial techniques for incorporating collective agreements, works rules and notices and custom and practice into individual contracts.

162. Two preliminary points must be stressed. The first is the optional nature of implied terms (including custom). A term will not be implied if it is contrary to an express term; and a custom may not be proved if it is contrary to an express or implied term. These principles of the common law distinguish it sharply from the civil law systems: there are no imperative norms in the legal relationship between employer and employee. In particular, implied terms can always be replaced by express ones, even if these are less favourable to the employee. This is particularly important in relation to collective agreements. The second preliminary point is that the written statement of particulars of terms of employment may facilitate proof of the express and implied terms of the contract, although this is not conclusive evidence of those terms.

§2. Terms Incorporated from Collective Agreements

163. British labour law remains rooted in the notion that terms and conditions are a matter of contract between individuals. Collective agreements are presumed not to be intended to be enforceable as contracts between the trade union and employer parties unless an intention to be so bound is expressed in writing.[212] However, the terms of collective agreements may achieve legal effect if they are incorporated into individual contracts of employment. Incorporation is not automatic, not even as minimum terms, and express agreement always takes precedence. In this respect, British labour law stands in sharp contrast to that of other countries, such as France, where the clauses of collective agreements apply to employment contracts except where there are provisions more favourable to the worker. The seriousness of this gap in British labour law has become apparent in times of recession when employers have been able to cut wages by the simple expedient of terminating contracts of employment and offering re-employment on revised terms and conditions less favourable than those laid down in the collective agreement.

164. Under what circumstances will a term of a collective agreement become legally enforceable as a term of the individual contract? Unfortunately, attempts to

212. Milward and Steven, *Workplace Industrial Relations in Britain*, London, 1986, p. 226.

construct a theory of incorporation which is both consistent with contractual principle and reflects reality have not been wholly successful. There are several difficulties. First, collective agreements usually apply to all workers of a particular category, whether or not they are members of a trade union which is party to the agreement, and even if they subsequently join or leave the union. Many workers may not even know of the existence of the agreement. This is difficult to reconcile with the contractual principle that parties should consent to the terms of their contract. Secondly, collective agreements contain procedural terms which may not be amenable to individual enforcement, or may not have been intended to create individual rights. Thirdly, collective bargaining may take place on several different levels at once, with a national or industry-wide agreement being supplemented by local or plant level agreements. The courts have to decide which of these should be incorporated. It should be noted that a worker cannot sue directly on the collective agreement, since he or she was not a party to it.[213]

165. The first major issue in any attempt at incorporation is that of 'bridging' the gap between the collective agreement and the individual contract. Several principles of incorporation have emerged:

(a) Express incorporation: this will occur where employer and employee expressly agree that the individual contract is subject to a particular collective agreement or agreements. Proof that such agreement has been reached may be facilitated by express reference to the collective agreement in the written statement of employment terms which the employer is obliged to provide.[214]
(b) Incorporation by custom: it is a well-recognized contractual principle that a contract can be taken to include terms which are sanctioned by custom unless the parties clearly specified otherwise. To become a term of a contract, a custom must be certain, reasonable and well-known, although the individual worker may be ignorant of its existence. Kahn-Freund characterized collective agreements as 'crystallized custom', arguing that this was the basis of incorporation.[215] This explains much of the reality of employment conditions, particularly the fact that collective agreements refer to all workers, regardless of their knowledge or approval. But it does not explain how new or varied collective agreements come to be incorporated.
(c) Implied incorporation: in practice industrial tribunals and courts are very willing to find even in the absence of express agreement or proof of custom, that the terms of collective agreements have become impliedly incorporated into contracts of employment, almost to the point of a presumption of fact that such agreements apply unless the contrary is shown.[216]

213. But this may be possible in Scots law: J. Casey, *Juridical Review* (1973) p. 22 at p. 39. It seems unlikely that the Contracts (Rights of Third Parties) Act 1999 will change the position in England and Wales.
214. ERA 1996, s. 1; see above, para. 132.
215. Kahn-Freund, *System of Industrial Relations in Great Britain* (ed. Flanders and Clegg), Oxford, 1954, pp. 58–59; *see* e.g. *Donelan* v. *Kirby* [1983] 1 IRLR 191 (EAT).
216. *Marley* v. *Forward Trust* [1986] IRLR 369 (CA).

166. The 'bridging' problem is resolved by these techniques of express or implied terms or custom and practice. In general, the trade union negotiating a collective agreement is not treated as the agent of its members even if it purports to act as their 'representative'. The only exceptions to this might be where the number of workers involved is very small and the issues are local or are personal to those workers. English law has not favoured the agency approach because, in Wedderburn's words, 'many puzzles would then arise'.[217] For example, the fact that collective agreements are generally regarded as applicable to non-unionists as well as trade union members is incompatible with the concept of the union as agent only for its own members. Another problem would arise with workers who joined the enterprise after the agreement was concluded. By the doctrines of the English law of agency, only those who were themselves capable of contracting at the time the agent made the contract may subsequently ratify the agent's action. This would mean that workers below the contractual capacity (18 years) at the time the collective agreement was made could not be bound by it. The most difficult question of all would be whether a member could revoke an agent's authority at any time in the same way as a principal could revoke an agent's authority. If this were possible, stable bargaining arrangements could be upset by individual withdrawals of authority.[218]

167. Several problems remain, common to all the above theories. First, not all terms of a collective agreement may be incorporated into individual contracts. The courts have distinguished between terms which are appropriate for individual enforcement and those which are not;[219] but the classification of any particular term must be determined on a case by case basis depending on the presumed intention of the parties.[220] Thus a collective agreement regarding hours of work,[221] dismissal procedure[222] and a redundancy selection procedure[223] has been held to be capable of individual incorporation, since such terms affect workers individually. However, a collective agreement between an employer and a union providing machinery for collective bargaining and for resolving industrial disputes has been held not be individually incorporated, even though it is of great importance to individual employees because 'it is almost inconceivable ... that it could have been intended to become legally enforceable at the suit of an individual worker'.[224] Instead such procedures are to be operated by the union and employers party to the agreement. Nor have the courts developed clear-cut principles to deal with collective bargaining at

217. Wedderburn, *The Worker and the Law*, 3rd edn, London, 1986, p. 327.
218. *Land* v. *West Yorks CC* [1979] ICR 452; *Singh* v. *British Steel Corporation* [1974] IRLR 131.
219. *National Coal Board* v. *National Union of Mineworkers* [1986] IRLR 439 at p. 454.
220. *Alexander* v. *Standard Telephones & Cables Ltd* [1990] IRLR 55.
221. *National Coal Board* v. *Galley* [1958] 1 WLR 16.
222. *Barber* v. *Manchester Regional Hospital Board* [1958] 1 WLR 181, *Irani* v. *Southampton and South West Hampshire Health Authority* [1985] IRLR 203.
223. *Alexander* v. *Standard Telephones* [1990] IRLR 55.
224. *National Coal Board* v. *National Union of Mineworkers* [1986] IRLR 439 at p. 454. Contrast, *City and Hackney Health Authority* v. *National Union of Public Employees* [1985] IRLR 263 (CA), where a shop-steward's recognition procedure was held to have been incorporated into an individual's contract.

both national and local level.[225] Some collective agreements do, however, make specific provision by their own terms as to what is to happen in case of conflict with other agreements. A further complication arises if an employer or union unilaterally withdraws from a collective agreement. Contractual theory requires consent by both parties to a variation; it has thus been held that, once a collective agreement has been incorporated into the individual contract, its terms cannot be removed by the employer's or union's unilateral withdrawal from the collective agreement.[226] The employee's consent may, however, be implied if he or she continues to work without objection. Moreover, it remains open to the employer to terminate the conditions incorporated from the collective agreement by terminating the individual contracts and offering to re-employ the relevant workers on the new terms.[227] If the collective agreement is varied with the consent of the trade union, individual contracts will usually be varied accordingly, on the basis of an express or implied term that the individual contract is subject to collective agreements for the time being in force.

§3. Terms Incorporated from Works Rules and Notices

168. The terms of individual contracts of employment may also be found in rules, notices and other documents issued by management to employees either at the time of engagement or subsequently. In some cases, such rules are collectively agreed, in which case the methods of incorporation are as set out above. Frequently, however, they are unilaterally imposed. In that case, they become terms of the contract in one of the following ways.

169. Unilaterally imposed rules may become part of the contract of employment:

(1) by express incorporation, for example by the worker signing an acknowledgement, at the time of making the contract or subsequently, that the rules are binding upon him, or if reasonable notice is given to the worker of the existence of the rules and he works under them without objection;
(2) by implied incorporation, for example where the worker has accepted employment on the 'usual conditions', which would be taken to include the works rules;
(3) by proof that the rules were recognized by custom and practice. Express rules take precedence over the second and third categories.

170. Works rules in British industry are of so many different kinds that no general statement can be made about their function as contractual terms. But it needs to

225. Compare *Clift* v. *West Riding CC*, *The Times*, 10 April 1964 (local agreement prevailed) with *Gascol Conversions Ltd* v. *Mercer* [1974] ICR 420 (national agreement prevailed).
226. *Robertson* v. *British Gas Corporation* [1983] ICR 351; *Gibbons* v. *Associated British Ports* [1985] IRLR 376; *Airlie* v. *City of Edinburgh DC* [1996] IRLR 516.
227. *Burdett Coutts* v. *Hertfordshire CC* [1984] IRLR 91 (QBD).

be stressed that not all works rules are contractual in character. For example, the Court of Appeal[228] decided in 1972 that the British Railways Rules Book setting out the duties of railway employees were not terms of the contracts of employment of those employees. They were simply 'instructions to a man as to how he is to do his work'. This meant that they could be unilaterally altered by the employer without the employee's consent, at any time. The employee, on the other hand, was obliged to obey the rules, as altered from time to time, because of his duty of obedience to the lawful instructions of the employer. In cases like this therefore, works rules will be treated simply as instances of lawful managerial commands. In other cases, they may be construed as being contractually binding on both parties.

§4. Terms Incorporated from Custom and Practice

171. The custom and practice of a trade or industry has traditionally been an important source of terms and conditions of employment, although this form of regulation has become less frequent with the greater formalization of conditions of work, encouraged by the obligation to supply a statutory statement of terms. A somewhat different type of custom and practice developed in manufacturing industry during the 1950s, in the form of informal workplace bargaining, displacing national agreements. This was increasingly recognized as an important source of terms of the contract. In the past decade, however, workplace bargaining has itself become increasingly formalized, and informal workplace bargaining is less prevalent. To become a term of a contract, a custom or practice must be certain, reasonable and well-known. Even if an individual worker is ignorant of the particular custom, he or she may be taken to know of local customs.[229]

228. *Secretary of State for Employment* v. *ASLEF* [1972] 2 QB 443.
229. The classic example is *Sagar* v. *Ridehalgh* [1931] 1 Ch. 310. But see now *Bond* v. *CAV Ltd* [1983] IRLR 360, where the requirement of notoriety was more strictly applied.

Chapter 3. The Duties of Cooperation, Fidelity and Care

172. Three of the most important duties implied in law into every contract of employment are discussed in this chapter. These are (1) the duty of mutual co-operation; (2) the duty of faithful service; and (3) the duty of reasonable care.

§1. The Duty of Mutual Cooperation

173. The general duty of cooperation between contracting parties has been developed in recent years by the courts into an obligation of mutual trust and confidence implied by law into every employment relationship. This has been said to be at 'the heart' of the modern contract of employment, dictating how employees should be treated.[230] However, this duty is ambiguous and a number of questions remain unresolved, such as how far the duty is reciprocal and whether the parties can contract out of it. The duty will be analysed here first from the viewpoint of the employee's duty to obey lawful and reasonable orders, and secondly the employer's duty.

I. The Employee's Duty to Obey Lawful and Reasonable Orders

174. One of the most important terms implied by common law into the contract of employment is the employee's duty to obey lawful and reasonable orders. This reflects a judicial endorsement of the employer's 'managerial prerogative' and of the notions of command and subordination inherent in the employment relationship. This has sometimes been treated as an aspect of the duty of faithful service (see below, para. ???). But case law suggests that the rationale of such an implied term lies in the duty not to frustrate the commercial objectives of the employer,[231] a perspective which assumes a unity of purpose between employer and employee in contrast with the pluralist premise of an intrinsic conflict of interest between the two sides. Thus it has been held to be an implied term that 'each employee will not, in obeying lawful instructions, seek to obey them in a wholly unreasonable way, which has the effect of disrupting the system, the efficient running of which he is employed to ensure'.[232]

175. The scope of this implied term is of particular importance in determining the extent of the employer's common law right of summary dismissal. In the 19th century, a single act of disobedience was treated as entitling the employer summarily to dismiss an employee, provided the order was 'lawful'. Thus, a refusal to

230. ILJ 27 (1998) 79 and ILJ 84 (2001) 30; Hepple and Morris, ILJ 31 (2002) 245, 253; and Barmes (2004) MLR 435.

231. *Secretary of State for Employment* v. *ASLEF* [1972] 2 All ER, 949 at pp. 971–972, *per* Buckley LJ; and see *Ticehurst* v. *British Telecommunications plc.* [1992] IRLR 219, CA.

232. *Ibid.*, at p. 980 *per* Roskill LJ; see too Lord Denning MR at p. 965.

allow an employee to visit her sick mother was held to be lawful,[233] as was an order to remain in a zone of danger so long as there was no immediate threat of violence or disease to the employee. More recent cases have held that one act of disobedience can only justify a dismissal if it in effect amounts to a repudiation by the employee of the contract.[234] It was judicially stated in 1974 that 'many of the decisions which are customarily cited date from the last century and may be wholly out of accord with current social conditions … . We have by now come to realize that a contract of service imposes upon the parties a duty of mutual respect'.[235] Moreover, recent cases suggest that an employee can refuse to work long hours or to undertake excessive duties which cause stress-related illness.[236]

176. Several cases have concerned the reasonableness of an order that the employee transfer to a new place of work. Where there is no express obligation to transfer, the courts have been willing to imply a reasonable term, taking into account such factors as the nature of the employer's business and whether the employee had been moved before.[237] Even where there is an express mobility clause which requires the employee to transfer to another location, an ET may imply a term that reasonable notice will be given to the employee when the employer decides to exercise its powers to require the employee to move.[238] Although the Court of Appeal has refused to imply a term that the employer's exercise of an express or implied right to require mobility should be exercised only for 'genuine operational reasons' (such a term being too uncertain in scope),[239] the EAT has recently utilized the implied term that the employer must not behave in a manner calculated to undermine the relationship of trust and confidence when exercising an express power to require mobility.[240] A requirement that an employee must move may in some circumstances amount to indirect sex discrimination where this has a disproportionate adverse impact on women, unless it can be objectively justified.[241]

II. The Employer's Duty to Take Steps to Achieve the Purposes of the Employment Relationship

177. In contrast to the extensive nature of the employee's implied duties, the employer's implied obligations have traditionally been limited to the duty not to prevent or hinder the occurrence of an express condition upon which the performance of the contract by the employee depends (e.g. the provision of piece-work to

233. *Turner* v. *Mason* (1845)14 M&W 112.
234. *Laws* v. *London Chronicle (Indicator Newspapers) Ltd* [1958] 1 WLR 698 (CA).
235. *Wilson* v. *Racher* [1974] ICR 428 at 430.
236. *Johnstone* v. *Bloomsbury AHA* [1991] IRLR 118 (CA); *Walker* v. *Northumberland CC* [1995] IRLR 35.
237. *Jones* v. *Associated Tunnelling Co. Ltd* [1981] IRLR 477 (EAT).
238. *Prestwick Circuits Ltd* v. *McAndrew* [1990] IRLR 191, Ct of Session; *United Bank Ltd* v. *Akhtar* [1989] IRLR 507, EAT.
239. *Murco Petroleum Ltd* v. *Forge* [1987] ICR 282.
240. *United Bank Ltd* v. *Akhtar* [1989] IRLR 507, EAT.
241. *Meade Hill* v. *British Council* [1995] IRLR 478 (see Part I, Ch. 8, below).

a worker paid on piece rates). Under the influence of the law of unfair dismissal (see below, Ch. 7), this duty has been developed into an implied duty of mutual trust and confidence.[242] Although this does not extend to a requirement that the employer should treat employees reasonably,[243] it does require that the employer should not behave in a manner calculated to damage the relationship of trust and confidence[244] and should be good and considerate to employees.[245] The employer should take positive steps to achieve the purposes of the employment relationship, not only with regard to the material conditions of employment such as pay and safety, but also in respect of the psychological conditions which are essential to the employee's performance. For example, it has been held that the employer is under a positive duty to protect the employee from harassment by fellow employees,[246] to refrain from severely criticizing a supervisor in the presence of subordinates,[247] to investigate the employee's genuine grievances,[248] and generally to treat the employee with dignity and respect.[249] The employer must not falsely accuse the employee of serious misconduct on the basis of scanty evidence[250] nor may he give unjustified warnings with a view to disheartening the employee.[251] Nor may he require an employee to submit to a medical examination or search (in the absence of an express term) and to suspend the employee when he or she refuses.[252] Although an isolated action by the employer may not amount to a breach of this term, a course of conduct may be established which does so.[253] This extended duty of cooperation is particularly important in the context of unfair dismissal, since an employee is entitled to resign and claim to have been 'constructively dismissed' if the employer breaches this duty.

178. A recent development has been the notion that the employer's express powers must be exercised in good faith, and the related requirement that the employer must not exercise discretionary contractual powers so as to defeat the objects of the relationship.[254] However, the case law has not developed, as some commentators expected it might, into regarding the contract of employment as a relationship of good faith.[255] So, for example, there is no positive duty on an employer to inform

242. E.g. *Woods* v. *W.M. Car Services (Peterborough) Ltd* [1982] ICR 693 (CA).
243. *Post Office* v. *Roberts* [1980] IRLR 347 (EAT).
244. *Courtaulds Northern Textiles Ltd* v. *Andrew* [1979] IRLR 84.
245. *Woods* v. *W.M. Car Services (Peterborough) Ltd*, above.
246. *Wigan Borough Council* v. *Davies* [1979] IRLR 1278; *Bracebridge Engineering Ltd* v. *Darby* [1990] IRLR 3, EAT.
247. *Courtaulds Northern Textiles Ltd* v. *Andrew*, above.
248. *British Aircraft Corporation* v. *Austin* [1978] IRLR 332.
249. *Garner* v. *Grange Furnishing Ltd* [1977] IRLR 206; *Palmanor Ltd* v. *Cedron* [1978] ICR 1008.
250. *Robinson* v. *Crompton Parkinson Ltd* [1978] ICR 401.
251. *Walker* v. *Josiah Wedgwood & Sons Ltd* [1978] ICR 744 at 754.
252. *Bliss* v. *South East Thames Regional Health Authority* [1987] ICR 700.
253. *Lewis* v. *Motorworld Garages Ltd* [1986] ICR 157.
254. *Imperial Tobacco Pension Trust Ltd* v. *Imperial Tobacco Co. Ltd* [1992] 2 QB 333; *Johnstone* v. *Bloomsbury AHA* [1991] IRLR 118; *Aspeden* v. *Webbs Poultry & Meat Group Holdings Ltd* [1996] IRLR 521.
255. D. Brodie (1998) 27 ILJ 79 at p. 87.

an employee that the way she is proposing to exercise rights in connection with a contractual early retirement scheme may not be the most financially advantageous for her.[256] The duty of mutual trust and confidence must not be confused with a fiduciary relationship, which requires good faith.[257] In the leading case of *Malik* v. *BCCI*,[258] the then House of Lords held that the following conditions must be fulfilled in order to establish a breach of the employer's duty of mutual trust and confidence. (1) The conduct of the employer must impinge on the relationship in the sense that 'looked at objectively, it is likely to destroy or seriously damage the degree of trust and confidence the employee is reasonably entitled to have in his employer.'[259] It is the impact on the employee not the motives of the employer that is relevant.[260] (2) The employee is entitled to terminate the contract without notice if he or she becomes aware during the relationship of such conduct. If the employee becomes aware only after termination, and can prove that the breach caused him or her loss which is not too remote, the employee can claim damages for economic loss. However, the duty does not survive the termination of the relationship with the result that the employee is not entitled to claim damages at common law for the manner of dismissal (e.g. causing a psychiatric disorder) or making it more difficult to find future employment.[261] (3) The conduct must be likely to destroy or seriously damage trust and confidence between employer and employee. So it is a breach of this duty to reveal in a reference to a prospective employer complaints against an employee of which she is unaware thereby blocking her progress in getting a job.[262] This means that, however unfair or unreasonable the employer's behaviour when dismissing the employee, he or she cannot claim damages in a wrongful dismissal action or compensation in an unfair dismissal claim for the manner of the dismissal: see *Johnson* v. *Unisys Ltd* (2001) and *Dunnachie* v. *Kingston upon Hull City Council* (2004).[263] If, on the other hand, the employer's behaviour *before* dismissal is such as to give rise to a claim for a breach of the implied term which can be said to exist independently of his subsequent dismissal, and financial loss flows directly from that failure, the employee may bring an action in respect of that loss. Such an action will not be barred by the availability of a claim in the employment tribunal for unfair dismissal. Further, since the claim is not an unfair dismissal claim there will be no ceiling on the compensation that may be awarded, though the claim will be subject to the rule against double recovery. This is the outcome of the important House of Lords decision in *Eastwood* v. *Magnox Electric plc* (2004).[264]

---

256. *University of Nottingham* v. *Eyett* [1999] IRLR 522; compare *Scally* v. *Southern Health and Social Services Board* [1991] IRLR 522 as explained by M. Freedland 125 21 ILJ (1992) 135 at 138–140.
257. *Nottingham University* v. *Fishel* [2000] IRLR 471.
258. [1997] IRLR 462.
259. *Ibid.* at p. 464 *per* Lord Nicholls.
260. *Ibid.* at p. 469 *per* Lord Steyn; and *see Macari* v. *Celtic Football and Athletic Club* [1999] IRLR 787.
261. *Johnson* v. *Unisys Ltd* [2001] IRLR 279, HL.
262. *TSB* v. *Harris* [2000] IRLR 157. There may also be liability for negligent misstatement in such circumstances: *Cox* v. *Sun Alliance Life Ltd* [2001] IRLR 448.
263. *Dunnachie* v. *Kingston upon Hull City Council* (2004).
264. *Dunnachie* v. *Kingston upon Hull City Council* (2004).

III. The Provision of Work

179. It is the duty of employer and employee to cooperate in fulfilling their obligations under the contract. From the employer's point of view, however, this generally means no more than a duty to pay remuneration. Failure to pay wages over a period of time is regarded as a breach of the employer's fundamental obligations, so entitling the employee to terminate the contract without notice. However, in general, the employer is under no obligation to provide work so long as he goes on providing remuneration.

180. There are three exceptional situations[265] in which the employer must provide work:

(1) in contracts in which the bargain is that the employer will provide a salary plus the opportunity of becoming better known, such as in the case of an actor or artist;
(2) in contracts with commission or piece-workers in which the employer promises to pay an agreed rate and impliedly promises to provide a reasonable amount of work;
(3) in contracts with skilled workers in which the employer promises to pay a salary and impliedly promises to provide a reasonable amount of work to maintain or develop skills.

181. It has been suggested by Lord Denning[266] that there is a general right to be provided with work, but this view is not generally accepted. In the exceptional situations mentioned where the employer is under a duty to provide work his failure to do so may entitle the employee to terminate the contract without notice. Occasionally the failure to provide work may be due to some supervening event, without the fault on either side, and so may be treated as a frustration of the contract bringing it to an end automatically (e.g. a fire burning down the place of work) (see para. 289, below).

§2. The Employee's Duty of Faithful Service

182. The employee must serve his employer faithfully and honestly.[267] This basic duty may be amplified by express terms but even if nothing is said it will be implied as a matter of law that the employee is not to misappropriate his employer's property or misuse his trade secrets or confidential information. (Restraints against competition by ex-employees are discussed in Ch. 9 below.) However, the relationship is not a fiduciary one. The employee's freedom to act in his or her own interests is regulated by express and implied contractual terms andf not by a general

265. *Langston* v. *AUEW* (No. 2) [1974] ICR 510, *per* Sir John Donaldson at p. 521.
266. *Langston* v. *AUEW* [1974] ICR 180 at p. 190.
267. See generally, B. Hepple, 'Employee Loyalty in English Law', *Comp. Lab. Law and Policy Jo.* 20.

fiduciary duty to act in the interests of the employer. Any fiduciary duties arise from the particular facts of a contractual relationship.[268]

I. Misappropriation of Property

183. The employee is obliged to keep proper accounts, and if he or she receives any secret profit or bribe this belongs to his employer and he can be made to account for it.[269] Misappropriation of property is a ground for summary dismissal at common law, even if the facts come to light only after the dismissal.[270] The dismissal will be lawful under the unfair dismissals legislation provided that the employer had reasonable grounds for his belief at the time of dismissal, and carried out as much investigation as was reasonable in the circumstances.[271] Where misappropriation is discovered only after the contract has been terminated with due notice, the employee is still entitled to the contractual remuneration for the period after the breach during which normal services were rendered.[272]

II. Spare-time Work

184. Unless the parties have expressly agreed to the contrary, there is generally no restriction on a worker taking spare-time work. However, he or she cannot take a job which might inflict harm on his principal employer. So an injunction may be granted to restrain an employee from working for a rival employer during his spare time, and competitive work would normally justify dismissal by the employer. It is probably not enough that the spare-time work is in the same field of activity as that of the principal employer. There must be substantial drain on the employee's time or energies or some clear danger causing loss to the employer.[273] Where this can be established, a negative injunction may be granted to prevent the employee from working for a competitor so long as the employee is not faced with the choice of 'work or starve'.[274]

III. Trade Secrets and Confidential Information

185. An employee must not disclose the employer's trade secrets to a third party, nor misuse confidential information acquired in the course of employment. In some

268. *Nottingham University* v. *Fishel* [2000] IRLR 471.
269. *Reading* v. *Attorney-General* [1951] AC 507, HL.
270. *Boston* v. *Ansell* (1888) 39 Ch. D. 339 (CA).
271. *British Home Stores Ltd* v. *Burchell* [1980] ICR 303; approved in *Weddell & Co. Ltd* v. *Tepper* [1980] ICR 286 (CA).
272. *Horcal* v. *Gatland* [1984] IRLR 291 (CA).
273. *Hivac Ltd* v. *Park Royal Scientific Instruments Ltd* [1946] Ch. 169; *Nova Plastics Ltd* v. *Froggett* [1982] IRLR 146.
274. *Warner Bros Pictures Inc.* v. *Nelson* [1937] 1 KB 207 (see further on 'garden leave' Part I, Ch. 9 below).

situations, this obligation may continue even after the employment has ended. In the absence of an express term on these matters, the obligations of the employee are the subject of implied terms. While the employee remains in the employment of the employer, the extent of the duty of fidelity will vary according to the nature of the contract. The duty will be broken if an employee makes or copies a list of the customers of the employer for use after his employment ends or deliberately memorizes such a list. The obligation not to use or disclose information clearly covers secret processes of manufacture, such as chemical formulae, or designs and other information which is of a sufficiently high degree of confidentiality to amount to a trade secret.[275] In *Thomas Marshall (Exports) Ltd* v. *Guinle*[276] a general test of the class of protected information was suggested, namely if (i) the owner reasonably believed that its release would be injurious to him or her; (ii) the owner reasonably believed that it was not yet in the public domain, and (iii) the information could be judged confidential in the light of the usage and practices of the particular industry or trade. However, in *Faccenda (Chickens) Ltd* v. *Fowler*,[277] a distinction was drawn between information amounting to a trade secret and less sensitive information. During employment, both types of information, which the employee 'could only acquire as a result of and in the course of his employment', fall within the scope of the implied term. But the Court of Appeal held that after the employment has ended, the implied term protects only information which is sufficiently confidential to amount to a trade secret. All the circumstances have to be taken into account, including the nature of the employment (a higher obligation being imposed where the employee habitually handles sensitive material because the employee can be expected to understand its nature), the nature of the information, whether the employer impressed upon the employee the confidentiality of the information, and whether the information can be easily isolated from other information which the employee is free to use or disclose. The employer may, of course, supplement the implied duty against Disclosure by an express covenant (see para. 365, below). Employees who deliberately copy or memorize information for their use after leaving the employment, obviously break the implied duty of good faith and fidelity, and as long ago as 1895 the Court of Appeal said that there was no need in such a case for the employer to show that the information was confidential.[278] This was reaffirmed by the Court of Appeal, when rejecting an argument by an employee who had taken with him his employer's card index containing the names and addresses of customers that he could have compiled a comparable list from trade journals and telephone directories.[279] It is important to note that an action for breach of confidence is based on conscience and a person can only be liable if they agree or know, whether actual or constructive knowledge, that the information being used is confidential.[280] Former employees who obtain the information from legitimate sources are as free as any other competitor to do so, but they may not make unlawful use of

275. *Faccenda (Chickens) Ltd* v. *Fowler* [1986] ICR 297 CA; *Herbert Morris Ltd* v. *Saxelby* [1916] AC 688 at 704.
276. [1978] ICR 905.
277. [1986] ICR 297.
278. *Robb* v. *Green* [1895] 2 QB 315, CA; *Wallace Brogan & Co.* v. *Cove* [1997] IRLR 453 (CA).
279. *Roger Bullivant Ltd* v. *Ellis* [1989] ICR 464, CA.
280. *Vestergaard Frandsen A/S & Ors v Bestnet Europe Ltd & Ors* [2013] UKSC 31.

the employers' own list. The so-called 'springboard doctrine' prevents an employee from getting a start without paying for it.

A. *Whistleblowing*

186. At common law, it is not a breach of the employee's duty of confidentiality if he discloses 'any misconduct of such a nature that it ought in the public interest to be disclosed to others'.[281] This category of 'misconduct' no doubt includes the commission of a crime or other unlawful act by the employer, but it is not clear what other matters must be disclosed 'in the public interest'. It was held in one case that an employee was entitled to reveal an arrangement by his former employers to maintain prices, allegedly in contravention of fair competition legislation, on the grounds that this affected the 'public interest'. In such cases the person to whom the information is disclosed must have a 'proper interest' in receiving it. It would be rare for the misconduct to be of such a nature to justify disclosure to the press.

187. The Public Interest Disclosure Act 1998 now provides protection to workers in respect of 'qualifying disclosures'. In order to qualify, the disclosure must be made by the worker in the reasonable belief that it tends to show that one or more of the following have occurred, or are likely to occur: the commission of a criminal offence: the failure of a person to comply with a legal obligation; the occurrence of a miscarriage of justice; the endangering of a person's health or safety; damage to the environment; or the deliberate concealment of information relating to any of these matters. In order to be protected the disclosure must be made in an authorized way. In general, this must be to the employer or a person authorized by the employer to receive such a disclosure, or to a person responsible for the failure in question. Disclosure may also be made to a legal adviser, a Minister of the Crown, or a regulatory person or body. External disclosures are protected only in very limited circumstances.

The worker must first show that he or she reasonably believed that the information disclosed was substantially true, and secondly, that the information concerned conduct of an 'exceptionally serious nature'. Where it is not exceptionally serious, the employee must show in addition that the employee believed at the time of the disclosure that he or she would be subject to a detriment by the employer if they raised the matter internally; that (in the case where there is no relevant regulatory body) the worker reasonably believed that internal disclosure would lead to concealment of evidence by the employer; that the worker had previously made disclosure of substantially the same information to the employer or to a regulatory body; and that in all the circumstances it was reasonable to make the disclosure. The Act states that reasonableness depends on factors such as the identity of the person to whom the disclosure is made, the seriousness of the conduct in question, whether the disclosure is made in breach of a duty of confidentiality owed by the employer to a third person, action previously taken by the worker's representative or regulatory body in response to the initial disclosure to them, and whether in making the

281. *Initial Services Ltd* v. *Putterill* [1968] 1 QB 396.

disclosure the employee had complied with any procedure for disclosure laid down by the employer. Until the relevant provisions of the Enterprise and Regulatory Reform Act 2013 came into effect on the 25 June 2013 there was also the requirement that the disclosure was made in 'good faith' in order to qualify for the protection. However, this has now been removed, and in effect reverses the position as previously held in *Parkins* v. *Sodexho Ltd.*[282] A worker may complain to an employment tribunal that he or she has been subject to a detriment by reason of having made the disclosure,[283] which included protection from harassment or bullying by his or her employer. This was extended to offer protection to a workers from bullying and harassment by fellow workers, unless the employer can establish that they had taken all reasonably practicable steps to prevent the detrimental treatment from occurring[284]. Dismissal in relation to a protected disclosure is automatically unfair.[285]

Any term of a contract purporting to preclude a worker from making a protected disclosure is void.

B. Remedies

188. The employer who alleges that his trade secrets or confidences have been betrayed may seek remedies in the ordinary civil courts. An injunction may be granted restraining the employee or ex-employee from acting in breach of his duties, and he may be ordered to account for the profits made through their use, and also to pay damages for breach of contract.[286] The employer may be able to dismiss the employee without notice provided proper procedures are followed (below, Ch. 7). If the employment Tribunal finds that a disclosure was not made in good faith it has the power to reduce any compensation awarded by up to 25 per cent. This is likely to mean that the case law relating to good faith will still be relevant in order. Of particular importance will be *Street* v. *Derbyshire Unemployed Works Centre*[287], where the Court of Appeal held that a disclosure made in pursuance of a personal grudge is not made in good faith, irrespective of the truth of the matter.

C. Disclosure for Bargaining Purposes

189. A consequence of the rules about confidential information is that individual employees are not at liberty to disclose information which may be relevant to collective bargaining to trade unions, and workers' representatives on company

282. *Parkins* v. *Sodexho Ltd* [2002] IRLR 109.
283. ERA 1996, s. 47B.
284. Section 19 of the Enterprise and Regulatory Reform Act 2013, which came into force on 25 June 2013.
285. ERA 1996, s. 103A.
286. *Attorney-General* v. *Blake* [2000] 4 All ER 385, where there were held to be exceptional circumstances justifying an account of profits for breach by a member of the secret intelligence service of his contractual duty not to disclose.
287. *Street* v. *Derbyshire Unemployed Works Centre* [2004] IRLR 687.

organs are likewise bound by the ordinary rules as to breach of confidence. A trade union official who induces an employee to disclose information for collective bargaining purposes before a claim has been prepared may be restrained by injunction and ordered to pay damages.[288] However if a dispute with an employer exists or is in immediate contemplation, the trade union official inducing the employee to disclose information would be immune from civil proceedings by reason of the statutory protection given to any person inducing a breach of contract 'in contemplation or furtherance of a trade dispute'.[289] The employee who disclosed such confidential information to a trade union may nevertheless be in breach of contract even during a trade dispute.[290]

190. An employer is under a duty to disclose information to trade unions for collective bargaining purposes in certain circumstances, which are discussed in Part II, Ch. 4.

D. Duty to Disclose Misconduct

191. The duty of fidelity does not, however, oblige the employee to disclose his or her own misconduct. In the leading case, Lord Atkin said:

> The servant owes a duty not to steal, but having stolen, is there a superadded duty to confess that he has stolen? I am satisfied that to imply such a duty would be a departure from the well-established usage of mankind and would be to create obligations entirely outside the normal contemplation of the parties.[291]

This decision of the then House of Lords seems to rest upon the general idea of the right not to incriminate oneself, and serves to protect the right to retain wages already paid, before the misconduct is discovered.[292] However, the principle of fidelity dictates that the employee, particularly if he or she is in a managerial or supervisory position, may be obliged to disclose the misconduct of fellow employees.[293]

§3. The Duty of Reasonable Care

I. The Employee's Duty

192. An employee is under a duty to exercise reasonable skill and care in the exercise of his or her duties. What is reasonable depends upon all the circumstances, and different standards may apply according to whether (1) the employer seeks damages or an indemnity from the employee for the financial loss to the

---

288. *Bent's Brewery Co. Ltd* v. *Hogan* [1945] 2 All ER 570.
289. TULRCA 1992, s. 219, see Part II, Ch. 5.
290. *Norbrook Laboratories* v. *Sands* [1984] IRLR 201 (Northern Ireland CA).
291. *Bell* v. *Lever Bros. Ltd* [1932] AC 161 at p. 813.
292. Mark Freedland, ILJ 13 (1984) 25 at 30.
293. *Sybron Corporation* v. *Rochem Ltd* [1983] ICR 801 (CA); *Nottingham University* v. *Fishel* [2000] IRLR 471; *Swain* v. *West (Butchers) Ltd* [1936] 3 All ER 261.

employer resulting from the negligence, or (2) the employer seeks to dismiss the negligent employee.

A. *The Employer's Claim for Damages or an Indemnity*

193. There are two legal bases upon which an employer may seek damages or an indemnity. The first arises under the Civil Liability (Contribution) Act 1978, which allows a joint tortfeasor (i.e. wrongdoer) who is liable to a third party in respect of any damage to recover a contribution (which may be a full indemnity) from any other tortfeasor who is, or would if sued have been liable, in respect of that same damage. The usual situation in which this applies is where an employee in the course of the employment negligently injures a fellow employee, who then claims damages from their common employer. The employer may then join the negligent employee as a third party to the proceedings, if he is not already a co-Defendant, and seek a contribution. The second basis for an indemnity rests on a controversial decision of the House of Lords in the case *Lister* v. *Romford Ice and Cold Storage Co. Ltd* (1957)[294] in which it was decided, as a matter of law, that there was an implied duty in a lorry-driver's employment contract to exercise reasonable care about his employer's business.

194. In practice, these rights are not often enforced against employees.[295] The reason is that usually the employer does not suffer any loss because it is insured in respect of liability to its own employees (such insurance has been compulsory since 1 January 1972)[296] and for liability to third parties suffering injuries in road accidents (such insurance is also compulsory). Only if the employer's insurance company chooses to exercise its rights of subrogation under the contract of insurance will an attempt be made to claim an indemnity from an employee. In fact, as a result of a threat of nationalization after *Lister's* case (above), most insurance companies are now parties to a 'gentlemen's agreement' not to enforce their rights of subrogation against employees. However, guidance from the Court of Appeal has refused to allow the right of subrogation to be enforced in an industrial setting, because of the potential disruption to labour relations, in circumstances where the 'gentlemen's agreement' did not apply.[297]

B. *The Power of Dismissal*

195. In general, a single act of negligence will not justify termination of the employment contract without notice.[298] Under the law of unfair dismissal it is only

294. [1957] 1 All ER 125.
295. An example of the use of the right of action is *Janata Bank* v. *Ahmed* [1981] ICR 791 (CA) where the damages exceeded £36,000.
296. Employers Liability (Compulsory Insurance) Act 1969.
297. *Morris* v. *Ford Motor Co. Ltd* [1973] QB 792.
298. *Jupiter General Insurance Co. Ltd* v. *Shroff* [1937] 3 All ER 67.

gross negligence which would justify dismissal without a warning and an opportunity to improve performance. It has been recognized, however, that there are certain occupations (such as the pilot of an aircraft and the driver of an express train) where a single act of negligence in a matter central to the employee's duties might render the dismissal fair although there has been no previous misconduct, and the employee has rendered long service (see Ch. 7, below).[299]

II. The Employer's Duty

196. An employee who is injured at work may seek to hold his employer responsible on two possible grounds: (1) the breach of a common law duty to exercise reasonable care for the safety of employees in the course of their employment, or a statutory duty to take specified precautions for the employee's safety; or (2) the breach of a common law or statutory duty owed by a fellow-employee to the injured employee, the employer being vicariously liable for the torts (delict(s)) of its employees. The first of these duties may be classified either as an implied term of the contract of employment or as arising in tort (*ex delicto*). The second is normally classified as a duty in tort alone. Prior to 1948,[300] an action against the employer on the second ground was barred by the doctrine of common employment. This subject of compensation for work accidents, which in part rests on the employer's liability, and in part on social security law, lies beyond the scope of this monograph. It must, however, be mentioned that, under Section 2(1) of the Unfair Contract Terms Act 1977 (in force since 1 February 1978) any term of a contract or notice which excludes or restricts liability for death or personal injury resulting from negligence is void. Section 2(2) of the Act of 1977 prohibits exclusion or restriction of liability for negligence in the case of 'other loss or damage' (e.g. to property or economic interests) unless the term or notice satisfies a test of 'reasonableness'. These provisions extend to the contract of employment, but only in favour of the employee not the employer. These provisions do not appear to affect the kind of indemnity clause in the *Lister* case.

299. *Turner* v. *Pleasurama Casinos* [1976] IRLR 151.
300. Law Reform (Personal Injuries) Act 1948, s. 1.

Chapter 4. Working Time and Holidays

§1. The Working Time Regulations

I. Implementation of the Working Time Directive

197. Until 1998[301] it was a distinctive feature of British labour law that there was no general legislation laying down minimum standards for the length of the working day or the number of rest days and holidays. The relatively few statutory controls, for example over the hours of young persons and of women in factories, were removed by the deregulatory measures of the Thatcher governments during the 1980s. One of the only restrictions which remained was that, in certain circumstances, it is automatically unfair to dismiss retail employees for refusing to work on Sundays.[302] Instead of legal enactment, the substantial gains which were achieved in most industries in respect of working time were the result of collective bargaining.[303]

Over the 100 years 1881 to 1981, annual hours worked by men fell by 35 per cent and lifetime hours fell by 43 per cent. For women the reductions in lifetime hours were much smaller, at one-tenth, as the increased number of years in the workforce offset reductions in weekly and annual hours. By 1992 the normal length of the working day was less than 8 hours, with a five-day working week, and a 37-hour week was becoming the average. At the same time, only a minority of workers worked a 'normal' day or 'standard' week and a substantial minority worked very long weekly hours. One million employees, 6 per cent of the total, usually worked for over 48 hours a week, excluding overtime, in their main job. If paid and unpaid overtime were included, then 3.2 million usually worked over 48 hours per week, accounting for 15 per cent of all workers.

Unlike in most EU Member States, there were no legal limits on the maximum weekly overtime. Apart from restrictions on certain employments there were no statutory requirements for weekly rest, and no general legislation on holidays. Even the custom of respecting 'bank' (i.e. public) holidays in many industries has been the result of collective bargaining, since the only legislation on this subject itself simply prohibits certain financial dealings on the days in question and gives no general right to public holidays.[304]

198. It was in this situation that the United Kingdom had to implement the Working Time Directive 93/104/EEC and the Young Workers Directive 94/33/EC. At first the UK unsuccessfully challenged the legal basis of the Working Time Directive (Article 118a EC Treaty).[305] The Conservative government issued a consultation paper in December 1996 which indicated that it did not intend to

301. Working Time Regulations 1998, as amended 1999 and 2006 (SI 2006/99).
302. Sunday Trading Act 1994, and ERA 1996, Part IV and s. 101.
303. See generally, B. Hepple and C. Hakim, 'United Kingdom' in R. Blanpain, E. Kohler and J. Rojot (eds.), *Legal and Contractual Limitations on Working Time in the European Union* (2nd edn, Leuven, 1997), pp. 659–93.
304. Banking and Financial Dealings Act 1971, s. 1, Sched. 1.
305. Case C-84/94 *United Kingdom* v. *Council* [1996] ECR I-5755.

over-implement or 'gold-plate' the directive, because it wanted to avoid unnecessary burdens on business. The New Labour government, elected in May 1997, was more sympathetic and in a White Paper [306] stated that the regulation of working time was central to the government's family-friendly policies, as well as to a more productive workforce. The Working Time Regulations[307] came into force on 1 October 1998.

The provisions of the Young Workers Directive were also implemented in these and other regulations concerning the obligations of employers to young persons, and the protection of children at work.[308] The main problem with the Regulations is that they simply copy out the wording of the directives without giving detailed legal guidance in the British context.[309]

II. Scope of the Regulations

199. The directive and regulations apply to 'workers', and not only 'employees' (see Part I, Ch. 1, above). This includes trainees who are on work experience or training other than on a course run by an educational institution or training establishment. Most agency workers are covered by the regulations, as are those in Crown employment, certain police activities and the armed forces and, in part, domestic servants. However, they exclude certain categories of employment completely, including air, rail, road sea and inland waterways and lake transport, sea fishing and all other work at sea; the activities of doctors in training; certain parts of the police, armed forces and civil protection services. These matters are now covered by later bespoke directives.

III. Basic Entitlements

200. The overriding principle of the directive and regulations is the principle of humanization of work,[310] explained in Article 13 of the directive as 'adapting work to the worker, with a view, in particular, to alleviating monotonous work and work at a pre-determined work rate, depending on the type of activity, and of health and safety requirements, especially as regards breaks during working time.' The specific provisions are:

- a minimum daily rest period of 11 consecutive hours in each 24-hour period;
- a minimum uninterrupted rest period of 24 hours every week; this can be taken as two uninterrupted rest periods in each 14-day period or one uninterrupted rest period of 48 hours in each 14-day period;

306. *Fairness at Work* Cmnd 3968, para. 5.6.
307. SI 1998/1833.
308. SI 1997/135, SI 1998/276, SI 1998/2411.
309. See C. Barnard, 'The Working Time Regulations 1998' (1999) 28 ILJ, 61–75. There are guidance notes, but some of the interpretations in these are controversial.
310. See S. Hardy, 'Harmonising European Working Time in an Enlarged EU': A Case of Failed 'Humanization'?, IJCLL (2006).

- an in-work rest break of at least 20 minutes where the working day is longer than six hours (a collective or workforce agreement can provide for a longer period);
- paid annual leave of at least four weeks; there are notice provisions and leave may not be replaced by payment in lieu except on termination of contract; where a worker leaves a job having taken more leave than he or she is entitled to pro rate, a relevant agreement can stipulate that the worker should compensate the employer;
- a weekly working week of not more than 48 hours on average, including overtime, over a reference period of (usually) 17 weeks;
- night work of not more than an average of 8 hours in any 24-hour period over a reference period of 17 weeks; the averaging does not apply in the case of work involving 'special hazards or heavy physical or mental strain';
- free and confidential health assessment for workers before taking in night work and at regular intervals thereafter; and,
- night workers assessed by a registered medical practitioner as suffering health problems connected with night work must be transferred, where possible, to suitable day work.

There have been a number of cases that have reached the higher courts, including the Court of Justice of the European on the issue of holiday pay entitlement following long term illness. Where an individual has been absent from work with sickness, and is thus prevented from taking their paid annual leave entitlement in that year, then the worker will be entitled to take paid annual leave at another time, even if this is in a subsequent annual leave period, and it is only where the employment relationship has been terminated that a payment in lieu of that holiday leave can be made.[311] However, it must be noted that this ability to carry over holiday leave across leave periods only extends to the basic four weeks' leave right provided for in the Directive, and does not extend to any additional leave over and beyond this period.

IV. Derogations

201. There are a number of complex derogations. The first and widest category relates to those whose working time is unmeasured, that is where 'on account of the specific characteristics of the activity in which he [or she] is engaged the duration of working time is not measured or pre-determined or can be determined by the worker himself [herself]'. Examples include managing executives or other persons with autonomous decision-making powers, family workers and workers officiating in religious etc. ceremonies. The second category covers five 'special' situations: (1) where the worker's activities and his or her place of work is distant; (2) where

311. *NHS Leeds* v. *Larner [2012] EWCA Civ 1034 CA. See also Stringer and others* v. *HM Revenue and Customs sub nom Commissioners of Inland Revenue* v. *Ainsworth and others; Schultz-Hoff* v. *Deutsche Rentenversicherung Bund* [2009] IRLR 214 ECJ; *KHS AG* v. *Schulte* [2012] IRLR 156 ECJ; *Pereda v. Madrid Movilidad SA [2009] IRLR 959 ECJ* and *Dominguez* v. *Centre informatique du Centre Ouest Atlantique* Case C-282/10 ECJ.

the worker is engaged in security or surveillance activities requiring a permanent presence; (3) where the worker's activities involve the need for continuity of service or production (e.g. hospitals, docks, press, etc.); (4) where there is a foreseeable surge of activity (e.g. agriculture, tourism and postal services); and (5) where the worker's activities are affected by, for example unusual and unforeseeable circumstances. The working time rules apply to those activities, but the reference period is extended to 26 weeks. The third category is shift workers who are exempted from the rules on daily and weekly rest periods when they change shift and the change makes it impossible for them to take a daily or weekly rest period between the end of one shift and the start of the next one. Workers whose work is split up over the day (e.g. cleaning staff) are also exempt from daily and weekly rest periods.

V. Collective, Workforce and Individual Agreements

202. The most important category of derogations is that which allows the modification or exclusion of the provisions on night work, daily and weekly rest and in work rest breaks by collective and workforce agreements. In addition such agreements can, for objective and technical reasons or reasons concerning the organization of work, increase the reference period over which working time is calculated from 17 to 52 weeks. This possibility is intended to encourage management and workers' representatives to negotiate and adapt the rules to meet their individual circumstances, so permitting controlled 'flexibility'. Where any limits are derogated from by agreement, the employer must 'wherever possible' allow workers to take an 'equivalent period of compensatory rest'. Where this is not possible, the worker must be given other appropriate protection. 'Collective agreements are agreements with independent trade unions'. 'Workforce agreements' allow employers to agree working time arrangements with workers who do not have any terms and conditions set by collective agreement. In other words, collective agreements take precedence. To be valid a workforce agreement must (1) be in writing; (2) have effect for a specified period not exceeding five years; (3) apply either to all of the relevant members of the workforce (other than those covered by collective agreement), or to all of the relevant members of the workforce who belong to a particular group (i.e. sharing a workplace, function or organizational unit within a business); and (4) be signed by the representatives of the workforce or the representatives of the group where appropriate. If the employer employed 20 or fewer workers on the date when the agreement was first made available for signature it must be signed either by the appropriate representatives or by the majority of workers (a 'majority' agreement. The employer has to make the agreement and guidance which might be required to understand it fully to all the workers for whom it is intended before the agreement is signed. 'Representatives of the workforce' or of the 'group' for this purpose are workers have to be duly elected in accordance with prescribed rules, and they are protected against suffering detriment or dismissal on the grounds of performance of their functions. They do not have an express right to time off to perform these functions.

203. Arguably there may be derogation by individual written legally-binding agreement, as well as by a workforce agreement, or by a collective agreement which forms part of the contract between the worker and the employer, in order to specify the dates from which reference periods start to run and to determine the meaning of working time. In addition, individual workers can choose to contract out from the 48-hour maximum working week, but not from any other provision, provided the following conditions are met: (1) the agreement must be in writing; (2) it may relate either to a specified period or indefinitely; (3) it must be terminable by the worker by giving not less than 7 days' notice in writing to the employer; but the agreement can provide for a different period of notice, up to a maximum of three months; (4) the employer must maintain up-to-date records which identifies each of the workers who has agreed to waive the 48-hour limit; and (5) the employer must permit any inspector appointed by the Health and Safety Executive (HSE) or other regulatory authority to inspect the records and must provide such inspector with information regarding any case in which a worker has agreed to waive the 48-hour limit.

VI. Enforcement

204. The limits relating to working time, night work, health assessment, pattern of work, record-keeping and compensatory rest are enforced through criminal sanctions against the employer. This is enforced by the HSE in respect of factories, building sites, mines, farms, fairgrounds, quarries, chemical plants, nuclear installations, schools and hospitals, or by local authority environmental health departments in respect of retailing, offices, hotels and catering, sports, leisure, and consumer services. Entitlements to minimum rest periods and to paid annual leave are enforced by way of complaint by the individual worker to an employment tribunal normally within three months of the act or omission complained of. Where a complaint is upheld the tribunal may make a declaration and may award compensation 'such as the tribunal considers just and equitable in al the circumstances' having regard to the employer's default in refusing to provide the entitlement, and any loss sustained by the worker as a consequence of that default. Employees who are dismissed for reasons connected with the Working Time Regulations may claim that their dismissal is automatically unfair.

VII. Reform

205. Working Time Directive 2003/88 seeks to introduce changes, in particular the removal of the UK's opt-out of working time. However, such radical reforms, including the increase in working time to 96 hours per week have been delayed by successive Presidencies of the EU.

§2. Time off Work

206. Employees have the statutory right to take time off during working hours in a number of situations.

I. Union Officials

207. Employees who are officials of independent trade unions recognized by the employer for purposes of collective bargaining are entitled to reasonable time off with pay.[312] (An official includes a shop steward.) The scope of this right was significantly narrowed in 1989. Previously, an official could claim paid time off to carry out all duties concerned with industrial relations between his or her employer or an associated employer and its employees, and the courts generally construed this phrase broadly. The Employment Act 1989, however, removed the right to paid time off for matters in respect of which the union is not recognized by the employer. Thus a union official is only entitled to paid time off for duties concerned with negotiations with the employer over those matters in relation to which the union is recognized by the employer, or for duties in relation to which the employer has agreed that the union may perform functions on behalf of his or her employees. Time off for training is restricted to approved training relevant to such duties, and there is no longer a right to time off for duties involving industrial relations with an associated employer.

II. Union Members

208. Members of independent trade unions recognized by the employer are entitled to reasonable time off for activities of their union and in order to represent the union.[313] This does not include time off for industrial action. It is time off without pay. An ACAS Code of Practice (2010) gives guidelines.

III. Public Duties

209. An employee must be allowed reasonable time off for certain specified public duties (such as justice of the peace, member of a tribunal, or member of a local authority or the governing body of any educational establishment).[314] This time off may be used only for attending meetings and for executive functions. This is time off without pay. No Code of Practice is to be issued.

312. TULRCA 1992, s. 168.
313. TULRCA 1992, s. 170.
314. ERA 1996, s. 50.

IV. Redundant Employees

210. An employee who has been given notice of dismissal by reason of redundancy has the right to reasonable time off during the notice period to seek new employment or to make arrangements for training.[315] The employee must have been continuously employed for two years or more.

V. Ante-natal Care

211. An employee who is pregnant has the right not to be unreasonably refused time off with pay during her working hours to enable her to keep an appointment to attend at any place for the purpose of receiving ante-natal care.[316] This has to be on the advice of a medical practitioner, midwife or health visitor and a certificate or appointment card must be produced for a second or subsequent appointment.

VI. Safety Representatives

212. The Safety Representatives and Safety Committees Regulations 1977[317] require employers to permit safety representatives[318] to take such time off with pay as is necessary for the purposes of performing his or her statutory safety functions and undergoing reasonable training in relation to those functions having regard to the Health and Safety Executive's Code in regard to training.

VII. Employee Representatives and Occupational Pension Fund Trustees

213. An employee who is an employee representative for the purposes of consultation on collective redundancies or transfers of undertakings or a candidate to be such a representative is entitled to reasonable time off during working hours, with pay, in order to perform his or her functions as such or to undergo training to perform such functions.[319] There is a similar right for employees who are occupational pension fund trustees.[320]

VIII. Dependants

214. An employee is entitled to take a reasonable amount of time off during working hours in order to take action which is necessary because of the illness, care or death of a dependant, or to deal with an incident which involves the child of an

315. ERA 1996, s. 52.
316. ERA 1996, s. 55.
317. SI 1977 500, reg. 3(1), as amended 1999.
318. See Part II, Ch. 3, below for the structure and functions of these committees and representatives.
319. ERA 1996, s. 63.
320. ERA 1996, s. 58.

employee and which occurs unexpectedly in a period during which an educational establishment which the child attends is responsible for the child.[321] For this purpose a 'dependant' is a spouse, child, parent, and certain persons living in the same household as the employee.

IX. Claims for Breach of Rights

215. In each of the above cases, an employee may complain to an Employment Tribunal within three months of the failure to give time off. If the complaint is well-founded, the tribunal may make a declaration. In the case of trade union officials, safety and employee representatives, trustees of occupational pension funds, and those seeking ante-natal care the tribunal may award the remuneration due as well as compensation, having regard to the employer's default and the employee's loss. The other categories of employees may be awarded compensation but no remuneration is due to them. A redundant employee may claim up to two-fifths of a week's pay.

§3. Part-time Work

216. According to the 2004 Workplace Employment Relations Survey,[322] full-timers accounted for 85 per cent of employment and part-timers 15 per cent, a decrease from previous years. Women held 81 per cent of the part-time jobs, which accounted for 42 per cent of all women's jobs. The concept of indirect sex discrimination has been important in removing obstacles to part-time work for women (see Part I, Ch. 8, below). The limitations of this approach, however, are that (1) a male comparator has to be found; (2) proof of significant adverse impact on women may be difficult; and (3) the objective justification may include the very market forces which cause discrimination. The ILO Convention No. 175 of 1994 and the accompanying Recommendation No. 182 contemplates specific rights for all part-time workers.

The significantly weaker Agreement between the Social Partners, implemented by Council Directive 97/81/EC, relies on (1) a general principle of non-discrimination which is subject to a defence of objective justification; and (2) encouragements to improve the quality and availability of part-time work.

The Part-Time Work Directive has been implemented in the United Kingdom by the Part-Time Work (Prevention of Less Favourable Treatment) Regulations 2000, which came into force on 1 July 2000. These regulations create a right for a part-time worker to be treated no less favourably in certain respects *pro rata temporis* than a comparable full-timer. Who is part-time is determined by the 'custom and practice' of the employer. There must be an actual full-time comparator, but (unlike

321. ERA 1996, s. 57A. Maternity and parental leave are dealt with separately.
322. WERS, DTI (see www.dti.gov.uk).

sex discrimination) this need not be a person of the opposite gender. The comparator must be currently employed by the same employer 'under the same type of contract'. This may be at another establishment of the same employer where there are no comparable full-timers at the same establishment as the part-timer. The comparator must be engaged on the same or broadly similar work having regard to whether the comparator has a similar level of qualification, skills and experience. There cannot be a claim (as in sex discrimination) for equal pay for work of equal value. The non-discrimination principle applies only to direct discrimination and (unlike sex discrimination) does not apply to indirect discrimination. The less favourable treatment must be 'on grounds of' being a part-timer, a narrower test than for discrimination 'related to' pregnancy or disability. Unlike sex discrimination, a defence of objective justification of direct discrimination is allowed. The directive, but not the UK regulations, requires employers to give consideration 'as far as possible' to measures to facilitate access to part-time work, but this applies only to jobs 'that become available in the establishment'. In the UK women who wish to return to work after pregnancy and confinement on a part-time basis or a job-share must, therefore, continue to rely on the concept of indirect sex discrimination. The refusal to allow her to do so may be objectively justified for reasons such as cost or administrative efficiency.

Chapter 5. Remuneration and Benefits

§1. Regulation of Remuneration

217. Apart from periods of incomes policy, there has been little state intervention into levels of pay. The main instances of pay regulation are the national minimum wage and the equal pay principles under the Equality Act 2010, which obliges employers to pay men and women at the same rates for like work or work of equal value (*see* Part I, Ch. 8, *below*). There have been significant changes over the past two decades in the way in which pay is determined.

According to successive Workplace Industrial Relations Surveys (WERS), the percentage of workplaces in which collective bargaining was the dominant mode of pay determination fell by half in the space of 14 years, from 60 per cent in 1984 to 42 per cent in 1990 and just 29 per cent in 1998.[323] There were also substantial changes in the nature of collective bargaining over pay in that period. The proportion of all workplaces in which multi-employer agreements were part of the arrangements for determining pay fell by about two-thirds from 41 per cent in 1984 to 13 per cent in 1998. In 1998 pay was set by management at a higher level of the organization in 25 per cent of workplaces and by management at workplace level in 30 per cent of organizations. In 14 per cent of workplaces pay was set externally to the organization. In private sector manufacturing and extraction in 1998 pay was set by collective bargaining in 23 per cent of workplaces, by management at workplace level in 48 per cent of workplaces, and by higher-level management in the organization in 24 per cent of workplaces. In private sector services in 1998, collective bargaining featured in only 14 per cent of workplaces, while management at workplace level fixed pay in 39 per cent of organizations, and higher-level management did so in 36 per cent of organizations. Only in the public sector was pay still mainly determined by collective bargaining, but even here there had been a decrease from 94 per cent of workplaces in 1984 to 63 per cent in 1998 to 52 per cent in 2003.

§2. Payment Systems

218. Methods of remuneration are a central feature of workplace industrial relations. They have an important influence on the opportunities available for bargaining and the extent of management control.[324] Factors influencing the size of pay awards in large bargaining units include the cost of living, general labour market conditions (the 'going rate'), and economic factors such as the employer's ability to pay, the performance of the workforce or organization and general economic conditions. The general economic factors have tended to become most important in recent years. In workplaces where collective bargaining is not the dominant form of

---

323. The information in this paragraph is drawn from Neil Milward, Alex Bryson and John Forth, *All Change at Work?* (London, 2000), pp. 184–222.

324. W. Brown (ed.), *The Changing Contours of Industrial Relations*, p. 110.

pay determination general economic conditions also appear to be of increasing importance.[325]

219. There is a wide variety of pay systems in Britain. One common form of payment is based on units of time (monthly, weekly, daily or hourly). Monthly payment is an indication of high ('staff') status and is usually associated with non-manual workers. Overtime, which is generally remunerated at a higher (premium) rate (e.g. time-and-a-half) constitutes an important element in the pay of manual employees. According to WERS, over half of all employees regularly worked overtime, with a quarter doing up to 5 hours a week, 17 per cent doing between 6 and 10 hours, and 11 per cent in excess of 10 hours. The main reason for working overtime is the need for money, but not all workers are paid for these extended hours. Managers and professionals frequently have no 'standard' hours and hence no 'overtime'. Clerks and technicians are likely to get time off in lieu of pay, while operatives and craft workers are paid.

220. Also important is the payment system known as payment by results (PBR), whereby pay is related to effort and output. Although the traditional aim of PBR is to encourage workers to raise their output, it has increasingly become an instrument of management control designed to ensure consistency of output. There is a wide variety of PBR systems, ranging from long established piece-working to complex systems of commission and bonus payments. According to WERS, PBR was more commonly used for non-manual than manual workers in 1998, whereas the reverse was true in 1990 and 2000.[326]

221. Profit-related pay systems were encouraged by the Conservative government in the 1980s through a series of tax exemptions. They have become fairly widespread, rising from 19 per cent of workplaces in 1984 to 46 per cent in 1998. This type of pay is found in the majority of workplaces with 1,000 or more employees. Share ownership schemes were found in 13 per cent of all workplaces in 1980. This rose to 30 per cent in 1990 but dropped to 24 per cent in 1998[327] and by a further 10 per cent by 2008.

§3. Fringe Benefits

222. Fringe benefits, which may be defined as payments in cash or kind additional to salary, bonus and commission, are an increasingly significant form of remuneration, particularly among high-income earners and high-status occupations. Examples of such benefits among higher-paid employees are company cars, subsidized lunches, medical insurance and share acquisition schemes (interest free or at a reduced rate). In order to prevent tax avoidance on non-cash benefits, there is a

325. Millward *et al.*, *op. cit.*, pp. 208–209.
326. Milward *et al.*, *op. cit.*, pp. 212–213.
327. Milward *et al.*, *op. cit.*, pp. 213–218.

complex system of taxation, the broad effect being to tax as many benefits as possible. Directors (with some exceptions) and higher paid employees are charged tax at the 'cash equivalent' of all benefits (normally the cost to the employer of providing the benefit). Special rules apply to provision of cars, petrol, beneficial loan arrangements and share purchase schemes. Although employees who are not directors or who earn less than the prescribed amount are generally in a more favourable position, special rules apply to living accommodation, credit cards and vouchers.

§4. Occupational Pensions

223. The provision of occupational pensions is regarded as primarily a matter of social security law rather than employment law, and fall outside the scope of this monograph.[328]

224. Occupational pensions have also been affected, from a different direction, by EC sex discrimination law (see Part I, Ch. 8, below) and the Pensions Act 1995, as amended, and adjoining Pension Regulations 2005. Auto-enrolment was introduced in 2014.

§5. National Minimum Wage

225. Before 1998, there was no general minimum wage legislation in Britain. The traditional approach from 1909 to 1993, distinguishing Britain from other countries such as France and the United States, was to be selective. Minimum wages were not fixed for the whole economy but only for specific categories of workers. The approach of successive governments prior to 1980 is best understood in the context of two parallel policy objectives, namely, the prevention of low pay and the encouragement of collective bargaining. The earliest minimum wage legislation, instituted in 1909, concentrated on combating low pay, particularly in relation to 'sweated labour', employment characterized by starvation wages and inhuman working conditions. Later legislation also embodied the policy of encouraging collective bargaining, in the belief that low pay was closely associated with the absence of adequate collective bargaining machinery and correspondingly, that the development of such machinery was the best way of counteracting low pay. This was reflected in legislation, which provided that minimum wage-fixing machinery could be established for a category of workers if the Secretary of State considered that no adequate machinery existed for the effective regulation of the remuneration of those workers.

However, after 1980, both policy objectives were set aside in favour of permitting employers to develop pay systems 'wholly in accordance with the best interests of their businesses'[329] even if this led to lower pay. Indeed, it was argued that minimum wage-fixing machinery in the form of wages councils caused poverty by

328. For a specialist work see Robin Ellison, *Pensions Law and Practice* (London, 1987, updated).
329. Department of Employment Wages Councils: 1988 Consultation Document, p. 5.

reducing jobs and increasing unemployment. According to the then Department of Employment's Consultative Paper, in 1985, 'wages councils interfere with the freedom of employers to offer and job seekers to accept jobs at wages that would otherwise be acceptable'.[330] This approach led to legislation severely restricting the operation of wages councils (which covered about 2.5 million workers or 10 per cent of the employed workforce) and to their abolition in 1993.

226. The Labour governments from 1997 to 2010 fulfilled their election commitment by rapidly introducing the National Minimum Wage Act 1998, which provides for the introduction of a minimum basic hourly rate of pay for workers over the age of 26, with the possibility of lower rates for younger workers. The Act and implementing regulations[331] came into force on 1 April 1999. Further development came when the Conservative Government introduced a new National Living Wage, which came into effect on 1 April 2016. The rates are increased annually on 1 April in accordance with recommendations from the Low Pay Commission. The current national living wage, which applies to workers over the age of 25, is £7.50 per hour. The rate is £7.05 per hour for workers aged 21 and over, with a rate of £5.60 for workers aged 18–20 years old, and a rate of £4.05 for workers aged 16–17 years old. The Low Pay Commission has proposed that 21-year olds should be included in the main rate, but this recommendation has not been accepted.[332] The most significant feature of the legislation is that it applies the prescribed rates to all workers irrespective of the sector or region in which they work. The coverage is almost universal. It applies to all 'workers' (see Part I, Ch. 1, above), including homeworkers. Those excluded are self-employed workers, volunteers, voluntary workers and company directors. It was previously the position that apprentices under the age of 26 during the first year of apprenticeship and certain other trainees were also excluded; however the current position is that apprentices under 19 or apprentices over 19 and in the first year of an apprenticeship must be paid an at least the apprenticeship rate of £3.50 per hour. The position of 'volunteers' is ambiguous. Students who undertake a placement with an employer as part of a higher education course do not have to be paid the national minimum wage. This provision applies to undergraduates only where the course is provided by a university or college in the United Kingdom.

227. The employer is under an obligation to pay the national minimum wage (a single hourly rate) on average in respect of hours worked in a given 'pay reference period'. The regulations provide a basis for calculating which hours are to count as working time within a given pay reference period according to four categories: time work, salaried work, output work and unmeasured work. Of particular importance is the fact that workers whose work involves 'standby' 'zero hours' or 'on-call' arrangements, or 'downtime', are entitled to the national minimum wage even for

330. DE Consultative Paper 1985, para. 7.
331. SI 1999/583, and SI 1999/584. *See generally*, Bob Simpson, 'A milestone in the legal regulation of pay: the National Minimum Wage Act 1999' ILJ 28 (1999) 1, and 'Implementing the National Minimum Wage: the 1999 Regulations' ILJ 28 (1999) 171.
332. *The National Minimum Wage: The Story so Far.* Seventh Report of the Low Pay Commission (2005); Simpson, B. 'The National Minimum wage five years on ... .', ILJ 33 (2004), pp. 22–41.

periods when required to be available at the place of work even if not actually working. But the minimum wage is not payable for periods of standby when the employee is away from the employer's premises, or is sent home because she or he is not required to be available for work. For workers required to sleep on the premises only the time when actually working affects the minimum wage. The minimum wage is also not payable for rest periods or when a worker is taking industrial action. Regulations provide for the circumstances in which tips and gratuities and overtime pay count towards the minimum rate.

228. The Act provides for the right to the national minimum wage to take effect as a term of the contract, giving rise, by implication, to a claim in an employment tribunal by the worker for payment in full under the Employment Rights Act 1996, Section 13, in the event of breach. Enforcement officers (from the Revenue and Contributions Agency) have the power to issue enforcement notices to require employers to pay the national minimum wage, and they may also institute proceedings on behalf of a worker. There is the possibility of criminal sanctions against an underpaying employer (six new criminal offences). There are requirements for recordkeeping, and for issuing a national minimum wage statement to employees. There is protection against suffering a detriment or being dismissed for asserting a right to the national minimum wage.

§6. Payment and Calculation of Wages

I. A Question of Contract

229. Apart from the national minimum wage, pay rates are fixed entirely as a matter of contract. As has been indicated above, pay may be determined by collective bargaining. In such cases, the relevant collective agreements will usually be incorporated into the individual's contract of employment, either expressly or impliedly (see above, para. 149). In a few isolated cases (e.g. where an employer has failed to comply with an operative order to disclose information to a trade union), there may be a binding arbitration award of the CAC which is incorporated into the contract. In other cases, where management unilaterally determines pay, this becomes legally enforceable only as a matter of express of implied agreement, and this may involve questions of interpretation. As explained earlier, these questions of interpretation may themselves be resolved through a dynamic on-going bargaining process. However, with the growing individualization of employment relations, such questions increasingly reach the courts and employment tribunals for interpretation. The CAC has power to interpret its own awards.

II. The Concept of a 'Week's Pay'

230. Special rules exist for the calculation of a 'week's pay' for statutory purposes. This precise calculation needs to be made, for example, to determine the amount of redundancy payment, and guaranteed payments during periods of lay-off and during the minimum periods of notice to determine the contract. These rules are set out in Part XIV, Ch. 2 of the Employment Rights Act 1996. This makes it necessary to determine whether there are 'normal working hours' (these exclude overtime unless the employee is required to work overtime and the employer is required to provide it). If there are, the amount of a 'week's pay' depends on whether or not the amount of pay varies with the amount of work done. If it does not, a 'week's pay' is the amount payable under the contract on the 'calculation date' (this date differs according to the statutory rights in question). If it does vary, the amount of the 'week's pay' is then usually the amount of pay for the number of normal working hours in a week calculated at an hourly rate of remuneration payable in respect of a 12-week period. In cases where there are no 'normal working hours' a week's pay is the amount of the employee's average weekly remuneration over a 12-week period. In calculating pay for these purposes, benefits in kind (such as travelling allowances) are disregarded. The maximum amount of a week's pay for various statutory purposes is varied from time to time.

III. No Agreement as to Amount

231. If there is no express or implied provision in the contract of employment regarding the rate of remuneration the employee may claim a reasonable remuneration. So long as it can be shown that the work was agreed to be done on the basis that some payment was to be made, the common law implies a promise to pay what the services are worth (*quantum meruit*). However, if the circumstances show that the employer and employee did not intend an agreement to come into effect until the rate of remuneration was agreed then such a term cannot be implied. For example, a promise to pay an employee 'such remuneration as the directors may determine' will prevent the employee from claiming any remuneration unless and until the directors make a determination.[333] Similarly an arrangement that the parties will agree a future rise in salary does not oblige the employer to reach such an agreement.

IV. Payment for Incomplete Periods

232. Remuneration is payable only in arrears at the end of each period for which it is due, in the absence of an agreement between the parties to make advances on pay. The period of the employment for which payment is due depends on the express or implied agreement of the parties; for example it may be hourly, weekly, monthly or quarterly. At common law, the rule appears to have been that an employee could not recover any remuneration at all for a period which he did not complete, for any reason other than a breach of contract by the employer.[334]

However, the Apportionment Act 1870, Section 2, provides that 'salaries' shall 'be considered as accruing from day to day and shall be apportioned in respect of

333. *Re Richmond Gate Property Co. Ltd* [1965] 1 WLR 335.
334. *Cutter* v. *Powell* (1795) 6 TR 320.

time accordingly'. It is usually assumed that 'salaries' includes 'wages' (i.e. all remuneration) but this has not been authoritatively decided by the courts.[335] Nor is it entirely clear whether an employee who fails to complete a period because he is summarily dismissed on grounds of his own misconduct can claim wages for that part of the period for which he has worked, although the weight of academic opinion believes that he is so entitled.[336] Where the contract has come to an end by reason of 'frustration' (i.e. supervening impossibility of performance) without the fault of either party, the Law Reform (Frustrated Contracts) Act 1943 allows the court to order payment of a 'just' amount in respect of services to which the employer has had the benefit before the frustrating event (e.g. a fire burning down the workplace). In practice, employers nearly always pay for services actually performed even though the period of payment has not been completed.

V. Manner of Payment and Deductions

233. As a general rule, employer and employees are free to agree as to the manner of payment, that is whether it is to be in cash or by cheque or otherwise. Similarly, the place of payment and the periods at which payment is to be made are left to the parties' determination. Until 1986, the manner of payment of manual workers and in some cases shop assistants was regulated by the Truck Acts 1831 to 1940, which required such workers to be paid in the 'current coin of the realm'. This was initially intended to prevent abuse of workers by enforced trading and payment in kind, but with the decline of payment in kind, such protection became obsolete. These provisions were repealed by the Wages Act 1986. It is now permissible to use any modern method of payment, including payment into a bank account.

234. The question of deductions from pay is more controversial. It is not uncommon for employers to deduct sums of money from employees' remuneration for negligent work, disciplinary offences, or cash and stock shortages, in some cases leading to a substantial reduction in wages.[337] A new framework for protecting workers in such circumstances was established by the Wages Act 1986, which is now consolidated in Part II of the Employment Rights Act 1996. Unlike its predecessors, this legislation gives a central role to the contract of employment.

Deductions are permitted if they are required or authorized by virtue of a provision in the worker's contract, or the worker has previously consented in writing to the relevant deduction. By contrast, under the previous framework, it was not sufficient for deductions to be authorized by contract; in addition, they had to be 'fair and reasonable'. In addition, deductions authorized by statutory provision (e.g. income tax or national insurance) are permitted. The Act sets no general limit on

335. *Moriarty* v. *Regent's Garage Co. Ltd* [1921] 1 KB 423.
336. Glanville Williams, *Law Quarterly Review* 57 (1941) at p. 383; but cf. Paul Matthews, *Legal Studies* 2 (1982), p. 302.
337. T. Goriely, 'Arbitrary Deductions from Pay and the Proposed Repeal of the Truck Acts' ILJ 12 (1983) 236.

the proportion of wages which may be deducted. For retail workers only, deductions or payments in respect of stock deficiencies or cash shortages are limited to 10 per cent of wages payable on any pay day. However, it is permissible to make deductions by instalments, and no limit is placed on the amount deductible from the final pay packet on termination of employment. Although the 1986 Act removed some of the anomalies of the previous framework, the overall result was to decrease the protection of workers, and to reassert the 'central nature of contract', regardless of the fact that contract is of little use to workers in vulnerable positions who lack the bargaining power to resist contractual provisions.

235. The 1986 Act also established a new method of enforcement. Whereas breach of the previous provisions was a criminal offence, and their operation was policed by an inspectorate, redress under the current legislation is through an ET, which can award only what has been unlawfully deducted, with no punitive or compensatory elements. The scope of the tribunal's jurisdiction over claims concerning deductions has led to conflicting case-law, since jurisdiction for claims arising purely out of breach of contract remains with the ordinary courts. In some circumstances, it may be difficult to distinguish a dispute over a deduction from one concerned with the amount properly payable under a contract. In *Delaney* v. *Staples*,[338] the House of Lords held that non-payment of wages due to an employee is a deduction from wages within the meaning of the Act, so that an ET can deal with a claim that an employer failed to pay an employee the full amount of his wages at the appropriate time. However, it was decided that there was no jurisdiction under the Act to entertain a claim for payment in lieu of notice, since this is in effect a claim for damages for wrongful dismissal payable in connection with the termination of employment. However, the tribunals do now have jurisdiction to deal with certain claims for breach of contract, and so it is possible for employees to choose between the ordinary courts and the tribunals in respect of such claims arising on termination of employment. On the other hand, recourse to an industrial tribunal is not available in respect of any deduction made where a worker has taken part in industrial action.

236. The Act permits the operation of the 'check-off', a widespread practice whereby the employer deducts trade union subscriptions from wages by the employer on behalf of a worker and pays them over to the union. Provided the worker's written consent to such an arrangement is obtained, the deduction is lawful. There is also statutory regulation of the check-off in respect of any deduction from wages of the political levy which some unions collect from members to support their political funds[339] (see Part II, Ch. 2, below).

237. The Act covers all workers, not only those under a contract of service or apprenticeship, but also those who work under any other contract to perform personally any work or services for another party to the contract, whose status is not that of a client or customer of any profession or business undertaking carried on by

338. [1992] IRLR 191, HL.
339. TULRCA 1992, s. 86.

the individual. The Act no longer distinguishes between manual and non-manual workers, but does introduce a complex distinction between retail and non-retail workers.

VI. Itemized Pay Statements

238. The Employment Rights Act 1996, Section 8, gives every employee the right to be given, every time payment of wages or salary is made, a written pay statement, itemizing (1) the gross amount of wages or salary; (2) variable and fixed deductions; (3) the net amount of wages or salary payable; (4) where different parts of the net amount are paid in different ways, the amount and method of each part payment. A remedy for non-compliance with this provision may be obtained in an employment tribunal.

§7. Rights to Remuneration on Employer's Insolvency

239. Unpaid wages or salary, owed to an employee by an employer, are treated as preferential debts on the insolvency of the employer. The priority over other creditors extends only to pay accrued during the four months before the date of insolvency and is limited to a prescribed amount.[340] Preference is also accorded to certain statutory payments.[341]

240. The Employment Rights Act 1996, Section 182 gives an employee the right to recover certain amounts owing to him by the insolvent employer from the National Insurance Fund. This includes up to eight weeks' arrears of pay, pay for the minimum legal notice period, up to six weeks' holiday pay; any basic award of compensation for unfair dismissal, and reimbursement of premiums paid for apprenticeship or articles of clerkship, subject to certain maximum amounts which may be varied from time to time. The trustees of an occupational pension fund may also obtain payment of unpaid contributions owing to the fund. The Secretary of State, upon making a payment from the Fund, is subrogated to the rights and remedies of the employee against the insolvent employer. Disputes are dealt with by employment tribunals. This provides a valuable safety net for employees in the event of their employer's insolvency. However, long delays have been experienced by employees. This is to some extent mitigated by provisions which permit the Secretary of State to make payments to employees before receiving a statement from the liquidator or receiver of the amount owed, if such a statement does not appear to be necessary to determine the amount due.

340. Insolvency Act 1986, ss. 386–387, and Sched. 6.
341. Insolvency Act 1986, Sched. 6, para. 13.

§8. Remuneration during Lay-off and Short-time

241. Workers may be 'laid off' or put on short-time for a variety of reasons, such as temporary fluctuations in production, closure of a plant due to causes, beyond the employer's control (e.g. a failure of power supplies), or recession. The term 'layoff' does not have a legal definition apart from the context of redundancy payments where it means that workers are not provided with work and, under their contracts, they are not entitled to pay. This, however, is not the meaning adopted in everyday industrial practice where the notion of 'lay-off' is taken to include any situation where the worker is not provided with work, and 'short-time' is a situation where the worker is provided with work for less than his or her normal working hours.

242. The legal rules regarding the maintenance of income during lay-offs and short-time are extremely complicated.[342] It is necessary, first of all, to appreciate that a lay-off may take one of four different legal forms depending on the circumstances. These are discussed in turn.

I. Frustration of the Contract

243. 'Frustration' means supervening impossibility of performance as by some event making the performance of the contract a physical impossibility or unlawful (e.g. the burning down of the factory). It is rare for a lay-off to occur in these circumstances, and if there is a possibility of the worker being re-employed within a short period there will be no frustration. If there is, then the worker loses any right to remuneration from the moment the event occurs.

II. The Employee is Dismissed

244. This is rare because lay-offs are generally of short duration. However, in a few exceptional cases, failure to provide work to an employee (such as an actor) may constitute a dismissal by the employer. In that event the employee has no right to continue to receive his contractual remuneration but he may have claims in respect of unfair dismissal or for a redundancy payment (below Ch. 7). However, in recent recessionary times and since 2008, Great Britain has seen an increase in its usage.

III. The Employee is Dismissed but Re-engaged when Work Resumes

245. This is frequent in certain industries such as shipbuilding and construction. Since he is dismissed he is not entitled to any contractual remuneration during the period of lay-off, but he may be able to claim a redundancy payment, or if he has

342. See generally, E. Szysczak, *Partial Unemployment: The Regulation of Short-Time Working in Britain* (London, 1990).

been unfairly selected for dismissal on grounds of redundancy he may be able to claim a remedy for unfair dismissal (below, Ch. 7). If he does not claim redundancy payment and is subsequently re-engaged, the 'temporary cessation of work' due to the lay-off will not affect his continuity of employment (i.e. seniority rights).

IV. The Employee is Suspended from Work

A. At Common Law

246. We have seen that although, at common law, an employer is under no general obligation to provide work, he must pay the employee. He cannot suspend an employee without pay, unless there is an express agreement to that effect. This means that whether the worker is paid according to time, or according to results (piece-work) he is entitled to his contractual remuneration even though there is no work for him to do.

247. There are, however, two exceptions to this general rule. First, the right to be paid may be excluded by express or implied agreement or by custom. An example of an express term was a case in 1936 where the contract provided that musicians would not be paid when they did not play, but the court interpreted this narrowly holding that the employers could refuse to pay only for those performances which it was reasonable for them to cancel.[343] Only one reported case is known to the authors in which an implied term or custom allowing the employer to refuse payment has been proved. This was where a boiler-scaler was employed whenever there was a job to be done. In between jobs he was laid-off. There was held to be an implied term, because of the casual nature of his employment, to lay him off without pay.[344] Where, however, the employer does have a contractual right to lay a worker off indefinitely without pay, there is no implied term that the duration of the lay-off should be reasonable. Thus an employee cannot claim that the employer has repudiated the contract and thus that he or she has been constructively dismissed.[345]

248. A second exception is where the employer's failure to provide work is due to circumstances beyond its control. For example, in a case in 1926 a colliery had to be closed to allow a dangerous state of affairs underground to be remedied. This had occurred through no fault of the employers. The court held that it was the implied intention of the parties that the risk of untoward events such as unsafe conditions or breakage of machinery should be shared.[346] It is not clear exactly how far this principle goes. What circumstances are 'outside the employer's control'? It

343. *Minnevitch* v. *Café de Paris (Londres) Ltd* [1936] 1 All ER 884.
344. *Puttick* v. *John Wright & Sons (Blackwall) Ltd* [1972] 1 ICR 457. Such a term is even less likely to be implied in the case of a white-collar employee: *Namyslo* v. *Secretary of State for Employment* [1979] IRLR 450U (Industrial Tribunal). A custom would have to be reasonable, certain and notorious: *Bond* v. *C.A.V. Ltd* [1983] IRLR 360.
345. *Kenneth MacRae & Co. Ltd* v. *Dawson* [1984] IRLR 5.
346. *Browning* v. *Crumlin Valley Collieries Ltd* [1926] 1 KB 572.

seems likely that lay-offs caused by strikes at premises of suppliers of the employer fall within this concept. On the other hand, the court in an earlier case regarded a lay-off due to a trade recession as being within the employer's control, and so the employees laid-off remained entitled to remuneration.[347] This means that English law draws a curious distinction between lay-offs due to the fluctuations in trade, when remuneration must continue to be paid, and lay-offs due to circumstances such as mechanical failure or lack of materials, when a principle of risk-sharing is applied. Recent cases have tended to limit the scope of this exception.[348]

B. Guaranteed Week Collective Agreements

249. The insecurity of workers' income during periods of lay-off has led to the negotiation of many different types of collective agreement to maintain income during the first few days or weeks or lay-off or short-time working. Most of these agreements require the employee to be willing to accept an offer of suitable alternative employment, and the amount guaranteed is normally less than a full week's pay. These agreements generally take effect as express or implied terms of the individual contract. In general the employer cannot unilaterally 'suspend' the guaranteed agreement without the consent of the employees concerned. If the standards laid down in the agreement are less favourable than the statutory guarantee payments they are superseded by the latter. Conversely, it is possible to obtain exemption from the statutory scheme where alternative collective arrangements have been made. Relatively few exemptions have been granted.

C. Guarantee Payments under the Employment Rights Act[349]

250. Collective bargaining has not provided adequate protection for earnings during lay-offs, and since 1 February 1977 every employee (with minor exceptions) is entitled to a guarantee payment for certain days when he is not provided with work, up to a prescribed amount.

251. In order to be eligible the employee must have been continuously employed by the same employer for one month. He or she can claim only in respect of a day on which he is normally required to work and he or she must have had no work throughout the whole of the day because of a diminution in the requirements of the employer's business for work of the kind he or she was employed to do, or because of any other occurrence affecting the normal working of the employer's business in relation to work of the kind which the employee was employed to do. Guarantee payments may not be claimed if the failure to provide work is the result of a strike, lock-out or other industrial action involving any employee of his or her employer or an associated employer; or if the employee unreasonably refuses an offer of suitable

347. *Devonald* v. *Rosser & Sons* [1906] 2 KB 728.
348. *Johnson* v. *Cross* [1977] ICR 872; *Bond* v. *C.A.V. Ltd* [1983] IRLR 360.
349. ERA 1996, ss. 28–34.

alternative employment for the workless day; or if the employee fails to comply with reasonable requirements imposed by his employer to ensure that the employee's services are available.

252. Although the rights to guarantee payments under statute are separate from rights to such payments under contract (including as we have seen collective agreements), a rule of mutual set-off applies. Any contractual remuneration received by an employee in respect of a workless day goes towards discharging the employer's liability to make the statutory payment. Conversely the statutory payment is set off against the contractual remuneration. Disputes regarding statutory guarantee payments may be referred to industrial tribunals.

D. Redundancy Payments

253. The Employment Rights Act 1996, Part XI, Ch. 3, allows an employee to claim compensation for redundancy based on age and length of service for lay-offs and short-time in two situations: (1) where the employee is dismissed for redundancy, and (2) where the employee is laid-off or put on short-time within the definition of those terms in Section 139 of the Act. The first situation is like any other redundancy dismissal and will be discussed in Ch. 7, below. In both situations the employee must have been continuously employed for two years or more to qualify. In the second situation, to claim a redundancy payment the lay-off or short-time (or combination of the two) must have continued for 4 consecutive weeks or have occurred during 6 out of 13 weeks (weeks affected by strikes or lock-outs do not count). The employee must give notice of intention to claim a payment and give the minimum notice needed to terminate the contract. The employer must then contest liability by serving a counter-notice within 7 days of the employee's notice to claim, and by proving that there is reasonable expectation of work being provided. In order to fall under these provisions the 'lay-off ' must be one in which the employee's pay depends upon being given work by the employer and the employee must not be being given this work and he must not be entitled to pay. The 'short-time' provisions apply where the diminution of work causes the employee's earnings to drop to less than half a week's pay. These provisions remain, little used in practice even in times of economic downturn.

Chapter 6. Incapacity for Work

§1. Reasons for Work Absence

254. Absence rates vary significantly between occupations and between industries. Research into the reasons for absence indicates that many factors contribute to absences. Among these are: (1) age structure, with 'old' labour forces having greater amounts of absence than 'young' labour forces; (2) size of firm, with smaller firms having lower absence rates; (3) length of journey to work with long journeys being associated with higher absence rates; (4) lack of supervision in the firm, this often resulting in high absence rates; (5) sick-pay schemes in firms with those providing leave with pay having higher absence rates than those which do not.

§2. Income Maintenance during Absence from Work due to Sickness or Injury

255. The maintenance of income of an employee who is absent from work because of sickness or injury depends on the interaction of three distinct sources: (1) the terms of the employee's contract of employment, express or implied or as a matter of custom and practice; (2) social security benefits and statutory sick pay; (3) lump-sum damages awarded by a court (or paid in settlement of a claim) where the sickness or injury is due to the fault of the employer or of those for whom he or she is responsible.

I. Remuneration under the Contract of Employment

256. Sick pay schemes set up either as a result of collective bargaining or unilaterally provided by management have become widespread in the past 70 post-war years. In practice, most organizations provide benefits, paying wages during sickness, although the duration of entitlement and level of payment varies considerably between employers, and typically this depends on factors such as length of service. Where there is a sick pay scheme this will usually be incorporated into the contract of employment either expressly or by implication. Proof of the employee's rights is aided by the employer's statutory obligation to give written particulars of any terms and conditions relating to incapacity for work due to sickness or injury, including any provisions for sick pay.[350]

257. If there is no sick pay scheme, there may be a custom relating to sick pay or a term may be implied. In some older cases, it was held that if the contract was silent as to the employee's right to sick pay, there was a presumption that the employer's obligation to pay wages continued until the contract was determined by

350. ERA 1996, s. 1.

notice.[351] However, the existence of such a presumption has been rejected in more recent cases.[352] Instead, the Court of Appeal has said that the evidence in each case should be approached with 'an open mind, unprejudiced by any precondition, presumption or assumption',[353] the aim being to discover what the agreement was. In seeking evidence of the agreement, the court is entitled to look at the subsequent conduct of the parties. Thus if an employee has never received sick pay, the court is likely to imply that he or she has no right to it. Moreover, if there is a contractual right to sick pay, but the duration is not specified, there is no presumption that sick pay lasts until the contract is determined. Instead the court will imply a reasonable term as to duration, and in an industry where the normal practice is to apply sick pay for a limited period only, the reasonable term to imply is the term normally applicable in that industry.[354] The only statutory requirement is that the employee should be paid in full during the compulsory minimum period of notice.[355]

II. Social Security Benefits and Statutory Sick Pay

258. The principle of compulsory insurance was adopted (following the example of Germany) in the National Insurance Act 1911. In return for contributions, manual employees and certain low-earning non-manual employees were entitled to free medical treatment from doctors who agreed to participate, and the contributor also received sickness benefit which lasted for 26 weeks but could be extended for disablement. The scheme was administered by Approved Societies, including friendly societies and trade unions. The number of persons covered gradually increased between 1911 and 1946. In 1942, in his famous report on Social Insurance and Allied Services,[356] Sir William Beveridge criticized the provision for sickness and invalidism on the grounds that it was insufficiently concerned with improving health, provided too low a level of benefits, and was inadequately administered by the Approved Societies. The scheme initiated in 1946 under the inspiration of the Beveridge Report retained the basic principle of social insurance conferring benefits at a flat-rate subsistence level in respect of major causes of income loss. Social insurance was made comprehensive, covering previously excluded groups and administration was unified under a Department of State. At the same time, a free and comprehensive National Health Service was established.

The Beveridge scheme failed to meet its basic objective of establishing a national minimum of income support for 'normal needs' while leaving 'room and encouragement for voluntary action by each individual to provide more than that minimum for himself and his family'.[357] Over some fifty years since Beveridge, successive governments have kept the level of flat-rate insurance benefits below the

351. *Marrison v. Bell* [1939] 2 KB 187; *Orman* v. *Saville Sportswear Ltd* [1960] 1 WLR 1055.
352. *Mears* v. *Safecar Security Ltd* [1982] ICR 626 (CA); *Howman* v. *Blyth* [1983] ICR 416.
353. [1982] ICR 626 at p. 649.
354. *Howman* v. *Blyth* [1983] ICR 416.
355. ERA 1996, ss. 87–91.
356. Cmnd 6404 (1942).
357. *Ibid.*, para. 9.

subsistence level, so that the number of those relying on means-tested supplementary benefits (formerly called national assistance) has steadily increased. The means-tested benefit, rather than contributory social insurance, provides the minimum level of income for the poorest section of injured and disabled persons. Moreover, the Beveridge scheme failed to make adequate provision for the long-term disabled. This has led governments, in response to pressure groups, to make *ad hoc* provision for specific sections of the disabled such as workers suffering from certain dust-related diseases whose former employers are no longer in business.[358] There was a departure from the flat-rate principle when earnings-related sickness benefits were introduced in 1966 and this was extended to certain other benefits such as invalidity pensions, so bringing the British social security system closer to that on the Continent of Europe. However, there was a radical reversal in 1982 when earnings-related supplements were abolished in respect of short-term sickness benefit. This was designed to save public expenditure and to facilitate bringing the relevant benefits into taxation. The Beveridge principle of flat-rate contributions failed to generate an adequate level of benefits, and as a result there was a shift to a system of earnings-related contributions.

259. Presently, there is a dual state benefit system for those unable to work because of sickness or disability, depending on what it is: the Employment Support Allowance (ESA) and the Personal Independence Payment (PIP)) . This replaced the former system under the Disability Living Allowane (DLA).

260. The ESA was introduced on 27 October 2008. It is a benefit for individuals who are considered to have 'limited capability for work' and are not entitled to SSP. What this means is that if it is unreasonable to require a person to work due to the nature of their sickness or disability then they may be enitled to the ESA. There are two types of ESA: the contributory ESA and income-related ESA. The contributory ESA is as it sounds, and is payable to those who have contributed into the social security system. Namely, this is payable to persons who satisfy the relevant National Insurance contribution conditions. Income-related ESA is means tested, and has no contributory element to it. Income-related ESA can be paid to supplement a contributory ESA. Determination of suitability is through an assessment by a suitable practitioner. Obviously if the assessment shows a claimant not to have limited capability for work then their claim for ESA fails. However, if a claimant is deemed to have limited capability for work following assessment then they will be placed in one of two categories: having limited capability for work-related activity, or being capable of work-related activity. Where a person is placed in the first of these two categories (these are called in the 'support group') they will receive the main rate of ESA along with an additional support allowance.[359] Those placed in the second group, the 'capable of work-related activity' group, will receive the main ESA rate plus an additional work-related component. Those in this category will be required

358. Pneumoconiosis etc. (Workers' Compensation) Act 1979.

359. There are certain conditions that will see an individually automatically placed into this category. This covers the most serious of conditions, such as individuals who are terminally ill, or where a person is undergoing chemotherapy.

to attend work-focused interviews amongst other requiements to maintain their eligibility for the full benefit.

261. PIP was initially introduced through a pilot scheme, which commenced in April 2013, and was introduced nationally in June 2013. The framework for PIP is contained within the Welfare Reform Act 2012. There are two elements that are considered when assessing eligibility for PIP: first is the person's ability to carry out daily living activities and whether this is limited or severely limited by the person's physical or mental condition. Secondly, there is assessment of a person's mobility activities, again with consideration of whether this is limited or severely limited by a physical or mental condition. As intimated through the consideration of two elements, there are two parts to the PIP allowance, a daily living component and a mobility component. Each of these are considered individually, and assessed against a matrix of factors contained within the Welfare Reform Act by a HCP practitioner. PIP is essentially a points based system. Points will be awarded against each of the listed factors. And the cumulative total of the points awarded will determine whether either of the components achieve the points threshold to receive the standard or enhanced weekly rate. PIP is often awarded for a period of up to two years, at which point reassessment will be needed for the allowance to continue. However, longer term awards can be made.

262. Since April 2000, the conditions for access to social security have been tightened: most people now need to have paid sufficient contributions in one of the last two tax years (previously any tax year would do); and half of any occupational or personal pension above a prescribed amount is deducted from incapacity benefit entitlement. It is not possible (since 2008) to claim ESA benefit as well as state retirement pension or jobseeker's allowance. Other benefits, such as for maternity and invalid care allowance, are known as overlapping benefits. The claimant can receive an amount equal to the highest of these benefits. Other benefits can be paid on top of ESA benefit, including PIP and/or attendance allowance (AA).

263. The major source of income support for those incapable of work for short periods owing to illness or injury since April 1983 has been statutory sick pay (SSP). Before that date a short-term industrial injury benefit was payable for work-related accidents and prescribed industrial diseases, and state sickness benefit for other illnesses. The value of these state benefits to high-earners was considerably reduced by the withdrawal of earnings-related supplements in 1982. Employers are now obliged to pay SSP to employees. This is usually for a maximum of 28 weeks for any one period of incapacity for work.[360] During this period the employee has no entitlement to state ESA. The main justification put forward for the introduction of SSP was the reduction of administrative expenditure by placing responsibility in the employer's hands. But in terms of the original scheme, the state retained ultimate financial responsibility: employers could recoup the SSP paid by them by recouping it from their national insurance contributions.

360. Social Security Contributions and Benefits Act 1992, Pt XI. See also the Statutory Sick Pay (General) Regulations 1982 (SI 1982, 894), as amended.

264. SSP is not payable for the first three days of sickness, but unlike ESA, there is no requirement that the employee fulfil contribution conditions. Thus, an employee may become eligible for SSP as soon as he or she begins working. Formerly, an employee was entitled to state benefit even if the employer paid sick pay under the contract of employment. The present scheme, however, allows the employer to discharge contractual liability for sick pay by paying SSP (and vice versa), thus preventing double recovery and relieving the employer of some contractual obligations. SSP is not designed to replace earnings, but provides flat rate recovery on two earnings bands. Many occupational sick pay schemes therefore operate by topping up the state entitlement to the level of the employee's earnings.

III. Lump Sum Damages

265. If the employee is able to establish that the employer was in breach of its common law duty to take reasonable care for the employee's safety, or in breach of a statutory safety duty, or that the employer is vicariously responsible for the negligence or breach of duty by a fellow-employee, then he or she may receive damages in the form of a lump sum payment. In assessing the amount of damages deductions will be made for remuneration received from the employer (or likely to be paid in future) since the basic principle of the damages award is compensatory. The law relating to the employers' liability for damages falls outside the scope of this monograph.

§3. Maternity Pay

266. An employee absent from work because of pregnancy or confinement may be able to receive two types of maternity benefit: (1) from her employer, under her contract of employment; (2) statutory maternity pay (SMP), payable by the state, but administered by employers on lines similar to SSP above. Women have four rights in relation to pregnancy and childbirth. These are: the right to maternity leave; the right to maternity pay; time off for ante-natal care; and protection from detriment or dismissal on the grounds of pregnancy or childbirth.

The Pregnant Workers Directive 92/85/EEC required Member States to provide women workers with at least 14 weeks' maternity leave. The relevant domestic law is now contained within ERA 1996, Sections 71–75 and the MPLR, as amended by the Maternity and Parental Leave (Amendment) Regulations 2002, SI 2002/2789 (MPLAR 2002), which apply to mothers of children born on or after 6 April 2003.

267. Women are entitled to a period of ordinary maternity leave (OML) of 26 weeks (extended from 18 weeks as from 24 November 2002), without the need to accrue a qualifying period of continuous employment): MPLR, reg. 7. A woman is entitled to OML and any holiday leave: in *Merino Gomez* v. *Continental Industrias del Caucho SA*, Case C-342/01 [2004] IRLR 407, the ECJ ruled that a woman is entitled to her statutory minimum annual holiday in addition to any maternity leave to which she may be entitled.

268. There are detailed notification requirements to be followed, failing which the maternity leave may be lost. The employee must notify her employer no later than the end of the 15th week before the expected week of childbirth (EWC) – or as soon as reasonably practicable – of the fact that she is pregnant, the expected date of childbirth and the date on which she intends to commence her OML (reg. 4). This date may be varied by notifying the employer at least 28 days before the date varied or before the new date, whichever is the earlier. The employer must then give the woman notice of the date on which her OML will end (reg. 8). If the employer fails to do this, she may return early and she is protected from detriment or dismissal if she does not return on that date (regs. 10(c), 13 and 14).

269. Under the statutory maternity pay scheme, a woman working in Britain with 26 weeks of continuous employment by the 15th week before the expected week of confinement (EWC) (i.e. birth) with average earnings at or above the lower earnings limit for the payment of National Insurance contributions is entitled to statutory maternity pay (SMP): see the Social Security Contributions and Benefits Act 1992, Sections 164–171. For the first six weeks, it is paid at the rate of 90 per cent of the woman's normal weekly earnings. For the remaining 20 weeks it is paid at a standard rate (equivalent to the maternity rate), which is currently £140.98 per week. A woman must give 28 days' notice of the day SMP should start. In calculating the earnings-related part of SMP, any pay rise awarded during a woman's absence on maternity leave must be taken into account, even where it was not backdated (see *Alabaster* v. *Woolwich plc*[2005] IRLR 576, CA, following the ECJ ruling in the case).[361] The mother can do up to 10 days' work during her maternity leave without losing any Statutory Maternity Pay; payment for these days should be agreed between the mother and her employer.

I. Under the Contract of Employment

270. Prior to the introduction of statutory provisions, only 15–20 per cent of employers operated schemes granting women paid maternity leave.[362] Now, a significant proportion of companies offer employees maternity benefits which are superior to those provided by statute, for example longer periods of leave and 6 to 12 weeks' leave at full pay.

II. Statutory Maternity Pay

271. As noted above statutory maternity pay (SMP), like SSP, is payable by the employer, but is recouped from national insurance contributions. In terms of the Social Security Contributions and Benefits Act 1992 SMP is payable to a woman

361. A. McColgan, 'Family Friendly Frolics: the Maternity and Parental Leave Regulations 1999', ILJ 29 (2000) 125–144.
362. N. Fonda, 'Statutory Maternity Leave in the UK' in P. Muss and N. Fonda, *Work and the Family* (London, 1980), p. 121.

who has been employed for 26 weeks up to the qualifying week, which is the 15th week before the EWC, and whose average weekly earnings in the eight weeks preceding the qualifying week exceed the lower earnings limit for national insurance contributions.[363]

272. SMP is available for a minimum period of 26 weeks. The state maternity allowance is payable to employees at the lower rate of SMP for that entire payment period, and to non-employees at a yet lower rate. Where an employee is also entitled to a contractual payment, she is entitled to either the contractual sum, or SMP for the relevant weeks, whichever is the greater; but not to both. The remedy for refusal to pay lies in a complaint to an adjudication officer, with appeals to the Social Security Appeals Tribunal and thence to the Social Security Commissioners.

§4. Suspension from Work on Medical Grounds[364]

273. Under health and safety legislation an employer may be required to suspend an employee from work on medical grounds, because of unsafe conditions, etc. During the period of suspension under these statutory requirements the employee is entitled to be paid by his employer for not more than 26 weeks, subject to certain qualifications.

§5. Right to Return to Work

I. Sickness or Injury

274. A long absence may bring the contract to an end automatically through 'frustration' (supervening impossibility of performance). The test, applied by the courts, is 'was the employee's incapacity of such a nature, or did it appear likely to continue for such a period, that further performance of [the employee's] obligations in the future would either be impossible or would be a thing radically different from that undertaken by him and accepted by the employer under the agreed terms of his employment?'[365] Among the relevant factors will be the sick pay provisions in the contract, whether the employee is in a key position, the nature of the illness and the employee's length of service. Recent cases have tended to limit the doctrine to long-term contracts with no notice provisions.[366]

363. See also the Pregnant Workers Directive (Council Directive No. 92/85/ EC) which requires the maintenance of a payment to and/or entitlement to an adequate allowance, which must be at least equivalent to that which a worker would receive in the event of a break in her activities on grounds connected with her state of health, subject to any ceiling laid down under national legislation.
364. ERA 1996, ss. 64, 65.
365. *Marshall* v. *Harland & Wolff Ltd* [1972] 1 WLR 899 at pp. 902–904.
366. *Harman* v. *Flexible Lamp Ltd* [1980] IRLR 418; cf. *Notcutt* v. *Universal Equipment Co. (London) Ltd* [1986] ICR 414.

275. If the contract has not been frustrated, then the employer who dismisses the employee by reason of sickness or injury ('incapability') will have to satisfy an employment tribunal, under the unfair dismissals law, that in all the circumstances (having regard to equity and the substantial merits of the case) it acted reasonably in treating the incapability as a sufficient reason for dismissal. This applies only to those who satisfy the eligibility requirements for unfair dismissal (see Ch. 7, below). The employer who acts slowly and is generous to the sick or injured employee is likely to satisfy the tribunal. There are no set rules, the only test being fairness in all the circumstances. In general it will be necessary for the employer to show that it has investigated the facts, warned the employee and heard the employee's side of the story. It will usually be found unfair to dismiss where the period of sick pay under the contract has not yet expired. The employer is not obliged to create a special job for a sick employee, suitable to his or her capacities, however long his service; but there may be cases, where other lighter jobs are available, that these should be offered to an employee not in good health. In some enterprises there are collective agreements which provide for sick employees to be transferred to a 'holding department' or 'inactive register' with clearly defined rights, normally after an agreed period of absence. This type of agreement does not give an automatic right to be put back in the old job but it preserves the employee's continuity of employment although he or she is not actually working. If the employee has not been dismissed, and the contract has not been frustrated, the employee has no automatic right to the identical job he or she was doing before absence from work. His or her right will depend on the terms of the job description in his contract of employment, which may allow flexibility. If the job has disappeared the employee may be entitled to a redundancy payment (below, Ch. 7).[367]

II. Dismissal for Pregnancy-related Reasons

276. The dismissal of an employee is regarded as automatically unfair if the reason or principal reason for the dismissal is connected with (1) the pregnancy of the employee; (2) the fact that the employee has given birth to a child, where the dismissal ends the employee's ordinary or additional maternity leave period; (3) the suspension of the employee under an enactment or a health and safety recommendation on grounds connected with her pregnancy; (4) the fact that she took, sought to take, or availed herself of the benefits of, ordinary maternity leave; (5) the fact that she took or sought to take (i) additional maternity leave, (ii) parental leave, or (iii) time off for ante-natal care guaranteed under Sections 55–57 of the ERA 1996; (6) the fact that she is redundant, and she was made redundant during her maternity leave period and was not offered suitable alternative employment.[368] This protection does not apply if (1) the number of employees employed by the employer does

367. Note the possible application of the Disability Discrimination Act 1995 if the cause of the absence is impairment which has substantial and long-term effects on the employee's ability to carry out normal activities (Ch. 8, below).
368. ERA 1996, as amended by ERelA 1999, and the Maternity and Parental Leave Etc. Regulations 1999 (SI 1999 3312) (MPL Regulations).

not exceed five, and it is not reasonably practicable for the employer or its successor to permit the employee to return to a job which is both suitable and appropriate for her to do in the circumstances; or (2) it is not reasonably practicable for a reason other than redundancy for the employer or its successor to permit the employee to return to a job which is both suitable and appropriate for her to do in the circumstances, but an associated employer offers her a job of that kind, and she accepts or unreasonably refuses that offer. The application of these rights is not restricted by reference to a qualifying period of service.

III. Maternity, Paternity, Adoption and Parental Leave

277. The former DTI published a Green Paper in December 2000 entitled, *Work and Parents: Competitiveness and Choice*, concerning the entitlements identified above, and a Work and Parents Taskforce was established in 2001 to consider ways of introducing 'family-friendly' and 'business-friendly' flexible working practices. The government published a document entitled 'Balancing work and family life: enhancing choice and support for parents', in January 2003, which considered further developments to improve work/life balance for the future. In late 2004, the government announced its 'family-friendly strategy' for the following decade. This contained a number of proposals, including the introduction of a Childcare approval scheme from 6 April 2005, which provides families on incomes not exceeding £59,000 with tax credit support to help pay for home child-care (this is now in place); the introduction of paid maternity leave of 12 months by the end of the next Parliament. Moreover, since April 2007, the maternity leave entitlement has been extended to 9 months. The Work and Families Act 2006, which received Royal Assent in June 2006, has implemented these changes.

The Government announced in November 2012 that legislation to introduce changes to flexible working was to be introduced in 2014, to introduce flexible parental leave. The Regulations giving effect to this came in to force on the 1 December 2014. This change enables parents flexibility to choose how they share the care of their child. This did not alter the 52 week entitlement that the mother has to maternity leave; however, it gives parents a greater choice as to apportioning the leave between them up to a total of 52 weeks, although this is still subject to the requirement that the mother takes at least the initial two weeks of leave after birth. This was brought in for parents where a baby is due, or a child placed for adoption, on or after 5 April 2015.

IV. Flexible Working

278. In November 2001, the Work and Parents Task Force delivered a report proposing that employees who were parents of children under 6 should be able to request flexible working arrangements, and that the employer should be required to take this request seriously. This was taken up by the government, and a provision was inserted into the ERA 1996 by the Employment Act 2002 (*see* ERA 1996, Sections 80F–80I), effective from 6 April 2003.

There are two sets of regulations on flexible working: the Flexible Working (Procedural Requirements) Regulations 2002, SI 2002/3207 ('the FE(PR) Regs'), and the Flexible Working (Eligibility, Complaints and Remedies) Regulations 2002, SI 2002/3236 ('the FW(ECR) regs'). The right is to request to work flexibly (i.e. a right to request a contractual variation), rather than an automatic right to do so. The change must relate to hours or times and place of work (ERA 1996, Section 80F(1)(a)).

279. To qualify for this right, the employee must be:

- a qualifying employee, i.e. with at least 26 weeks' of continuous employment (FE(PR) Regs, reg. 3(1)(a);
- having or expecting to have responsibility for the upbringing of a child aged under 6 (or under 18 if the child is disabled): ERA 1996, Section 80F(3) and (7);
- either the parent, foster parent, guardian, or adopter of the child, or the husband, wife or partner (including civil partner) of such a person (FE(PR) Regs, reg. 3(1)(b).

280. The application to request the right must be made in writing, and must specify the change applied for, the date from which the employee wants it to be effective, and the effect (if any) the applicant thinks the change would have on the employer: FE(PR) Regs, reg. 4; ERA 1996, Section 80F. The application must be made before the fourteenth day before the day on which the child reaches the age of 6 (or 18 if disabled). The employer must hold a meeting within 28 days of the request, and inform the employee of the decision within 14 days of the meeting (FE(PR) Regs, regs. 3 and 4). The employee may be accompanied by a fellow worker. The employee may appeal against the decision within 14 days and, if an appeal is made, an appeal meeting must be held within 14 days of the appeal being lodged, unless the appeal is upheld within 14 days of the appeal being lodged (FE(PR) Regs, regs. 6 and 8).

281. The employer may only refuse the request on 'business grounds' (ERA 1996, Section 80G(1)(b)). These are:

- burden of additional costs;
- detrimental effect of the ability to meet customer demand;
- inability to reorganize work among existing staff;
- inability to recruit additional staff;
- detrimental impact on quality or performance;
- insufficiency of work during periods that the employee proposes to work planned structural changes;
- any other ground that the Secretary of State may specify.

These grounds seem very wide, giving great scope to the employer to refuse the request.

§6. PROTECTION OF SENIORITY RIGHTS[369]

282. An employee will be credited with certain weeks of absence from work for purposes of calculating continuity of employment, and continuity will not be broken by those absences. These are weeks of absence: (1) during all or part of which the employee is incapable of work in consequence of sickness or injury, up to a maximum of 26 weeks; and (2) during which the employee is absent from work wholly or partly because of pregnancy or confinement.

369. ERA 1996, s. 212.

Chapter 7. Job Security

§1. Development of the Concept of Job Security

283. Since 1963 there has been a spate of legislation intended to give employees a measure of security against abrupt or unfair dismissal and to provide compensation when jobs disappear for economic reasons. A variety of imprecise concepts has been applied by commentators. One is the idea of 'property in the job' or the right to undisturbed possession of a job which cannot be taken away without due process of law.[370] This, as Professor H.A. Turner has remarked, 'is the employee's compensation for his relative lack of property in the capital that employs him'.[371] Another concept is the 'right to work' which in Britain means 'not only access to a new job after having quit or lost an old one, but also a right to continue at the old'.[372] It has, however, been argued that so far from increasing job security or job-property rights, the effect of the legislation has been to encourage British workers to abandon their 'protective' attitudes to jobs and to accept dismissals in return for cash payments. [373] It has also been suggested that the emphasis on individual rights in respect of disciplinary action by management has weakened the collective control of jobs by workers and, to some extent, strengthened managerial control.[374]

284. Before 1875 the employee was, in fact, bound to his or her employer because desertion (breach of contract) was punishable as a criminal offence and employees could also be imprisoned for debts (such as wage advances) owed to the employer. The criminal liability for desertion was modified in 1867 and abolished in 1875. 'This fundamental revolution in the law' (as Sidney and Beatrice Webb called it)[375] meant that from then on employer and employee became equal parties to a civil contract. The contractual classification of the relationship means that, in formal legal terms, the employer cannot compel the employee to continue in service – that would 'turn contracts of service into contracts of slavery'[376] – and, on the principles of reciprocity and mutual confidence, the employee cannot compel the employer to keep him or her in service. As a general principle, therefore, the remedy of specific performance (or compulsion to perform contractual obligations) has not been available for breach of the contract of employment.

285. Proposals for improving job security in the early 1960s generally took the form of a requirement that employers should give longer formal notice of dismissal.

370. The classic exposition is by F. Meyers, *Ownership of Jobs: A Comparative Study* (Los Angeles, 1964), p. 1; see generally B. Hepple, 'A Right to Work?', ILJ 10 (1981) 65 and H. Collins, *Justice in Dismissal* (Oxford, 1992); R. Upex and S. Hardy, *Law on Termination* (8th edn, Jordans, Bristol, 2012).
371. H.A. Turner *et al.*, *Labour Relations in the Motor Industry* (London, 1967), p. 337.
372. Meyers, *op. cit.*, p. 18.
373. R.H. Fryer, 'The Myths of the Redundancy Payments Act', ILJ 2 (1973), 1.
374. M. Mellish and N. Collis-Squires, 'Legal and Social Norms in Discipline and Dismissal', ILJ 5 (1976), 164.
375. S. & B. Webb, *History of Trade Unionism* (rev. edn, London, 1919), p. 291.
376. *Per* Fry LJ in *De Francesco* v. *Barnum* (1890) 45 Ch. D. 430 at p. 438.

The original Contracts of Employment Bill 1963 (the first general legislation in Britain on terms of employment since 1875) placed a reciprocal obligation on employers and employees to give one another the same minimum periods of notice. The trade unions were concerned that this would restrict the right to strike after giving notice to terminate contracts, and, under pressure, the Conservative Government modified the original proposals so as to make the minimum period of notice to be given by an employee to terminate his or her contract the period of one week. The minimum period to be given by the employer, on the other hand, varied from one week (in respect of employees with between 26 weeks' and two years' service) to four weeks (for those with five years' or more service). These periods of notice by the employer have been extended in later Acts (now contained in the Employment Rights Act 1996).

286. The Redundancy Payments Act 1965 (now included in the Employment Rights Act 1996, Part XI) made employers liable to pay lump-sum compensation based on age and length of service, to redundant employees. It was originally envisaged that this cost should be shared among employers. Hence, employers were entitled to recover a proportion of the redundancy payment from a Redundancy Fund made up of contributions from all employers. With the increase in redundancies after 1980, the Fund was found to be in financial difficulties, and in order to increase available resources, employee contributions were instituted in April 1982, at the rate of 0.35 per cent of earnings. The result of this was that redundancies were subsidized in part by fellow employees: indeed, since 1982, employee contributions exceeded those of employers, as a percentage both of earnings and of the Fund.

During the 1980s, the Redundancy Fund paid out about £200 million. In 1986 the right to a rebate was confined to employers with fewer than 10 employees, and in 1989, it was abolished entirely.[377] It has been estimated that only about 45 per cent of employees made redundant have been eligible for payments under the Act, and the average lump sum payment is only about one-fifth of the median adult average wage.[378] Part of the reason for this is that there is a two-year qualifying period, and the definition of 'redundancy' is far more restrictive than the circumstances in which a worker in France can obtain severance pay or a worker in Belgium or Italy can receive payments supplementary to unemployment insurance following workforce reductions. The stated purposes of the Act included the mitigation of the economic consequences of redundancy, compensation for the loss of job property rights, and the encouragement of mobility. A survey of the main groups actually or potentially involved in redundancy[379] found that the Act has had some impact on attitudes and behaviour, increasing mobility and flexibility of labour and reducing the level of dispute activity over redundancies. One of the most important demonstrated consequences of the Act has been to increase the significance of age as a criterion for redundancy because the larger payments to older workers with long service acts as

377. Employment Act 1989, s. 17.

378. *Labour Market Trends*, May 1999, p. 253; R.H. Fryer, 'Redundancy, Values and Public Policy', *Industrial Relations Journal* 4 (1973) 12; *see too* ILJ 2 (1973), 1.

379. S.R. Parker *et al.*, *Effects of the Redundancy Payments Act*, London, HMSO, 1971.

a mechanism to induce them to leave employment.[380] In this sense, the Act has facilitated movement out of the labour force.

287. In 1971, as part of the then Industrial Relations Act, the Conservative government introduced unfair dismissals legislation, in large measure based on and owing its main inspiration to the ILO Recommendation No. 119 (1963) concerning termination of employment. Unfair dismissals legislation, improved in a number of ways, became one of the centrepieces of the labour law introduced by the Labour government during the so-called 'Social Contract' period of 1974–9. It was, however, progressively narrowed by the Conservative government after 1979 as part of its philosophy of 'reducing burdens on business'. Thus its coverage was significantly reduced by increasing the qualifying period of service from six months to one year and then to two years. The standard of proof of fairness was also weakened and levels of compensation kept low. When the New Labour government came into power in 1997, some of these changes were reversed. In particular, the period of service was reduced to one year,[381] and the maximum levels of compensation significantly increased. However, this did not last long, with the Conservative led coaltion government of 2010 re-introducing the two year qualification period[382] for the right not to be unfairly dismissed, and introducing a cap of 12 months' pay for the unfair dismissal compensatory award.[383] The present British legislation is less extensive than that found elsewhere in Europe, and law and practice is in some respects below the standards in the ILO Termination of Employment Convention 1982, which the UK government has not ratified. The provisions are now found in the Employment Rights Act 1996, Part X, as amended.

288. The right to complain of unfair dismissal marked a major departure from the common law.[384] The employer's power to terminate employment without any reason by lawful notice or payment in lieu of notice, has been restricted. The employer has to prove the reason for dismissal (or, if more than one, the principal reason) and that this was one of a number of potentially fair reasons, namely the capability or conduct of the worker, or that he or she was redundant, or that he or she could not be employed without breach of some statutory requirement, or that there was some other substantial reason of a kind such as to justify the dismissal of an employee holding the position in question. Certain reasons are automatically unfair, such as trade union membership or activities or non-membership of a trade union. In other cases, the tribunal has to determine whether the dismissal was fair or unfair in the circumstances, having regard to the reason shown by the employer, in 'accordance with equity and the substantial merits of the case'.[385] Control over

380. Department of Employment, 'Age and Redundancy', *Employment Gazette* 86 (1978), 1038.
381. Unfair Dismissal and Statement of Reasons for Dismissal (Variation of Qualifying Period) Order 1999, SI 1999 1436.
382. This was brought in with effect from 6 April 2012.
383. This statutory cap on compensatory awards came in to effect on 29 July 2013.
384. See generally, B. Hepple, 'The Fall and Rise of Unfair Dismissal', in W. McCarthy (ed.), *Legal Intervention in Industrial Relations* (Oxford, 1992), pp. 79–102; B. Hepple, and G. Morris, 'The Employment Act 2002 and the crisi of individual employment rights', ILJ 31 (2002), 245–269.
385. ERA 1996, s. 98(4)(b).

jobs has been depersonalized in the sense that the employer can only dismiss certain workers after due process of law.[386] Moreover, there is a relatively cheap, informal and expeditious remedy for an aggrieved employee by way of complaint to an Employment Tribunal within three months of the effective date of termination. Unlike the common law, the legislation (since 1976) provides that the successful employee may be granted an order of reinstatement or re-engagement (previously only a recommendation to this effect could be made).

289. In reality, however, the right to be continuously employed, unless in the words of Article 4 of the ILO Termination of Employment Convention 1982, 'there is a valid reason connected with the capacity or conduct of the worker or based on the operational requirements of the undertaking, establishment or service', has been far less effective than might have been expected. First, the proportion of dismissed workers utilizing the statutory remedy has been modest. This was particularly so after the qualifying period was increased to two years:

290. Secondly, employees who bring claims have found themselves at a relative disadvantage *vis-à-vis* the employer. One reason which has been suggested for this is the unequal representation of employees and employers before tribunals, with employers more likely than employees to have skilled lay or legal advocates.[387] However, a more important reason is the judicial interpretation which has been given to the standard of fairness in the legislation. As will be seen below, the courts and tribunals have interpreted the statutory concept of unfair dismissal as resting upon the foundation of the common law contract of employment. The underlying assumption is the natural authority of management emanating from the property rights of the owners of the business.

This has led to a wide interpretation of the potentially fair reasons for dismissal (in particular the residual category of 'other substantial reason'), it being sufficient for the employer to show a subjective belief in the existence of that reason. In addition, the standard of fairness has been based on the view that it is not for tribunals to impose their own opinion as to whether they would have dismissed in the same circumstances but rather to decide whether the dismissal was within the range of responses which reasonable employers *might* adopt. This non-interventionist approach has recently been reiterated, countering attempts to assert a more activist role for tribunals. It has been somewhat mitigated by the recent emphasis on procedural requirements regardless of the outcome of the case.[388] But there have been some recent signs of a resurgence of the view that a procedural defect did not in itself render a dismissal unfair if the employer could reasonably have dismissed the employee had a fair procedure been followed.

In this way, the overall approach of tribunals has reinforced traditional contractual notions that the employee's interest in job security must take second place to

---

386. It was in this sense that Meyers, *op. cit.*, p. 1 spoke of the 'ownership of jobs'.
387. Dickens, *op. cit.*, pp. 85–93.
388. *Polkey* v. *A.E. Dayton Ltd* [1988] ICR 142.

the employer's right to manage. By considering how a reasonable body of employers might behave the tribunals have become, in Patrick Elias's words,[389] norm-reflecting rather than norm-setting. Not surprisingly tribunal decisions reflect conceptions of common practice rather than more radical notions of worker control of jobs. The result has been that, until very recently, success rates in ETs have been relatively low.

291. Thirdly, the legislation has failed to secure re-employment of unfairly dismissed employees. This remedy is rarely awarded by tribunals, although on paper it has been the primary remedy since 1976, with compensation an alternative. In 2005, the tribunal ordered reinstatement or re-engagement of the applicant in only 2 per cent of successful cases.[390] Although the then Labour Government introduced significant increases in the maximum compensation level, which has since been reduced by the Conservative led coalition government, the current levels of compensation cannot be said to meet the point made by the ILO Committee of Experts in 1974 that compensation is most effective as a remedy where it can act as a deterrent against unjustified termination.

292. Fourthly, the legislation appears to have had relatively little success in providing an impetus for collective bargaining to improve on the basic rights. It was originally intended that collective agreements should replace statutory provisions: hence the provision in the legislation allowing collective agreements to replace the statutory provisions where the standards in the agreement were at least as high as those in the legislation and ministerial approval is granted.[391] In fact, these exemption arrangements have rarely been used: only three exempted agreements for redundancy payments in 20 years and one for unfair dismissal in 13 years.[392] Collective agreements play only a supplementary role to legislation, for example providing for 'add-on' voluntary payments over and above the statutory minima or prescribing voluntary procedures but not replacing the legislation.

293. In many respects, the legislation has done little more than support the power of managers to buy-out jobs. Nevertheless, the unfair dismissals legislation has had some positive effects. It has provided some protection to individual workers against arbitrary action, where trade union organization is ineffective or non-existent. It has also enabled trade unions to offer better services to members in small and dispersed groups on whose behalf it is difficult to negotiate collectively. Most importantly, the legislation, together with successive ACAS Codes of Practice, has provided the impetus for the spread of formal procedures for dealing with discipline and dismissals. Survey evidence indicates that in 1998, formal disciplinary procedures were in operation in at least 92 per cent of workplaces. Although these were

389. P. Elias, ILJ 10 (1981), 201.
390. ACAS *Annual Report* 1999–2000, p. 33; Employment Tribunals Service *Annual Report* 1999–2000.
391. Employment Rights Act 1996, s. 110.
392. Millward and Stevens, *op. cit.*, p. 176; see too W.W. Daniel and N. Milward, *Workplace Industrial Relations in Britain*, pp. 163–170; W. Brown, *op. cit.*, pp. 35–37, 43–48; Dickens, *Dismissal: A Study of Unfair Dismissal and the Industrial Tribunal System*, pp. 232–234, 252–255.

more common in larger workplaces, they were very much the norm even in smaller workplaces.[393] They were particularly widespread in unionized workplaces, with such procedures found in 97 per cent of such workplaces. Equally significant, these procedures were agreed with recognized trade unions in nine-tenths of cases.[394] This involvement by trade unions is likely to be enhanced by the new right, instituted by the Employment Relations Act 1999, for a worker to be accompanied to a disciplinary hearing by a companion of his or her choice, and represented under the 2004 Employment Relations Act. The companion, who may be a trade union official or another worker of the employer, must be permitted to address the hearing and to confer with the worker during the hearing, but does not have the right to answer questions on behalf of the worker.[395] The fact that the companion may be a trade union official, whether or not the trade union is recognized by the employer, is an important opportunity for trade unions to provide services for workers and thereby both to retain existing members and recruit new ones.

294. Since 1997, neo-liberal policies of persistent narrowing of individual employment rights have been replaced by an attempt to find a 'third way', in which social justice is no longer perceived as costly in terms of economic efficiency; but as potential contributing to economic growth and well-being. The neo-liberal argument favoured restricting or removing unfair dismissal rights, on the grounds that the legislation imposed additional costs of employment (including administrative costs of screening and supervising workers) and deterred recruitment by reducing the flexibility of undertakings to respond to market changes by dismissals. It was also argued that the legislation induces inefficient use of labour because of the fear of claims for unfair dismissal, particularly for small firms and those establishing new or expanded operations. Support for the opposite view is, however, provided by surveys of management attitudes and responses[396] which have shown that few employers are reluctant to recruit additional labour because of the legislation. What the legislation has done is to induce greater care in the selection of recruits so as to improve quality rather than to restrict quantity.[397] This tends to support the view of those who argue that the legislation aids efficiency by achieving labour forces closer to the needs of the undertaking. There is evidence that the use of temporary contracts and casual labour is increasing, but this seems to have been prompted more by economic than legal considerations.[398] Another argument for deregulation is that the legislation has introduced greater formalism into labour relations which undermines flexible management control of the workforce. Against this, it has been strongly argued that the widespread adoption of fair procedures has made the

393. M. Cully, *et al.*, *The 1998 Workplace Employee Relations Survey: First Findings* (1999), p. 14.
394. N. Millward, A. Bryson, and J. Forth, *All Change at Work* (2000), pp. 156–157.
395. Employment Relations Act 1999, s. 10(2).
396. W.W. Daniel, and E. Stilgoe, *The Impact of Employment Protection Laws* London (Policy Studies Institute, 1978); R. Clifton, and C. Tatton, Brown, *Impact of Employment Legislation on Small Firms*, Department of Employment Research Paper No. 6, London, 1979; S. Evans, J. Goodman, and L. Hargreaves, *Unfair Dismissal Law and Employment Practice in the 1980s*, Department of Employment Research Paper No. 53, London, 1985; Dickens, *op. cit.*, Ch. 8.
397. This is a conclusion from all the above surveys.
398. S. Evans *et al.*, *op. cit.*, pp. 15–18.

administration of discipline more open and acceptable and has removed legitimacy from collective industrial action against dismissals.[399] A survey has indicated[400] that the vast majority of employers now take more care in preparing for a dismissal so as to ensure that it is legally 'safe', although many small firms continue to act informally. About two-thirds of the sample of employees and trade union representatives felt that generally management dealt fairly with disciplinary matters, but some concern was expressed that procedures and unfair dismissal legislation were undermining the scope for unions to negotiate over disciplinary cases.[401]

§2. Continuity of Employment

295. In order to qualify for statutory job security rights, including statutory periods of notice, unfair dismissal, and redundancy payments, an employee must have a requisite period of 'continuous employment'. For example, unless the employee has been continuously employed for two years there is no right to statutory redundancy payment, and the amount of the payment depends upon age and length of continuous employment. Likewise, the employee cannot complain of unfair dismissal unless he or she has been continuously employed for two years in most cases. The length of continuous employment also affects other job rights, such as maternity pay, guarantee payments and so on. Other rights, however, require no such qualifications. These include the right not to be discriminated against on grounds of race or sex, the right to time off for ante-natal care, and the right not to be dismissed for trade union reasons.

296. The method of determining whether a person has been continuously employed is set out in the Employment Rights Act 1996, Part XIV, Ch. 1. These provisions are extremely complex and only the main principles are set out here. Essentially there are two elements in the concept of 'continuous employment'. The first is continuity, that is the existence of an employment relationship based on a contract of employment or a series of contracts with the same employer or, in some cases, successors to that employer. The second is that the employee must have continuity for a requisite period of employment, that is he or she must have been credited with the requisite period of weeks. For a week (which always ends on Saturday) to count the employee's relationship with his or her employer must have been governed by a contract of employment in some part of that week.

297. The general rule is that if a week occurs which cannot be credited to an employee then not only does that week not count as a period of employment, but also it destroys continuity of employment. If continuity is broken then any weeks credited to the employee are cancelled and the employee has to start from week one

---

399. S. Henry, *Private Justice*, London, 1983; K. Williams, 'Unfair dismissal, myths and statistics', ILJ 12 (1983) 157. The available evidence indicates that the introduction of statutory protection has not, in fact, reduced the level of strikes over dismissal: see Dickens, *op. cit.*, pp. 224–232.
400. Evans *et al.*, *op. cit.*, pp. 33–35.
401. *Ibid.*, pp. 35–40.

again when he or she resumes work. There is a presumption that employment is continuous and it is for the employer to produce evidence to rebut this presumption. It is necessary for the written statement of employment terms to include particulars of any period of continuity of employment with a previous employer which counts as a period of employment with the present employer. The effect of such a statement may be to prevent an employer contending that a change of employer had broken continuity.

298. There are two main exceptions to the general rule. First, there are certain weeks which do not count as a period of employment but which do not break continuity. These are weeks during any part of which the employee took part in a strike or was absent from work because of a lock-out, where the employee worked abroad or where the employee was on military service. Secondly, there are weeks during which there was no contract in existence but the employee is still entitled to have counted as periods of employment and treated as not breaking continuity. These are weeks during all or part of which the employee is absent because of sickness or injury, or a temporary cessation of work,[402] or by arrangement or custom he or she is regarded as continuing in the employment, or because of pregnancy or confinement. Where an employee is absent for a continuous period of more than 26 weeks because of sickness or injury, this will not break continuity. But only the first 26 weeks will count.

§3. Acquired Rights on Transfer of Undertakings

299. Changes in the control of an undertaking may have a significant effect on the job security of employees.[403] This was recognized by the European Community when it made provision for the protection of employees in the event of change of employer by means of the Acquired Rights Directive, first adopted in 1977 (77/187) and repealed and replaced in 2001 by the Acquired Rights Directive 2001.[404] This was originally put into effect in UK domestic law by means of the Transfer of Undertakings (Protection of Employment) Regulations 1981, then 2006 (TUPE), as amended by the Collective Redundancies and Transfer of Undertakings (Protection of Employment) (Amendment) Regulations 2014.[405] It should be stressed at the outset that these provisions do not cover the most common form of takeover in Britain, namely the transfer of share capital. In such cases, shares in the company which is the formal employer become vested in an acquiring company of which it becomes a subsidiary; or the shares may be taken over by the shareholders of the acquiring company; or the undertaking may be managed by the acquiring company while the

402. E.g. where a teacher was engaged on a series of fixed-term contracts for the academic session (October to June), it was held that the interval between contracts was a 'temporary cessation of work': *Ford* v. *Warwickshire CC* [1983] 2 AC 71 (HL).

403. See S. Hardy, *Understanding TUPE* (Oxford, 2001); S. Hardy, *et al.*, *TUPE 2006* (London, 4th edn, 2013). J. McMullen, 'An analysis of the TUPE Regulations 2006', ILJ 25 (2006), pp. 113–139.

404. OJ L61/26, 5 March 1977, as amended by Directive 98/50 of 29 June 1998, OJ 1998, L201/88, as consolidated by Directive 01/23.

405. SI 1981 1794, as amended. In force on 31 January 2014,

undertaking remains nominally the property of the company taken over. In these cases the identity of the employer, for purposes of the collective agreement and the contract of employment, remains the same. But the repercussions for trade unions and employees may be considerable.

At present, labour law provides no protection in these circumstances except where they involve 'hiving down' in the sale of an insolvent company. However, if the takeover, merger or amalgamation takes the less usual form of acquisition of the ownership of the undertaking in a way that there is a change of the identity of the employer, then the acquired rights legislation provides some protection for employees. The statutory rules aim to overcome the inadequacy of the common law according to which a change of employer terminates the contract of employment and the new employer does not automatically succeed to the old employer's rights and obligations.[406]

300. The 1977 directive was subsequently amended by Directive 98/59/EC and both directives have now been consolidated into Council Directive 2001/23/EC, whose provisions are quoted in the text below. The original directive was transposed into domestic law by the Transfer of Undertakings (Protection of Employment) Regulations 1981 (as amended). The 2001 directive has been transposed into UK Law by the Transfer of Undertakings (Protection of Employment) Regulations 2006,[407] which came into effect on 6 April 2006, as amended in 2014.

301. The provisions of the Consolidation Directive (Directive 2001/23); Article 1(1)(a) of the Directive states that it is to apply to 'any transfer of an undertaking, business or part of an undertaking or business to another employer as a result of a legal transfer or merger.' Article 1(1) goes on to state:

> (b) … there is a transfer within the meaning of this Directive where there is a transfer of an economic entity which retains its identity, meaning an organized grouping of resources which has the objective of pursuing an economic activity, whether or not that activity is central or ancillary.
>
> (c) This Directive shall apply to public and private undertakings engaged in economic activities whether or not they are operating for gain.

Article 3 provides for the automatic transfer to the transferee of the transferor's rights and obligations arising from a contract of employment or from an employment relationship existing on the date of the transfer. In *CELTEC Ltd* v. *Astley* (2005)[408] the ECJ said that the phrase 'date of a transfer' is a particular point in time which cannot be postponed to another date at the will of the transferor or transferee and is the date on which responsibility as employer for carrying on the business of the unit transferred moved from the transferor to the transferee. It went on to hold that, for the purposes of applying Article 3(1), contracts of employment or employment relationships existing on the date of the transfer, as so defined, are deemed to

---

406. *Nokes* v. *Doncaster Amalgamated Collieries Ltd* [1940] AC 1014 (HL).
407. SI 2006/246.
408. *CELTEC* v. *Astley* [2006] HR 992, HL.

be handed over on that date, regardless of what has been agreed between the parties. Article 4(1) (as substituted) states:

The transfer of the undertaking, business or part of the undertaking or business shall not in itself constitute grounds for dismissal by the transferor or the transferee. This provision shall not stand in the way of dismissals that may take place for economic, technical or organizational reasons entailing changes in the work force.

Article 4(2) goes on to provide that if the contract of employment or the employment relationship is terminated because the transfer involves a substantial change in working conditions to the detriment of the employee, the employer is to be regarded as having been responsible for the termination.

302. The question is important since it relates to the coverage of the Directive and the sorts of transfers which are embraced by it. In *Allen* v. *Amalgamated Construction Co. Ltd* (2000) the Court said:

> It is ... clear that the Directive is intended to cover any legal change in the person of the employer ... and ... it can, therefore, apply to a transfer between two subsidiary companies in the same group, which are distinct legal persons each with specific employment relationships with their employees. The fact that the companies in question not only have the same ownership but also the same management and the same premises and that they are engaged in the same works makes no difference in this regard.

Thus a transfer between subsidiary companies in the same corporate group is covered by the directive.

303. The final case to consider in this context is the most recent decision of the ECJ, the case of *Abler* v. *Sodexho MM Catering Gesellschaft mbH and Sanrest Großküchen Betribsgesellschaft mbH* (2004).[409] The case involved a transfer of catering services, after a tendering process, to Sodexho. It refused to take over the materials, stock and employees of the previous contractor, Sanrest. The ECJ said that in a sector such as catering, where the activity is based essentially on equipment, the failure of a new contractor to take over an essential part of the staff which the predecessor contractor employed to perform the same activity is not sufficient to preclude the existence of a transfer of an entity which retains its identity within the meaning of the directive, whose main objective is to ensure the continuity, even against the wishes of the transferee, of the employment contracts of the employees of the transferor. The Court said that catering could not be regarded as an activity based essentially on manpower since it requires a significant amount of equipment. Thus, the transfer of the premises and the equipment provided by the hospital was sufficient to make this a transfer of an economic entity. The Court added that the fact that the tangible assets taken over by the new contractor did not belong to its predecessor but were provided by the contracting authority could not preclude the

409. *Abler.* v *Sodexho MM Catering GmB* [2004] 1RCR 168, ECJ.

existence of a transfer, since it was clear that the directive applied whenever there was a change in the legal or natural person who was responsible for carrying on the business. See also *Temco Service Industries SA* v. *Imzilyen* (2002),[410] in which the ECJ held that there may be a transfer where the transferor is a sub-contractor of the original contractor.

304. In reg. 3 of the TUPE 2006 Regulations (which is headed 'A relevant transfer') two situations are treated as relevant transfers. The first is similar to the one found in the 1981 Regulations. Regulation 3(1)(a) of the 2006 Regulations defines this first type of transfer as:

a transfer of an undertaking, business or part of an undertaking or business situated immediately before the transfer in the United Kingdom to another person where there is a transfer of an economic entity which retains its identity.

Regulation 3(2) defines the phrase 'economic entity'; this is considered in the next section, in the context of the discussion of the meaning of the words 'undertaking' and 'business'.

305. The second type of relevant transfer is what is called 'a service provision change'; it is defined in regulation 3(1)(b) as a situation in which:

(i) activities cease to be carried out by a person ('a client') on his own behalf and are carried out instead by another person on the client's behalf ('a contractor');
(ii) activities cease to be carried out by a contractor on a client's behalf (whether or not those activities had previously been carried out by the client on his own behalf) and are carried out instead by another person ('a subsequent contractor') on the client's behalf; or
(iii) activities cease to be carried out by a contractor or a subsequent contractor on a client's behalf (whether or not those activities had previously been carried out by the client on his own behalf) and are carried out instead by the client on his own behalf.

The conditions set out in regulation 3(3) must also be satisfied. These are:

(a) immediately before the service provision change –
    (i) there is an organized grouping of employees situated in Great Britain which has as its principal purpose the carrying out of the activities concerned on behalf of the client;
    (ii) the client intends that the activities will, following the service provision change, be carried out by the transferee other than in connection with a single specific event or task of short-term duration; and
(b) the activities concerned do not consist wholly or mainly of the supply of goods for the client's use.

410. *Temco Service Identities SA* v. *Imzilyen* [2002] IRLR 214, ECJ.

306. The following points should be noted here:

- there must be 'an organized grouping of employees';
- such a grouping may consist of one person only;
- these provisions do not apply to situations where a contractor is engaged to organize a single specific event or task and the event or task is of short-term duration;
- the provisions do not apply where a client engages a contractor to supply goods for the client's use.

The above provisions are intended to apply to three situations: (1) contracting out or 'out-sourcing'; (2) assignment of a contract to a new contractor on subsequent retendering; and (3) contracting in or 'insourcing', i.e. where a contract with an outside contractor ends and the service is brought back 'in house' by the former client.

In all cases, however, there must be 'an organized grouping of employees ... which has as its principal purpose the carrying out of the activities concerned on behalf of the client'. This is intended to confine the coverage of the regulations to cases where the transferor has in place a team of employees dedicated to carrying out the activities that are to transfer and would exclude cases where there was no identifiable grouping of employees.

307. The starting-point of any discussion of whether there has been a transfer of an undertaking is the ECJ decisions in *Süzen* v. *Zehnacker Gebdudereinigung GmbH Krankenhausservice, Lefarth GmbH (Party joined)* (1997) and *Sánchez Hidalgo* v. *Asociacion de Servicios ASER* (1999). Following this decision was the EAT decision in *RCO Support Services and Aintree Hospital Trust* v. *UNISON* (2002), which was upheld by the Court of Appeal. The case involved cleaners and caterers. The cleaners were employed by Initial Hospital Services Ltd at Walton Hospital, one of two hospitals run by the Aintree Hospitals NHS Trust. Initial tendered for the cleaning contract at Fazakerley, the other hospital run by the Trust, but it was won by RCO. None of the Walton cleaners applied for jobs with RCO and none were taken on. Subsequently the employment of cleaners at Walton ended and a number of them brought unfair dismissal proceedings. The catering staff were employed at Walton by the Trust itself. Three of the support staff were dismissed for redundancy. Applications were invited by RCO, who held the catering contract at Fazakerley. One applicant was not offered a job and another declined the job offered to her. The ET held that there was a relevant transfer from Initial to RCO in respect of the cleaners and from the Trust to RCO in respect of the caterers. The EAT dismissed the appeals. They said that the absence of movement of significant assets or of a major part of the workforce does not necessarily deny the existence of a relevant transfer and expressed the view that *Süzen* can no longer be safely relied upon. The Court of Appeal upheld the EAT's decision, favouring the approach taken by the Court of Appeal in *ECM* over that taken by the earlier CA in *Betts* v. *Brintel*. The Court of Appeal's decision signals a preference for the *Spijkers* approach. Mummery LJ, with whom the other two members of the Court agreed, said that the mere fact that a putative transferee carries on the same activities or supplies the same services as the putative transferor is not by itself determinative in favour of a transfer, nor does it by itself support a conclusion that an entity retains its identity.

Similarly, the fact that none of the workforce is taken on is not necessarily conclusive on the issue of retention of identity. He said that these matters are all factors to be considered in making an overall assessment of all the facts characterizing the transaction, with no single factor being considered in isolation.

308. The regulations are only triggered if there has been an 'undertaking' which has been 'transferred'. It is therefore helpful to decide first whether there is an undertaking and second whether it has been transferred.[411] There was at first an attempt to exclude non-commercial undertakings; but it is clear now that an undertaking includes any stable economic entity whose activity is not limited to performing one specific works contract. The rise in service industries, and the growing tendency to 'out-source' or contract out labour intensive activities has prompted the ECJ to hold that an undertaking need not necessarily have significant assets, tangible or intangible, provided that it is sufficiently structured and autonomous. This means that in sectors such as cleaning and surveillance, where assets are reduced their most basic and the activity is essentially based on manpower, it is still possible to demarcate an 'undertaking' for these purposes.[412] Indeed, an organized grouping of wage-earners who are specifically and permanently assigned to a common task may mount to an economic entity. The question of whether the undertaking has been transferred is even more complex and controversial, particularly in cases in which a contract has been assigned first to one contractor and subsequently to another.

According to the directive, a transfer is included where 'there is a transfer of an economic entity which retains its identity'.[413] Case-law has held that an entity retains its identity if its operation is actually continued or resumed. This is more difficult to ascertain in a labour-intensive sector. It has therefore been held that an entity is capable of maintaining its identity where the new employer does not merely pursue the activity in question, but takes over a major part of the employees assigned by the previous employer to that task. This principle has led to the particularly influential but controversial decision in *Suzen*.[414] This case held that the directive does not apply if there is no transfer of significant tangible or intangible assets or taking over by the new employer of a major part of the workforce assigned by its predecessor to the task in question. This would mean that if a local authority contracted out its cleaning services to one undertaker, and subsequently, on the termination of the first contract, hired a new contractor, there would be no transfer if the new contractor did not take on any of the existing staff. This appears to act as an incentive to the second undertaker to refuse to hire existing staff, counteracting the very purpose of the directive. The British Employment Appeal Tribunal has, however, emphasized, that it is wrong to consider any particular factor in isolation. Thus it is necessary to consider such factors as the type of undertaking, whether or not its tangible assets are transferred, the value of its intangible assets at the time of transfer, whether or not the majority of employees are taken over by the new

411. This paragraph follows the helpful guidance given by Lindsay P. in *Cheesman* v. *Brewer Contracts* [2001] IRLR 144 EAT.
412. *Sanchez Hidalgo* Case C-173/96 [1999] IRLR 136 ECJ; *Francisco Hernandez Vidal SA* Case C-127/96 [1999] IRLR 132 ECJ.
413. Acquired Rights Directive Article 1(a).
414. *Suzen* Case C-13/95 [1997] IRLR 255 ECJ.

company, whether or not its customers are transferred, and the degree of similarity between the activities carried on before and after the transfer.[415]

However, the question of whether there has been a transfer is far from settled. In a very recent ECJ case, involving a change of bus contractor, it was held that the fact that the majority of existing drivers were re-engaged by the new operators was not sufficient to establish a transfer because no tangible assets, such as the buses themselves, were transferred.[416] This seems to give unnecessary weight to a single factor, regardless of the other factors, such as the similarity of customers and the transfer of employees.

309. The Regulations provide that collective agreements existing at the time of transfer shall continue in force after the transfer as if made with the transferee, and also that trade union recognition is transferred provided that the undertaking retains a distinct identity under the new employer.[417] These provisions, modelled on the EC directive, do not generally provide any *legal* safeguard in the British context because of the general presumption that collective agreements are not intended by the parties to be legally enforceable contracts, although they will bite where there is statutory recognition or where the agreements are legally enforceable. More important are the duties imposed by the regulations to inform and consult with recognized trade unions.[418] The duty to inform trade union representatives of the fact and timing of the transfer, the 'legal, economic and social implications' and the measures envisaged, rests on both the transferor and the transferee in relation to any employee who may be affected by the transfer, whether or not a union member, and whether or not employed in the undertaking or the part to be transferred. The duty to consult also rests upon both the transferor and the transferee. The remedy for a breach of these obligations is by way of complaint to an employment tribunal. Where the union's complaint is well-founded the tribunal must make a declaration and may award 'just and equitable compensation' to affected employees. If this is not paid the employee, not the union, must present a further complaint and the tribunal may then order the employer to pay the amount. The maximum award is £500 in respect of any employee.

§4. Methods of Termination of Employment

310. Every employee, with certain exceptions set out below, has the right not to be unfairly dismissed by his or her employer. At the first stage it must be established that the employee was 'dismissed'. This means either (1) termination of the contract by the employer; (2) expiry without renewal of a fixed term contract; or (3) 'constructive dismissal'. Once this has been established, the employer must then show the reason (or if there was more than one, the principal reason) for the dismissal. The third stage involves determining whether the dismissal for the reason given is unfair. Some reasons are automatically unfair; while others are only unfair

415. *Cheesman* above note 1.
416. *Oy Likenne Ab* v. *Liskajarvi* Case C-172/99 [2001] IRLR 171.
417. Regs. 5 and 6.
418. Regs. 13–16.

if the tribunal is not satisfied that the employer acted reasonably in treating the nominated reason as a sufficient reason for dismissal.

I. Frustration

311. The contract of employment is regarded as essentially personal in nature and so some events lead automatically to its termination, for example the death of the employer, the dissolution of a partnership, or an order for the compulsory winding up of a company. There is also a broad general principle of frustration (supervening impossibility of performance). Under this principle, if a change of circumstances makes performance of the contract unlawful, or physically impossible, or its objects incapable of achievement, the contract will be automatically brought to an end, without the need for dismissal by the employer or resignation by the employee. The effect of a finding of frustration is serious: for the purposes of the unfair dismissal legislation, an employee is not treated as dismissed, and therefore cannot claim compensation regardless of the reasonableness or otherwise of the dismissal. Similarly, no redundancy compensation can be claimed, unless the frustrating event relates to the employer, not the employees. The two most common instances of frustration occur in relation to illness or imprisonment of the employee.

A number of important principles in this respect have been formulated by the courts.[419] Factors which may help to decide the issue include the length of previous employment, how long it had been expected that the employment would continue, the nature of the job, the nature, length and effect of the illness or disabling event, together with the prospects of recovery, the need of the employer for the work to be done, the risk to employer of acquiring obligations to the replacement employee, whether wages have continued to be paid, the acts and statements of the employer, including contractual provisions for sickness pay, and whether in all the circumstances a reasonable employer could be expected to wait any longer. In recognition of the seriousness of the consequences of a finding of frustration, the court should guard against too easy an application of the doctrine, especially in the context of redundancy. However, a suggestion that frustration should never operate where a periodic contract was terminable by short notice has been rejected by the Court of Appeal. Where the employee had become incapacitated from ever again performing his or her contract of employment, the doctrine of frustration could terminate the contract before notice of its termination, and the employer was not obliged to pay the employee in respect of any period of notice, nor to defend the dismissal on the basis of reasonableness.[420] A sentence of imprisonment may amount to a frustrating event if it renders the performance of the contract impossible or radically different from that which the parties contemplated. In this situation, the employee cannot argue that he or she has repudiated the contract, and that the employer's acceptance

419. *Egg Stores (Stanford Hill) Ltd* v. *Leibovici* [1976] IRLR 376, *Notcutt* v. *Universal Equipment* [1986] ICR 414, *FC Shepherd Ltd* v. *Jerrom* [1986] ICR 802, *Williams* v. *Watsons Luxury Coaches* [1990] IRLR 164.

420. *Notcutt* v. *Universal Equipment* [1986] ICR 414.

of that repudiation amounts to a dismissal for the purposes of the law of unfair dismissal: an employee cannot rely on his or her own fault.[421]

II. By Agreement

312. The parties may agree that the contract is to last (i) for a limited period of time; or (ii) until the happening of an uncertain event (e.g. until war is declared); or (iii) until the happening of a certain event, the time of which is uncertain (e.g. for the life of the sovereign); or (iv) to perform a specific task (e.g. deliver a course of lectures, or chop down a tree) where the time of completion is uncertain. Certain statutory rights (e.g. to guarantee and medical suspension payments) do not apply to employment under a contract for a fixed term of three months or less, unless the employee can show three months' continuity. An employee whose contract is for a fixed term of two years or more may agree in writing to exclude any right to a redundancy payment.[422] A similar provision under which an employee could waive unfair dismissal rights in respect of fixed term contacts for one year or more was rightly perceived as opening short term workers to the risk of exploitation and abolished in 1999.[423] The Court of Appeal has held that a contract for a fixed term covers only category (i) above, that is for a specified stated time; this is the case even if the contract is determinable by notice within that term.[424] The statutory definition of dismissal[425] includes, where the contract is for a fixed term, the expiry of the term without its being renewed under the same contract. Since this does not cover contracts in categories (ii), (iii) and (iv) above, persons in those categories have no grounds to complain of unfair dismissal or to claim redundancy payments when the event occurs or the task is completed.[426] Some difficulty has arisen where employer and employee agree that the employment will end automatically if the employee fails to fulfil a condition (e.g. that the employee return from extended leave by a given date). A series of earlier cases held that this would be an agreed termination rather than a termination by the employer if the condition was clear and the employee could be shown to have genuinely agreed.[427] However, the courts are reluctant to uphold agreements which affect employee's statutory rights. In an important case, it was held that if the agreement had the effect of limiting the statutory right not to be unfairly dismissed, it fell foul of Section 203(1) of the Employment Rights Act 1996, which declares that any provision in an agreement will be void insofar as it purports to exclude or limit the operation of any provision of the Act or to preclude any person from presenting a complaint under the Act to an employment tribunal.[428] This was an important recognition of the inequality of bargaining power of employer and employee in these contexts.

---

421. *FC Shepherd* v. *Jerrom* [1986] ICR 802. See R. Fentiman, 'Frustration of Contracts of Employment' (1986) 15 ILJ 54.
422. ERA 1996, s. 197(3).
423. EPCA 1978, s. 142(1), revoked by ERA 1999, s. 18 from 25 October 1999.
424. *Dixon* v. *BBC* [1979] ICR 282 (CA).
425. ERA 1996, ss. 95(1), 136(1).
426. *Wiltshire County Council* v. *NATFHE* [1980] ICR 455 (CA).
427. *British Leyland UK Ltd* v. *Ashraf* [1978] ICR 979 (EAT); *Midland Electrical Engineering* v. *Kanji* [1980] IRLR 185 (EAT); *Tracey* v. *Zest Equipment Co. Ltd* [1982] ICR 481 (EAT).
428. *Igbo* v. *Johnson. Matthey Chemicals Ltd* [1986] ICR 505.

III. Dismissal by Employer with Notice

313. An employee is treated as 'dismissed' for the purposes of unfair dismissal and redundancy law, if the contract under which he or she is employed by the employer is terminated by the employer, whether it is so terminated by notice or without notice. At common law, the employer is entitled to terminate a contract for an indefinite period by giving a reasonable period of notice. The parties may expressly limit the right of either side to terminate by notice except for specified reasons. For example, the contract may be stated to be one 'until reaching the retirement age' or 'for life' or 'permanent and pensionable'. In such cases it may not be terminated by notice.

314. Where the length of notice is not specified by the contract expressly or by custom, then the length of a reasonable period of notice depends upon all the circumstances. Among relevant factors are the employee's status, the nature of the job and the general character of the services to be rendered. The frequency of payment (e.g. weekly or monthly) may be a convenient guide but this is not conclusive. These common law rules are now subject to the provisions of Section 86 of the Employment Rights Act 1996 which lays down the following minimum periods of notice:

- one week to a person continuously employed for between one month and 2 years;
- one week for each year of continuous employment, to a person continuously employed for 2 years or more but less than 12 years;
- twelve weeks to a person continuously employed for 12 years or more.

The notice period will not commence until the dismissed employee has been given a 'reasonable opportunity' to read the dismissal letter.[429] The employee may accept payment of wages in lieu of notice, or may waive his or her right to notice, but the provision in a contract of employment for shorter periods of notice than those laid down in the Act is ineffective.

315. The Act of 1996 also guarantees the employee's income during the statutory minimum notice period. The detailed rules are set out in Sections 87 to 91 of the Act.

316. In *Rai* v. *Somerfield Stores Ltd* (2004), the EAT said that a notice which enables an employer to terminate an employee's contract of employment only if the employee does or does not perform a particular act specified in the notice which only the employee can choose whether or not to perform is not an unequivocal notice to terminate the employment. In the case in question the employee was told that if he did not return to work by a specified date his contract would be regarded as terminated. The EAT said that this did not amount to a dismissal with notice. A final point to be noted here is that a dismissal with notice may be converted into a

429. *Gisda Cyf* v. *Barratt* [2010] UKSC 41.

summary dismissal if the employer dismisses the employee on the spot during his or her notice period. Such an action would amount to a wrongful dismissal.

IV. Dismissal by Employer without Notice

317. At common law, an employer is entitled to dismiss an employee summarily, that is without notice, if the employee has disregarded an essential term of the contract. This is an area of law in which old cases are of little assistance because of changing judicial attitudes. Early decisions were often not concerned with the rights of 'master' and 'servant' but with the question which arose under the Poor Laws as to whether a particular community was legally obliged to provide aid to a destitute person because he or she had acquired a settlement by virtue of having been employed there for a certain period. Other decisions, before 1867, arose under the criminal law of desertion. Modern cases have moved towards the general principles of repudiatory breach in contract law, by stressing factors such as whether an important term of the contract has been broken, whether the employee's actions have undermined mutual confidence, and whether the employee has a reasonable excuse for his or her conduct. Each case depends on its own circumstances. The contract is terminated not by the employee's repudiatory conduct, but by the employer's act in accepting that repudiation.[430] Dismissal by the employer without notice is treated as a dismissal for the purposes of the statutory law of unfair dismissal. This is the case even if the employer is entitled to dismiss at common law. However, the dismissal is not necessarily unfair.

V. Variation of Contract Distinguished from Dismissal

318. In some situations the employer may introduce changes in working conditions, either with or without notice, which affect the employee adversely. At common law, if the employee consents either expressly or impliedly to such a change in terms this is called a 'consensual variation' and the employee may not then complain that he or she has been 'dismissed'. However, the courts will 'be slow to find that there has been a consensual variation where the employee has been faced with the alternative of dismissal and where the variation has been adverse to his interest'.[431] If there has been no consent, the employee may have an action for breach of contract. Employers have on occasion attempted to circumvent the need for consent by arguing that the change in working conditions was not a variation at all but notice terminating employment and offering re-employment on new terms. However, it has been held that a termination by notice will not readily be implied in such circumstances.[432] It has also been argued that consent to a variation can be implied from

430. *London Transport Executive* v. *Clarke* [1981] ICR 334 (CA) *Rigby* v. *Ferodo* [1988] ICR 29, *Dietman* v. *London Borough of Brent* [1988] IRLR 299.
431. *Sheet Metal Components Ltd* v. *Plumridge* [1974] ICR 373. Unilateral withdrawal by the employer from a collective agreement is not a variation unless the employee consents.
432. *Burdett-Coutts* v. *Hertfordshire County Council* [1984] IRLR 91.

the fact that an employee has continued to work under the changed terms. Again, the courts have been reluctant to imply consent from conduct too readily. Provided that employees make it abundantly clear that they are not willing to accept the new terms, the fact that they have remained in their posts does not amount to consent.[433] The situation is somewhat different in respect of the statutory right to unfair dismissal. Whereas at common law, the employer will try to show a dismissal with notice and re-employment on new terms, under the statute it is the employee who wishes to show that the variation has amounted to a dismissal for the purposes of the statutory remedy. The courts have been generally sympathetic to this claim, making it clear more than once that they dislike an attempt by an employer to make 'use of the employee's willingness to work, and to work for a lower wage' as a means of avoiding 'dismissal' and resultant liability for a redundancy payment or unfair dismissal. Thus, courts have accepted the argument that a unilateral variation of contract terms may be challenged under unfair dismissal legislation where the employee continues working, so long as the variation is enough to amount to termination of the old contract and replacement by a new one.[434]

319. Due to this difficulty, employees have been given a statutory right in respect of claims for redundancy payments to a month's trial period in any changed terms of employment. This means that a claim for redundancy can still be made if the employment is terminated during the trial period. But in unfair dismissal cases (and in redundancy cases where the employee has stayed in the changed job for more than one month) the employees may lose the right to claim that they were 'dismissed' if they do not make it clear that they are working under protest, or if they continue for a long time in the changed job.

VI. Termination by the Employee

320. At common law the employee may terminate the contract by giving the agreed notice, or where no period is specified by giving reasonable notice, depending on the circumstances. Under the Employment Rights Act 1996 the statutory minimum period of notice which an employee must give after continuous employment of one month or more is one week. In some employments the period required by contract is much longer.

321. At common law, the employee is entitled to terminate the contract without notice if the employer breaks a fundamental term of the contract. This is the reverse of the situation in which the employer is entitled to dismiss the employee summarily. Unilateral changes in the contract by the employer will amount to a repudiation of the employer's fundamental obligations only if they go to the basis of the contract; for example by reducing the employee's pay, suspending the employee without pay where the contract does not provide for this, making drastic changes in the working hours, forcing an employee to join a trade union, requiring an employee

433. *Rigby* v. *Ferodo* [1987] IRLR 516 (HL), *Burdett-Coutts* above.
434. *Hogg* v. *Dover College* [1990] ICR 39; *Alcan Extrusions* v. *Yates* [1996] IRLR 327.

to work under unsafe conditions or forcing him or her to hand in his or her resignation. Sexual harassment will also amount to a repudiatory breach.[435] Generally speaking, changes made as a result of collective agreements will not amount to a repudiation of contract by the employer unless the terms of that agreement cannot be said to have been incorporated into the individual employment contract. For example, where employees have resigned from a union and have made it clear that they will not accept terms of employment negotiated after their resignation, it may be that freshly negotiated terms are not binding on them.[436]

322. The main importance of these common law rules is that the employee may claim that he or she has been dismissed for the purposes of unfair dismissal and redundancy law if he or she terminates his or her contract, with or without notice, in circumstances such that he or she is entitled to terminate it at common law without notice. This is popularly known as 'constructive dismissal'. The test is whether the employer has repudiated the contract.[437] It should be stressed that a constructive dismissal is not necessarily unfair.

§5. Reasons for Dismissal and References

323. At common law, an employer is not required to give any reason for dismissal. Moreover, if the employee brings an action for damages for wrongful dismissal the employer is entitled to justify the dismissal by proving reasons which were not known to him or her at the time of the original dismissal.[438]

324. Both these common law rules have now been modified by legislation. An employee who has 12 months' continuous employment is entitled, under Section 92 of the Employment Rights Act 1996 to be provided by his or her employer within 14 days of his or her so requesting 'a written statement giving the particulars of the reasons for the employee's dismissal'. There is no requirement for a period of continuous employment where the employee is pregnant or on maternity leave; and reasons must be given regardless of whether she requests them. If the employer 'unreasonably refuses' an employment tribunal shall award the employee a sum equivalent to two weeks' pay. The written statement of reasons is admissible in unfair dismissal and other proceedings. The common law rule regarding subsequently discovered misconduct does not apply to proceedings for unfair dismissal, in which the employer may rely only on those facts which were known to him or her at the time of dismissal.[439]

325. There is no obligation on an employer to provide an employee with a character reference. If the employer does provide a reference he or she must take care

435. *Bracebridge Engineering Ltd* v. *Darby* [1990] IRLR 3.
436. *Singh* v. *British Steel Corporation* [1974] IRLR 131; cf. *Land* v. *West Yorkshire CC* [1979] ICR 452.
437. *Western Excavating (ECC) Ltd* v. *Sharp* [1978] ICR 221 (CA).
438. *Boston Deep Sea Fishing Co.* v. *Ansell* (1888) 39 Ch. D. 339.
439. *W. Devis & Sons* v. *Atkins* [1977] ICR 662 (HL).

not to say anything defamatory, deceitful or without reasonable care as to its accuracy.[440] An employer may not refer to certain spent convictions of a rehabilitated offender or to any circumstances ancillary to those convictions.[441] An additional remedy is now provided by Section 13 of the Data Protection Act 1998, which gives an employee the right to claim compensation in respect of data which are factually inaccurate, provided he or she has suffered damage because of the inaccuracy of the data. This would apply to an action in respect of an inaccurate reference based on any information stored by the employer. The employee may also be able to have the inaccurate data rectified or deleted.

§6. Remedies for Wrongful Dismissal

326. The concept of 'wrongful dismissal' is applied to any dismissal where the employer, not being entitled at common law to terminate the contract summarily, fails to give the period of notice required by law. The employee's sole remedy will usually be a claim for damages in the county court or the High Court. The measure of damages for wrongful dismissal will normally be the remuneration which the employee has lost by not being given the requisite period of notice. Damages are not awarded for hurt feelings, or for the manner in which the dismissal took place[442] or, traditionally, for the fact that dismissal made it more difficult to find alternative employment. The House of Lords has recently reaffirmed that an employee cannot recover damages for psychiatric damage caused by the manner of dismissal (e.g. in breach of fair procedure).[443] The damages are awarded net of tax and social security contributions and subject to deduction of certain other benefits received, such as wages earned in an alternative employment, jobseekers' allowance and supplementary benefits.[444] The employee is under a duty to mitigate his or her loss by taking reasonable steps to find alternative employment and by claiming such benefits as he is entitled to.

327. In general, the courts will not order specific performance of a contract of employment. The accepted rationale for this is that to compel performance of a contract of employment is inconsistent with the principle that the relationship depends on mutual confidence.[445] This means that the most effective remedy for a wrongful dismissal, namely reinstatement, is in general denied to the employee. Although similar principles apply to injunctions restraining the employer from acting in

---

440. *Lawton* v. *BOC Transhield Ltd* [1987] ICR 7; *Spring* v. *Guardian Assurance plc.* [1994] ICR 596.
441. Rehabilitation of Offenders Act 1974, s. 4(4). There are detailed rules as to when a conviction becomes 'spent'.
442. *Addis* v. *Gramophone Co.* [1909] AC 488 (House of Lords); *Bliss* v. *South East Thames RHA* [1985] IRLR 308 (CA); *Dunnachie* v. *Kingston-upon-Hull* [2004] UKHL 36.
443. *Johnson* v. *Unisys Ltd* [2001] IRLR 279, distinguishing *Malik* v. *BCCI SA* [1997] IRLR 462 where damages were awarded for breach of a duty of trust and confidence; see too *BCCI SA* v. *Ali (No. 3)* [1999] IRLR 508 and *Eastwood* v. *Magnox Electric* [2004] UKHL 35.
444. *Lincoln* v. *Hayman* [1984] 2 All ER 819.
445. *Hill* v. *Parsons* [1972] 1 Ch. 305; *Chappell* v. *Times Newspapers Ltd* [1975] ICR 145 at pp. 173, 176, 178.

breach of contract, the courts have recently evinced a greater willingness to grant injunctions.[446] This is particularly so when a dismissal has taken place in breach of a contractual disciplinary procedure, and an application is made for an interim injunction in interlocutory proceedings pending the full trial. In general, the courts will only grant an injunction if damages are inadequate]and complete confidence in the relationship has been maintained. Injunctions are more likely to be granted where the employer is a large company or public authority, since it is more likely that confidence will be maintained in such a situation than in the case of a small business or partnership. The requirement that confidence be maintained may, however, be relaxed where the plaintiff does not demand full reinstatement, but merely wishes to be suspended on full pay while internal disciplinary proceedings are taking place.[447] An injunction will only be granted if the contractual relationship remains alive. This puts great emphasis on the question of when a repudiatory breach by an employer will effectively terminate the contract. Several cases have held that ordinary contractual principles, whereby a breach only terminates a contract if the innocent party accepts the repudiation, do not apply to the contract of employment.

Instead, it has been held that a repudiation by the employer can automatically terminated the contract.[448] If this were the case, then the contract would be at an end, and it would be futile to grant an injunction preventing the employer from terminating. However, if ordinary contractual principles do apply, as the preponderance of authority suggests they do,[449] then the contract of employment remains alive until the employee has accepted the repudiation, and an injunction can be effective. However, the court will readily infer that the employee has accepted the repudiation. Delay in bringing proceedings will be construed as acceptance, as will seeking alternative employment. Nevertheless, the availability of injunctions entails that, in a limited class of cases, the contractual remedy may be more effective than the remedies under unfair dismissal.

§7. Unfair Dismissal

328. Every employee, with certain exceptions set out below, has the right not to be unfairly dismissed by his or her employer. At the first stage it must be established that the employee was 'dismissed'. This means either (1) termination of the contract by the employer; (2) expiry without renewal of a fixed term contract; or

---

446. *Jones* v. *Lee* [1980] IRLR 67; *Irani* v. *Southampton AHA* [1985] IRLR 755; *Powell* v. *London Borough of Brent* [1987] IRLR 466 (CA); *Hughes* v. *London Borough of Southwark* [1988] IRLR 55, *Wadcock* v. *London Borough of Brent* [1990] IRLR 223.

447. *Robb* v. *London Borough of Hammersmith and Fulham* [1991].

448. *London Transport Executive* v. *Clarke* [1981] IRLR 166 *per* Denning MR; *Gunton* v. *Richmond on Thames LBC* [1980] IRLR 321 *per* Shaw LJ; *R* v. *East Berkshire AHA* [1984] IRLR 278 *per* May LJ.

449. *London Transport Executive* v. *Clarke* [1981] IRLR 166 *per* Templeman LJ; *Gunton* v. *Richmond on Thames LBC* [1980] IRLR 321 *per* Buckley LJ; *Thomas Marshall* v. *Guinle* [1978] IRLR 174 *per* Megarry VC; *Dietman* v. *Brent LBC* [1988] IRLR 299; *Burdett Coutts* v. *Hertfordshire* [1984] IRLR 91 but see *Boyo* v. *Lambeth London Borough Council* [1995] IRLR 50.

(3) 'constructive dismissal'. Once this has been established, the employer must then show the reason (or if there was more than one, the principal reason) for the dismissal. The third stage involves determining whether the dismissal for the reason given is unfair. Some reasons are automatically unfair; while others are only unfair if if the tribunal is not satisfied that the employer acted reasonably in treating the nominated reason as a sufficient reason for dismissal.

I. The Former Statutory Dispute Resolution Procedures

329. The Employment Act 2002 introduced provisions whose aim is to improve the resolution of disputes in the workplace.[450] The relevant provisions of the Act (Sections 29–33 and Sched. 2) came into force on 1 October 2004. The implementing Regulations, the Employment Act 2002 (Dispute Resolution) Regulations 2004 (SI 2004/752), came into force at the same time.

330. Section 30(1) of the 2002 Act provided that every employer and employee must comply with the requirements of the procedure in relation to any matter to which the statutory procedure applies. Sched. 2, Pts. 1 and 2 sets out the procedures which consist of (i) dismissal and disciplinary procedures and (ii) grievance procedures. Each set of procedures consists of a standard procedure and a modified procedure. The Regulations set out the situations in which the procedures apply, and the exceptions to them. It should be noted that the statutory dismissal and disciplinary procedures apply where an employer is contemplating dismissing an employee. In the case of constructive dismissals by employees, the statutory *grievance* procedures apply. Failure on the part of either the employer or the employee to observe the procedures will lead to certain consequences. In the case of the *employer*, a failure to complete the applicable procedure will mean that the dismissal is automatically unfair, provided that the non-completion of the procedure is 'wholly or mainly attributable' to the employer's failure to complete the requirements of the procedure: *see* ERA 1996, Section 98A (inserted by EA 2002, Section 34).

In addition, any award of compensation made against the employer was subject to a minimum adjustment of 10 per cent and a maximum adjustment of 50 per cent: see EA 2002, Section 31(3). The tribunal may make a lesser increase in cases where there are 'exceptional circumstances' and it considers that it would be 'unjust or inequitable' to make a smaller increase: see EA 2002, Section 31(4). A failure by the employee to complete the applicable procedure will have two consequences.

First, he or she will not be able to present a complaint of unfair dismissal to the tribunal (subject to exceptions) until the procedures have been complied with: see EA 2002 Section 32. Second, as with the employer, any award of compensation made in his or her favour by the tribunal, is liable to be reduced by a minimum of 10 per cent and a maximum of 50 per cent, again subject to the possibility of a smaller reduction in 'exceptional circumstances': see EA 2002, Section 31(2) and (4).

450. Hepple and Morris, *op. cit.*

II. The Repeal of the Disciplinary and Dismissal Procedures

331. On 6 April 2009 the technically loathsome statutory procedures were repealed under the Employment Act 2008 (cf. Sanders [2009] ILJ, vol. 38, pp. 30–49, for fuller detail and useful commentary). These were to be found in Sched. 2, Part I of the Employment Act 2002, which provided for a 'standard' and a 'modified' procedure. The standard procedure comprises three steps: (i) the statement by the employer of the grounds for action and an invitation to a meeting to discuss the matter; (ii) the meeting itself; and (iii) appeals. The modified procedure consisted of only *two* stages: (i) the statement by the employer of the grounds for action; and (ii) appeals. The difference between the two procedures lay in the nature of the statement which the employer must make.

332. The standard procedure intended to apply to all cases where the employer is contemplating dismissing, or taking 'relevant disciplinary action' against, an employee: see reg. 3(1) of the regulations. The standard procedure applied to actual dismissals and dismissals arising on the expiry of a limited-term contract: see reg. 2(1). It did not apply to constructive dismissals, since they are not included within the definition of 'dismissed' given in reg. 2(1). Thus, an employee claiming to have been constructively dismissed falls within the provisions relating to grievance procedures.

333. The modified dismissal procedure applied in the following circumstances: (a) the employer dismissed the employee by reason of his or her conduct without notice; (b) the dismissal took place at the time when the employer became aware of the conduct or immediately afterwards; (c) the employer was entitled, in the circumstances, to dismiss the employee without notice or pay in lieu of notice by reason of the conduct; and (d) it was reasonable for the employer, in the circumstances, to dismiss the employee before enquiring into the circumstances in which the conduct took place: reg. 3(2) of the regulations. In effect, the modified procedure applied where there is a summary dismissal for gross misconduct.

334. The 2004 Regulations provided for a number of situations in which the statutory procedures do not apply. If a particular case fell within one of the exceptions the effect will be that the consequences (set out above) will not apply. A dismissal and disciplinary procedure would not apply, or, if it had started, will be treated as having been complied with, where the employer or employee's failure to start or complete the procedure is for one of the following reasons:

(a) the party has reasonable grounds for believing that starting or completing the procedure would result in a significant threat to the party or their property, or any other person or their property;
(b) the party has been subjected to harassment and has reasonable grounds to believe that following the procedure would result in further harassment;
(c) it is not practicable to start or complete the procedure within a reasonable period.

335. The 2004 regulations (reg. 4) also provide that the dismissal and disciplinary procedures do not apply to the following types of dismissal, for example dismissals of a whole group of employees and dismissals of employees taking part in industrial action.

III. (Statutory) Grievance Procedures

336. As with the dismissal and disciplinary procedures, the grievance procedures were of two types: the 'standard' and the 'modified' procedure: see EA 2002, Sched. 2, paras. 6–10. Similarly, the standard procedure comprised three steps: (i) the statement of grievance by the employee, which must be sent to the employer; (ii) the meeting itself; and (iii) appeal: see EA 2002, Sched. 2, paras. 6–8. The modified procedure consisteds of only *two* stages: (i) the statement of grievance by the employee; and (ii) the employer's response: see EA 2002, Sched. 2, para. 9. It consisted in effect of an exchange of letters. In the case of the standard procedure the employee is required to set out the grievance in writing and send the statement or a copy of it to the employer.

337. Regulation 2(1) of the 2004 regulations defined 'grievance' as: 'a complaint by an employee about action which his employer has taken or is contemplating taking in relation to him.' Regulation 2(2) went on to say that, in determining whether a written communication fulfils a requirement of Sched. 2 of the 2002 Act, it is irrelevant whether it deals with any other matter. The EAT has said that it is not necessary for the employee *personally* to write the letter said to constitute the grievance and that such action may be taken on the employee's behalf by an agent, for example a solicitor: *see Warner Ltd* v. *Apsland.*[451] The question which has caused most of the problems was: what requirements are necessary for a communication written by an employer to constitute a 'grievance' for the purposes of the 2004 regulations. In *Commotion Ltd* v. *Rutty*[452] the EAT said that a letter applying for a variation of an employee's working pattern (under ERA 1996, Section 80) may fulfil the requirements of para. 2(2) provided that it sets out a grievance.

338. In the later case of *Shergold* v. *Fieldway Medical Centre* (2005) the then President of the EAT, Burton J, dealt with the above issue and other questions arising under the 2004 regulations. The facts of the case were that the employee resigned her employment and complained of unfair dismissal. Her resignation, which was with notice, was contained in a letter in which she set out at length her reasons for leaving. A meeting took place between the employee and the employer; she was advised to put in a formal grievance but her employment ended without her having done so. The EAT said that it was satisfied that the letter of resignation was sufficient to comply with Section 32 and Sched. 2 of the EA 2002. Burton J observed that the requirements of paragraph 6 of the grievance procedure are 'simple' and 'minimal' and said that the requirement 'is simply that the grievance

451. [2006] IRLR 87, EAT.
452. [2006] ICR 290, EAT.

must be set out in writing'. It followed that it may be contained within a letter of resignation. The EAT also said that it is not necessary to make it plain in the writing that it is a grievance, or is an invocation of a grievance procedure. Nor is it necessary for the employee to have complied with any company or contractual grievance procedure.

339. The 2004 Regulations provided for various situations in which the statutory procedures do not apply. A grievance procedure would not have been applied, or, if it has started, will be treated as having been complied with, where the employer or employee's failure to start or complete the procedure is for one of the following reasons:

(a) the party has reasonable grounds for believing that starting or completing the procedure would result in a significant threat to the party or their property, or any other person or their property;
(b) the party has been subjected to harassment and has reasonable grounds to believe that following the procedure would result in further harassment;
(c) it is not practicable to start or complete the procedure within a reasonable period (*see* reg. 11).

IV. Non-compliance under the Repealed Procedures

340. The Employment Act 2002 introduced provisions whose aim is to improve the resolution of disputes in the workplace. The important point for the purpose of this section is that an employee who fails to comply with the applicable procedure will not be able to present a complaint to the employment tribunal until the procedures have been complied with (subject to exceptions): *see* Section 32. In addition, any award of compensation made in his or her favour by the tribunal is liable to be reduced by a minimum.

341. Section 32 of the Act applies to unfair dismissal cases and has the effect of depriving tribunals of jurisdiction in cases where the employee is obliged to go through a grievance. So an employee who is dismissed is not affected by that provision and will be able to present a complaint immediately.

342. Decisions of the EAT concerning these provisions have now started to appear. The first requirement of Section 32 (above) has been considered in *Galaxy Showers Ltd* v. *Wilson* (2006) and *Shergold* v. *Fieldway Medical Centre* (2006). In both cases, the issue was whether the employee had raised a grievance and whether the tribunal had jurisdiction under Section 32. The EAT in both cases made it clear that a grievance may be contained in a letter of resignation. In the latter case, Burton J said that the requirements of paragraph 6 of the Dispute Resolutions Regulations are 'simple' and 'minimal'. He also said that it is not necessary to make it plain in the written document that it is a grievance or is an invocation of a grievance procedure. He drew attention to reg. 2(2) which states that it is irrelevant whether the written communication 'deals with any other matter'. It should be noted that, in both cases, the employee in question resigned with notice. It is not clear what would be the position if the employee resigned with immediate effect.

343. The second aspect of the new legislation is the extension of the time limits, which is effected by Regulation 15(1) of the Dispute Resolution Regulations. If Regulation 15 applies, the time limit will be extended by three months from the day after the day on which the limitation period would otherwise have expired. Regulation 15(1)(a) comes into play where either of the dismissal and disciplinary procedures applies and the employee presents a complaint to the tribunal after the expiry of the normal time limit 'but had reasonable grounds for believing, when the limit expired, that a dismissal or disciplinary procedure was being followed in respect of matters that consisted of or included the substance of the tribunal complaint'. In *Piscitelli* v. *Zilli Fish Ltd*[453] the EAT held that a letter seeking a cash settlement of an employee's potential unfair dismissal claim did not raise an internal appeal against his dismissal. This meant that the time for presenting a complaint of unfair dismissal was not extended by reg. 15(1) and his complaint was therefore out of time. Regulation 15(1)(b) applies to constructive dismissals, amongst other things, and comes into play where 'the circumstances specified in para. (3) apply'. These are that the employee presents a complaint to the tribunal in one of two sets of circumstances: *either* within the normal time limit but in circumstances in which Section 32(2) or (3) does not permit a complaint to be presented *or* after the expiry of the normal time limit but after compliance with the requirements of Sched. 2, para. 6 or 9 within the normal time limit.

A. The New/Old Regime Restored – the Employment Act 2008

344. Since 6 April 2009, the demise of the statutory procedures allowed for change, or as is more accurate a refined return to the former regime under the Employment Act 2008.

The Act comprises of 23 sections and is divided as follows:

- Sections 1–7 make certain changes to the law relating to dispute resolution in the workplace.
- Sections 8–12 make changes to the enforcement of the national minimum wage.
- Section 13 clarifies that CFAVs do not qualify for the NMW.
- Section 14 amends section 44 of NMWA 1998 to broaden the type of expenses that can be reimbursed to voluntary workers without triggering eligibility for the NMW.
- Sections 15–16 amend the employment agency standards enforcement regime by making offences under EAA 1973 each way offences and conferring additional inspection powers on the Employment Agency Standards Inspectorate.
- Section 18 allows officers appointed under the NMWA 1998 and officers appointed under the EAA 1973 to share information with each other for the purpose of their respective enforcement functions.

453. [2006] Unreported, 12 January, EAT.

- Section 19 amends trade union membership law to ensure UK compliance with the ruling of the European Court of Human Rights on *Aslef* v. *UK*.
- Sections 20–23 deal with general details of the Act.

Section 1 of the Act abolishes the statutory procedures. 'Dismissal' is defined in the Commencement Order by incorporating the definition in s.95(1) Employment Rights Act 1996, which provides that an employee is dismissed if the contract under which he or she is employed is terminated by the employer (whether with or without notice). That definition does not however identify *when* the employee is to be regarded as dismissed. The 'effective date of termination' is defined (in s.97) as the date of expiry of notice, where the dismissal is with notice, but that term is nowhere incorporated into the Commencement Order. Since a notice of dismissal, on a given, cannot be unilaterally withdrawn, it is clearly arguable that the giving of notice is sufficient. It is a pity that the Order has not made the position clear.

345. Broadly, the 'new law' of unfair dismissal is the old law, ie that which applied before October 2004. In all cases the appropriate test for dismissal not to be unfair, the appropriate test for dismissal not to be unfair, the employer having shown a potentially fair reason for the dismissal, will be whether the Tribunal concludes that in all the circumstances the employer acted reasonably in relying on that reason to dismiss the employee. That has both a substantive and a procedural element, and in relation to both the Tribunal must not substitute its own view but ask whether it was open to a reasonable employer to have done what the Respondent did, and in the way it was done.

Instead of statutory procedures, ACAS has produced a new Code. Consequently, before reaching its decision however, the Tribunal is required to have regard to any relevant provision in an ACAS Code of Practice:

- The Code covers both conduct and capability/performance issues, but not redundancy, or ill health dismissals.
- Rules and procedures should be specific, clear and in writing, and employees or their representatives should be involved in the development of them.
- Employers and employees should raise issues promptly and not unreasonably delay procedures, meetings etc.
- Consistency is important.
- Employers need to investigate as necessary, inform employees of issues and give them an opportunity to put their case before decisions are made (with a right to be accompanied at formal meetings) and to appeal against any formal decision.
- In misconduct cases, wherever practicable, different people should carry out the investigation and disciplinary hearing.
- If there is an investigatory meeting with the employee, the employer's procedure *may* allow accompaniment, but this is not otherwise a right.
- Suspension (with pay) should be as brief as possible, and it should be made clear it is not a disciplinary sanction.
- Notice of a disciplinary hearing should give enough information to enable the employee to prepare an answer, and copies of written evidence, including any witness statements, should normally be provided.

- Both parties should 'make every effort to attend' disciplinary meetings, as should the companion.
- At the meeting, the employee should be entitled to call relevant witnesses (having given notice of the intention to do so).
- Guidance is given on what is reasonable in relation to the employee's choice of companion.
- A first warning may be a final one if the employee's actions (or poor performance) have had or are liable to have a serious impact on the organization.
- A fair disciplinary process should 'always' be followed before dismissing for gross misconduct.
- Where the employee is persistently unable or unwilling to attend a disciplinary meeting without good cause the employer should make a decision on the evidence.
- Appeals should be heard if possible by a manager not previously involved (but there is no statement that the appeal manager need be more senior than the dismissing manager).
- Conviction of a criminal offence does not of itself normally justify disciplinary action – whether it does depends on its effect on suitability to do the job and relationship with employer, colleagues and customers.

The repeal of Section 98A(2) Employment Rights Act 1996 will restore the principle established in *Polkey* v. *A E Dayton Services Ltd* [1988] ICR 142 that if an unfair procedure has been followed, the resulting dismissal will usually be unfair, and that is that affected by the fact (if such it be) that the employee would still have been dismissed if a fair procedure had been followed.

346. However that question *is* relevant to compensation. What has become known as the *Polkey* reduction is a reduction in the compensatory award (not the basic award, which can only be reduced for compensatory fault, or offset by a redundancy payment) in some cases to nil, on the ground that the employee would or might have been dismissed had a fair procedure been followed.

This approach to compensation survived the changes under the 2002 Act, and has been applied more widely than its original area of application, redundancy cases (and most recently it has even been extended to discrimination claims: *Abbey National plc* v. *Chagger* [2009] IRLR 86). The issue has however become complicated by the presence of Section 98A(2), which reversed *Polkey* in relation to the *fairness* of dismissal, but not, in terms, its application to compensation. The complication arises from *YMCA Training Limited* v. *Stewart* [2007] IRLR 185, where the EAT held that if the employer shows that it was at least 51 per cent likely that the employee would have been dismissed anyway, the dismissal has been shown on the balance of probabilities to be *fair*.

B. Grievances

347. There will no longer be any requirement for employees to invoke the statutory grievance procedure before pursuing a Tribunal claim. However there is some encouragement to do so in the ACAS Code, which provides that 'if it is not possible to resolve a grievance informally employees *should* raise the matter formally and without unreasonable delay' and that this '*should* be done in writing and *should* set out the nature of the grievance' (para 31, emphasis added). Employees are also advised to make every effort to attend grievance meetings. An unreasonable failure to follow these precepts may lead to a reduction of up to 25 per cent in any compensation awarded.

Tribunals will have a discretion to increase or reduce compensation where:

- the claim is within the Schedule;
- it concerns a matter to which 'a relevant Code of Practice' applies; and
- the employer, or employee, as the case may be has unreasonably failed to comply with the Code.

The increase or decrease may be of up to 25 per cent of the award. Unlike the position now, it appears that this includes the basic as well as the compensatory award for unfair dismissal. The increase or decrease in the compensatory award is to be applied *before* any reduction for contributory fault, or to give credit for a redundancy payment above the statutory limit, and before the cap on an award (from 6 April 2017 this is £80,541) is applied (see on this Section 124A Employment Rights Act 1996, as amended by Section 3(4) Employment Act 2008).

As the level of increase or decrease, the Act gives no guidance. The sanction serves a similar purpose to Section 31 Employment Act 2002, so it is likely that Tribunals will rely on the guidance given by the Courts on how Section 31 should be applied. The approach of most Tribunals has been to look at the seriousness of the default, including its consequences for the employee, and such matters as whether it was deliberate, and whether the size of the organization was such that ignorance was excusable. For a complete failure to follow the relevant statutory procedure, the starting point has tended to be 50 per cent (the current maximum) but this is then often reduced by whatever factors point in favour of the employer.

V. Reasons Allowed for Dismissal

348. In order to potentially justify a dismissal, the employer must show a set of facts known to him or her, or beliefs held, at the time of dismissal which caused him or her to dismiss the employee. These facts must fall within one of the following categories:[454] (1) 'The capability or qualifications of the employee for performing work of the kind that he was employed by the employer to do' ('capability' is assessed by reference to skill, aptitude, health or any other physical or mental quality). (2) 'The conduct of the employee'. (3) The employee was 'redundant'. This concept is defined by reference to the redundancy payments legislation. (4) 'The employee could not continue to work in the position which he held without contravention (either on his part or on the part of his employer) of a duty or restriction

454. ERA 1996, ss. 98(1), 98(2) [EPCA 1978, ss. 57(1), 57(2)].

imposed by or under any enactment' (e.g. safety legislation, or a driving disqualification imposed on a lorry driver). (5) 'Some other substantial reason of a kind such as to justify the dismissal of an employee holding the position which the employee held'. The most common examples of reasons falling within this category relate to the business needs of the employer, such as refusal to agree to changes in employment terms, pressure from an important customer to dismiss the employee, the temporary nature of the employment, and an irreconcilable conflict of personalities. This last category functions merely as a filter: according to the Court of Appeal, it is designed only to deter employers from dismissing employees for a trivial or unworthy reason.[455] By statute[456] dismissal of a temporary replacement for an employee who is absent from work because of a pregnancy or confinement or medical suspension is treated as a 'substantial reason', provided fair warning of the temporary nature of the job was given to the replacement. Moreover, dismissal for an 'economic, technical or organizational reason entailing changes in the workforce of either the transferor or transferee' on the transfer of an undertaking is deemed to be a 'substantial reason'.[457] In all these cases the tribunal still has to determine whether the employer acted reasonably in all the circumstances.

349. A dismissal is not capable of giving rise to a complaint of unfairness if a certificate is produced signed by a Minister of the Crown that the dismissal was taken 'for the purpose of safeguarding national security'.[458] This does not cover dismissals unfair on the grounds of family reasons, health and safety or employee representation, and a discrimination case may still be brought under the appropriate legislation. It used to be the case that a dismissal during a strike or lock-out was automatically fair, but recent legislation has provided, for the first time, a remedy for employees dismissed while on strike (this is discussed in Part II, Ch. 5).

VI. Automatically Unfair Reasons

350. The list of reasons which render a dismissal automatically unfair has been expanded dramatically by recent legislation, and now covers: trade union membership and activities; refusal to belong to a trade union; selection for redundancy in breach of an agreed procedure; pregnancy, confinement or other family leave; assertion of statutory rights against the employer (including working time, minimum wage or tax credit rights and refusal to work on Sunday as a shop or betting worker); action as a health and safety representative, employee representative or trustee of an occupational pension scheme; dismissal in connection with a transfer of an undertaking (except where the dismissal is for an economic, technical or organizational reason); spent convictions; and whistleblowing. The inclusion of trade union membership and activities as an automatically unfair reason constitutes one of the chief means of protecting freedom of association, reinforced for the first time after

455. *Kent County Council* v. *Gilham* [1985] IRLR 18 (CA).
456. ERA 1995, s. 106 EPCA 1978, s. 61.
457. Transfer of Undertakings (Protection of Employment) Regulations 1981 (as amended 2006).
458. ERA 1995, s. 193.

October 2000 by the right to freedom of association incorporated from the European Convention of Human Rights by the Human Rights Act 1998. The right, as defined in the statute, is that it is unfair to be dismissed because the '(a) was, or proposed to become a member of an independent trade union; (b) had taken, or proposed to take, part in the activities of an independent trade union at an appropriate time, or (c) was not a member of any trade union, or of a particular trade union, or of one of a number of particular trade unions or had refused, or proposed to refuse, to become or remain a member.'[459]

The definition of an 'appropriate time' envisages that an employee may participate outside working hours off the employer's premises, or on the premises while there with the express or implied permission of the employer (e.g. during meal breaks) but while not actually at work. The right to participate during working hours depends on the employer's consent, which may be gathered from the circumstances. Enlisting the help of a trade union officer in negotiating terms of employment is an important incident of union membership.[460] ACAS has issued a Code of Practice containing guidelines. The effect of these provisions on union membership agreements (i.e. the closed shop) is discussed, in connection with trade union freedom, in Part II, Ch. 1. The dismissal of a pregnant employee and the right to return to work after confinement were discussed in Ch. 6, *above*. Selection for redundancy is discussed *below*.

VII. Fairness

351. The long-standing notion of 'reasonableness' was modernized to a popular, more normative condition of 'fairness'. Still, unless the dismissal was for a reason which was automatically unfair, the tribunal is required to decide whether the employer acted reasonably. Section 98(4) of the Employment Rights Act 1996 states:

> ... the determination of the question whether the dismissal is fair or unfair (having regard to the reason shown by the employer) –
>
> (a) depends on whether in the circumstances (including the size and administrative resources of the employer's undertaking), the employer acted reasonably or unreasonably in treating it as a sufficient reason for dismissing the employee; and
> (b) shall be determined in accordance with equity and the substantial merits of the case.

Since 1980, there has been no formal burden of proof in the determination of this question. The tribunal, with its tripartite composition, is expected to act as an 'industrial jury', drawing on the industrial experience of its lay members to reach a conclusion based on common sense and common fairness. The statute has, however, been interpreted to mean that the tribunal members should not substitute their

459. TULRCA 1992, s. 152(1).
460. *Discount Tobacco & Confectionery Ltd* v. *Armitage* [1990] IRLR 15.

own opinion for that of management. Lord Denning said that 'It must be remembered that in all these cases there is a band of reasonableness, within which one employer may reasonably take one view: another quite reasonably take a different view'.[461] Thus, the function of the employment tribunal, 'as an industrial jury, is to determine whether in the particular circumstances of each case, the decision to dismiss the employee fell within the band of reasonable responses which a reasonable employer might have adopted'.[462] The 'band of reasonable responses' test clearly gives the employer considerable latitude in decision-making, particularly if the concept of the reasonable employer simply reflects actual practices of most employers.

A recent attempt by the Employment Appeal Tribunal to institute a more interventionist test was, however, emphatically rejected by the Court of Appeal.[463]

352. One way of circumscribing this managerial prerogative without interfering too much with the ultimate substance of the decision has been to require the employer to follow certain procedures in order to ensure that a dismissal is fair. Requirements of this sort include the need to warn an employee and to give him or her the opportunity of being heard before being dismissed. The approach of tribunals and courts to procedural requirements was transformed by the House of Lords decision in *Polkey* v. *A.E. Dayton Services*.[464] Prior to this decision, procedural requirements had been considerably diluted in cases in which the tribunal considered that the employee suffered no injustice by the absence of procedure.[465] In *Polkey*, however, the House of Lords reinstated the importance of procedure, holding that the reasonableness of the dismissal could only be determined on the basis of the employer's knowledge at the time of dismissal, not in the light of facts which subsequently emerged even if they showed that no injustice had been caused.[466] This means that failure to follow a fair procedure may in itself render a dismissal unfair, even though, had the procedure been followed, it might have been fair to dismiss the employee. In such circumstances, according to *Polkey*, compensation should be reduced but the unfairness of the dismissal remains. At the same time, failure to follow a procedure does not inevitably entail an unfair dismissal. 'If the employer could reasonably have concluded in the light of the circumstances known to him at the time of dismissal that consultation or warning would be utterly useless, he might well act reasonably even if he did not observe the provisions of the [ACAS Code of Practice].'[467] The width of this exception remains unclear, but it does have the potential to erode the basic principle.[468] Cases since *Polkey* have elaborated on the standards of procedure required. The most difficult area concerns

461. *British Leyland UK Ltd* v. *Swift* [1981] IRLR 91 (CA) at p. 93.
462. *Iceland Frozen Foods* v. *Jones* [1983] ICR 17 (EAT) at p. 25.
463. *Foley* v. *Post Office* [2000] ICR 1283 (CA).
464. [1988] ICR 142.
465. *British Labour Pump* v. *Byrne* [1979] ICR 347 at 353–354, *W. & J. Wass* v. *Binns* [1982] ICR 486 (CA).
466. See also *Devis* v. *Atkins* [1977] ICR 662 (HL); *Sillifant* v. *Powell Duffryn Timber Ltd* [1983] IRLR 91.
467. [1988] ICR 142 at p. 153, *per* Lord Mackay, and see Lord Bridge at p. 163.
468. See for example *Mathewson* v. *RB Wilson Dental Laboratory* [1988] IRLR 512; *Fuller* v. *Lloyds Bank* [1991] IRLR 336. Contrast *McLaren* v. *National Coal Board* [1988] ICR 370.

disciplinary hearings. Here the guidelines set out in the early case of *British Home Stores* v. *Burchell*[469] generally apply. According to this test, in cases of alleged misconduct, it must first be established that the employer in fact believed that it had occurred.

Secondly, did the employer have reasonable grounds upon which to sustain that belief? And thirdly, had the employer at the stage at which he or she formed that belief carried out as much investigation into the matter as was reasonable? There is no need for a quasi-judicial inquiry;[470] in this respect, the tribunal should take into account the business needs of the employer. Nevertheless, some basic principles apply: the employee should know the case against him or her, and where the case depends on written witness statements, these should generally be revealed to the employee.[471] An appeal can only rectify defects in the original proceeding if it is a re-hearing *de novo* rather than a mere review.[472]

353. The question of reasonableness is one of fact for the tribunal, appeals being limited to points of law. Thus an appeal is only available where either the tribunal misdirected themselves in law in that they misconstrued their function in considering the question of reasonableness, or they reached a conclusion which no reasonable tribunal, properly directed in law, could have reached.[473] This approach has been criticized for leading to inconsistent decisions as between tribunals. However, in the words of the Court of Appeal:

Whether or not an employer has behaved reasonably in dismissing an employee is a question of fact, and it is a question upon which different people, looking at the same set of circumstances, may reasonably come to different conclusions. It is therefore endemic in a system where there is no appeal on fact that from time to time different [employment tribunals] will give different answers to broadly similar situations, and neither decision can be challenged. It is therefore important that this court should resist the temptation to seek to overturn a factual decision with which it may not agree, by searching for some shadowy point of law on which to hang its hat for the purpose of bringing uniformity to the differing decisions. If we were to take this course, it would have the very undesirable effect of encouraging innumerable appeals which raised no point of law, but depended upon comparative findings of fact.[474]

In recent cases and particularly those on procedure, the EAT has nevertheless been prepared to lay down detailed guidelines for tribunals to follow. However, failure to follow these does not necessarily constitute an error of law.

354. There are now several situations in which selection for redundancy must be treated as unfair. These include those where the employee shows that the principal reason for selection was trade union membership or activities or refusal to join

469. [1980] ICR 303.
470. *Ulsterbus Ltd* v. *Henderson* [1989] IRLR 251.
471. *Spink* v. *Express Foods Group Ltd* [1990] IRLR 320; *Louies* v. *Coventry Hood & Seating Co. Ltd* [1990] IRLR 324; cf. *Fuller* v. *Lloyds Bank* [1991] IRLR 336 (EAT).
472. *Whitbread & Co. plc* v. *Mills* [1988] ICR 776.
473. *Gilham* v. *Kent County Council (No. 2)* [1985] ICR 233 (CA) at 243–244.
474. *Ibid.*, *per* Griffiths LJ at p. 240.

a trade union[475] and most (but not all) of the automatically unfair reasons for dismissal.[476] Where the selection is not automatically unfair, it must still be reasonable within the meaning of Section 98(4) of the 1996 Act. This means that both the system for selection and its application must be fair.[477] The process must be objectively justified, although this will take into account the size of the employer.[478] Other criteria of reasonableness include whether attempts were made to find suitable alternative employment for the redundant employee and whether his or her union was consulted. A clear and objective selection procedure should be used, but there is no obligation to provide a right of appeal against selection for redundancy.[479]

VIII. Remedies for Unfair Dismissal

355. The primary remedies available under the Employment Rights Act 1996 are (1) *reinstatement*, which means that the employer must treat the employee in all respects as if he or she had not been dismissed, restoring pay, pension and other benefits; and (2) *re-engagement*, which differs from reinstatement in that the employee may be re-engaged in a different job from that which he or she formerly held, provided that the new job is comparable to the old or is otherwise suitable. Re-engagement may be by a successor or associated employer. In exercising its discretion whether to grant reinstatement or re-engagement the tribunal must consider the complainant's wishes, whether he or she caused or contributed to the dismissal, and whether it is practicable for the employer to comply with an order for reinstatement or re-engagement.[480] The mere fact that the employer has engaged a permanent replacement does not automatically make these remedies 'impracticable'. If the employee is reinstated, but the terms of the order are not fully complied with, the tribunal must award compensation to the extent that partial noncompliance has caused the employee's loss, with a maximum award, fixed at £80,541 (6 April 2017) or the equivalent of 12 months' pay, which ever is lowest. If the order for reinstatement or re-engagement is not complied with at all, then the tribunal must award a basic and compensatory award (see below) and, unless the employer can show that compliance was not practicable, an *additional* award of compensation. The additional award is between 26 and 52 weeks' pay (the maximum week's pay from 6 April 2017 is £489).

356. If orders for reinstatement or re-engagement are not made, the tribunal must award compensation under two heads. (1) A basic award is calculated similarly to a redundancy payment, on the basis of age and years of service. The employee receives one and a half week's pay for each year in employment at the age of 41 or over; one week's pay for each year from 22 to 40; and half a week's

475. TULRCA 1992, s. 153.
476. ERA 1996, s. 105.
477. *British Aerospace plc.* v. *Green* [1995] IRLR 433, 437 (*per* Millett LJ).
478. *Williams* v. *Compair Maxam Ltd* [1982] ICR 156.
479. *Robinson* v. *Ulster Carpet Mills Ltd* [1991] IRLR 348 (NICA).
480. ERA 1996, s. 116.

pay for each year under 22. This is reduced by one-twelfth for each calendar month over the age of 64 for all employees.[481] The maximum week's pay is £489 (from 6 April 2017) subject to a maximum of 20 years' employment. There is no minimum basic award, except in two cases. First, where the dismissal is unfair on the grounds of redundancy, but no redundancy payment is payable because the employee accepted or unreason-ably refused alternative employment, a fixed award of two weeks' pay must be ordered. Secondly, where the dismissal is automatically unfair because of trade union membership or activities or non-membership of a trade union, or on grounds of activities in health and safety, working time, trusteeship of occupational pension schemes or employee representation the minimum award is £5,970 (6 April 2017) before deductions.

The basic award may be reduced, to nil if necessary, in the following circumstances: (a) the employee has unreasonably refused an offer which would have amounted to reinstatement as if he had not been dismissed; (b) the employee's pre-dismissal conduct was such that it is just and equitable to reduce the basic award; (c) the employee has received an amount in respect of dismissal under designated dismissal procedures agreement or on the grounds of redundancy.[482]

357. (2) A compensatory award is such amount as the tribunal 'considers just and equitable in all the circumstances having regard to the loss sustained by the complainant in consequence of the dismissal insofar as that loss is attributable to action taken by the employer'.[483] This is calculated according to principles laid down by the courts, and includes loss of earnings and benefits up to the date of hearing and subsequently, and loss of pension rights, expenses and statutory employment protection rights. It excludes injury to feelings, inconvenience or other non-pecuniary loss (compare sex and race discrimination and wrongful dismissal). Deductions are made in respect of the employee's failure to mitigate his or her loss, the employee's contribution to the dismissal and any other payment received from the employer or earnings elsewhere except during the period of notice. In addition, compensation can be decreased where an employer failed to follow the required procedure, but the dismissal would otherwise have been fair.[484] For any dismissals which take effect on or after 6 April 2017, the compensatory award shall be the lower of £80,541 or 52 weeks' gross pay.

358. A special procedure, called interim relief, is available for those who claim that they have been dismissed for trade union membership or activities, refusal to join a trade union, health and safety activities, employee representation, working time complaints, protected disclosure or trusteeship of an occupational pension scheme. This procedure enables the tribunal to order that the employee be reinstated, or if both parties agree, re-engaged in another job, or if the employer refuses to do either, suspended on full pay ('an order for the continuation of the contract of

481. ERA 1996, s. 119.
482. ERA 1996, s. 122.
483. ERA 1996, s. 123(1).
484. *Polkey* v. *AE Dayton* [1988] ICR 142.

employment') until final determination of the complaint.[485] The claim has to be presented within seven days of dismissal, there must be a likelihood of the employee succeeding at the final hearing and, in the case of a trade union member, it must be supported by a certificate from an authorized official of an independent trade union. This is the only situation under the statute in which a dismissal may be suspended pending the determination of the question. (For interlocutory injunctions at common law, see above.)

IX. Relationship with other Claims

359. Although fewer claims are brought before the ordinary courts for wrongful dismissal at common law than before tribunals for unfair dismissal, the common law remedy remains important in several classes of cases. These include cases in which the worker is not eligible for statutory protection; where the relatively short statutory limitation period for unfair dismissal has expired; where it is considered that an injunction is a likely remedy or where an employee was dismissed in circumstances which would be fair under the statute, but no wages have been paid in lieu of notice. It should be noted that it is not relevant to the question of unfair dismissal (in respect of which proceedings may be brought only in an ET) whether or not the dismissal was wrongful at common law. If damages are awarded in a court in respect of loss of earnings then these would be deducted from the compensatory award for unfair dismissal. Tribunal hearings will usually be completed long before an action before the ordinary courts comes to trial. If the tribunal has awarded compensation for unfair dismissal this will include loss of pay in lieu of notice and so there is unlikely to be any loss left to compensate by an award of damages. Nevertheless, for employees in the higher earnings brackets, it may well be worth pursuing both claims if the total loss resulting from the dismissal exceeds the statutory maximum compensation awardable in an unfair dismissal claim. In such a case, the court will not set off the compensation awarded in the unfair dismissal claim against the contractual compensation.[486]

360. A statutory redundancy payment or a payment voluntarily made by the employer, will be deducted from the award of compensation for unfair dismissal. Double awards may not be made in respect of an act which is both an unfair dismissal and compensatible as sex or race discrimination under other legislation.

X. Exclusions from Unfair Dismissals Legislation

361. The following is a summary of those classes of employee who may not bring a complaint of unfair dismissal. (1) Employees who have been continuously employed for less than two years, unless the dismissal was on medical grounds (one month) or for trade union membership or activities or non-membership of a trade

485. TULRCA 1992, ss. 161–166; ERA 1996, ss. 128–132.
486. *O'Laoire* v. *Jackel International* [1991] IRLR 170 (CA).

union, family reasons, health and safety activities, refusal to do retail work on Sundays, trusteeship of an occupational pension scheme, employee representation, making a protected disclosure or asserting a statutory right, including working time, minimum wage or tax credit (no minimum period).[487] (2) Share fishermen. (3) Persons employed on United Kingdom registered ships wholly outside Great Britain, or not ordinarily resident in Great Britain. (4) Persons employed under fixed-term contracts made before 28 February 1972, or fixed-term contracts for two years or more made after that date if they have waived their rights in writing. (5) Persons who do not present claims within three months of the date of termination, or such further period as the tribunal considers reasonable in a case where it is satisfied that it was not reasonably practicable for the complaint to be presented before the end of three months; (6) Persons having the benefit of a dismissal procedures agreement exempted by the Secretary of State.

A. Resignation

362. The requirements in the case of a resignation by an employee are very similar to those for a dismissal. It is important for employers to know whether an employee has resigned, since if they treat the employee as having resigned when that is not in fact the case, they may be held to have dismissed the employee. If the employee's resignation is prompted by a repudiatory act or breach of contract by the employer, that may be treated as a constructive dismissal by the employer. A resignation does not require acceptance by the employer and, if the employee wishes to change his or her mind and withdraw the resignation, the withdrawal requires the employer's agreement. Failure to give it does not amount to a constructive dismissal.

B. Constructive Dismissal

363. Different considerations arise where the employee's resignation is prompted by a breach of contract or repudiatory act committed by the employer. In that case, the resignation will be called a 'constructive dismissal'. It should be noted that this term has no statutory authority and is merely a convenient shorthand expression for a resignation on the part of the employee prompted by an action on the part of the employer which may be categorized as a repudiatory act or a breach of contract. In *Western Excavating (ECC) Ltd* v. *Sharp* (1978) (at p. 226), Lord Denning MR said:

If the employer is guilty of conduct which is a significant breach going to the root of the contract of employment, or which shows that the employer no longer intends to be bound by one or more of the essential terms of contract, then the employee is entitled to treat himself as discharged from any further performance ... [T]he conduct must ... be sufficiently serious to entitle him to leave at once ...

487. ERA 1996, s. 108, TULRCA 1992, s. 154.

364. Historically, in cases of constructive dismissal, the first question to ask is whether the employer's action is in breach of its contractual obligations or is a repudiation of them. That will involve ascertaining the express terms of the contract and considering whether any terms should be implied. Once the breach or repudiation has been established, it must be serious enough to entitle the employee to leave without notice. Further, the employee's resignation must have been caused by the breach. Finally, there will be no constructive dismissal if the employee waived the right to terminate the contract, for example by affirming the contract. See also the decisions of the Court of Appeal in *Meikle* v. *Nottinghamshire CC* (2004) and of the EAT in *Greenhof* v. *Barnsley Metropolitan Borough Council* (2006). In both cases an employer's failure to make reasonable adjustments in the case of a disabled employee was treated a breach of the implied duty of mutual trust and confidence. In *Horkaluk* v. *Cantor Fitzgerald International* (2005) the Court of Appeal held that an employee who was subjected to a campaign of bullying and intimidation, accompanied by foul and abusive language, had been constructively dismissed. However, since *GAB Robins (UK) Ltd* v. *Triggs*[2008] EWCA Civ 17, the question to be scrutinized by Employment Tribunals, guides the Court of Appeal, is whether an unreasonable and/or unjustifiable act being capable of amounting also to a breach of the implied term of mutual trust and confidence. Such actions being likely to destroy or seriously damage the employment relationship between the parties, so as to succeed in constructive dismissal claims.

§8. Redundancy

I. Meaning

365. With the enormous increase in unemployment since 1979, redundancies have been a central feature of labour relations. Advance notifications of pending redundancies reached a peak of 1.5 million in 1980, from which it declined to 376,314 in 1990 and 348,848 in 2000 and 411,000 in 2005.[488] In 2010, it peaked at 621,000 redundancies.

Employees have a statutory right to a redundancy payment under the provisions of the Employment Rights Act 1996, Part XI. Subject to some exclusions there are two main criteria for a redundancy payment. The first is that the employee has been dismissed, and dismissal for these purposes is defined in the same way as for unfair dismissal. Secondly, the dismissal must be by reason of 'redundancy'.

This concept has a special meaning in the 1996 Act, Section 139, namely that the employee's dismissal is attributable wholly or mainly to:

- (a) the fact that his employer has ceased or intends to cease –
  - (i) to carry on the business for the purposes of which the employee was employed by him; or

488. Note that employers are now only required to notify impending redundancies of more than 20, rather than 10 workers.

(ii) to carry on that business in the place where the employee was so employed; or

(b) the fact that the requirements of that business –

(i) for employees to carry out work of a particular kind; or

(ii) for employees to carry out work of a particular kind in the place where the employee was employed by the employer; have ceased or diminished or are expected to cease or diminish.

There is a statutory presumption that the dismissal is by reason of redundancy. The burden therefore rests on the employer to prove otherwise.

366. The statutory definition, stressing as it does the necessity for diminished requirements for employees to do work of a particular kind, is a narrower concept than that to be found in the ILO Termination of Employment Convention 1982 which refers to 'the operational requirements of the enterprise' or the EC Collective Redundancies Directive[489] which refers to 'reasons not related to the individual workers concerned'. As interpreted by the courts, the definition does not include all cases in which, in order to diminish labour costs or increase productivity, the employer has changed the terms and conditions of work or re-organized the workforce. Even if the employer's actions amount to a repudiatory breach of contract, or if the dismissal is wholly a result of the employer's operational requirements rather the employee's conduct, this will not entitle the employee to redundancy compensation unless the employer's requirements for employees to do work of the particular kind the employee was employed to do have ceased or diminished. Thus, an employer was not required to pay redundancy payments to employees who could not make their own transport arrangements to and from work after the employer withdrew a free bus service. This was despite the fact that the employer was in breach of contract.[490] Similarly, a change in working arrangements and shift systems is not necessarily a redundancy situation, even if the change is a response to a fall-off in sales and leads to a substantial drop in earnings,[491] provided the employer still requires employees to do work of the particular kind. Nor will the courts question the employer's reasons for declaring employees to be redundant,[492] and conversely, if the employer honestly believes that the dismissal is justified by a reason other than redundancy, the employee is not 'redundant'.[493]

As a result of the limited definition of redundancy, only straightforward cases are covered. The references in Section 139(1) to the 'place where the employee was so employed' have been judicially interpreted to mean the place where the employee could be required by his or her contract of employment to work. Thus an employee who had worked at one place for seven years was not redundant when his employer moved his work to another establishment, since his contract required him to work

489. Directive 98/59, OJ 1998 L225/16.

490. *Chapman* v. *Goonvean and Rostowrack China Clay Co. Ltd* [1973] ICR 50 (CA).

491. *Johnson* v. *Nottinghamshire Combined Police Authority* [1971] ICR 170 (CA); *Lesney Products & Co. Ltd* v. *Nolan* [1977] ICR 235 (CA).

492. *Moon* v. *Homeworthy Furniture* [1977] ICR 117 (EAT).

493. *Hindle* v. *Percival Boats Ltd* [1969] ITR 86 (CA).

at any of the employer's establishments.[494] It has been suggested that where an employee can be required by contract to do a wide range of types of work, no redundancy compensation is payable provided the employer requires employees to do any of the work within the contractual range. Thus an employee whose contract requires him to do any work within his capabilities may not be entitled to a redundancy payment so long as the employer requires employees to do work within that range.

367. The *Safeway* decision was approved by the House of Lords in *Murray* v. *Foyle Meats Ltd* (1997), Lord Irvine of Lairg LC said:

The language of Section 139(1)(b) ... asks two questions of fact. The first is whether one or other of various states of economic affairs exists. In this case, the relevant one is whether the requirements of the business for employees to carry out work of a particular kind have diminished. The second question is whether the dismissal is attributable, wholly or mainly, to that state of affairs. This is a question of causation ... The key word in the statute is "attributable" and there is no reason in law why the dismissal of an employee should not be attributable to a diminution in the employer's needs for employees irrespective of the terms of his contract or the function which he performed.

368. The Court of Appeal has looked at this issue again, in *Shawkat* v. *Nottingham City Hospital NHS Trust* (2002). In that case, the employee was employed as a staff grade doctor in thoracic surgery. Following the establishment of a cardiothoracic unit, he was required to perform both cardiac and thoracic surgery. He refused and was dismissed. The tribunal rejected his claim that his dismissal was for redundancy, but the EAT allowed his appeal and remitted the case to the tribunal, on the footing that it was not clear that a tribunal could only have reached one conclusion. On remission, the tribunal again concluded that there was no diminution in the employers' requirements for employees to carry out work of a particular kind, i.e. thoracic surgery. It said that there was no reduction in the amount of thoracic surgery or the number of employees required to do that work. It said that the reason why the employee's thoracic sessions was reduced was because they wanted him to do cardiac work in part of his time. It therefore concluded that he was not dismissed by reason of redundancy. The EAT dismissed the employee's appeal, as did the Court of Appeal, which said that the question whether the requirements of Section 139 have been satisfied is a question of fact. Here, the tribunal's decision did not disclose an error of law and should not be disturbed.[495]

369. The statute provides a limited incentive to employers to attempt to redeploy redundant workers, in that an employee is not entitled to a redundancy payment if he or she unreasonably refuses an offer of suitable alternative employment, or an offer to renew the contract on the same terms immediately or within four

494. *UK Atomic Energy Authority* v. *Claydon* [1974] ICR 128 (NIRC), following *Sutcliffe* v. *Hawker Siddeley Aviation Ltd* [1973] ICR 560 (NIRC). *See also Rank Xerox* v. *Churchill* [1988] IRLR 280.

495. See also *Lambe* v. *186K Ltd* (2004), (CA). It should be borne in mind that a reorganization which does not fall within the statutory definition of redundancy may amount to 'some other substantial reason', the fifth potentially fair reason.

weeks of the dismissal.[496] The employee is entitled to a trial period of four weeks before deciding to accept the new job. An employee who does not remain on beyond the end of the trial period may be entitled to a redundancy payment in the same way as if no trial period had been embarked upon.

II. Calculation of Compensation

370. Section 162 of the Employment Rights Act 1996 provides that for each year of employment between the ages of 18 and 21 the employee is to receive a half-week's pay; for each year of employment between 22 and 40 one week's pay; and for each year of employment between 41 and 64, one and a half week's pay. Remuneration over £489 per week, and employment for longer than 20 years are ignored. A week's pay is calculated in accordance with the 1996 Act, Part XIV, Ch. 2. In effect the maximum award for a person with 20 years' service over the age of 41 is £14,670.

III. Exclusions

371. The following is a summary of the main classes of employee not entitled to receive a redundancy payment. (1) Employees who have not been continuously employed for two years or more. (2) Employees who have reached the normal retirement age applicable to their particular job, if that age is the same for men and women, and below 65; or, in other cases, employees who have reached 65. (3) Employees unreasonably refusing an offer of suitable alternative employment from the employer, or from his successor in the case of a change of ownership. (4) Employees accepting a renewal of contract or re-engagement from the employer, or from his successor in the case of a change of ownership. (5) Employees who leave their employment during the period of their notice, unless they comply with certain formal requirements to give the employer counter-notice. (6) In some cases where the employee is guilty of misconduct or where he or she takes part in a strike during the period of notice.[497]

§9. Collective Redundancies

372. Domestic legislation giving effect to the EC Directive on Collective Redundancies,[498] is now governed by Part IV, Ch. 2 of the Trade Union and Labour Relations (Consolidation) Act 1992. The Act requires an employer contemplating the dismissal of 20 or more employees at one establishment by reason of redundancy within a period of 45 days (previously 90 days) or less to consult the appropriate

---

496. ERA 1996, s. 138.
497. See below and *Sweet and Maxwell's, Encyclopedia of Employment Law*, para. 1-6503.
498. OJ 1975, L48/29 of 22 February 1975, consolidated by Directive 98/59 of 20 July 1998, OJ 1998, L225/16.

representatives of employees who may be affected and also to notify the BIS (the government). The obligation is to consult the union recognized by the employer for bargaining purposes in respect of the descriptions of employees from whose number the employer intends to select for redundancy or, if none, then 'employee representatives' as appointed or elected by the employees. The obligation is to consult 'in good time'. If the employer is proposing to dismiss 100 or more employees at one establishment over a 45-day period, consultation must take place not less than 45 days before the first dismissal.

373. The consultation must cover ways of avoiding or reducing the number of redundancies and mitigating the consequences of the redundancies, and must be undertaken by the employer with a view to reaching agreement with the representatives. The Act specifies the information to be given to the representatives, including the detailed reasons for the proposed dismissals, the numbers and descriptions of employees to be dismissed, and the total number of employees of such descriptions from whom the redundant employees are to be selected, the method of selection to be used, and the method of dismissal including the timing.

374. If the employer fails to carry out his or her duty to consult, the trade union concerned may complain to an employment tribunal which may make a *protective award*. The effect of the award is that the employees are to be kept on the payroll for the period of the award. This means that in addition to any other claims arising out of the dismissal (such as redundancy payments) the employees are entitled to be paid their wages for this period. The length of the period is within the discretion of the tribunal subject to a maximum of 45 days. An employee not paid the amount of an award due to him or her may present a complaint to an employment tribunal. The employer must notify BIS of the proposed redundancies within the same time periods. There is no obligation to notify the BIS where fewer than 20 employees are involved. In the notice employers must state the date on which they began consultation with any recognized union. They must also provide the Department with such other information as it may require. The penalty for failure to notify is a fine of up to £5,000 on conviction. Where the employer is a limited liability company, a director or manager who fails to notify the BIS may incur personal liability if he or she is guilty of fault or neglect.

Chapter 8. Equality and Non-discrimination

§1. The Development of the Legislation

375. In Great Britain, there are a number of grounds on which discrimination is prohibited. They are sex (including sexual orientation and a change of sex, i.e. transsexuality), race, disability, religion or belief and age.[499]

Historically until around the turn of the 21st century, three predominant areas of non-discrimination (now equality) activity existed under three key statutes: the Sex Discrimination Act 1975 the SDA, together with the Equal Pay Act 1970 the EqPA comprising the legislation on sex discrimination (and discrimination on the ground of marital status), and the Race Relations Act 1976 the RRA covering discrimination on the ground of race. From 19 July 2003, the RRA has been amended to provide, *inter alia*, an extended definition of indirect discrimination on the grounds of race, ethnic or national origin (Section 1(1), (1A)) and a definition of harassment (Section 3A) *see* the Race Relations Act 1976 (Amendment) Regulations 2003 SI 2003/1626 which introduced these and other changes, which were required to give effect to Council Directive 2000/43 of 29 June 2000 the Race Directive. The SDA, too, has been significantly amended recently, as required by the Equal Treatment Framework Directive (Directive 2002/73/EC) the ETFD. Important changes have been made, *inter alia*, to the definition of indirect discrimination in the fields of employment and vocational training, and the inclusion of a separate ground of discrimination in the form of harassment (i) on the ground of sex and (ii) harassment of a sexual nature. These amendments were introduced by the Employment Equality (Sex Discrimination) Regulations 2005 (SI 2005/2467) as from 1 October 2005.

376. The ETFD requires Member States to introduce legislation making age discrimination unlawful by 2006. The draft Employment Equality (Age) Regulations 2006, which implement this strand of the ETFD, were laid before Parliament on 9 March 2006. It is intended that these draft Regulations will come into force on 1 October 2006.

377. As in race discrimination, the common law developed no protection against discrimination on grounds of sex. Indeed, the attitudes of the all-male judiciary were often openly hostile. In the notorious case of *Roberts* v. *Hopwood*,[500] the House of Lords decided that it was unlawful for a local authority to provide equal pay for women doing the same work as men. Similarly, the courts consistently upheld the policies of local education authorities in the 1920s to dispense with the services of all married women teachers.[501]

499. S. Fredman, 'Equality: a new generation?', ILJ 30 (2001), 145–168.

500. [1925] AC 578 (HL).

501. *Short* v. *Poole Corporation* [1926] 1 Ch. 66 (CA); *Price* v. *Rhondda UDC* [1923] 2 Ch. 372 (Ch. D.).

378. Prior to 1970, the only legislation relating to sex discrimination was the Sex Disqualification (Removal) Act 1919, which made it unlawful to disqualify a person on the grounds of sex or marriage from the exercise of any public function or any civil office or vocation. However, this statute was too limited to have any great impact and remained largely a dead letter. Sex discrimination remained widespread; for example, it was commonplace for women to be paid less than men doing the same work. Throughout this period, the TUC had been conducting a campaign for equal pay for women workers, culminating in 1963 with the publication of a Charter for Women Workers. For the first time, the demands included a call for legislation to secure equal pay.

379. The first legislative fruits of the TUC's equal pay campaign came with the enactment of the Equal Pay Act 1970, which requires equal terms of employment for men and women workers. This Act did not come into force until 29 December 1975, thus giving employers a full five years to meet its requirements. By this time, both the Conservative and Labour Parties were committed to equality legislation. Equal pay trundles on, exposing a continuing inequality (cf. Fredman's excellent exposition on 'Reforming Equal Pay Laws [2008] vol. 37, ILJ, pp. 193–218).

In 1975, the Sex Discrimination Act 1975 was passed, prohibiting discrimination on grounds of sex or marital status in matters other than terms of employment. This Act departed from the model of the Race Relations Act 1968, in particular by allowing aggrieved individuals a right of direct access to employment tribunals (or, in cases outside the employment field, to county courts). At the same time, strategic enforcement was entrusted to an Equal Opportunities Commission (EOC), which deals with discriminatory practices by employers and encourages positive action against discrimination. This Act was used as a model for a new Race Relations Act, enacted in 1976. The new Act abolished enforcement through voluntary industry machinery, and replaced this with individual enforcement through employment tribunals, coupled with strategic enforcement by a Commission for Racial Equality (CRE). The CRE has similar powers to the EOC. In a parallel set of developments, the UK signed the UN Inter-national Covenant on Social and Cultural Rights, which requires action in respect of a large number of discriminatory contexts.

380. In the meantime, the UK had entered the EEC and, by the European Communities Act 1972, agreed to be bound by Community legislation. This legislation has exerted a fundamental influence on the later development of UK antidiscrimination legislation. In one of its very few provisions on social law, the foundational Treaty of Rome itself required equal remuneration for men and women doing equal work. This provision became particularly powerful because of the decision by the ECJ, in the famous case of *Defrenne* v. *Sabena* that its provisions are directly applicable, both vertically (against the State) and horizontally (against private employers).[502] The practical application of then Article 119 was facilitated by EEC Directive 75/117, specifying equal pay for work of equal value. Of particular significance were the enforcement proceedings brought against the UK in which the ECJ held that the absence of a requirement for equal pay for work of equal value in

502. *Defrenne* v. *Sabena* (No. 2) (Case 43/75 EEC) [1976] ECR 455.

the UK legislation constituted a breach of ex Article 119 and the equal pay directive. This in turn led to the amendment of the Equal Pay Act in 1983. Article 119 was strengthened and modernized by the Treaty of Amsterdam, where it appeared as Article 141. Among other things, Article 141 (now Article 257) incorporates the Equal Pay Directive in its text, and gives express legislative power to the Community to act in the field of equal pay.

Outside of equal pay itself, there has been a stream of directives on equal treatment of men and women, the most important being EC Directive 76/207 on equal treatment as regards access to employment, training, promotion and working conditions. This directive is directly applicable, but only against the state (vertically) and not against private employers (horizontally).[503] This has caused several anomalies, particularly in that state employees are able to rely directly on it, whereas private employees are not. This directive is further augmented by directives requiring equal treatment in state social security (EC Directive 79/7), occupational social security (EC Directive 86/378) and the self-employed (EC Directive 86/613). More recently, important progress has been made in requiring equal treatment of women with family responsibilities. Three significant directives have been adopted in this field, one on the protection at work of pregnant women before and after birth (EC Directive 92/85); one on parental and family leave (EC Directive 96/34) and one on part-time work (EC Directive 97/81). Also of importance is EC Directive 97/80 on the burden of proof, which, in addition to reversing the burden of proof, defines the concept of indirect discrimination (see below). A wide-ranging new directive on equal treatment of men and women, incorporating new judicial and statutory developments, is now in the pipe-line. Most important is the proposed inclusion of sexual harassment, previously only governed by 'soft law'.

381. Over the past couple of decades, non-discrimination legislation has been extended in a number of areas. Discrimination on grounds of disability, up until the introduction of the Equality Act 2010 (discussed below), was prohibited by the Disability Discrimination Act 1995, supported by Disability Rights Commission. The UK belatedly ratified ILO Convention No. 111 concerning discrimination in respect of occupation and employment on 8 June 1999. In addition, the incorporation of the European Convention of Human Rights by the Human Rights Act 1998 has meant that Article 14 of the Convention is now applicable in domestic law. This requires that all Convention rights be enjoyed without discrimination on a number of grounds. Particularly important developments have occurred in the area of race relations. At domestic level, the disturbing finding that the police forces were riddled with institutional racism, led to an important set of amendments of the Race Relations Act in the form of the Race Relations (Amendment) Act 2000. At the same time, the EU was given power, for the first time, to enact equality legislation in the field of race. This led to the adoption, under Article 13 of the Treaty of Amsterdam (now contained at Article 18 of the Treaty on the Functioning of the European Union), of a directive prohibiting discrimination on grounds of racial or ethnic origin (EC Directive 2000/43). A second directive, prohibiting discrimination on

503. *Marshall* v. *Southampton and South – West Hampshire Area Health Authority* [1986] ICR 335 (ECJ); *Integrity* v. *Rouvroy* (Case 373/89) [1991] IRLR 176 (ECJ).

grounds of religion or belief, disability, age or sexual orientation (EC Directive 2000/78) was enacted soon afterwards. These were mostly implemented into UK law by the transposition deadline of 19 July and 2 December 2003 respectively. However, the UK took advantage of the provision in Directive 2000/78/EC allowing legislation providing for protection against age discrimination to be delayed until 2006.

§2. THE IMPACT OF THE LEGISLATION

382. Women form an increasingly important part of the workforce. In 2005 there were 14.0 million women of working age in employment in Great Britain, constituting 44.2 per cent of all those of working age in employment. This constitutes an increase of 7 per cent in the decade since 1990; itself an increase of 19 per cent since 1979.[504] Nevertheless, despite the Equal Pay Act 1970 and the Sex Discrimination Acts 1975, women remain disadvantaged in British society. In particular, women as a group earn markedly less than men. Although the initial effect of the Equal Pay Act 1970 was to increase women's average gross hourly earnings from 63.1 per cent of those of men in 1970 to 75.1 per cent in 1976, progress towards equal pay has subsequently been slow and halting. In 2000 women's gross hourly earnings over all occupations were still only 81.6 per cent of those of men, representing a narrowing of the gap of only 5 per cent over the decade since 1990. When overtime and other additional payments are taken into account the gap is even wider: in 2000, women's weekly earnings were a mere 74.5 per cent of men's.

In non-manual occupations, the position was worse still: in 2000 women's gross hourly pay in these occupations was only 70.1 per cent of that of their male counterparts. If we focus on the total average gross weekly income, including not just earnings, but occupational pensions, benefits income and other sources of income, we find that women's gross individual income was on average only 51 per cent of men's in 1998/9. Although the gap in earnings has narrowed in most cases by between 5 and 7 per cent over the decade since 1990, the remaining gap is still substantially wider than in other EC countries, particularly Sweden and the former East Germany. In 1995 the average gap in the UK was 34 per cent as against the EU average of 27.5 per cent.[505] A central factor accounting for the continuing disadvantage of women is that the primary responsibility for childcare remains with women. As a result, women form the bulk of part-time workers: in 2000, only 8 per cent of male employees of working age worked part-time, compared with as many as 43 per cent of female employees. Women part-time workers earn substantially less than their full-time counterparts and male part-timers: indeed in 2000 women part-time workers earned on average 61 per cent of the average hourly earnings of male fulltime workers.

504. Figures in this section are derived from the 2000 *Labour Force Survey* and the 2000 *New Earnings Survey*; Women and Men in Great Britain (EOC 2000).

505. *Earnings Differentials between Men and Women*, European Commission 1998.

383. The continuing differential between men's and women's pay is partly accounted for by the concentration of women in lower-paid occupations ('vertical segregation'), and in the lower-paid grades of mixed occupations ('horizontal segregation'). Thus, women workers are largely concentrated in relatively few occupations and industries, frequently those with a high demand for part-time labour. In 2005, women constituted 93 per cent of care assistants, 87 per cent of nurses, 90 per cent of primary and nursery teachers, and 83 per cent of cleaners and domestics. At the other end of the spectrum, they constituted only 2 per cent of drivers of road goods vehicles, 7 per cent of production, works and maintenance managers, and 22 per cent of computer analysts or programmers. In craft and related occupations, only 7 per cent were women, while women formed the vast majority (76 per cent) of those employed in clerical and secretarial occupations.

Even where women work in mixed professions, there are far higher proportions of men than women in the better-paid grades. Similarly, women are seriously under-represented in senior positions.[506] Trade unions are scarcely better. Although in 1999, women constituted two in five trade union members, they formed only a tiny proportion of trade union leadership. Of a total of 78 general secretaries in 2000, only seven were women.[507] Of the biggest ten unions, the best female representation in leadership positions is found in the T&G general union, with women comprising 20 per cent of its membership and 32 per cent of its national executive. By contrast, in the National Union of Teachers (NUT), the membership is 75 per cent female, but women comprise a mere 41 per cent of the national executive.

384. There have been important changes in the position of ethnic minorities in the labour force. Over the past few decades, there has been a clear upward movement in job levels of ethnic minorities and a narrowing of differentials between ethnic minorities and the ethnic majority. Particularly important is the finding that different groups with the same qualifications doing the same types of jobs in the same areas are generally paid similar amounts. Nevertheless ethnic minorities continue to suffer serious discrimination and disadvantage in the labour market.[508] Unemployment rates for ethnic minority groups in 2000 were appreciably higher than those for the white population: 12.0 per cent compared with 5.1 per cent. But the most striking finding of the 1990s is that the differences between the minorities are often as great as those between the majority and the minority. By far the most disadvantaged group consists of families of Bangladeshi and Pakistani origin and their British born children. In 1994, more than four out of five Pakistani and Bangladeshi households had an equivalent income below half the national average, four times as many as white non-pensioner house-holds. Unemployment rates among Pakistani and Bangladeshi men are high and for those in work, pay tends to be low. By contrast, East African Asians and Chinese have reached parity with whites and Indians are fast closing any remaining gaps. The average Indian household has a slightly higher total income than a white house-hold (including pensioners), the unemployment rate for Indians is only slightly higher than whites and a 1999 study

506. *Women and Men in Great Britain 2000* (EOC).
507. *Labour Research*, March 2000, p. 17.
508. *Ethnic Minorities In Britain*: CRE Factsheet (1999).

found that young Indian men had almost the same earning power as their white counterparts; compared to young Pakistani and Bangladeshi men, which had not much more than half of whites' earning power. A more complex pattern is found among Caribbeans and Africans, where there is a very strong variation between individual members of the groups. Thus a study published in 1999 showed that young Caribbean men were more than twice as likely to be unemployed as young white men, and had lower earnings. Overall, the rate of poverty among Caribbeans is only slightly higher than that among white households. So far as Africans are concerned, the earning power of young African men tends to be considerably less than whites'. In addition, they have a high average risk of unemployment.

For those in work, many individuals receive a substantially lower return for the same level of qualification than their white counterparts. In addition, there is a disturbing persistence of violence, harassment and prejudice on the grounds of race, religion and ethnicity. Perhaps the most serious is the lack of confidence in the police. Home Office statistics for 1998–9 found that black people were six times more likely than whites to be stopped and searched under police powers to detect and investigate crime. These issues were forced to the surface by the case of Stephen Lawrence, the victim of a racist assault and murder. The report of the inquiry into allegations of racism about the police failure to investigate the murder properly found that 'institutional racism' was a pervasive influence in police decisions and the broader culture and structure of both the police and other agencies. Institutional racism was defined as the 'collective failure of an organization to provide an appropriate and professional service to people because of their colour, culture, or ethnic origin. It can be seen or detected in process, attitudes and behaviour which amount to discrimination through unwitting prejudice, ignorance, thoughtlessness and racist stereotyping which disadvantage minority ethnic people.'[509]

385. In view of the persistence of discrimination against women and blacks, it seems surprising that little use has been made of the legislation. In 1976, the first year of operation of the Equal Pay Act there were 1,742 applications to employment tribunals; in 1984 there were only 33 applications. This number increased somewhat after the scope of the Equal Pay Act was widened by the 1984 amendments; reaching 2570 cases in 2000.[510] A similar picture emerges in relation to the former Sex Discrimination Act: there were only 1,046 applications under that Act in 1989/1990, which rose to 5243 in 2000, while under the Race Relations Act applications rose from a mere 939 to 3074. There were 1,704 applications in 2000 under the Disability Discrimination Act. This rise in the number of applications is, however, less encouraging when the success rates are considered. In 1998/99, only 7 cases under the Equal Pay Act were successful (2.2 per cent of those proceeding to tribunal), although 517 were settled through ACAS. Similarly in that year there

---

509. Home Office *Report of the MacPherson Inquiry*, Cmnd 4262, 24 February 1999, especially para. 6.34.

510. The figures in this section are based on statistics published annually in the *Employment Gazette*, the most recent being *Employment Gazette* May 1991, 303, and in the Council on Tribunals Annual Report 2000.

were 131 successful race discrimination cases (15.6 per cent, with 813 settled), 270 successful sex discrimination cases (33.9 per cent, with 1,791 settled).[511]

386. Significant changes were made to the SDA on 1 October 2005. These amendments implemented the changes required by the Equal Treatment Framework Directive (Directive 2002/73/EC) (see the Employment Equality (Sex Discrimination) Regulations 2005 (SI 2005/2467). They included a new definition of indirect discrimination and a separate definition of harassment on the ground of sex and harassment of a sexual nature. The changes, which applied to employment and vocational training, aligned the SDA with the other legislation concerning unlawful discrimination in these fields.

387. Legal protection against discrimination on grounds of race is a relative newcomer in Britain, when compared to sex discrimination. Judge-made common law failed to develop such protection; prior to 1965, no English or Scottish case declared racial discrimination to be against public policy. The first statutory measure, the Race Relations Act 1965, covered only a limited area and was largely ineffective. Its failure prompted a remarkable political campaign to improve the social position and employment opportunities of Britain's immigrants from the New Commonwealth and their British-born children. This was assisted by a report published in 1967 which revealed substantial discrimination against immigrants.[512] It was notable that this campaign was based not on the trade unions, but rather on organizations of ethnic minorities and sympathetic liberals, the Labour Party, and other left-wing political organizations.[513] The result was the Race Relations Act 1968, which was consciously modelled on anti-discrimination legislation in the United States and Canada. It was enforced, not by individual action, but by a Race Relations Board. In the employment field, voluntary industrial disputes procedures were used as the primary means of enforcement in some 40 industries covering about one-third of the labour force. However, so few opinions of unlawful discrimination were formed by the voluntary industry machinery that the Race Relations Board concluded that the experiment of using industry panels had failed.[514] The Act was not, however, replaced until 1976.

388. The Race Directive, which was issued to combat discrimination across a number of grounds, was implemented by the Race Relations Act 1976 (Amendment) Regulations 2000. Unfortunately, the scope of the Directive and that of the RRA was not the same: the Directive concerns discrimination on the ground of race, or ethnic or national origin, while the RRA had an extendedremit and also covered discrimination on the grounds of colour or nationality. Therefore, although the 2003 Regulations amended the RRA in a number of respects, these amendments did not

511. *Labour Market Trends*, September 1999, p. 494.
512. W.W. Daniel, *Racial Discrimination in England* (1968).
513. The background is fully described in B. Hepple, *Race, Jobs and the Law in Britain* (2nd edn, Harmondsworth, 1970).
514. Report of the Race Relations Board January 1975 to June 1976, Home Office, 1976, para. 60.

apply to discrimination on the grounds of colour or nationality, which was unsatisfactory and seemed to make the application of the RRA even more complex. However, in practice it did not present too many difficulties to complainants, as these two terms could usually be linked with race in some way.

The position of non-discrimination legislation changed with the introduction of April 2010, which was introduced to consolidate all the different pieces of non-discriminaiton legislation in to one place. The idea was that this Act would harmonise the protections, and ensure consistency across the different protected characteristics.

§3. EQUALITY ACT 2010

389. The Equality Act 2010 received Royal Assent in April 2010.

The main provisions of the Act, commenced on 1 October 2010, harmonized and sought to simplify the plethora of current equality laws, replacing them with this single Act.

390. The variant type of discrimination under the EqA 2010 are as follows.

Direct discrimination occurs when someone is treated less favourably than another person because of a protected characteristic they have or are thought to have (see perceptive discrimination below), or because they associate with someone who has a protected characteristic.

Associative discrimination already applies to race, religion or belief and sexual orientation, and is now extended to cover age, disability, gender reassignment and sex. This is direct discrimination against someone because they associate with another person who possesses a protected characteristic.

Perceptive discrimination also already applies to age, race, religion or belief and sexual orientation. It is now extended to cover disability, gender reassignment and sex. This is direct discrimination against an individual because others think they possess a particular protected characteristic. It applies even if the person does not actually possess that characteristic.

Indirect discrimination applies to age, race, religion or belief, sex, sexual orientation and marriage and civil partnership. But under the EqA 2010 it is now extended to cover disability and gender reassignment. Indirect discrimination can occur when an employer has a condition, rule, policy or even a practice that applies to everyone but particularly disadvantages people who share a protected characteristic. Indirect discrimination can be justified if it can be shown that the act was reasonable, ie that it is "a proportionate means of achieving a legitimate aim". A legitimate aim might be any lawful decision made in running an organisation or business, but if there is a discriminatory effect, the sole aim of reducing costs is likely to be unlawful.

Harassment is 'unwanted conduct related to a relevant protected characteristic, which has the purpose or effect of violating an individual's dignity or creating an intimidating, hostile, degrading, humiliating or offensive environment for that individual'. Harassment applies to all protected characteristics except for pregnancy and maternity and marriage and civil partnership.

Third party harassment applies to sex. Now extended to cover age, disability gender reassignment, race, religion or belief and sexual orientation.

Victimization occurs when an employee is treated badly because they have made or supported a complaint or raised a grievance under the Equality Act; or because they are suspected of doing so. An employee is not protected from victimization if they have maliciously made or supported an untrue complaint.

391. The touchstone protected characteristics are:

- age;
- disability;
- gender reassignment;
- marriage and civil partnership;
- pregnancy and maternity;
- race;
- religion or belief;
- sex;
- sexual orientation.

392. The Act protects people of all ages. However, different treatment because of age is not unlawful direct or indirect discrimination if you can justify it, i.e. if you can demonstrate that it is a proportionate means of meeting a legitimate aim. Age is the only protected characteristic that allows employers to justify direct discrimination.

393. The Act has made it easier for a person to show that they are disabled and protected from disability discrimination. Under the Act, a person is disabled if they have a physical or mental impairment which has a substantial and long term adverse effect on their ability to carry out normal day-to-day activities, which would include things like using a telephone, reading a book or using public transport. As before, the Act puts a duty on employers to make reasonable adjustments for their staff to help them overcome disadvantage resulting from an impairment (eg by providing assistive technologies to help visually impaired staff use computers effectively). The Act includes a new protection from 'discrimination arising from disability'.

394. The Act provides protection for transsexual people. A transsexual person is someone who proposes to, starts or has completed a process to change his or her gender. The Act no longer requires a person to be under medical supervision to be protected – so a woman who decides to live permanently as a man but does not undergo any medical procedures would be covered. It is discrimination to treat transsexual people less favourably for being absent from work because they propose to undergo, are undergoing or have undergone gender reassignment than they would be treated if they were absent because they were ill or injured. Medical procedures for gender reassignment such as hormone treatment, should not be treated as a 'lifestyle' choice.

395. The Act protects employees who are married or in a civil partnership against discrimination. Single people are not protected.

396. A woman is protected against discrimination on the grounds of pregnancy and maternity during the period of her pregnancy and any statutory maternity leave to which she is entitled. During this period, pregnancy and maternity discrimination cannot be treated as sex discrimination. An employer must not take into account an employee's period of absence due to pregnancy-related illness when making a decision about her employment.

397. For purposes of the Act 'race' includes colour, nationality and ethnic or national origins (including gypsies and travellers). A racial group can be made up of two or more different racial groups (e.g. Black Britons).

398. In the Equality Act, religion includes any religion. It also includes a lack of religion, in other words employees or jobseekers are protected if they do not follow a certain religion or have no religion at all. Additionally, a religion must have a clear structure and belief system. Belief means any religious or philosophical belief or a lack of such belief.

399. Both men and women are protected under the Act. The Act protects bisexual, gay, heterosexual and lesbian people.

400. By s.123 of the Act proceedings on most discrimination complaints to the Tribunal:

'may not be brought after the end of –

- the period of 3 months starting with the date of the act to which the complaint relates, or
- such other period as the employment tribunal thinks just and equitable.'

401. Under Part 8 of the Act (ss 108-112 EqA 2010) there are important provisions dealing with:

- relationships that have ended (s.108);
- liability of employers and principals (s.109);
- liability of employees and agents (s.110);
- instructing, causing or inducing contraventions of the Act (s.111);
- aiding contraventions (s.112).

Broadly speaking, these sections replicate the existing legislation, although with some redrafting. However, s.110 (liability of employees and agents) incorporates some of the elements in the 'aiding unlawful acts' provisions in previous discrimination legislation, but it takes a more direct approach and, unlike the previous provisions, it is not necessary to show that the employee or agent knew that the act was unlawful (*Weathersfield* v. *Sargent* [1999] IRLR 94).

402. In turn, the definitions of prohibited conduct refer to the protected characteristics. They are defined in Part 2, Chapter 1:

- age (s.5);
- disability (s.6 and Sch1);
- gender reassignment (s.7 and see also s.16);
- marriage and civil partnership (s.8);
- pregnancy and maternity (not defined, but see ss. 17-18);
- race (s.9);
- religion and belief (s.10);
- sex (s.11);
- sexual orientation (s.12).

There is also a general interpretation section in s.212 and a very helpful index to defined expressions in s.214 and Sch 28. NB s.213 on references to maternity leave.

403. Section 136 applies to any proceedings relating to a contravention of the EQA 2919 (including a breach of an equality rule, but not including an offence).

404. In order to breathe life into the new Act and embolden its aims, the Equality and Human Rights Commission (EHRC) has issued three new codes:

- Code of Practice on Employment;
- Code of Practice in Equal Pay;
- Code of Practice on Services, Public Functions and Associations.

A statutory Code does not impose legal obligations. It is not an authoritative statement of the law. Only the tribunals and the courts can provide such authority.

405. The general powers of the ET in respect of remedies in a successful complaint are to be found in s.124. The Tribunal may:

- make a declaration as to the rights of the complainant and the respondent in relation to the matters to which the proceedings relate;
- order the respondent to pay compensation to the complainant (on a tortious measure, including injury to feelings);
- make an appropriate recommendation;
- award interest (s.139).

An appropriate recommendation is a recommendation that within a specified period the respondent takes specified steps for the purpose of obviating or reducing the adverse effect of any matter to which the proceedings relate: (a) on the complainant; and/or (b) on any other person (s.124(3) EqA 2010). See s.124(7) EqA 2010, where R fails to comply with a recommendation.

406. Discrimination 'arising from' disability: this is a new form of unlawful discrimination which is intended to address problems that had occurred with "reason related" discrimination under the old law.

- Duty to make reasonable adjustments**:** the duty which existed previously under the Disability Discrimination Act 1995 is now extended to require employers to take such steps as are reasonable to provide auxiliary aids or services to a disabled employee who would otherwise be put at a substantial disadvantage in relation to a non-disabled employee.
- Harassment**:** the Act extends the definition of harassment to harassment related to an employee's race, colour or nationality. Thus unlawful harassment can now relate to any of the protected characteristics set out above, save for pregnancy, maternity, marriage and civil partnership.

Another key change to the old law relates to an employer's responsibility for harassment of its employees by a third party.

- Enquiries about disability and health prior to appointment: The Equality Act 2010 prohibits pre-selection questions of a candidate (whether orally or in writing) about their health save as set out below. These rules apply to the appointment process for an employee or the process for offering employment. Questions *can* be asked where the question is necessary for the purpose of:

  (i) establishing whether the applicant will be able to undergo an assessment in order to determine whether the employer will be under a duty to make reasonable adjustments;
  (ii) establishing whether the applicant will be able to carry out a function that is intrinsic to the work involved in the job being applied for;

- Victimization: there is no longer a need to ask whether a person has been treated less favourably than someone who did not commit the protected act. Rather than comparing the treatment of the Claimant with someone else's treatment, the question is simply whether the Claimant was treated to their detriment because of a protected act.

§4. Grounds for Prohibited Conduct

407. Direct discrimination is defined in s.13(1). A person (A) discriminates against another (B) if, because of a protected characteristic, A treats B less favourably than A treats or would treat others. It requires an actual or hypothetical comparator. This is a broad definition. The key wording is the phrase 'because of' instead of the previous phrasing of 'on the ground(s) of'.

408. If the protected characteristic is age, A does not discriminate against B if A can show A's treatment of B to be a proportionate means of achieving a legitimate aim (s.13(2)). Note that the defence does not use the term 'justification'.

409. If the protected characteristic is disability, and B is not a disabled person, A does not discriminate against B only because A treats or would treat disabled persons more favourably than A treats B (s.13(3)).

410. If the protected characteristic is marriage and civil partnership, s.13 applies to a contravention of Part 5 (work) only if the treatment is because it is B who is married or a civil partner (s.13(4)).

411. If the protected characteristic is race, less favourable treatment includes segregating B from others (s.13(5)).

412. If the protected characteristic is sex, in a case where B is a man no account is to be taken of special treatment afforded to a woman in connection with pregnancy or childbirth (s.13(6)(b) and (7)).

413. The pre-existing law required a Claimant to bring separate claims: for example, under the race, sex or religious discrimination provisions. See *Bahl* v *The Law Society*[2004] IRLR 799 CA. Multiple discrimination occurs when a person is treated less favourably because of more than one of the protected characteristics. The problem of combined discrimination is now dealt with by EQA 2010 s.14. A person (A) discriminates against another (B) if, because of a combination of two relevant protected characteristics, A treats B less favourably than A treats or would treat a person who does not share either of those characteristics (s.14(1)) (Note that the draftsman did not say 'both of those characteristics'). The relevant protected characteristics are age; disability; gender reassignment; race; religion or belief; sex and sexual orientation only (s.14(2)). However, at this moment in time section 14 has not been brought in to effect. So although it remains within the Equality Act, and has potential to deal with combined discrimination, it will not have application until the government of the day takes action to make it effective. There does not appear to be any impetus to dow this with the current Conservative Government.

414. In a disability-specific provision, s.15(1) of the 2010 Act states that a person (A) discriminates against a disabled person (B) of A treats B unfavourably because of something arising in consequence of B's disability, and A cannot show that the treatment is a proportionate means of achieving a legitimate aim. Discrimination arising from a disability does not apply if A shows that A did not know, and could not reasonably have been expected to know, that B had the disability (s.15(2)). The Explanatory Notes suggest that s.15 provides that it is discrimination to treat a disabled person unfavourably – not because of the person's disability itself, but because of something arising from, or in consequence of, his or her disability, such as the need to take al period of disability-related absence. However, such treatment may be justified if it is a proportionate means of achieving a legitimate aim. Nevertheless, in order to establish discrimination arising from disability, the alleged discriminator must know (or be reasonably be expected to know) that the disabled person has a disability.

415. Section 24(1) provides that, for the purpose of establishing a contravention of the Act by virtue of direct discrimination (s.13(1)), it does not matter whether A has the protected characteristic. For the purpose of establishing a contravention of the Act by virtue of combined discrimination (dual characteristics) (s.14(1)), it does not matter whether A has one of the protected characteristics in the combination or whether A has both (s.24(2)). The effect is that it is no defence to a claim of direct discrimination that the alleged discriminator shares the protected characteristic with the victim.

416. Section 26 of the Equality Act 2010 addresses harassment. The Act preserves existing legislative provisions on harassment. Harassment will probably amount to direct discrimination. The Act introduces a unified provision for harassment within a single enactment, thus extending free-standing harassment provisions to other strands not previously protected by specific harassment provisions.

417. Section 111 addresses instructing, causing or inducing discrimination. A person (A) must not instruct another (B) to do in relation to a third person (C) anything which contravenes Part 5 (work) of the Act (s.111(1)).

418. The characteristic of 'disability' is one of the protected characteristics listed in EQA 2010 s.4. The definition of "disability" is supplied by s.6 and Sch.1. A person (P) has a disability if:

P has a physical or mental impairment; and

- the impairment has a substantial and long-term adverse effect on P's ability to carry out normal day-to-day activities (s.6(1)).

The key questions are:

- Does P have a physical or mental impairment?
- Does the impairment have an adverse effect on P's ability to carry out normal day-to-day activities?
- Is that adverse effect substantial?
- Is that adverse effect long-term?

The Equality Act 2010 (Disability) Regulations SI 2010/2128 ('the Disability Regs') which have been made under the Equality Act 2010 contain additional provisions some of which concern the definition disability. Regulation 4 states that the following conditions are not to be treated as amounting to impairments:

- a tendency to set fires;
- a tendency to steal;
- a tendency to physical or sexual abuse of other persons;
- exhibitionism;
- voyeurism;

– seasonal allergic rhinitis (hay fever) unless it aggravates the effect of any other condition.

419. Schedule 8 to the EQA 2010 explains how the duty to make reasonable adjustments in s.20 of the Act applies to an employer or other persons under Part 5 of the Act (Work).

In summary, Schedule 8 establishes the three requirements of the duty which apply where an interested disabled employee, job applicant or person in another relevant work relationship (eg office holder, contract worker etc) is placed at a substantial (more than minor or trivial) disadvantage compared to non-disabled employees or applicants. the duty is not an anticipatory duty. An employer is not required to anticipate the needs of potential disabled employees or job applicants. An employer is also not expected to make reasonable adjustments in advance of being faced with an actual disabled employee or job application.

Schedule 8 applies where a duty to make reasonable adjustments is imposed on A by Part 5 of the EQA 2010 (work). The duty requires A to comply with the first, second and third requirements in s.20 of the Act (Schedule 8 Part 1).

The first requirement arises where a provision, criterion or practice of A's puts an interested disabled person at a substantial (more than minor or trivial) disadvantage in relation to a relevant matter in comparison with persons who are not disabled.

The second requirement arises where a physical feature puts an interested disabled person at a substantial (more than minor or trivial) disadvantage in relation to a relevant matter in comparison with persons who are not disabled.

The third requirement arises where a disabled person would, but for the provision of an auxiliary aid, be put at a substantial (more than minor or trivial) disadvantage in relation to a relevant matter in comparison with persons who are not disabled.

420. This new section provides:

> 124 *Remedies general*
>
> This section applies if an employment tribunal finds that there has been a contravention of a provision referred to in section 120(1).
>
> (2) The tribunal may:
> (a) make a declaration as to the rights of the complainant and the respondent in relation to matters to which the proceedings relate;
> (b) order the respondent to pay compensation to the complainant;
> (c) make an appropriate recommendation;
>
> (3) An appropriate recommendation is a recommendation that within a specified period the respondent takes specified steps for the purpose of obviating or reducing the adverse effect of any matter to which the proceedings relate:
> (a) on the complainant;
> (b) on any other person;
>
> (4) Sub-section (5) applies if the tribunal:
> (a) finds that a contravention is established by virtue of Section 19, but

(b) is satisfied that the provision, criterion or practice was not applied with the intention of discriminating against the complainant.

(5) It must not make an order under sub-section (2)(b) unless it first considers whether to act under sub-section (2)(a) or (c).

(6) The amount of compensation which may be awarded under sub-section (2)(b) corresponds to the amount which could be awarded by a County Court or the sheriff under Section 119.

(7) If a respondent fails, without reasonable excuse, to comply with an appropriate recommendation insofar as it relates to the complainant, the tribunal may:

(a) if an order was made under sub-section (2)(b), increase the amount of compensation to be paid;

(b) if no such order was made, make one.

This provides for more proactive enforcement, in particular extensive usage of recommendations.

§5. Closing the Gap and Widening the Protection

421. Some of these gaps have now been filled as a result of important new initiatives at EU level and the incorporation into domestic law of the ECHR by the HRA 1998, which came into effect in October 2000. As a result of new powers given by the Treaty of Amsterdam, a directive 'implementing the principle of equal treatment between persons irrespective of racial or ethnic origin' was adopted in June 2000.[515] A second directive extending the principle of equal treatment to prevent discrimination on grounds of age, disability, religion and sexual orientation (the 'framework directive') was adopted five months later.[516] Member States have two years within which to implement these directives. The list is further extended by the incorporation of Article 14 ECHR into domestic law. This states that the enjoyment of Convention rights must be secured without discrimination on any grounds such as sex, race, colour, language, religion, political or other opinion, national or social origin, association with a national minority, property, birth or other status. Finally, the Northern Ireland Act 1998, includes in Section 75 a long list of grounds to which public bodies must have due regard, including religion, political opinion, racial group, age, marital status, sexual orientation, gender, disability and persons with dependants and persons without.

The Burden of Proof Directive (Directive 97/80/EC) was intended to address this problem by changing the burden of proof in sex discrimination cases (it is sometimes erroneously stated that the directive reverses the burden of proof, which it does not). The Sex Discrimination (Indirect Discrimination and Burden of Proof) Regulations 2001 implement the directive by inserting a new section in the SDA, Section 63A. This means that, if the complainant proves facts from which the ET

515. Council Directive 2000/43/EC of 29 June 2000 [2000] OJ L180/22.

516. Council Directive 2000/78/EC of 27 November 2000 [2000] OJ L303/16.

could conclude, in the absence of an adequate explanation, that the respondent committed an act of discrimination against them, the ET will uphold the complaint, unless the respondent proves that he did not commit it. The same burden of proof provision applies in the RRA (Section 54A). Although this might appear to be a significant change in the law, courts and tribunals had reached a similar position, i.e. they would take adverse inferences once the complainant had established a prima facie case (*see King* v. *Great Britain China Centre* (1991), CA). The EAT set out guidelines on how the burden of proof provisions should be applied in a sex discrimination case, *Barton* v. *Investec Henderson Crosthwaite Securities Ltd* (2003). The *Barton* guidelines have been approved by the Court of Appeal (with slight amendments) in *Igen Ltd and ors* v. *Wong* (2005), CA.

§6. Areas of Unlawful Discrimination

422. The EQA 2010 make discrimination unlawful in certain defined areas of employment. Among the main areas covered are selection arrangements, job offers, promotion, training, and other benefits. Dismissals are covered; in fact if the employee is dismissed before one year of continuous employment, the only remedy will be under anti-discrimination. Outside of the areas specified in the legislation, discrimination remains lawful. In particular, the anti-discrimination laws do not apply to immigration control.[517] In a recent case it was held that individual police constables could be liable for racial discrimination when providing assistance to or protection of members of the public, but it was strongly suggested that the Act did not refer to the police when performing their duties of preventing and detecting crime. Equally problematic was the express finding that the Act did not make the Chief Commissioner of Police vicariously liable for discriminatory acts by police officers.[518] It was these limitations which led to the enactment of the Race Relations (Amendment) Act 2000. The new legislation makes it unlawful for public authorities to discriminate in any of their functions; not just employment, education and the provision of services, to which the earlier RRA is confined. Law enforcement, the core functions of the prison and probation services, and the implementation of the Government's economic and social policies will for the first time be subject to discrimination laws.[519]

Also significant is the fact that the government's wide powers of patronage in conferring public appointments and honours, including the granting of peerages, must now be exercised in a non-discriminatory manner. The prohibition on discrimination applies not only to the appointment itself, but also to the terms and conditions on which the appointment is offered, and a decision to refuse to appoint. In addition, the new provisions fill a significant lacuna by making chief officers of police vicariously liable for acts of discrimination carried out by officers under their

517. *Kassam* v. *Immigration Appeal Tribunal* [1980] 2 All ER 330 (CA) at 342–343 (*per* Stephenson LJ).
518. *Farah* v. *Commissioner of Police of the Metropolis* [1997] 1 All ER 289 (CA).
519. HC (1999–2000) Standing Committee D (11 April 2000).

direction and control. Even more importantly, it is not sufficient for public authorities to refrain from discriminating. In addition, the Act imposes positive obligations on such authorities to promote race equality. However, immigration control is still not subject to anti-discrimination law. The legislation states that it is not unlawful for a Minister of the Crown or an official acting with express statutory authorization to discriminate against another person on grounds of nationality or ethnic or national origins in carrying out immigration and nationality functions. A key safeguard is provided in the form of a monitor appointed by the Secretary of State.

I. Religion and/or Belief

423. Despite the fact that there has been discrimination legislation at domestic level concerning sex and race since the middle of the 1970s, there has been a gap concerning other grounds of discrimination, i.e. sexual orientation, religion or belief and age (with disability not being addressed until 1995 under the DDA). Impetus for change came once again from the EU with the introduction under the Amsterdam Treaty in 1997 of a new Article 13 to be incorporated in the Treaty of Rome (which can now be found at Article 18 of the Treaty of the Functioning of the European Union following renumbering under the Treaty of Lisbon). This empowered the Council of Ministers to take action to combat discrimination across a wide range: sex, racial or ethnic origin, religion or belief, disability, age or sexual orientation. The EU used this power to adopt the Equal Treatment Framework Directive (2000/78EC), which required Member States to legislate against these forms of discrimination by 2003, with the exception of age and disability, for which the implementation date was 2006.[520]

Much litigation has began to develop the area of religious discrimination. For instance, in *Saini* v. *All Saints Haque Centre and Others* UKEAT/0227/08/ZT, the EAT held that the Tribunal had erred in considering only whether or not the employer mistreated the claimant on the grounds of his religion in circumstances where they found as fact they mistreated him for the purpose of seeking to get rid of another employee on the grounds of that employee's religion. Further, in *Eweida* v. *BA plc* [2010] EWCA 80, the CA held where a Christian employee, who objected to BA's policy of requiring jewellery to be worn concealed by the uniform, that there was no discrimination because there was no evidence that a group of Christians were put at a particular religious disadvantage when compared with non-Christians. However, the Court of Appeal in *LB of Islington* v. *Ladele* [2009] EWCA Civ 1357 confirmed that discrimination can be justified where a Registrar who, among other things, registered marriages, refused to participate in registering a civil partnership (a gay marriage) because to do so was inconsistent with her religious beliefs. The council insisted that she should undertake at least some of these duties, and disciplined her and threatened her with dismissal when she refused. She alleged that she had been discriminated against by reason of her religious belief in various

520. The Employment Equality (Sexual Orientation) Regulations 2003 (SI 2003/1661), which came into force on 1 December, 2003 and the Employment Equality (Religion or Belief) Regulations (2003 SI 2003/1660), which came into force on 2 December 2003.

ways. The allegations were that there had been direct discrimination, indirect discrimination and harassment. The indirect discrimination argument was based on the fact that the council had chosen to designate the claimant as someone suitable to do civil partnership work notwithstanding that they knew that she had genuine and strong religious reasons for not wanting to do it. The Council had a legitimate aim of providing civil partnership service on non-discriminatory basis; it was proportionate to require C to carry out service.

A total of four cases, including *Eweida* and *Ladele* formed part of a combined application to the European Court of Human Rights in *Eweida, Ladele, McFarlane and Chaplin* v. *The United Kingdom*[521] where the focus was on the protection of religion or belief under Article 9 of the ECHR. The four Christian applicants in this case sought to question the extent to which domestic legislation protected their right to manifest their religion within the workplace as required under Article 9. The ECtHR repeated a position that it has traditionally held, that the right to freedom of thought, conscience and religion is afforded where views attain cogency, seriousness, cohesion and importance. It further stated that in order to be a manifestation of a belief it need not be a mandatory requirement of the religion/belief in question, and that the courts would be required to examine whether there is a 'sufficiently close and direct nexus between the act and the underlying belief'. In terms of the outcome of the case, the ECtHR held that:

- Ms Eweida succeeded as BA's uniform policy in not permitting her to wear a cross interfered with her right to manifest her religious belief. BA's argument that the ban on wearing a cross was due to its desire to maintain its corporate image failed – none more so as it had been able to protect this perfectly well since altering their uniform policy to permit the wearing of religious symbols. It was further considered that there had been no evidence of real encroachment on the interests of others. In such circumstances the state had failed to sufficiently protect Ms Eweida's Art 9 rights.
- Ms Chapin, a nurse also complaining of the prohibition on her wearing a cross on a necklace at work, failed in her application. Her employer's obligation to maintain health and safety in a hospital environment succeeded as the Court did not see fit to interfere with decisions made domestically.
- Both Ms Ladele who objected to officiating at same sex civil partnership ceremonies, and Mr McFarlane who objected to providing psycho sexual counselling to same sex couples, based their objections on their Christian beliefs. It was stated that those manifestations were to be protected unless interference was necessary in a democratic society for the protection of the rights and freedoms of others. It was accepted that the equal opportunities policies of the employers in these cases were designed to ensure the provision of services without discrimination—including on the ground of sexual orientation. In these circumstances it was held that the state had not been found to have failed to protect Art 9 rights of either of these applicants in seeking to strike a balance between the

521. *Eweida, Ladele, McFarlane and Chaplin* v. *The United Kingdom* [2013] IRLR 231. See M. Hill, 'Religious symbolism and conscientious objection in the workplace: an evaluation of Strasbourg's judgment in *Eweida and others* v. *United Kingdom*' Ecc. L.J. 2013, 191–203.

rights of the two employees to manifest their religious belief and the employer's interest in securing the rights of others.

Of significance, is the case of *Grainger Plc* v. *Nicholson* (EAT 0219/07), which reminds us that belief, need not necessarily be related to religion, since Nicholson's belief that carbon emissions must be cut to avoid the catastrophic consequences of climate change was capable of amounting to a philosophical belief. Again, this widens the frontiers of the necessary protection from inequality envisaged by the Directive.

424. Until the 21st century, there was no protection in Great Britain concerning discrimination on the ground of sexual orientation. The SDA renders unlawful discrimination 'on the ground of sex', whereas gay and lesbian complainants were bringing claims under the SDA on the ground of sexual orientation.[522]

Following *English* v. *Thomas Sanderson Ltd* (2009) ICR 543, at last the Court of Appeal has grappled with the idea that the Employment Equality (Sexual Orientation) Regulations 2003 cover an individual who was target of homophobic abuse even though he was not gay, so widening the protection afforded by the Directive.

425. The courts and tribunals took a restrictive view: the SDA requires a comparison between the complainant and an actual or hypothetical comparator of the *opposite sex*, so the complainant would succeed only where it could be established that an actual or hypothetical person of the opposite sex but with the same sexual orientation, i.e. homosexuality, would not have been treated less favourably. Where such a comparator would have been treated in the same way as the complainant, i.e. badly, there was no contravention of the SDA. Thus, in *Pearce* v. *Governing Body of Mayfield Secondary School* (2003) a case concerning homophobic abuse by pupils of a female teacher who was lesbian, the House of Lords held that this was not direct sex discrimination as a male homosexual teacher would have been subjected to such abuse (see also *Smith* v. *Gardner Merchant Ltd* (1998)). The acts complained of in *Pearce* took place before the coming into force of the Human Rights Act 1998 on 2 October, 1998, so no claim could be brought on the basis of an infringement of human rights.

426. The previous Employment Equality (Sexual Orientation) Regulations 2003 extended protection to persons who face discrimination on the ground of their sexual orientation. Regulation 2 defines 'sexual orientation' as orientation towards persons of the same sex, the opposite sex, or both the same sex and the opposite sex. The legislation therefore covers homosexuals, heterosexuals and bi-sexuals, making it unlawful to discriminate against a person in any one these categories because of his or her sexual orientation.

427. Further, the former Employment Equality (Religion and Belief) Regulations 2003 (SI 2003/1660) were drafted in similar terms, with the relevant changes

522. H. Oliver, 'Sexual orientation discrimination: perceptions, definitions and genuine occupational requirement', ILJ 33 (2004), 1–21.

being made.[523] The four forms of discrimination rendered unlawful are direct, indirect, harassment and victimization, with similar definitions. Thus, for direct discrimination the definition is less favourable treatment on the grounds of religion[524] or belief, while indirect discrimination involves, (i) the application by A of a provision, criterion or practice which he applies or would apply to persons not of the same religion or belief as B, but (ii) which puts or would put persons of the same religion or belief as B at a particular disadvantage when compared with other persons, (iii) which puts B at that disadvantage, and (iv) which cannot be shown to be a proportionate means of achieving a legitimate aim (reg. 3). The religion or belief must not be that of A (reg. 3(2)).

II. Age

428. The Age Regulations were laid before Parliament on 9 March 2006 and came into force on 1 October 2006. They implement the age discrimination strand of the ETFD. They now are enshrined under the EQA 2010.

429. The objective justification defence is subject to a number of general exemptions, i.e. where justification is not required. These include: requiring retirement at age 65 or more ; benefits related to length of service, which are excepted unless the disadvantaged employee has more than five years' service, in which case the employer must establish that it 'reasonably appears' to him that the criterion of length of service 'fulfils a business need', e.g. encouraging loyalty or motivation, or rewarding experience (reg. 32); pay related to the national minimum wage (this will apply only to those situations where the employees in the lower age group (below, age 22) are paid less than the adult minimum wage pay related to the national minimum wage. This will not cover all pay differences based on the age bands used in the national minimum wage. Only those situations are covered where the employees in the lower age group (below, age 22) are paid less than the adult minimum wage (reg. 32); age-related provisions in occupational pension schemes (Sched. 2).

§7. Pensions, Death and Retirement

430. A major source of litigation has concerned provisions relating to death and retirement. The original Sex Discrimination Act excluded all provisions in relation to death or retirement, and this was broadly interpreted to include anything which was 'part and parcel of the employer's system of catering for retirement.'

The rationale for this exception was the fact that the retiring age for the purposes of state pensions was 65 for men and 60 for women; and similar age limits were

523. L. Vickers, 'Freedom of Religion and the workplace: the draft employment equality (religion or belief) regulations 2003', ILJ 32 (2003), 23–36.

524. A. McColgan, 'Class wars? Religion and (In)equality in the workplace', [2009] vol. 38, ILJ, pp. 1–29.

applied in a wide variety of non-statutory schemes, particularly in respect of retirement ages. This permitted discrimination not just in retirement and pension ages, but in a wide range of related circumstances, such as the restriction to wives of the right to survivors' benefits and the use of sex based actuarial data which assumed greater longevity in women, and therefore permitted lower pensions or higher contributions in respect of women. Such discrimination was initially legitimated at EC level. Despite Directive 79/7 on Equal Treatment in Social Security, which provides for the principle of equal treatment in statutory schemes, including protection against the risks of old age, Member States were expressly permitted to set pension ages which were different for men and women. Both this directive and the Occupational Social Security Directive, Directive 87/378, contained explicit derogations for provisions concerning survivors' benefits; and the 1987 directive also permitted the use of separate actuarial data for men and women in the fixing of levels of workers' contributions for up to 13 years after the notification of the Directive. It was the ECJ that provided the impetus for change. In the important case of *Marshall*,[525] it was held that an earlier retirement age of 60 for women compared with 65 for men constituted discrimination contrary to the Equal Treatment Directive. This effectively outlawed differential retirement ages. Of even greater importance was the series of decisions, particularly that in *Barber* v. *Guardian Royal Exchange*,[526] in which the ECJ interpreted 'pay' widely so that many aspects of occupational pensions would be governed by Article 141 (now Article 157 TFEU), thus effectively sidestepping the derogations in the two directives. In these cases, the court held that 'pay' only excludes social security schemes or retirement pensions which are directly governed by legislation without any element of agreement and which are obligatorily applicable to general categories of workers. Article 141 has also been held to apply to survivors' pensions, supplementary occupational schemes, other non-contracted-out occupational schemes, public service scheme, benefits on early retirement and transfer values.[527] It should be noted, however, that the *Barber* decision has prospective effect only: Article 141 of the Treaty cannot be relied on to claim entitlement to a pension from a date prior to 1990, unless legal proceedings have been initiated before that date.

431. Other exceptions to the Sex Discrimination Act include jobs for which being a man or woman is a genuine occupational qualification, such as models, actors, toilet attendants, hospital and prison staff, and personal welfare counsellors. This exception also includes work in a private home involving close physical or social contact with a person living in the home, or knowledge of intimate details of such a person's life.

432. The previous Race Relations Act (now incorporated into the EqA 2010) narrowed list of genuine occupational qualifications, including actors, models,

525. *Marshall* v. *Southampton AHA* C-152/84 [1986] ECR 723.
526. [1990] IRLR 240 (ECJ).
527. See e.g. *Ten Oever* C-109/91 [1993] IRLR 601 ECJ, para. 9; *Moroni* C110/91 [1994] IRLR 130 ECJ; *Coloroll* C-200/91 [1994] IRLR 586 (ECJ); *Beune* C-7/93 [1995] IRLR 103 (ECJ). On pensions equality, *see generally* Fredman, S. *Women and the Law* (OUP, 1997), Ch. 8.

personal welfare counsellors and jobs involving working in a place where food and drink is provided in a particular setting for which, in that job, a person of a particular racial group is required 'for reasons of authenticity' (e.g. Chinese restaurants). It also covers jobs where 'the holder of the job provides persons of that racial group with personal services promoting their welfare and those services can most effectively be provided by a person of that racial group'. This last provision has been narrowly construed, to cover only personal services generally requiring face to face contact, or susceptibility to personal, physical contact. This means that the exception cannot be used as a way of facilitating 'positive discrimination' (below).[528] Notably, the new EC equality directives restrict the availability of genuine occupational requirements as an exception to the equality principle to those which can be justified on the grounds that the objective is legitimate and the requirement is proportionate.

§8. Positive Action

433. Nothing in the legislation requires 'reverse' discrimination in favour of women, married persons or blacks. Indeed, the definition of discrimination means that, apart from a few exceptions, such discrimination is itself unlawful. Positive action is currently provided for in sections 158 and 159 of the EqA 2010, and in effect extends the positive action exceptions that were permitted under the previous legislation. This enables an employer for the first time to take positive action in the context of recruitment and promotion[529] to favour a candidate with a particular protected characteristic where there are two or more candidates deemed to be of otherwise equal merit; previously this was only enabled in the context of training.[530]

Section 158 EqA 2010 provides that where person who share a protected characteristic and either (i) suffer a disadvantage connected to that disadvantage; or (ii) have particular needs that are different from persons who do not share that characteristic; or (iii) those with that particular characteristic who have had a disproportionately low participation in a particular activity, positive action can be utilized if it is a proportionate means of achieving a legitimate aim, where that aim is either to overcome or minimise the disadvantage suffered, meeting the particular needs in question or enabling or encouraging participation

Section 159 of the EqA 2010 has five hurdles to overcome. It must be established that:

- the successful candidate shares a protected characteristic;
- the protected group in which the candidate is part of is at a disadvantage connected to the characteristic or that group has had disproportionately low participation in an activity;

528. *London Borough of Lambeth* v. *CRE* [1990] IRLR 231 (CA); *cf Tottenham Green Under Fives Centre* v. *Marshall* [1989] IRLR 147 (EAT); *Tottenham Green Under Fives Centre* v. *Marshall* (No. 2) [1991] IRLR 162 (EAT).
529. Section 159 of the EqA 2010.
530. This has been retained in section 158 EqA 2010.

- the successful applicant is 'as qualified' to be recruited or promoted as other candidates;
- they do not have a policy of treating people who share the protected characteristic more favourably in connection with recruitment and promotion than people who do not share it and;
- the positive action is proportionate.

Another exception is that trade unions and similar bodies may reserve seats on elective bodies for members of one sex. It is also lawful to take positive action short of reverse discrimination, including monitoring the proportion of female or ethnic minority employees in order to identify and remove possible barriers to their recruitment and advancement. Similarly, it may be necessary to take positive measures to remove what might otherwise be indirectly discriminatory barriers, for example by removing word-of-mouth recruitment and by advertising in the minority press.

A further development in this area came under the Race Relations (Amendment) Act 2000, which imposed a positive duty on public authorities to promote racial equality setting down the pathway for the EqA 2010, as it is enacted today. At s.149 EqA 2010, a public sector duty is imposed which builds upon the earlier equality duties. This currently applies across all of the protected characteristics, except for marital status and civil partnership. This requires public authorities to advance equality of opportunity, which is arguably an expansion on the previous requirement to merely promote it.

§9. Enforcement

434. The experience under the Race Relations Act 1976 was regarded by some as proof that investigation of all individual complaints by a public agency was 'costly and wasteful' and as creating 'resentment and hostility' among those whom it was designed to assist because they were denied direct access to the courts.[531] On the other hand, it was argued that private individuals did not have the resources to find and prove discrimination, and that it was through individual casework that patterns of discrimination emerged. The current Acts try to meet these points by allowing both individual enforcement, in some cases with the assistance of the Commissions, and also action against discriminatory practices by the Commissions.

435. An individual may complain to an employment tribunal within three months of the alleged discriminatory act (the period may be extended) and the EHRC may, in their discretion, assist individuals, for example by giving advice, procuring settlements, arranging for legal assistance or representation. Officers of ACAS have to attempt conciliation, encouraging the use, where appropriate, of voluntary industrial grievance procedures. The most serious obstacle facing the complainant is that of proving unlawful discrimination, although a procedure does exist by which the complainant may obtain information from the respondent to help him

531. *Equality for Women*, Cmnd 5724, 1974, para. 28; *Racial Discrimination*, Cmnd 6234, 1975, paras. 40, 41.

or her to decide whether or not to institute proceedings and, if he or she does, to assist in presenting a case. The tribunal may (1) make an order declaring the rights of the parties; (2) award compensation and (3) recommend that the respondent take within a specified period action appearing to the tribunal to be practicable for the purpose of obviating or reducing the adverse effect of the unlawful discrimination on the complainant. Compensation aims to make good, so far as possible, the loss suffered by the victim by putting him or her into as good a position as if no wrong had occurred. The statutory maximum of £10,000 was removed after the decision of the ECJ in *Marshall No. 2*, which held that compensation should ensure that the loss and damage actually sustained as a result of the discrimination be made good in full.[532] As a result there has been an upward trend in the levels of compensation awarded. Nevertheless, compensation levels remain low. There is no power to order reinstatement or re-engagement or that the next job be offered to the complainant, although these measures may be recommended. If a recommendation is not complied with, without reasonable justification, the amount of compensation awarded may be increased. One particularly problematic anomaly concerns unintentional indirect discrimination.

Both the RRA and SDA initially prohibited the recovery of damages for unintentional indirect discrimination, but, in order comply with EC law, the Sex Discrimination Act was amended in 1996 so that a tribunal can award compensation for unintentional indirect discrimination in employment cases. However, no such amendment was made to the RRA, and damages are still unavailable in non-employment cases of unintentional indirect sex discrimination. It has also been held that punitive damages should not be awarded in a race or sex discrimination case.[533] This is also anomalous, in that such damages are available in other cases, and may constitute a breach of EC law.

§10. Equal Pay

436. The previous Equal Pay Act 1970 and the Sex Discrimination Act 1975 were mutually exclusive, in that the former applies only to discrimination relating to payment of money or other terms under the contract (including terms such as holidays, holiday pay, hours and sick pay), while the latter applies only to matters not included in a contract. Although the Acts are intended to be read as a code, there is a discrepancy between them, in that the Equal Pay Act requires a comparison to be made with a specific member of the opposite sex in the same employment whereas the Sex Discrimination Act covers situations where there is no comparable member of the opposite sex. i.e. a 'hypothetical' male. This has proved to be a serious limitation on the impact of the Equal Pay Act since, as has been pointed out above, many women work in predominantly female occupations or grades and are thus unable to find a suitable comparator. Moreover, the area of comparison which a woman may draw with a man's job is limited to a man in the same employment,

532. *Marshall* v. *Southampton and South West Hampshire Area Health Authority* (No. 2) Case C-271/91 [1993] ECR I-4367 ECJ.
533. *Deane* v. *London Borough of Ealing* [1993] IRLR 209 EAT.

that is employed by one employer or an associated employer at the same establishment in Great Britain. A comparison may be drawn with other establishments elsewhere in Britain only if common terms of employment are observed in those establishments. Such terms need not be identical; indeed, the House of Lords has held that the concept of 'common terms and conditions' necessarily includes terms applicable to a wide range of employees, whose individual terms could vary greatly. Terms and conditions governed by the same collective agreement 'represent the paradigm, though not necessarily the only example of common terms and conditions'.[534] The need to find a comparator in the same employment has been particularly problematic with the increase in outsourcing, or 'contracting out' of services previously done by in-house employees. In such situations, the outside contractor may reduce the pay of women whose pay had previously been protected by the availability of male comparators doing work of equal value; because the comparators are no longer in the same employment, this comparison is not available. In a case now pending before the ECJ, the domestic courts have asked for a ruling as to whether EC law requires a broader comparison, to include employees of the previous employer. The woman is entitled to choose the man or men with whom she wishes to be compared,[535] but has to be careful not to cast her net too wide. References in the Act to women apply equally to men and vice versa.

437. The EqA 2010, like the Equal Pay Act, entitles a woman to claim equal treatment with a man in three situations. First, it allows a woman the right to equal treatment when employed on work of the same or a broadly similar nature to that of a man in the same employment. In making the comparison, regard must be had to the frequency or otherwise with which any differences between their work occur in practice, as well as the nature and extent of the differences. This is a necessarily limited basis of comparison, and has been narrowly interpreted by tribunals and courts. Secondly, a woman is entitled to equal treatment with a man if her job and his have been given an equal value under a job evaluation study (JES). A 'job evaluation' is defined as a study undertaken with a view to evaluating jobs to be done by all or any employees in an undertaking or group of undertakings, where the evaluation is made in 'terms of the demands made on the worker under various headings (for instance effort, skill, decision)'.[536] This type of JES is known as an 'analytical' job evaluation, in contrast with more subjective evaluations based on 'whole job' or 'felt fair' comparisons. An existing JES can operate as a bar to a claim for equal pay for work of equal value, but only if it is analytical in this sense.[537] However, the employer is not obliged to undertake such a study. Even where a JES does exist, it may give disproportionate weight to traditionally 'male skills' such as physical strength or experience. However, a JES which is itself discriminatory is not a bar to an equal value claim.

534. *Leverton* v. *Clwyd County Council* [1989] IRLR 28 (HL).
535. *Ainsworth* v. *Glass Tubes Ltd* [1977] IRLR 74 (EAT); *Pickstone* v. *Freemans plc* [1988] IRLR 357 (HL).
536. EqPA, s. 1(5).
537. *Bromley* v. *H&J Quick Ltd* [1988] IRLR 249 (CA).

438. The third basis of comparison allows a woman to claim equal treatment with a man doing work of equal value.[538] This was introduced in 1983 as a result of infringement proceedings under ex Article 141 of the Treaty of Rome.[539] It is broader than the first two methods, since it does not require like work, nor does it rely on an employer-initiated job evaluation exercise. The equal value provisions were intended to be a residual claim, only operative if neither 'like work' nor 'work rated as equivalent' were applicable. However, the House of Lords has held that such an interpretation would conflict with European law.[540] Therefore, even if there is a man doing the same work as the complainant, she may still claim equal pay work of equal value provided that she is able to find a suitable comparator who is not himself employed on like work or work rated as equivalent. However, a claim for equal value cannot be made if a job evaluation study has been carried out unless the existing study can be shown to be discriminatory. In practice, this has proved to be a very difficult hurdle to surmount. If the tribunal is satisfied that there are reasonable grounds for determining that the work is of equal value, or that the existing JES is discriminatory, it may appoint an independent expert, one of a panel appointed by ACAS, to conduct a job evaluation exercise. The expert is given considerable discretion, the only guidelines being that the evaluation should be carried out according to the demands made on the employee, rather than using other methods of job evaluation such as market value or marginal productivity. The expert's report is only challengeable on limited grounds. Because of unconscionable delays in the preparation and submission of the expert's report (para. 360, *below*), the tribunals have recently been given new powers to determine the question of equal value themselves. The equal value provisions have been successfully used to establish entitlement to equality of pay between a female canteen worker and three skilled manual workers in a shipyard,[541] female ship packers and a male labourer[542] and a house-mother and a house-father.[543] However, the provisions are still limited in that the woman must find a comparator in the same employment doing work of the same value. There is still no redress for women in a segregated establishment, nor for a woman whose work is admittedly of lower value than a male comparator, but whose pay is disproportionately low. For example, a woman whose work is worth 75 per cent of that of a man, but who is paid only 50 per cent of his pay, has no grounds for complaint under the Act. On the other hand, European law will give redress to a woman whose work is of higher value than that of a male comparator.[544]

439. Where a woman has established the relevant comparison, it is still open to the employer to argue in defence that the difference in pay was genuinely due to a

538. Equal Pay (Amendment) Regulations 1982, SI 1983 1794.
539. *Commission of the European Communities* v. *United Kingdom* [1982] ICR 578 (ECJ).
540. *Pickstone* v. *Freemans plc.* [1988] IRLR 357 (HL).
541. *Hayward* v. *Cammell Laird Shipbuilders Ltd* [1984] IRLR 463, [1987] IRLR 257.
542. *Wells* v. *F. Smales & Son Fish Merchants* EOR, No. 2, July/August 1985, p. 24.
543. *Scott* v. *Beam College*, EOR, No. 4, November/December 1985, p. 6.
544. *Murphy* v. *Bord Telecomm Eirean* [1988] IRLR 267 (ECJ); cf. *Waddington* v. *Leicester Council for Social Services* [1977] IRLR 32 (EAT).

material factor, other than the differences of sex.[545] The crucial question in this context is the extent to which market forces are allowed to justify a pay discrepancy. For example, could an employer argue that the reason for the difference in pay is that the male employee was in a position to demand higher pay just because he was paid more in a previous job than the female employee? In the early case of *Clay Cross* v. *Fletcher*,[546] Lord Denning recognized that such a reason could simply replicate existing discrimination within the market, and held that the employer's defence was limited to personal factors such as merit and experience. However, in *Rainey* v. *Greater Glasgow Health Board* the House of Lords expressly overruled the *Clay Cross* exclusion of market forces.[547] It is therefore permissible to justify a discrepancy in pay by reference to any economic or administrative grounds, whether the claim is based on the like work or JES provisions, or on work of equal value. The market forces defence is potentially a significant limitation on the impact of the Equal Pay Act particularly where 'women's work' is undervalued by the market due to traditional stereotypes, inferior training or responsibilities for child-care.

440. The impact of the 'market forces' defence is mitigated to some extent by the principle that it is not sufficient for the employer to show an intention to achieve an objective. Instead the difference in pay must actually achieve that objective.[548] In applying this test, there are three matters to which national courts must have regard, namely that the means chosen by the employer corresponds to a real need on the part of the undertaking, that they are appropriate to achieving the objectives pursued and are necessary to that end.[549] Although the EqA 2010 does not explicitly include the concept of indirect discrimination it has been held that the Equal Pay Act 'operates to counteract all discrimination, whether direct or indirect and whether intentional or unintentional; it looks at the effect of the contractual terms, not whether they were expressed in overtly discriminatory words or with any particular intention'.[550] Moreover there is now no difference between the defence of justification thus interpreted in the Equal Pay Act and that relating to indirect discrimination in the Sex Discrimination Act.

441. The individual may enforce the right to equal treatment through a statutory term in the contract of employment (called the 'equality clause'). The effect is that any term of the woman's contract which is less favourable than a similar term in the comparator's contract is modified so as not to be less favourable. In making the comparison, each term is to be considered independently: thus basic pay should be compared with basic pay, sickness benefit with sickness benefit etc. An employer

545. EqPA 1970, s. 1(3).
546. *Clay Cross (Quarry Services) Ltd* v. *Fletcher* [1979] ICR 1 (CA).
547. *Rainey* v. *Greater Glasgow Health Board* [1987] IRLR 26 (HL).
548. *Jenkins* v. *Kingsgate (Clothing Productions) Ltd (No. 2)* [1981] IRLR 388 (EAT).
549. *Bilka–Kaufhaus GmbH* v. *Weber von Hartz* Case 190/84 [1986] IRLR 317 (ECJ), held applicable to domestic law by the House of Lords in *Rainey* v. *Greater Glasgow Health Board* [1987] IRLR 26; see also *Enderby v. Frenchay Health Authority* [1993] IRLR 591.
550. *Jenkins* v. *Kingsgate (Clothing Productions) Ltd (No. 2)*, above at p. 724. This goes beyond the interpretation placed on Article 141 of the Treaty of Rome by the European Court of Justice: [1981] ICR 592.

cannot argue that less favourable treatment in respect of one term, such as basic pay, is off-set by better treatment in respect of another term, such as holiday entitlement or sick leave, although it is possible that the defence of justification might apply. The claim may be referred to the employment tribunal either by the employee, or by the employer, and in exceptional cases (so far never used) by the Secretary of State. The tribunal may award up to two years' arrears of pay and damages for breach of an equality clause. The proceedings must be instituted within 6 months of the termination of the woman's employment. Claims in respect of like work and work rated as equivalent under a JES follow a similar procedure to the tribunal proceedings, but where there is an equal value claim a much more complicated and lengthy procedure has to be followed. This includes a compulsory preliminary hearing to weed out cases where there is no reasonable prospect of success. In cases with multiple applicants, delays have been described by the EAT as 'scandalous and a denial of justice to women through the judicial process'.[551] Claims by 1280 women against British Coal are still going through the adjudicative process 15 years after the first applications were made. It took as many as 14 years for speech therapists' claims against health authorities to be concluded.

442. There is at present no mechanism in English law for correcting discriminatory collective agreements. Until 1986, such agreements could be referred to the Central Arbitration Committee (CAC) under Section 3 of the Equal Pay Act. However, because of the restrictive interpretation of its powers by the High Court, the CAC's ability to correct discrimination was limited, and references soon dried up. Its jurisdiction was abolished entirely in 1986. At the same time, the UK was required, under European law, to introduce legislation providing for any provision contrary to the principle of equal treatment in a collective agreement to be declared void or amended.[552] To this end, the Sex Discrimination Act 1986 provides that terms of collective agreements incorporated into contracts of employment are void and unenforceable if they contravene the EqA 2010. The more effective strategy of permitting correction of the whole collective agreement was rejected. This unsatisfactory position has now been partially remedied by an important decision of the European Court, which held that a discriminatory collective agreement could be challenged directly under ex Article 141.[553] The central significance of this case lies in its insistence that the offending clause in the agreement be amended to remove the discrimination rather than, as in the UK legislation, simply being avoided.

443. It is clear from the above that the EqA must be read subject to Article 157 TFEU (ex Article 141). In addition, Article 157 forms an independent cause of action. Since it is directly effective, both against the State and against private employers, an individual may bring a claim in an ordinary court or tribunal in the UK based on ex Article 141.

The most important question in establishing a claim under Article 157 is what counts as 'pay' in this context. The direct effect of the article can only be brought

551. *Arldridge* v. *British Telcommunications plc.* [1990] IRLR 10 at 14.
552. *Commission of the European Communities* v. *United Kingdom* [1984] ICR 192 (ECJ).
553. *Kowalska* v. *Freie und Hansestadt Hamburg* [1990] IRLR 447.

to bear if the claim concerns pay. The Treaty provision defines pay as the ordinary basic minimum wage or salary and any other consideration, whether in cash or in kind, which the worker receives, directly or indirectly, in respect of the employment from his or her employer. The area which has been the subject of most litigation has concerned the boundary between employment related benefits, which are pay within the meaning of the Article, and benefits paid by the state directly or indirectly, which are not pay. Examples of benefits which fall into a possible grey area are redundancy payments, sick pay and pensions, all of which may be voluntary, contractual, or statutory. In general, and especially in recent cases, the European Court of Justice has construed 'pay' broadly.[554] The most important case in this context has been *Barber* v. *Guardian Royal Exchange Assurance Group*,[555] in which the Court stated that the central question was whether the benefit arises in respect of employment, and this can be so even if it is required to be paid by statute, or is *ex gratia*. Thus statutory redundancy compensation was held to fall within the definition of 'pay', even thought it is a result of a statutory obligation. Similarly, retirement benefits count as 'pay' even though they are paid as part of a 'contracted out' scheme, because in both cases, the payment is an intrinsic part of the employment relationship. Statutory sick and maternity pay are more complex. The European Court has held that where sick pay is fully funded by the employer, it falls within Article 141.[556] (The application of Article 141 to pensions and related issues is discussed above.)

444. The EqA 2010 applies to persons employed on contracts of service or contracts personally to execute any work or labour. However, the Act excludes complaints by men that women are more favourably treated by way of maternity leave or other special treatment in connection with pregnancy or childbirth. There is no statutory right to paternity leave, although there is now a right to parental leave.

445. A number of initiatives have been introduced which have the aim of enhancing transparency of pay structures. This is with a view to removing discriminatory pay practices that are hidden. By enhancing transparency the potential of the equal pay provisions themselves are enhanced. A notable amendment in this respect is through the The Equality Act 2010 (Gender Pay Gap Information) Regulations 2017. The Regulations impose an obligation on employers with at least 250 employees to publish information relting to the gender pay gap within their organisation. This will include information on any differences in average hourly pay, differences in average bonuses paid, and information on proportions of males and females in each pay quartile of the workforce. This will highlight significant gender pay issues, which in turn ought to encourage action to redress such issues. However, although the regulations appear to have great potential, at least in terms of highlighting matters that would previously not be highlighted, they have great weakness in their

554. *Worringham* v. *Lloyds Bank Ltd*, Case 69/80, [1981] IRLR 178 (ECJ); *Garland* v. *British Rail Engineering Ltd*, Case 12/81, [1982] IRLR 111 (ECJ); *Bilka-Kaufhaus Gmbh* v. *Weber von Harz* [1986] IRLR 317 (ECJ); cf. *Defrenne* v. *Belgium* Case 80/70, [1971] ECR 445 (ECJ).

555. [1990] IRLR 240 (ECJ).

556. *Rinner-Kuhn* v. *FWW Spezial-Gebaudereinigung GmbH and Co. KG*, Case 171/89 [1989] IRLR 493 (ECJ); noted by Szyszczak in [1990] ILJ 114.

enforcement. Much of this relies on action taken by the Commission for Equality and Human Rights.

§11. Reform

446. In a major review of UK anti-discrimination legislation, concluded in 2000, that their has been a tidal wave of equal pay litigation across the UK, namely in the public sector affecting local authorities and NHS Trusts. Two landmark rulings have shaped the landscape of the litigation since, namely: *Hartlepool Borough Council* v. *Llewellyn; Middlesborough Borough Council* v. *Matthews; South Tyneside Borough Council* v. *McAvoy; Middlesborough Borough Council* v. *Ashcroft* (2009) ICR 1426.

In these landmark cases, the EAT held male employees doing same job as female Cs who brought successful equal pay claims could bring piggy back equal pay claims using female Cs as comparators; and, *Somerset County Council* v. *Pike* (2009) IRLR 870 which held pool for comparison should be restricted to those who had actually retired and re-entered employment where considering the existence of indirect discrimination in a rule that governed pension scheme access for employees who has retired and returned to work. Similarly, in the Scottish Courts in *Dumfries and Galloway Council* v. *North* (2009) ICR 1363, the EAT held that an employee can only rely upon comparator at different establishments where there is a real possibility of the comparator doing the same or a broadly similar job at the employee's place of work as he does at his current place of work. This is a significant ruling, given its engagement with Article 157 of the Treaty (formerly 141/119).[557] However, the Supreme Court (*North* v. *Dumfries* (2013) UKSC 45) historically upheld the right to compare terms and conditions with comparators who are employed by the same employer but work in or from different workplaces.

557. C. Kilpatrick, 'The ECJ and labour law: a 2008 retrospective review', [2009], vol 38 ILJ, pp. 180–208.

Chapter 9. Competition by Former Employees

447. This is a subject entirely regulated by rules of public policy formulated by the courts. Since early times restraints against competition have been regarded as void, and those who tried to control business competition were once even liable to imprisonment. It was however recognized that an employer might be unwilling to train apprentices if he could not restrain them from competing with him at the end of their time. In 1711, the rule was formulated that a restraint was prima facie valid if it did not extend over the whole country and was the result of a bargain between the parties. Since then, the rule has been changed in various ways and the modern doctrine is that restraints of trade are prima facie void but they can be justified if they are reasonable and are not contrary to the public interest. Moreover, a restraint may extend over the whole country or even the whole world, provided that this is reasonable and in the public interest.[558]

448. We have seen that the duty of faithful service obliges an employee not to disclose trade secrets of the employer or his confidential information so long as the employment lasts. The duty not to disclose secrets or information may even continue after the employment has ended, and no covenant is needed for this purpose.

However, this duty is more restricted than that imposed on the employee while the employment lasts. The obligation not to use or disclose information might cover secret processes of manufacture, or designs or special methods of construction, and other information of a sufficiently high degree of confidentiality as to amount to a trade secret. The obligation, after the employment has ended, does not extend to information only 'confidential' because the employee was told to keep it confidential and it remained in the employee's head and became part of his skill and knowledge. If the employer wishes to protect this latter kind of information after the employment has ended, he must enter into a restrictive covenant.[559] Another reason for a covenant is that there is no general restriction on an ex-employee canvassing or doing his business with customers of his former employer. The doctrine of restraint of trade then becomes relevant.[560]

449. The interests which an employer can protect by a covenant of this kind are narrowly defined. The employer cannot protect himself simply on the ground that competition by the ex-employee will harm the business in which he once worked. It has been suggested that the reasons for this are that the employer pays only for the services he receives and not for restraints against future competition, and that the employee is not an equal bargaining partner who is capable of protecting his own interests. Whatever the reasons it seems clear that an employer may expressly protect his trade secrets and confidential information (which, as we have said, might

558. *Nordenfelt* v. *Maxim Nordenfelt Guns & Ammunition Co.* [1894] AC 535.

559. Compare *Faccenda Chicken Ltd* v. *Fowler* [1986] ICR 297, CA, with *Balston Ltd* v. *Headline Filters Ltd* [1987] FSR 330, *Systems Reliability Holdings plc.* v. *Smith* [1990] IRLR 377, where differing views were expressed as to the permissible extent of protection by restrictive covenant.

560. This topic is extensively discussed in the *Sweet and Maxwell's Encyclopedia of Employment Law*, Part I.

be impliedly protected anyway, but an express covenant puts it beyond doubt) and probably his 'know-how'. The employer may only restrain the employee from soliciting customers after leaving the employment if the employee's position enabled him to gain influence over them, e.g. a sales representative or hairdresser's assistant.

450. In order to be regarded as reasonable the covenant must not go beyond what is necessary to protect the employer's interests. In this regard the courts have distinguished between 'area covenants' and 'solicitation covenants'. The former prohibit *working* in a particular area, the latter prohibit soliciting former customers. The courts are more inclined to uphold solicitation covenants than area covenants, but an area covenant may be upheld provided that the area covered is not too large. Similarly a restraint for an excessive length of time will not be upheld, nor will one which restrains an activity which bears no relation directly to the business of an employer, such as a tailor being restrained from working as a seller of shoes.

451. Even if the restraint is reasonable, it may still be held to be against the public interest. This has rarely been used as a ground for invalidity and has been strongly criticized by academic writers largely because the court is unlikely to pay much attention to general economic conditions, such as whether large-scale unemployment renders restraints unreasonable and in the public interest.[561] In one case (1967)[562] a restraint contained in the rule of a pension fund to which an employee had agreed as a term of his employment was struck down as not being in the public interest. The rule which was held to be invalid stated that the employee would lose his pension if he engaged in any competitive activity. Instead of using the ground of public interest, the court could have decided that the employer had no sufficient 'interest' to protect or that the restraint was not reasonable.

561. A.L. Goodhart, *Law Quarterly Review*, 49, p. 465.
562. *Bull* v. *Pitney -Bowes Ltd* [1967] 1 WLR 273. *See too Sadler* v. *Imperial Life Assurance Co. of Canada Ltd* [1988] IRLR 389.

Part II. Collective Labour Relations

Chapter 1. Trade Union Freedom

§1. Government Policies

452. Until the 1980s, successive governments in the UK generally adopted policies encouraging trade union organization and freedom of association. For most of the century, such policies were expressed primarily through the example set by the state to private employers, although after 1970, this was supplemented by legislation. From 1906, there was an official policy of encouraging public service employees to join trade unions (apart from the police, whose freedom of association is strictly limited by law).[563] In addition, the state used its vast purchasing powers as a means of influencing private sector employers.

From 1946 until its repeal in 1983, the Fair Wages Resolutions of the House of Commons required government departments to include in their contracts with suppliers a clause which provided that 'the contractor shall recognize the freedom of his workpeople to be members of trade unions.' Although in practice this clause had limited effect, it was a significant gesture of support on the part of government.[564] On the international level, the UK Government expressed further official support by ratifying international treaties guaranteeing freedom of association. These include four ILO Conventions, namely, Convention No. 87 (1948) on Freedom of Association, Convention No. 98 (1949) on the Right to Organize and Collective Bargaining, Convention No. 151 (1978) on Protection of the Right to Organize in the Public Service, and Convention No. 135 (1972) Concerning Protection and Facilities to be Afforded to Workers' Representatives in the Undertaking. The UK has also accepted the obligations in Article 11 of the European Convention on Human Rights and Fundamental Freedoms, which include the right to form and join trade unions, and Article 5 of the European Social Charter on the right to organize. Apart from Article 11 of the Human Rights Convention (which has enforceable since 2 October 2000 under the Human Rights Act 1998), these obligations are not directly enforceable as part of domestic law (for the reasons explained above), but before the 1980s successive governments sought to comply with their obligations.

453. The policy of encouragement of trade union membership changed radically when Mrs Thatcher's Conservative government came into power in 1979 and there

563. *Police Act 1919*, now the *Police Act 1996*, s. 64.
564. See the late Brian Bercusson, *Fair Wages Resolutions* (Mansell, London, 1976).

has been only a limited retreat under the new Labour government since 1997. A central tenet of Thatcherism was the view that trade unions impede the operation of the 'free market' and threaten individual freedoms. This led to much greater government intervention. Legislation was introduced placing increasing restrictions on trade union freedom, and the government no longer aimed by its own practices to encourage employers in the private sector to permit and recognize trade union organization. In total, there were six pieces of legislation introduced all with the aim of increasing legal control on the activities of trase unions. In 1983, the Fair Wages Resolution was repealed, an action which necessitated the denunciation of ILO Convention No. 94 on labour clauses in public contracts. This policy was extended to local authorities by the Local Government Act 1988, which makes it unlawful for local authorities to require government contractors to permit trade union organization as a condition of their contracts. Although this may be changed by order under the Local Government Act 1999, Section 19, no such changes have yet been made.

Similarly, the Conservative government changed the policy of advocating trade union membership among civil servants. The most striking expression of the new policy direction was the then Prime Minister's decision in January 1984 that trade union membership at the intelligence gathering unit, Government Communications Headquarters (GCHQ), posed a threat to national security. Without advance warning or consultation, the government banned the trade unions which had been firmly established there since the inception of GCHQ. It is now a condition of service of all civil servants employed at the intelligence gathering unit that they will not belong to a trade union or staff association, other than the internal, management sponsored staff association which has subsequently been established. A legal challenge to this unilateral change in conditions of service was unsuccessful.[565] The unions argued that the failure to consult them before the decision was a breach of natural justice, rendering it void. This contention was upheld by Glidewell J, but dismissed by the Court of Appeal and the House of Lords. The Law Lords unanimously held that the long history of encouragement of trade union membership and consultation over terms of employment gave rise to a duty to consult trade unions before making important changes. However, this duty was outweighed by the interests of the state in national security.

The Law Lords did not require the Prime Minister to provide evidence of the alleged threat to national security beyond proving that the real reason for her action was her genuine fear of such a threat. The union's complaint to the ILO was more successful: the ILO's Committee of Experts held that the UK Government had breached Convention No. 87, which gives workers the right to join organizations of their own choosing.[566] Nevertheless, the government took no steps to reverse the ban. As a last resort, the unions took their case to the European Court of Human Rights, complaining of a breach of Article 11 of the Convention, which gives the right to form and join trade unions. However, the European Commission of Human Rights declared their case inadmissible. Interestingly, this was not on the basis of the exception for national security, but because the article permits the imposition of

565. *Council of Civil Service Unions* v. *Minister for the Civil Service* [1984] 3 All ER 935, HL.

566. ILO Governing Body, 234th Report of the Committee on Freedom of Association, 1984, Case No. 1261.

restrictions on members of 'the administration of the State'.[567] The restrictive policy on trade unions is reflected too in the removal of well-established collective bargaining rights from schoolteachers, an act which was held to be in breach of ILO Convention No. 98 on the right to bargain.

454. Under Tony Blair's premiership, the then Labour Government yet again considered the position of trade unions and sought to introduce less intrusive measures. A key piece of legislation in this regard was the Employment Relations Act 2004. The centre piece of the revising 2004 Act were the provisions to increase the protections against the dismissal of employees taking official, lawfully-organized industrial action by extending the 'protected period' from 8 to 12 weeks; exempting 'lock out' days from the 12-week protected period; and, defining more closely the actions which employers and unions should undertake when taking reasonable procedural steps to resolve industrial disputes. Furthermore, measures to simplify the law on industrial action ballots and ballot notices, as well as a power to make regulations to introduce information and consultation in the workplace (in Great Britain and Northern Ireland), by implementing the Directive on Information and Consultation Directive were introduced. This Act also clarified the role of the companion in grievance and disciplinary proceedings. Lastly, it grants greater powers to strike out weak and vexatious claims.

455. Trade union protections are once more on the political agenda. The current Conservative Government has once more sought to introduce legislative action to limit Trade Unions. This has come in the form of the Trade Union Act 2016. This Act has introduced more stringent requirements that need to be satisfied for industrial action to be protected. This includes introducing tougher notice requirements being placed on unions.

§2. The Right to Belong to and Participate in the Activities of an Independent Trade Union

456. At common law, there is no prohibition against membership of trade unions. However, there is likewise no common law protection against discrimination by employers on the basis of trade union membership. It was not until the Industrial Relations Act 1971 that a statutory right to belong to a trade union of one's choice was first introduced. After the repeal of that Act there was no comprehensive legal guarantee of the right to organize. Instead three individual legal rights were introduced to protect trade union membership and activity at the workplace. These individual are now found in TULRCA 1992. The first of these is that officials and members of independent trade unions have the right to time off to participate in union activities. The second is that every employee has the right not to be unfairly dismissed by reason of membership of, or activities, at an appropriate time, in an independent trade union.[568] The third is that every employee has the right 'as an

567. *Council of Civil Service Unions* v. *United Kingdom*, Application No. 11603/85.
568. TULRCA 1992, s. 152.

individual' not to be penalized for, or deterred or prevented from joining an independent trade union or taking part in its activities at an appropriate time, by sanctions short of dismissal imposed by the employer.[569] There is no upper age limit or qualifying period of service for claiming these rights. A fourth right was introduced in 1990, which makes it unlawful to refuse employment to a person because he or she is a member of a trade union.[570] Although the 1990 Act was primarily aimed at preventing compulsory trade union membership, the need for formal equality led to the introduction of parallel protection for union members. However, the impact of this right is likely to be limited. Most discrimination at the point of employment occurs against union activists; and the legislation was deliberately phrased so as to exclude protection for those who are refused employment on the grounds of union activities rather than merely union membership.[571] In addition, rights have recently been introduced restricting the use of information relation to union membership or activities.[572]

457. This set of negative protections is now significantly enhanced by the incorporation into domestic law of the ECHR by the Human Rights Act 1998, which came into effect in October 2000. Article 11 of the Convention gives the right to freedom of association, which expressly includes the 'right to form and to join trade unions for the protection of his [or her] interests'. Article 11 is wider than existing law, since it is not confined to employees. Although the HRA on its face only applies to public authorities or private bodies when exercising functions of a public nature, the courts are themselves obliged to act consistently with Convention rights, so that common law actions between two individuals must be interpreted in conformity with Article 11.

458. A number of points may be made about the statutory rights. The first is that they belong to individuals. Although they protect a collective freedom, they cannot be enforced by the trade union, but only by the employee against his or her employer. Although the union may be expected to support the individual in any action he or she takes, it may be a weakness of this approach that the individual is more likely than a trade union to be deterred from bringing an action against the employer, especially during the subsistence of the employment relationship. A second point is that these rights do not extend to those who are not employees, for example, 'self-employed' construction workers.[573] A further limitation was introduced in 1977 by the Employment Appeal Tribunal, which held that an employee was not protected against dismissal for trade union activities in a previous job.[574] This left the way open to employers to blacklist trade union activists.

569. TULRCA 1992, s. 146.
570. TULRCA 1992, s. 137.
571. B. Simpson, 'The Employment Act 1990 in Context', MLR 1991, 418.
572. Data Protection Act 1998; Employment Relations Act 1999, s. 3, allowing regulations (none have been made yet) to prevent compilation of blacklists of union members or activists with a view to use for discrimination by employers or employment agencies.
573. This may be extended by regulation under ERA 1999, s. 23, but this has not so far happened.
574. *City of Birmingham District Council* v. *Beyer* [1977] IRLR 210 (EAT).

However, in an important decision, the Court of Appeal has held that protection extends to dismissal on the basis of the employee's previous union activities,[575] since the real reason for the dismissal must be the likelihood of activism in the present job. However, if the real reason for the dismissal was that the employee deceitfully failed to reveal relevant factors, then the section does not apply.

459. A third point is that the right to belong is not unlimited. It is a right to belong to an independent trade union and so properly excludes employer dominated 'company unions'. Nevertheless, the employee may belong to any union and not necessarily the union which the employer recognizes for collective bargaining purposes.

460. A fourth point is that the ambit of legitimate trade union activities has been severely limited by judicial interpretation. Most serious has been the restrictive definition given by the House of Lords in the cases of *Associated Newspapers* v. *Wilson* and *Associated British Ports* v. *Palmer*,[576] both of which concerned attempts by an employer to replace collectively bargained terms and conditions of employment with personal contracts. As an incentive to agree to depart from well established collectively bargained terms and conditions and agree to a personal contract, employees were offered a special pay rise. Any employee who refused to agree a personal contract and instead insisted on adherence to well-established bargaining arrangements was denied the pay increase. Employees who wished to continue to be subject to collective bargaining claimed that this course of action was a breach of the statutory protection against action short of dismissal 'taken against him [or her] as an individual for the purpose of preventing or deterring him from being or seeking to become a member of an independent trade union, or penalizing him for doing so'. In a particularly restrictive interpretation, the House of Lords held that 'action' for these purposes did not include omissions, so that a failure to pay additional pay increases to employees who refused to agree to accept personal contracts in place of collectively agreed terms and conditions of employment, did not amount to a breach of this section. In addition, and even more seriously, the House of Lords held that the employer's purpose in withholding pay increases from those who did not accept personal contracts was not to deter the employees from remaining members of the union or to penalize them for doing so, since they were free to retain their union membership cards. In other words, the right to freedom of association was reduced to bare membership of a union, with no credence given to the primary role of the union in protecting its members' interests through collective bargaining. The Conservative government, then in power, nevertheless endorsed this view of trade union freedom, passing an amendment, known as the Ullswater amendment[577], which stated that if the purpose of an employer was to further a change in his or her relationship with a class of employees, then that purpose should prevail, even if it coincided with the purpose of deterring or penalizing trade union activities.[578] Nor

575. *Fitzpatrick* v. *British Railways Board* [1991] IRLR 376 (CA).
576. [1995] IRLR 258 HL.
577. TULRCA 1992, s. 146.
578. TULRCA 1992, s. 148(3).

has the position been fully reversed by the Labour Party, in power since 1997. Although the legislation has been amended so that 'action short of dismissal' includes 'a deliberate failure to act',[579] no attempt has been made to repeal the Ullswater amendment or otherwise reverse the House of Lords decision in *Wilson*.

The 1999 legislation gives the Secretary of State the power to make regulations about cases where a worker is subjected to detriment or dismissed on the grounds that he refuses to enter into a contract which includes terms which differ from the terms of a collective agreement which applies to him' but no regulations have yet been made under this section; and in any event, the section goes on to state that as long as there is no prohibition on the individual receiving the payment from being a member of a trade union, and the higher rates of pay are provided for in the contract and reasonably relate to services provided by the worker under the contract.[580] In other restrictive decisions, the, the Court of Appeal has held that the employee is protected only if the employer's action is a response to the individual's activities as part of a trade union and not in respect of a general reprisal against the union itself. So a management decision to dismiss employees as a direct response to a union's request for recognition, after the employees had joined the union, was not unlawful.[581] In other words, only where the employer's action is taken against employees for their *individual* participation in the *collective* activity does the legislation provide any remedy. Finally it is to be noted that the right to participate is confined to activities at 'an appropriate time'. This in effect means times outside working hours, or times when the employee is on the employer's premises with permission but is not required to be at work (e.g. during meal or other recognized breaks). While the employee is at work the employer's permission is required.[582]

461. In *Wilson and Palmer* (2002),[583] their respective employers had offered pay increases on the relinquishing of their trade union rights. The House of Lords held that such action did not deprive the employees, who desired to exercise their freedom of association and remain in their trade unions, of their statutory rights and protection. The European Court of Human Rights in Strasbourg, took a different view, upholding that the UK law had failed to protect trade union members and that the British employers concerned had violated the freedom to associate. Section 2 of the Employment Relations Act 1999, contained a change of wording to Section 146 TULRCA 1992, so as to effectively reverse the ruling in *Wilson and Palmer* (above). Section 2 ERelA 1999, makes it unlawful for an employee to be 'subjected to any detriment' for trade union reasons.

462. The employee's remedy for breach of these rights is to make a complaint to an employment tribunal within three months of the act complained of. In the case of unfair dismissal, the special procedure of 'interim relief ' is available to continue the employee's contract of employment until his or her rights are determined.

579. ERA 1999, s. 2 Sched. 2, paras. 1, 4.
580. ERA 1999, 17.
581. *Carrington* v. *Therm-a-Stor Ltd* [1983] ICR 208, CA.
582. TULRCA 1992, s. 146(1), s. 152(1).
583. See K. Ewing, 'The Implications of Wilson and Palmer', ILJ 32 (2003), 1–22. Also, K. Ewing, 'Freedom of association and the Employment Rights Act (1999)', ILJ 28 (1999), 283–298.

Where reinstatement or re-engagement is not ordered, there is a minimum basic award of compensation and the Employment Relations Act 1999 increased the additional award for all cases where an employer fails to comply with an order for reinstatement or re-engagement which was practicable. In the case of action short of dismissal, the tribunal will grant a declaration as to the employee's rights and may award compensation for the loss sustained (e.g. loss of earnings) and also in respect of 'the infringement of the complainant's rights' (a statutory penalty not limited in amount). In cases of refusal to employ on grounds of trade union membership, the tribunal may, in addition to a declaration to that effect, make an order requiring payment of compensation and a recommendation that the respondent take appropriate action, failure to comply with which may result in increased compensation.

§3. The Right Not to Belong

463. The right not to belong to a trade union has frequently been treated differently from the right to belong. The question is of particular relevance where membership of a trade union is a precondition for obtaining or retaining employment (the 'closed shop'). It has been argued that whereas freedom of association is essential to the protection of workers in a pluralist society, the right not to belong is of a different character and may lead to disruption of orderly industrial relations.

The Donovan Commission, for example, argued that 'the two are not truly comparable. The former condition [the right not to belong] is designed to frustrate the development of collective bargaining, which it is public policy to promote, whereas no such objection applies to the latter'.[584]

464. A persistent argument against the closed shop centres on the alleged threat to individual freedom. The debate about whether the right to freedom of association is infringed by the closed shop depends to some extent on whether freedom of association is seen as an aspect of individual autonomy, or as a social right, to which exclusively individual interests are to some extent subordinate. One question which arises is whether the closed shop infringes Article 11 of the European Convention on Human Rights and Fundamental Freedoms, which states that freedom of association should not be subject to any restrictions except such as are prescribed by law and are necessary in a democratic society for the protection of the rights and freedoms of others. In the discussions leading up to the formulation of Article 11, it was explicitly agreed that it would be undesirable to include a right not to be compelled to join a union parallel to the right to join a union. In 1981, this question was raised directly before the European Court of Human Rights.[585]

Three former employees of British Rail complained that their rights under Article 11 had been infringed when they were dismissed for refusal to belong to the unions

584. Report of the Royal Commission on Trade Unions and Employers' Associations Cmnd. 3623, 1968, para. 599, and see generally R. Lewis and B. Simpson, ILJ, 11 (1982), 227; cf. Industrial Relations Act 1971, s. 5.

585. *Young, James and Webster* v. *United Kingdom* [1981] IRLR 408 (ECHR); and see also *Sigurour A Sigurjonsson* v. *Iceland* (1993) 16 EHRR 462.

with which British Rail had concluded a union membership agreement. Although the Court refused to review the closed shop system as such, it upheld the applicants' complaint in the particular circumstances of the case. The fact that the closed shop had been imposed on the applicants after their employment had begun and under the threat of dismissal was held to be an unacceptable infringement of their freedom of association. In addition, the Court held that the applicants' freedom of association had been infringed by the limitation on their choice of which union to join.

465. The Industrial Relations Act 1971, reflected an individualist philosophy by conferring a general right not to associate, in parallel with the new right to associate. This clashed with the collectivist aims of trade unions, most of whom had in any case refused to register as required by the Act. Competition for members developed between unregistered TUC unions and new or splinter unions who utilized the new rights as a platform to organize. As a result stable bargaining arrangements were threatened with disruption. After the repeal of the 1971 Act, the right not to belong to a union was recognized in only two specific instances, by legislation enacted between 1974 and 1976. First, there was a right not to be compelled to be a member of a non-independent (employer-dominated) trade union. Secondly, where a closed shop existed, an employee who genuinely objected on grounds of religious belief to being a member of any trade union whatsoever was protected from dismissal on grounds of non-membership.

466. The Conservative government elected in 1979 took the view that the right not to belong to a trade union was equivalent to the right to belong. This was reinforced by the view that the closed shop was an unwarranted restriction on individual freedom of choice, and an unnecessary fortification of trade union power, distorting the free market. The statutory protections of the right to belong were therefore expanded to include similar protections for the right not to belong. Thus the right not to be unfairly dismissed for membership of a trade union was extended, so that it is automatically unfair to dismiss an employee where the principal reason for dismissal was his or her non-membership of or refusal to belong to a particular or any trade union.[586] As in the case of trade union membership, dismissal for non-membership attracts an increased basic level of compensation (see Part I).

Similarly, employees are protected from action short of dismissal compelling them to be or become a member of any trade union or a particular trade union, or to enforce a requirement to make a payment as an alternative to joining a trade union.[587] In addition, interim relief is available to those dismissed for non-membership in the same way as for membership.

467. A further significant innovation of the Employment Acts 1980 and 1982 was the introduction of a right to include the trade union as a third party or co-defendant in proceedings against the employer for unfair dismissal or action

586. TULRCA 1992, s. 152(1)(c) and see above (automatically unfair reasons for dismissal).
587. TULRCA 1992, s. 146. For closed shop provisions see below.

short of dismissal.[588] Both the employer and the employee have the right to join the trade union as a party to the proceedings if it is claimed that the union took industrial action or threatened to do so in order to put pressure on the employer to dismiss the employee or take action short of dismissal. The tribunal may then make an award against the union only, or against both the employer and the union.

§4. The Closed Shop

468. The closed shop has been defined as a 'situation in which employees come to realize that a particular job is only to be obtained and retained if they become and remain members of one of a specified number of trade unions'.[589] The closed shop is normally maintained by unions threatening to take industrial action unless the employer dismisses or refuses to employ non-members. The phenomenon takes many different forms. A distinction is sometimes drawn between the pre-entry closed shop, in which a worker cannot apply for a job unless he or she is a union member, and the post-entry closed shop (called the 'union shop' in America), in which the worker is required to join a union within a stated period after having taken up the job. In Britain, the line between these two is often blurred in practice. Another distinction is between the requirement that the worker should become a member of any union or that he or she should belong to a specified union, or even a section of a specified union. Closed shops of all these varieties are found in Britain.

469. The function of the closed shop has changed over the years. In a major study published in 1964, McCarthy found that the closed shop was a response by unions and workers to certain organizational problems, such as high turnover, scattered workforces, inter-union competition and the existence of an alternative workforce which might undermine industrial action. The closed shop assisted unions in establishing and maintaining membership, in disciplining the members, and (in the case of a pre-entry closed shop only) in controlling an alternative workforce.[590]

More recent studies show, however, that in the 1970s the closed shop became less an instrument of employee control and more an instance of joint trade union and employer regulation in the interests of orderly industrial relations.[591] Employers not infrequently regarded the closed shop as a useful means of preventing inter-union disputes, of ensuring that collective bargaining arrangements cover all workers, and of maintaining effective discipline by union officials over the workforce. Indeed, during the period 1971–4 when the closed shop was prohibited by law, it appears that employers and trade unions colluded to maintain closed shops in existence.

588. TULRCA 1992, ss. 150, 160.
589. W.E.J. McCarthy, *The Closed Shop in Britain* (Oxford, 1964). This definition was followed by the Royal Commission on Trade Unions & Employers' Associations, Cmnd 3623, 1968.
590. McCarthy, *op. cit.*
591. S. Dunn and J. Gennard, *The Closed Shop in British Industry* (London, 1984); and Ch. 4 in *Industrial Relations and the Law in the 1980s: Issues and future Trends* (eds. P. Fosh and C.R. Littler) (London. 1985).

Moreover, closed shop agreements are now more likely to be formal and in writing than they were 20 years ago.

470. By the end of the 1970s, closed shop arrangements covered about a quarter of the workforce, more than 5.2 million people.[592] About 800,000 of these (4 per cent of the workforce) were in pre-entry closed shops, nearly all of these having been established in the era of craft unionism and in industries, such as merchant shipping, dock work and acting, in order to counteract the employers' use of a plentiful supply of casual non-union labour.[593] In the early 1960s post-entry closed shops covered 3 million people (12 per cent of the workforce), and were concentrated in a few industries, in particular engineering and coalmining.[594] By the end of the 1970s, the number in post-entry closed shops had grown to at least 4.5 million, an increase of over 50 per cent since the early 1960s. Post-entry closed shops had emerged in industries where they were little known previously, such as food, drink, clothing, footwear and chemical manufacture, local authorities and the nationalized industries.[595] However, even before the Conservative government's Employment Acts of 1980, 1982, 1988 and 1990 (below) had begun to take effect, the closed shop had reached a point of stagnation and decline. By mid-1982, it had fallen by 13 per cent to approximately 4.5 million in both pre- and post-entry closed shops.[596] The shrinking of industries such as coalmining, steel, shipbuilding, clothing, footwear, vehicles and railways where the closed shop was widespread, has not been compensated by extension in other industries. The continuation in these economic trends, with an overall decline in union membership, coupled with the impact of the Employment Acts means that the closed shop has continued to decline since 1982. A recent survey of 558 UK companies, largely in the private sector, found that the coverage of the closed shop had substantially declined during the 1980s, and the decline was most marked after 1985.

However, it also found that the closed shop remained widespread: nearly a quarter of firms in the survey that recognized trade unions were still operating some form of closed shop arrangement in 1990.[597] Nevertheless, Government estimates that there were as many as 1.3 million employees in pre-entry closed shops in 1989[598] were treated with widespread scepticism, the better view being that there were no more than 150,000.[599] By 1998 only 1 per cent of employers continued to operate any kind of closed shop (2 per cent of those with union recognition).[600]

592. J. Gennard *et al.* (1980) 88 *Employment Gazette* 16.
593. *Ibid.*
594. McCarthy, *op. cit.*, pp. 14–22.
595. Gennard *et al.*, *op. cit.*, p. 147.
596. Dunn and Gennard, *op. cit.*, p. 147.
597. P. Gregg and A. Yates, 'Changes in Wage-setting Arrangements and Trade Union Presence in the 1980s', *British Journal of Industrial Relations*, 361 (1991) at 366.
598. Department of Employment *Removing Barriers to Employment* (Cmnd 655, March 1989) paras. 2.6 and 2.7.
599. B. Simpson, MLR 418 (1991) at 423.
600. N. Millward, A. Bryson, and J. Forth, *All Change at Work?* (Routledge, 2000), pp. 89, 146.

471. Successive governments have displayed differing attitudes to the closed shop. It remained outside the scope of legal regulation until the Industrial Relations Act 1971 directly challenged the practice by making all pre-entry closed shop agreements void and allowing the post-entry closed shop only in two exceptional situations (the 'agency' shop and the 'approved closed shop'). The legitimacy of the closed shop was subsequently recognized by the Trade Union and Labour Relations Acts 1974–6 in that a dismissal for refusing to belong to a union was deemed fair if there was a 'union membership agreement' made with an independent trade union, under which employees had to belong to a trade union. A limited exception was provided in the case of employees who genuinely objected to union membership 'on grounds of religious belief'. With some amendments, this remained the legal framework until 1980.

The Conservative government of the 1980s, by contrast, repeatedly avowed to put an end to the closed shop. Initially, there was a perceived need to compromise. Hence the Employment Acts 1980 and 1982 amended the legal framework in order to undermine the closed shop as far as possible without outlawing it directly. Union membership agreements or closed shops were given limited protection, but only if they received exceptionally high levels of support. Where there was such support, dismissal of a non-member remained possible, but so many exceptions were introduced that in most cases dismissal was in fact unlawful.

472. The incremental approach to restriction of the closed shop was finally abandoned by the Employment Act 1988, which effectively outlawed the post-entry closed shop. It is now automatically unfair to dismiss an employee for non-membership of a trade union, even if a closed shop is in operation.[601] This deprives unions and employers of their main sanction against non-members. The prohibition was further extended by the Employment Act 1990, which was aimed at the pre-entry closed shop. The new Act provided a right of complaint to an employment tribunal for any individual whom an employer refuses to engage on the ground of non-membership of a trade union, or on the ground of refusal to agree to become a member after the employment begins. Protection extends widely, to include situations in which an employer refuses or deliberately omits to entertain and process an application, or makes an offer of employment the terms of which are such as no reasonable employer would offer, or places an advertisement which might reasonably be understood as indicating that a job is open only to union members.[602] Other avenues for securing employment to union members are similarly barred: employment agencies may no longer refuse to provide services to job seekers who do not belong to a union;[603] and employers may no longer enter into arrangements with unions whereby employment is offered only to persons put forward or approved by the union.

473. The impact of the restrictive provisions on the coverage of the closed shop has been dramatic. Although closed shops survived the incremental restrictions of

601. TULRCA 1992, s. 152.
602. TULRCA 1992, s. 137.
603. TULRCA 1992, s. 138.

the 1980s, so that some three-quarters of companies with a closed shop in 1984 still had some arrangement in 1990,[604] this was largely due to management support which has faded away in the 1990s.[605] As noted above, by 1998 only 1 per cent of employers continued to operate any kind of closed shop. Nonetheless, there remain areas, such as theatre and broadcasting, where the need to maintain professional skills and the excess of supply over demand for labour have meant that pre-entry closed shops have provided a valuable stabilizing influence, which may well be lost if the closed shop is prohibited. It is noteworthy that the government refused to bring professional associations within the scope of these provisions.

474. The restrictive effect of the above provisions is further reinforced by the compensation available in cases in which a dismissal is unfair by virtue of these provisions (*see* Part I), and the possibility of using the interim relief procedure to continue the contract of employment until a tribunal has resolved a complaint. In cases of refusal to engage a person because of non-membership of a union, the tribunal may order the employer to pay compensation up to the maximum limit in an ordinary unfair dismissal case (£85, 200 from February 2012), assessing compensation on the same basis as damages for breach of statutory duty. In addition, the tribunal may make a recommendation that the respondent take action to obviate or reduce the adverse effect on the complainant. This could include a recommendation that the employer consider the complainant for the next available job vacancy. If the respondent refuses to comply with such a recommendation, the tribunal may increase compensation, up to the maximum above.[606] As described above, it is possible for either the applicant or the employer to join the trade union as a respondent or third party in the proceedings, where the dismissal or refusal to engage is a result of pressure by the union.

Clearly, it will not be infrequent for the union to make direct or indirect threats of industrial action where necessary to preserve the closed shop. In such cases, the tribunal may award compensation against the union, or against both the union and the employer.

§5. Exclusion or Expulsion from the Union

475. Legislative intervention in the internal affairs of trade unions was one of the hall-marks of the Conservative legislation of the 1980s and 1990s. Once of the most intrusive of these was the right, first enacted in 1980, not to be excluded or expelled from a trade union except on specified grounds. These essentially allow exclusion or expulsion only where the employee does not meet union rules which restrict membership by occupation, qualifications, experience, employer or location, or by reason of certain types of individual conduct.[607] An employee who has been excluded or expelled from a union for other reasons has the right to complain

604. Gregg and Yates, *op. cit.*
605. Millward *et al.*, *op. cit.*
606. TULRCA 1992, s. 140.
607. TULRCA 1992, ss. 174–7.

to an employment tribunal, which may declare that the exclusion or expulsion was unlawful. The statutory provisions give little credence to the union's interest in autonomy in respect of its internal procedures. Thus, there is no requirement that workers first exhaust internal complaints or appeals procedures before applying to a tribunal. This may be contrasted with the strict common law requirements that a trade union abide by its own rules. It has been held that it is not necessary for the applicant to show that he or she was denied a particular job; it is sufficient to be seeking work in the particular field of industry to which the closed shop relates.[608]

476. If the union admits or re-admits the person, he or she may apply for compensation to the employment tribunal; if the union does not admit or re-admit the person after a tribunal has declared his or her complaint to be well-founded, he or she may apply for compensation to the Employment Appeal Tribunal. Both tribunals must award such compensation as they consider just and equitable in the circumstances, up to a maximum of £95,211 in either tribunal and with a minimum of £9,118 in the EAT (from 6 April 2017). This includes loss of earnings, loss of earning opportunity in the industry where the closed shop operates, and non-pecuniary loss, such as injury to feelings and upset in the person's personal life resulting from the refusal of membership.[609] The award may be reduced if the applicant caused or contributed to the refusal or exclusion and the applicant has the duty to mitigate his or her loss. (The common law controls on the relationship between unions and their members are described *below*). The right not to be unreasonably excluded or expelled has been exercised very infrequently.[610]

§6. UNION-ONLY PRACTICES

477. One way of supporting union membership and recognition, apart from the closed shop, is the 'union-only' or 'recognition-only' practice, whereby contracts for the supply of goods or services are made subject to the condition that the supplier's employees are trade union members, or that the supplier recognizes, negotiates or consults with a union. For example, in 1982, about one in eight local authorities imposed such requirements for manual workers.[611] As part of the present government's strategy of preventing such aids to the maintenance of union membership, the Employment Act 1982 introduced provisions preventing such practices.[612] This is done in three ways: First, a clause imposing either a union-only or a recognition only requirement in a contract for the supply of goods or services is made void; Secondly, a right to sue for breach of statutory duty is created when a person is excluded from a list of suppliers, or from those from whom tenders are invited, or when a

608. *Clark* v. *NATSOPA (Sogat '82)* [1985] IRLR 494 (EAT).
609. *Howard* v. *NGA* [1985] ICR 101 (EAT). Compare unfair dismissal, where compensation for injury to feelings is not *per se* compensatable.
610. For example, in 1990, only four such cases were heard by an employment tribunal: ACAS Annual Report 1990.
611. M. Ingham, and A. Thomson, *Dimensions of Industrial Relations in Local Authorities* University of Glasgow, 1982, Table 5A.
612. TULRCA 1992, ss. 144–5.

supply contract is terminated, or when no supply contract is entered into with a person, on the grounds that that person does not recognize, bargain with or consult unions, or the work to be done under the contract is likely to be done by non-unionists. Any person adversely affected has the right to sue. These would include, for example, a sub-contractor to the supplier affected, or an employee made redundant by that supplier; and, Thirdly, the Act lays down certain circumstances in which industrial action intended to put pressure on employers to maintain union only or recognition-only practices is not protected from civil liability by the immunities afforded to other types of industrial action.

To date there have been no reported cases on this provision. This clear 'preference for non-unionism'[613] is further reinforced by the Local Government Act 1988, which prevents local authorities and several other public bodies from using 'non-commercial matters' as a criterion when drawing up tender lists, selecting contractors or sub-contractors, or terminating contracts.[614] The list of non-commercial matters is a wide one, and includes clauses referring to freedom of association, the terms and conditions of employment of the relevant workforce and whether contractors promote equal opportunities or policies. Any person suffering loss or damage as a result of an authority breaching these provisions has a right to sue the authority for damages. These provisions have not been significantly amended by the Labour government: the only relevant provision is the power to provide by order that any of the prescribed matters cease to be a 'non-commercial' matter, and therefore be permitted in a contracting process.[615] No orders have yet been made under this provision.

613. J. Clark and Lord Wedderburn in *Labour Law and Industrial Relations: Building on Kahn- Freund* Oxford, 1983, p. 143. See also S. Evans and R. Lewis, ILJ (1988), 209.
614. Local Government Act 1988, s. 17.
615. Local Government Act 1999, s. 19.

Chapter 2. Trade Unions and Employers Associations

§1. Trade Union Membership

478. During the 1980s, British trade unions were confronted with a Conservative government explicitly committed to reducing trade union influence at the workplace and excluding unions from national political representation. This, combined with very high levels of unemployment, left the unions in a far weaker position than they were in at the start of the decade. This has been especially evident in respect of membership figures; after many years of steady growth, trade union membership in Britain declined steeply during the 1980s.[616] In 1989, there were 10.2 million trade union members, compared with the 1979 peak of 13.3 million, a fall of 24 per cent. By the end of the decade, there was little sign of a reversal of the downward trend: the fall in union membership in 1989 was the tenth consecutive fall in membership since 1979, despite strenuous attempts by unions to recruit new members among 'atypical' workers such as part-time workers and women. This trend has continued into the 1990s, with 7.9 million trade union members in 1998 (the first increase since 1979, but at 0.6 per cent statistically insignificant).

A similar pattern is evident in respect of union density (the proportion of employees in unions). Labour Force Survey figures show that union density dived from 39 per cent of all employees (excluding self-employed) in 1989 to 29.6 per cent in 1998, stabilizing in 1999 at about 29.5 per cent. Density is higher for men (31 per cent in 1999) than women (28 per cent). Successive studies by Workplace Industrial Relations Surveys[617] show that despite wholesale privatization and reorganization, the energy and water supply industries remained the sector with the highest levels of membership; while the lowest levels have always been found in distribution, hotels and catering. The recent fall was most rapid in the private sector: by 1998, private sector union density was less than half the density in the public sector. Thus aggregate union density in the private sector fell from 56 per cent in 1980 to 36 per cent in 1990 and still further to 26 per cent in 1998. Only 2 per cent had densities of 90 per cent or more compared to 17 per cent in 1980. But there were also steep declines in the public sector, and in fact, the greatest falls in aggregate density occurred between 1990 and 1998. Here density, which had been as high as 84 per cent in 1980, fell to 72 per cent in 1990 and plummeted to 57 per cent in 1998. Millward *et al.* have examined various causes for this decline. They point to several factors, of which three are worth highlighting. The first is the succession of statutory restrictions imposed on the closed shop during the 1980s, culminating in their prohibition in 1991. Whereas 23 per cent of all workplaces had a closed shop for some employees in 1980, this had fallen to as little as 1 per cent of all

616. Figures in this and subsequent paragraphs come from N. Millward, A. Bryson, and J. Forth, *All Change at Work* (Routledge, 2000).

617. *Annual Report of the Certification Officer 1991* and *1999–2000*, and *Employment Gazette*, June 1991, p. 337.

workplaces in 1998. A second major contributory factor was the extent of union recognition, with extremely low densities at workplaces without recognition, but density of about 53 per cent in workplaces where the union was recognized. This means that the steep decline in the number of establishments which recognized unions contributed substantially to the decline in overall membership. Whereas 64 per cent of all establishments had recognized unions in 1980, this had dived to only 42 per cent in 1998. Notably, however, the extent of union recognition in the public sector has remained high: although it declined from its high point of 94 per cent in 1980, it has remained stable at 87 per cent from 1990 to 1998. This means that the decline in recognition was almost wholly a private sector phenomenon. At the same time, one of the most striking findings was the decline in density even in workplaces with recognized unions down from 66 per cent in 1990 to 53 per cent in 1998. A final factor was concerned the differences between well-established workplaces and newly established ones. Union density was much lower among newly formed workplaces; and in the public sector, privatization had a particularly dramatic effect, since many of the public sector workplaces that were privatized had extremely high levels of density prior to privatization. It is as yet too soon to tell whether the more supportive political environment since 1997 has had the effect of slowing or reversing the decline in trade union membership and density, or whether the new statutory recognition procedure will contribute to this change.

§2. Trade Union Structure

479. Since 2000, there has been a trend towards concentration of union membership into fewer and larger unions. Whereas in 1920, there were 1,384 trade unions, this had fallen to 519 in 1973, 9 in 1991 and 243 in 2000 and 187 in 2005. This reflects the continuing process of merger and transfer of membership. In 1998, over 80 per cent of the total membership was covered by the 16 largest unions, all of which had more than 100,000 members.

The largest union was UNISON with over 1.27 million members. At the same time, there remain a large number of small unions: in 1998 almost half of all trade unions had fewer than 1,000 members together accounting for only 0.4 per cent of the total membership of all unions. The process of concentration has been stimulated by a number of pressures, including the difficulties faced by smaller unions in remaining solvent in the face of inflation and falling membership, changes in technology which have eroded traditional crafts and skills, and the active policy of expansion adopted by some unions. Hyman comments that 'two decades ago the pattern of British union membership differed little from the structure consolidated around the turn of the century: dominated by a handful of general, ex-craft and single industry sections of 19th century British capitalism. Unionism in the 1980s is far more broadly based: a reflection in part of the decline of traditional strongholds and the growth of 'tertiary' employment, in part of increased density in areas of former weakness, particularly in the public sector. Occupational shifts in employment and unionization have led to the current prominence of 'white-collar' organizations.'[618] Of particular note is the change in gender composition of unions. In 2000 women constituted 40 per cent of all trade union members, as against only 20 per cent in 1960. This amounts to a union density of women of 28 per cent as against that of men of 31 per cent.

480. Three principal categories of trade union structure are to be found in Britain – craft, industrial and general. But these categorizations have to be used with caution because many of the larger unions spill over the categories. The craft unions, organizing those with a particular skill, are particularly important in printing, engineering, shipbuilding and construction industries. Some unions have been regarded as craft unions, although skills are learned through a process of promotion from labourer to skilled worker rather than through an apprenticeship system, and the union may in fact also be an *industrial* one because it covers most workers in an industry. An example is the steel industry union, the Iron and Steel Trades' Confederation.

481. There are few remaining industrial unions in Britain. Traditionally, the nearest to an industrial union in Britain is the National Union of Mineworkers, which until a breakaway Union of Democratic Mineworkers was formed in 1985, included the vast majority of the National Coal Board's employees, manual and clerical and some supervisory, although most of the latter belong to a separate union. Others with a claim to the description of 'industrial' include the Communications Workers Union and the banking, insurance and finance union UNIFI . *461.* The general unions, who organize workers regardless of skill or industry, whatever the job they perform, include the Transport & General Workers' Union (now UNITE) and GMB. In some industries these unions organize nearly all the workers in the industry; in some they organize only certain occupations or gradings; in some they cover white-collar employees; in some they compete with other unions. They are spread over nearly all industrial groups. Consequently, there is an overlap between the avowedly general unions and these former skilled craft unions. All these large unions are showing increasing interest in technicians and white-collar employees. Indeed, in 1988, the large white-collar union, the Association of Scientific Technical and Managerial Staffs, amalgamated with the technical, administrative and supervisory section of the engineering union (AEUW-TASS) to form the MSF (the Manufacturing Science and Finance Union), which is now part of UNITE, one of the largest unions. The greatest trend in recent years has been towards multi-industry membership.

§3. Trades Union Congress

482. The Trades Union Congress (TUC), formed in 1868, lacks the power of some central trade union organizations in other countries. Nevertheless, it is almost unique in West Europe as a single trade union federation to which almost all major unions are affiliated. In 1999, there were 74 affiliated organizations, with a total

618. R. Hyman, Ch. 2 in G.S. Bain (ed.), *Industrial Relations in Britain* (Oxford, 1983), pp. 35–36.

membership of just over 6.8 million workers.[619] During the mid-1970s, the TUC played a central role in the corporatist decision-making processes instituted by the then Labour government. However, the influence and stature of the TUC was deliberately undermined during the Conservative rule, and its status has not been fully revitalized under the new Labour government. Nevertheless, it is playing an increasingly prominent role in the EU, under the Social Dialogue procedure, which gives important decision-making powers to the European TUC, of which the British TUC is an active member.

483. The TUC has power under its constitution to intervene in jurisdictional disputes between affiliated unions. A set of principles for avoidance of inter-union disputes was first laid down by the TUC in 1924 (the Hull Main Principles) and revised at the annual Conference held in 1939 at Bridlington. The so-called 'Bridlington' principles (which have been subsequently revised) advise unions to reach agreement on spheres of influence, recognition of membership of other affiliated bodies, and transfers of members. The Principles prohibit a TUC-affiliated union from commencing organizational activities in any grades of workers in which another TUC union has organized a majority of the workers and negotiates on behalf of those workers. Majority membership may not, however, be required in order to protect a union where organization has been 'exceptionally difficult'. The Principles are also aimed at preventing unions from 'poaching' members of another union, and, until 1993, required that a union should refuse to accept into membership any applicant who was or recently had been a member of another affiliated union, unless the other union agreed. The TUC internal Disputes Committee could issue an award that individuals accepted into membership in breach of the principles should be expelled, and expulsions to give effect to such orders were upheld at common law provided they were properly authorized by the union's rules.

However, the Principles have had to be revised in the light of the statutory protection for members against exclusion or expulsion (see TULRCA Section 174). The revisions, now contained in the 2000 edition of the Principles still require unions to affirm that they will not knowingly and actively seek to take into membership existing or recent members of another union without the agreement of that organization. If the other union objects, an attempt at resolution should include a moral obligation on the part of the respondent union to offer compensation to the complainant union for any loss of income that it has suffered as a consequence of knowing and active recruitment of its members. A complaint may be referred to the Disputes Committee, which now only has power to order financial compensation, not expulsion. The Disputes Committee must give a fair hearing must be given. Awards of the Committee are 'binding' on affiliates and a number of sanctions, including suspension of an affiliate, are available to the General Council in cases of refusal to obey. The awards as such are probably not binding in law, because of the general view that the TUC Constitution and the Bridlington Principles are 'not intended to create legal relations'.

619. National Statistics, *Britain 2001, The Official Yearbook of the United Kingdom* (HMSO, 2000), p. 159.

§4. Trade Union Amalgamations

484. Another way of combating the harmful consequences of multi-unionism is through the formation of federations of trade unions in certain industries, such as the Confederation of Shipbuilding and Engineering Unions. These federations handle negotiations in several industries and adopt joint policies. A further form of cooperation in particular industries where Joint Industrial Councils exist (*see* Ch. 4, *below*) is that achieved by the holding of joint meetings and the appointment of a joint secretariat by all the unions which sit on the 'workers' side' of such Councils. Perhaps the most important way of reducing multi-unionism has been by amalgamations between unions.

The total number of unions has fallen and this process is likely to continue. Amalgamations have played an important role in this. Legislation has existed since 1876 to facilitate amalgamations, and the relevant provisions are now found in TULRCA 1992 (Sections 97–106). The Act provides for mergers in two ways, by amalgamation and by transfer of engagements. The first method requires the consent of the majority of those voting in each amalgamating union, while the second method requires a vote only of the members of the transferor union. Certain minimum standards are laid down for the conduct of the ballots so as to ensure that every member has a proper opportunity to vote and that he has full knowledge of the terms. Complaints may be made to the Certification Officer with a right of appeal on questions of law to the EAT.

485. In 1999–2000, for example, ten mergers took place, involving a total of 508,370 members. Such mergers can be on a very large scale. In the public services, UNISON was created in 1993 by the merger of three major unions, the Confederation of Health Service Workers (COHSE), the National and Local Government Officers' Association (NALGO) and the National Union of Public Employees (NUPE). Similarly, in 1999 the Banking Insurance and Finance Union, UniFI and the NatWest Staff Association merged to form UNIFI. The result of amalgamations has not, however, been to simplify union structure. On the contrary it has helped to produce several large unions which cover nearly all industries – such as the Transport & General Workers' Union, GMB and the Amalgamated Engineering and Electrical Union. In the words of Professor Clegg the 'consequence has not been a rationalization of trade union structure, but increasing complexity'.[620]

§5. Definition and Objects of a Trade Union

486. For legal purposes a workers' organization is a 'trade union' only if it satisfies the definition in Section 1 of TULRCA, 1992. This lays down that the organization (which may be temporary or permanent) must: (1) consist wholly or mainly of workers of one or more descriptions; and (2) be an organization whose principal purposes include the regulation of relations between workers of that description or those descriptions and employers or employers' associations. It will be seen that

620. H.A. Clegg, *The Changing System of Industrial Relations in Great Britain* (London, 1979), p. 177.

although the definition is wide enough to cover an *ad hoc* negotiating committee, the organization must be directly involved in negotiation with employers: a body whose sole concern is to support strike action or to exert political influence is not a 'trade union'.

487. The definition does not, however, *limit* the purposes of a trade union. A trade union may include in its rule book (constitution) any lawful purposes at all, including political objects. Many unions do in fact include the socialization of the means of production, or support for the Labour Party, among their objects. In this respect the definition of a 'trade union', when introduced in 1974, cleared up a long-standing controversy as to whether objects other than labour–management relations could be validly pursued by a trade union.

§6. Expenditure on Political Objects

488. There is, however, one limitation on the freedom of trade unions to support political objects. In the *Osborne* case in 1909,[621] the House of Lords decided that it was beyond the powers of a trade union to levy a contribution on members to support the Labour Representation Committee, the forerunner of the Labour Party. The Trade Union Act 1913 effectively overruled this by permitting a trade union to have any lawful objects. At the same time the Act laid down a complicated set of conditions which must be observed before the union may expend funds on political objects. The purpose of these conditions is to protect political dissentients within the union. As part of the restrictive legislative programme of the Conservative Government, the conditions for the maintenance of political funds were made substantially more rigorous. They are now found in TULRCA 1992.

489. If a union wishes to expend money on 'political objects' as defined by the Act, it must set up a separate fund (the 'political fund') for that purpose. Such a fund may only be set up if a majority of the members of the union vote in favour of the fund in a secret ballot. Prior to 1984, no further ballots were required to maintain the fund. Since 1984, however, however, legislation has required the union to win majority support for the continuation of the fund in a ballot held every 10 years.[622] For unions which had a political fund for more than 9 years at the commencement of the Act (31 March 1985), a new ballot had to be conducted within 12 months of that date. The ballot must be fully postal, and an independent scrutineer must be appointed to supervise the election. Such ballots therefore impose substantial costs on the union. The Act also provides for several controls over the operation of the political fund. The Certification Officer (above, para. 78) must approve the rules governing the fund. In addition, the fund may only be financed by contributions specifically earmarked for political purposes, and it may not go into deficit.

621. *Amalgamated Society of Railway Servants* v. *Osborne* [1910] AC 87; see generally on this subject K.D. Ewing, *Trade Unions the Labour Party and the Law* (Edinburgh, 1982).
622. TULRCA 1992, ss. 71–96.

490. If no ballot has been held, or a majority of members has voted against the formation of a political fund, the union cannot spend money on 'political objects' as defined by the Act. Thus the definition of political objects is crucial. This definition, as revised and expanded by the 1984 Act, includes the expenditure of money, directly or indirectly, on 'party political' matters such as contributions towards a political party, or provisions of a service or property for use by that political party, as well as the selection of candidates and the maintenance of holders of political office.

In addition, a meeting or conference whose main purpose is the transaction of business in connection with a political party must be funded from the political fund, as must any advertising, literature, film or sound recording whose main purpose is to persuade people to vote or not to vote for a political party or candidate.[623] This last provision has led to fears that a union without a political fund would not be able to conduct campaigns which oppose government policy even on matters which directly affect its members such as privatization of State enterprises. Such fears were partially vindicated in *NALGO* v. *Paul and Fraser*.[624] Shortly before the local authority elections of 1987, NALGO (now part of UNISON), which at the time did not have a political fund, mounted a campaign of leaflets discussing the impact of government cut-backs and privatization in the public services. The leaflets were distributed in marginal constituencies. Such expenditure was declared unlawful, on the basis that the timing of the campaign demonstrated that its purpose was to persuade people how to exercise their votes. Browne-Wilkinson VC stressed that disapproval of government policy at a time other than an election was not necessarily unlawful. Nevertheless, the line between criticism of government policy and persuasion is thin, and in any case, unions without a political fund cannot campaign against government policy at a time when it would be most effective. As a result, several public sector unions, including NALGO and at least four civil service unions, voted in favour of establishing political funds, and UNISON maintains a political fund resolution.

491. If a political fund has been approved, union members will usually be charged a political levy, unless they choose to 'contract out'. The government has thus far refrained from implementing suggestions that members be required to 'contract in' to political subsidies. However, members must be notified of their right to contract out and they are protected against discrimination if they exercise their rights. A complaint of breach of the rules may be made to the Certification Officer with a right of appeal on questions of law to the EAT. In addition, the TUC has issued a Statement of Guidance which encourages trade unions to ensure that no obstacles are placed in the way of members wishing to contract out. Section 86 of TULRCA 1992 requires an employer to ensure that a political contribution is not deducted from the emoluments of a contracted-out worker who has certified that he has notified the union of his or her objection to contributing to the political fund and Section 87 gives the worker a right to sue the employer in the employment tribunal.

623. TULRCA 1992, s. 72.
624. [1987] IRLR 413.

492. Although the statute does not refer to any particular political party, the Labour Party has traditionally been the chief beneficiary of most political funds. Indeed, the Conservative government expected to weaken the Labour Party by requiring periodic ballots. However, the campaigns preceding the ballots increased political awareness among union members, and all unions with an existing political fund voted by a substantial majority to retain the fund. In addition, a number of unions (eight in 1988 alone) established political funds for the first time. There were 36 political fund resolutions in force as at 31 March 2000. In 1999, two review ballots were held to renew the resolution after 10 years in force and in both a majority of over 80 per cent in favour of retaining the fund was obtained. However, in a ballot held by the civil service union PCS in 1999, a majority of members voted against the establishment of a new fund. Total funds at the end of 1998 were £15.8 million.[625]

§7. Legal Classifications of Trade Unions

493. A list of trade unions is maintained by the Certification Officer (*see* para. 78). This system of listing is far less intrusive than the previous system of registration under the Industrial Relations Act 1971, according to which registration was a pre-condition for the exercise of many collective bargaining rights and carried with it a high degree of control of internal trade union affairs. Registration was abolished in 1974, and listing is automatically granted to any organization which is a 'trade union' as defined in the Act, provided it complies with some simple formalities.[626] The main advantages of listing are that a *listed* union may be able to obtain relief from tax on the income from its benefit funds, and it may seek a certificate of independence. There is a right of appeal on questions of fact and law from the Certification Officer's decision to refuse to list, or his removal from listing, of a trade union.

494. It is crucial for a trade union which is listed to obtain a certificate of independence in order to exercise a number of rights or to secure those rights for its members and officials. The certificate is conclusive proof that a trade union is independent. It is needed by a trade union in order to (1) enforce a right to disclosure of information; (2) be consulted in respect of collective redundancies; (3) appoint safety representatives; (4) be consulted about occupational pension schemes; (5) be consulted in respect of transfers of undertaking; (6) be consulted about training and (7) to conclude a disciplinary agreement, eligible for exemption by the Secretary of State. In addition, the rights to participate in trade union membership and activities, and to claim time off for trade union activities are reserved to members of independent trade unions. The definition of 'independent trade union' in Section 5 of TULRCA 1992 is one which:

625. Annual Report of the Certification Officer, 1999–2000.
626. TULRCA 1992, ss. 123–125.

(a) is not under the domination or control of an employer or a group of employers or of one or more employers' associations;
(b) is not liable to interference by an employer or any such group or association (arising out of the provision of financial or material support or by any other means whatsoever) tending towards such control. The decision whether or not a trade union falls within this definition is in the sole discretion of the Certification Officer, with a right of appeal on questions of fact or law to the EAT.

495. A special category of organizations enjoying, broadly speaking, the same rights as trade unions are special register *bodies*. Unlike ordinary trade unions these are corporate bodies, that is, either companies registered under the legislation relating to limited liability companies or incorporated by royal charter or letters patent. Such bodies are found mainly in the public services – such as the Royal College of Nursing – and their principal purposes are to maintain professional standards, but they have become involved in recent years to an increasing extent in negotiating terms and conditions of employment with employing authorities, often in competition with ordinary trade unions. In order to protect these bodies, the Industrial Relations Act equated them with trade unions for most purposes. This special position has been maintained by subsequent legislation.[627] However, those special register bodies whose principal purposes do not include labour-management relations may not be listed or seek a certificate of independence. In the private sector such bodies are of relatively little importance.

§8. Legal Status of Trade Unions

496. Trade unions (with the exception of special register bodies, above) are not corporate bodies. This leads to several difficulties. For example, if a union cannot enter into contracts, who is the party to the contract of membership? How can a trade union be sued? Property ownership in unincorporated associations is complex. To resolve these difficulties, a series of cases invested trade unions with certain attributes of corporate bodies. For example, in the *Taff Vale* case,[628] the House of Lords held that a trade union registered under the Trade Union Act 1871 could be held liable in tort (delict) for the acts of its officials in the course of a strike. Similarly, in the *Osborne* case,[629] the *ultra vires* doctrine was applied to trade unions as quasi-corporate bodies. Parliament intervened in the Trade Disputes Act 1906 to give trade unions a complete immunity from actions in tort (removed from 1971–1974 and again since 1982) and in the Trade Union Act 1913 to override the *Osborne* decision, but neither statute resolved the underlying question of the status of trade unions. Trade unions were given corporate status for the brief currency of the Industrial Relations Act 1971, but this depended on their willingness to submit to registration within the schema of the Act.

627. TULRCA 1992, s. 117.
628. *Taff Vale Railway Co.* v. *ASRS* [1901] AC 426.
629. *Amalgamated Society of Railway Servants* v. *Osborne* [1910] AC 87 (HL), above, para. 410.

497. The present formula, introduced in 1974, restored trade unions to unincorporated status. At the same time, it resolved some of the practical problems which flow from the unincorporated character of trade unions. The 1992 Act provides that (i) trade unions are capable of making contracts; (ii) all the property belonging to a union must be vested in trustees in trust for the union; (iii) trade unions are capable of suing and being sued in their own names; (iv) trade unions are amenable to criminal prosecution in their own names, and (v) judgments, awards, and orders may be enforced against any property held in trust for the union.[630] Nevertheless, some problems remain unresolved. Trade unions are probably not corporate bodies for the purposes of maintaining a defamation suit,[631] but the doctrine of *ultra vires* applicable to incorporated bodies has been held applicable to trade unions.[632] Similarly, trade unions have been held to be subject to the rule in *Foss* v. *Harbottle*,[633] by virtue of which only the association, not the individual member can sue for wrongs done to the association or for internal irregularities, unless a member's individual rights have been breached, or the acts done were fraudulent or *ultra vires*.[634]

§9. Liability of Trade Unions in Tort

498. For much of the 20th century, trade unions were given statutory immunity from liability in tort.[635] The immunity enjoyed by trade unions was broader than that afforded to individuals in respect of acts in contemplation or furtherance of a trade dispute. The immunity of trade unions was not confined to specific torts, nor to acts taken in contemplation or furtherance of a trade dispute. Thus liability for torts committed in the course of industrial action attached to the individual organizers rather than the union, although the union generally supported its officials financially in the conduct of the case and the satisfaction of any judgment.

One of the most significant changes brought about in 1982 was to remove this immunity, leaving trade unions, like individuals, exposed to tort action unless the more limited immunities now contained in Section 219, TULRCA 1992 applied. Further restrictions were imposed in 1984, by virtue of which Section 219 immunities would be of no avail to a union which had engaged in industrial action without conforming with the statutory balloting requirements. Subsequent legislation introduced yet more stringent provisions, including a separate right of action against trade unions. All these provisions have had dramatic implications for labour relations, particularly since they have meant that interlocutory injunctions are available against trade unions. Recent experience has demonstrated an increasing willingness

630. TULRCA 1992, s. 10.
631. *EEPTU* v. *Times Newspapers* [1980] QB 585 (QBD) although see also *Derbyshire County Council* v. *Times Newspapers Ltd* [1993] 1 All ER 1011 (HL).
632. *Hopkins* v. *National Union of Seamen* [1985] ICR 268 (Ch. D.); *Thomas* v. *National Union of Mineworkers* [1985] 2 All ER 1 (Ch. D.); *Taylor* v. *National Union of Mineworkers* [1985] IRLR 99 (Ch. D.); see Wedderburn 14 *Industrial Law Journal* (1985), 127.
633. (1843) 2 Hare 461.
634. *Cotter* v. *National Union of Seamen* [1929] 2 Ch. 58.
635. Trade Disputes Act 1906, s. 4, repealed by the Industrial Relations Act 1971. A more limited but still extensive immunity was contained in TULRA 1974, s. 14 (repealed in 1982).

on the part of employers to use legal remedies, both in the form of injunctions and damages.[636]

499. Since a trade union can act only through its officials and members, it is necessary to determine in what circumstances trade unions will be held liable for the tortious acts of their officials and members. At common law, a broad concept of trade union liability for actions of its members was established by the House of Lords in the famous case of *Heaton's Transport (St. Helens) Ltd* v. *TGWU*,[637] where a trade union was held liable for the unofficial acts of shop stewards, on the basis that shop stewards have general authority and discretion to act on the trade union's behalf. The trade union could only escape liability if it had expressly forbidden its members to take particular actions, possibly by disciplining members or withdrawing shop stewards' credentials. This could put trade unions in the difficult position of having to 'police' collective agreements and the law as against its own members'.[638] These common principles were partially superseded by a statutory scheme introduced in the 1980s and now contained in TULRCA 1992. Industrial action is taken to have been authorized or endorsed by a trade union if it was called by (a) anyone empowered by the rules to do so; (b) the principal executive committee, the president or general secretary or (c) any other committee of the union constituted by the rules, or any other official, whether employed or not.[639]

The union is liable in (b) and (c) even if the rules do not empower these committees or officials to call for industrial action. In the case of unofficial action only, the union may escape liability if the action is repudiated by the president, the general secretary or the principal executive committee. Repudiation provisions are harsh. A union must give written notice of repudiation not only to the committee or official who called the action, but also to every member of the union who the union has reason to believe is or may be participating. This extends even further: such notice must also be given to the employer of participating members, and, on request, to a party to a commercial contract whose performance is or may be interfered with as a result of the call to industrial action. In addition, repudiation may be negated by subsequent inconsistent behaviour of the union. These provisions raise grave dilemmas for many unions. 'Can any union dependent on localized bargaining and the work of many hundred of lay activists so centralize its control procedures as to prevent all forms of potentially unlawful industrial action without effectively alienating just those lay activists on which it depends?'[640] It should be noted that the statutory formula only applies in relation to the central industrial action torts, namely, inducing breach of contract, intimidation and conspiracy. The common law

636. Stephen, Evans, 'The use of injunctions in Industrial Disputes May 1984–April 1987', *British Journal of Industrial Relations*, 25 (1987), p. 419. *Labour Research*, 77 (1988), p. 7; and B. Simpson, 'The Labour Injunction, Unlawful Means and a right to strike', MLR, 50 (1987), pp. 506–516.
637. [1972] ICR 308, HL.
638. O. Kahn-Freund, 'The Industrial Relations Act 1971 – Some retrospective reflections' ILJ 3 (1974), 186 at 188.
639. TULRCA 1992, s. 20.
640. Michael Terry, 'Annual Review Article 1990', *British Journal of Industrial Relations* (1991), 104 at 109.

concept established in *Heaton's* continues to apply in other cases, such as nuisance or interference with business by unlawful means.

500. In order to avoid the risk of bankruptcy, Section 22 of TULRCA 1992 limits the amount of damages which may be awarded against a union in a tort action. The maximum in any single proceedings in favour of each Claimant is £10,000 if the union has less than 5,000 members, £50,000 if it has 5,000 but less than 25,000 members, £125,000 if it has 25,000 but less than 100,000 members and £250,000 if it has 100,000 or more members.

The amounts may be varied from time to time. A trade union's provident benefit funds and political fund (if it has one) are protected, as are the private property of the union's trustees, officials and members. But no property is safe, nor are there any limits in respect of the enforcement of fines imposed for contempt of court, i.e. refusal to obey a court order. Nor do the limits on damages include the legal costs which the unsuccessful union is likely to have to pay, and awards of interest need not be confined within the statutory maxima.[641] The possibility of a single strike with a small employer causing severe financial damage to a union is illustrated by the Stockport Messenger action in 1983 against the National Graphical Association as a result of which the union may have lost as much as one-tenth of its assets. The damages against the union were assessed at £131,051 plus interest (which included aggravated and exemplary damages in addition to proved losses).[642] When this was added to the £675,000 fines for contempt of court for non-compliance with an injunction, and legal costs of sequestration, it was estimated in December 1985[643] that the union had lost over £1 million. The NGA was again the subject of a stiff award of damages in 1988, when the court awarded the statutory limit of £250,000, and a further £90,000 in interest.

501. Failure by the union to pay damages or fines for contempt of court exposes the union to the risk of sequestration of its assets, the effect being to deny the union and its officers any control over its funds and premises until the court judgments have been satisfied and the union has 'apologized' to the court or otherwise 'cleared' its contempt. Sequestration has become an increasingly common method of enforcing the law. It was used, often with devastating effect, in some of the major disputes in the 1980s, including those of the miners in 1984–1985,[644] the print-workers who took action against News International at Wapping in 1985, and the seafarers in 1988. In the miners' strike, this was taken a step further. After the sequestration order, it was discovered that most of the union's funds had been moved abroad and the sequestrators could not get hold of them. The court therefore ordered the dispossession of the union's trustees, and their replacement by a court-appointed receiver.[645]

---

641. *Boxfoldia Ltd* v. *NGA* [1988] IRLR 383.
642. *Messenger Newspaper Group Ltd* v. *NGA* [1984] IRLR 397.
643. *Financial Times*, 27 December 1985.
644. The action against the NUM arose out of breach of the union's rules, below, para. 430.
645. *Clarke* v. *Heathfield* [1985] ICR 203, and *see* [1985] ICR 606; Rules of the Supreme Court Order 30, rule 1; Wedderburn, *The Worker and the Law* (3rd edn), p. 737, Elias and Ewing, *Trade Union Democracy* (Mansell, 1987), pp. 119–132.

This was the first occasion on which a receivership had been imposed on a trade union. Nevertheless, the use of receivership was reinforced and extended by the Employment Act 1988, reflecting the government's hope that the appointment of receivers would be a normal step for a court to take in an industrial dispute. Under the new provisions, a member has the right to complain to the court that union funds have been or are to be used 'unlawfully'.[646] Where trustees apply or propose to apply union funds in contravention of a court order, the court must remove all trustees, unless it is satisfied that there is good reason not to do so. This is not restricted to the trustees of the union against which a court order has been made, but may apply where one union gives financial support to another union which is in contempt.

§10. Trade Union Rules

502. Trade union government in Britain depends in part on what is written down in the formal rules and in part on unwritten but well-understood procedures ('custom and practice'). Rule books differ widely and display varying degrees of precision. Moreover, the courts have recognized that the rules are not the constitution; they are capable of modification by the proof of custom and practice. The TUC, in words which were adopted in a leading case by the House of Lords, has said that: 'Custom and practice may operate either by modifying a union's rules as they operate in practice, or by compensating for the absence of formal rules.'[647]

503. For most of the 20th century, the primary means of regulating trade union rules has been by judge-made common law. In 1971, as part of its general policy of legal regulation, the Industrial Relations Act imposed detailed requirements as to the matters to be specified in trade union rules, a legislative package with which the trade unions refused to cooperate. The mandatory requirements were repealed by the Trade Union and Labour Relations Acts 1974 and 1976, except for detailed rules relating to union accounts and members' superannuation schemes. The return to 'voluntarism' so far as internal trade union affairs were concerned reflected the belief that the needs of the many types of union in Britain were not capable of fitting into a single legislative model. The reform of union rule books advocated by the Donovan Commission was left to voluntary action by the unions themselves. Many unions have improved the scope and precision of their rule books, but the differences between rule books are still enormous. No two unions have the same system of government.

504. Since 1980, little credence has been given to the value of trade union autonomy, and legislation has made significant inroads into the voluntarist approach. In particular, under the guise of instituting a greater measure of 'democracy' into trade unions, detailed legislative requirements have been imposed in a

646. TULRCA 1992, s. 16.
647. *Heatons Transport (St. Helen's) Ltd* v. *TGWU* (1972) ICR 308 (HL).

number of important areas. Trade unions are required to hold elections in the prescribed form for certain trade union posts, and to ballot their members before taking industrial action. Periodic ballots are also required to retain the political fund. In addition, a union may not discipline or expel a member who has refused to take industrial action, even if the majority of the members have supported the action in a properly conducted ballot.[648] This last provision constitutes a grave incursion into the ability of trade unions to carry out their functions of protecting their members' collective interests, and contradicts the government's assertions that its true intentions are to promote trade union democracy. Statute also lays down that where a closed shop is in operation, a trade union may not unreasonably expel or exclude a member or applicant for membership. The rules relating to union accounts[649] and members' superannuation schemes[650] remain in force, but in 1988, two further rights were included. First, members must be given access to the union's accounting records,[651] and secondly, a member of a union has been granted a remedy against trustees of the union who have caused or permitted an unlawful application of the union's property.[652] Finally, there are special legislative rules protecting workers from discrimination by trade unions in respect of their colour, race, nationality, ethnic or national origins,[653] their sex or marital status,[654] or their disability.[655]

505. In parallel with the statutory provisions, the judges have developed a set of principles regulating the relationship between individual members and the trade union. This common law control of internal union activities is exercised through the notion that when a worker joins a union he or she becomes a party to a contract of association. This contract is subject to the same general principles as apply to other contracts, with some important modifications. There are four principles specifically applicable to contracts of membership. First, the rules are not to be construed literally or like a statute, but so as to give them a reasonable interpretation which accords with the court's view of what they must have been intended to mean, bearing in mind their authorship, their purpose and the readership to which they are addressed.[656]

506. The second principle relevant to a contract of membership is that the rules must be construed, in cases of ambiguity, against those who made them (*contra proferentem*). In particular, a union may not take disciplinary action against its members unless it has the express power to do so under the contract. Where it does have

648. TULRCA 1992, ss. 64–67; see generally S. Fredman, 'The New Rights: Labour Law and Ideology in the Thatcher Years', OJLS 12 (1992), 24.
649. TULRCA 1992, s. 28.
650. TULRCA 1992, ss. 38–42.
651. TULRCA 1992, s. 30.
652. TULRCA 1992, s. 16.
653. Race Relations Act 1976, s. 11; EEC reg. 1612/68, Art. 8.
654. Sex Discrimination Act 1975, s. 12.
655. Disability Discrimination Act 1995, s. 12.
656. *Heatons Transport (St. Helens) Ltd* v. *TGWU* [1972] ICR 398 (HL); *British Actors Equity Association* v. *Goring* [1977] ICR 393 (HL); *Porter* v. *National Union of Journalists* [1980] IRLR 404 (HL).

such power, it must act strictly in accordance with its rules: procedural requirements in the rules should be adhered to and decisions may only be taken by the body which has the power to do so under the rules. The courts have taken this further, and introduced a third principle, namely the imposition of axioms of public policy, as interpreted by the judges, to override or supplement the rules where the courts consider this to be justified. In recent years, the analogy has been drawn between union rules and a legislative code drawn up by some members to be imposed on all members, and this has enabled the courts to treat the actions of the organs and officers of a union like those of a governmental agency. Doctrines of administrative law have, in this way, infiltrated into the former contractual analysis of union rules. For example, the courts have insisted that, like administrative authorities, the so-called rules of natural justice must be followed when disciplinary action is taken, even if the rules state the contrary. Natural justice is similar in concept to the concept of 'due process'. In essence, it means that a person accused of a serious offence must be given a fair hearing before an unbiased body. Moreover, the administrative law analogy has led the courts to require discretions conferred on officials and committees to be exercised for proper purposes.

507. Finally, the most jealously guarded of the heads of public policy is that unions cannot oust the jurisdiction of the courts as the final arbiters on questions of law. The courts have said that even where there is an express requirement in union rules that internal remedies must be exhausted before a member can take his or her grievance to the court, the court is not bound by such a requirement. In deciding whether or not to intervene the court will consider the nature of the issue. If it is a question of legal interpretation of the rules, the court is likely to intervene even before internal appeals procedures laid down in the union rules have been exhausted.

508. These principles were particularly strictly applied in the miners' strike of 1984-5, when several trade union members sued the union for breach of the rules in declaring a strike without balloting the members as required by the rules. In several cases, trade union officials were held to be acting *ultra vires* (i.e. beyond their powers), with the result that actions taken in pursuance of the strike, such as the expulsion of members who refused to strike, or the use of union funds for strikers' families, were declared to be unlawful. The court granted injunctions (including mandatory injunctions) requiring the union to desist from the unlawful action. The refusal to comply with such injunctions in turn led to contempt proceedings and sequestration of the union's assets.[657]

509. The Employment Relations Act 1999 ensures that the Certification Officer (CO) should be the primary adjudicator in respect of complaints of breach of trade union rules. The Act abolished the Commissioner for the Rights of Trade Union Members and expanding the powers of the CO to deal with a range of additional complaints that had previously been presented to the court with assistance from the

---

657. *Taylor* v. *National Union of Mineworkers (Derbyshire Area)* [1984] IRLR 440; *Taylor* v. *NUM* [1985] IRLR 99; *Hopkins* v. *NUS* [1985] ICR 268; *Thomas* v. *NUM* [1985] IRLR 136 (Ch. D.).

Commissioner. These powers include complaints about a breach or threatened breach of the union's rules, including such matters as elections, ballots other than industrial action and the constitution and proceedings of the executive committee. Stress is also placed on recourse to internal proceedings: the CO may refuse to accept an application unless satisfied that the applicant has taken all reasonable steps to resolve the claim by use of an internal complaints procedure. The jurisdiction of the court and the CO are now mutually exclusive: an application put before the CO cannot be considered by the Court and vice versa.[658] The CO must provide an opportunity for both parties to be heard, and give reasons for his or her decision in writing. As well as the power to issue a declaration, the CO now has the power to make an enforcement order requiring the union to take steps to remedy the breach. An appeal on a question of law lies to the EAT. No decisions were issued in the first six months after these provisions came into effect, but 10 applications against four unions are pending, and a total of 132 inquiries had been made, many of them concerning inadequate representation of members by their union. Of these a third could lead to applications within the CO's jurisdiction.

§11. Trade Union Elections

510. As we have seen, trade unions have, for most of this century, been left to determine their own methods of appointing their officials. There is therefore a wide variety of methods, ranging from direct periodic elections, to life-time appointments to indirect elections via delegates. The Trade Union Act 1984, however, introduced a statutory scheme for electing certain union officials, despite trade union opposition to what was considered an unwarranted incursion into internal affairs. These provisions strengthened by later legislation, are now found in TULRCA 1992.

511. The relevant provisions require the trade union to hold periodic elections for members of the 'executive', defined as the principal committee of the union exercising executive functions. These requirements are not confined to election of the voting members of the executive; the obligation to stand for periodic election extends to a complex network of officers. Most importantly, the Act includes the general secretary and president, even if the rules of the union deny these officers the right to vote on the executive. This gives no scope to unions who regard these officers as senior bureaucrats, employed for their professional expertise rather than their popularity among members. Also included are those who may attend and speak at some or all the committee's meetings, otherwise than to provide factual information or technical or professional advice.[659] There is no requirement that other officials, such as shop stewards or branch officials, be elected. No member of the executive may hold his or her position for more than five years without being re-elected.

512. The Act imposes a particular model of democracy on trade unions. First, elections must be direct, in that each relevant member must vote directly for the

658. TULRCA 1992, s. 108A as inserted by Sched. 6, ERA 1999.
659. TULRCA 1992, s. 46.

official, rather than electing a delegate who then has the power to cast a block vote for a particular candidate. All members must have an equal vote, but the trade union may define particular constituencies, provided no member is deprived of a vote in all relevant elections. (The union's rulebook may, however exclude unemployed members, members in arrears, and apprentices, trainees, students or new members.) Secondly, voting must be by secret ballot, rather than by show of hands, a method which before the Act was used by many unions. Thirdly, the primary method of voting is a full postal method, with the trade union being required to send ballot forms and a list of candidates to voters at their home addresses, and votes being returned by post. This slow and costly method (unions are now required to keep an up-to-date register of members) was imposed in preference to voting at workplace or branch meetings on the assumption that voters may be subject to pressure at such meetings. Unions who have traditionally conducted elections at branch or workplace meetings argue in response that it is important to hear the debate before casting a vote.

Finally, the voters must not be subject to interference from or constraint imposed by the union, its members or its officials. It is noteworthy that there is no restriction on interference by third parties, such as the employer. In the past, government funds were available to meet the cost of ballots.[660] Initially, the TUC opposed the use by its affiliates of such money, and in 1991, for example, the Certification Officer paid out a total of £4.08 million (compared to £2.64 million in 1990) in respect of 692 ballots.[661] However, government subsidies were withdrawn in March 1996, and since then unions have had to bear their own costs.

513. There are several other detailed requirements with which trade union elections must comply. Firstly, every member of the union has a prima facie right to stand as a candidate free from unreasonable exclusion. The union may exclude a class of members provided all members of the class are so excluded and the class is not determined by reference only to those members which the union chooses to exclude. Nor may the union require a candidate, directly or indirectly to be a member of a political party.[662] This will affect unions which have rules requiring officers, once elected, to be members of the Labour Party, or to attend the Labour Party conference. On the other hand, there is nothing to prevent a union prohibiting membership of a political party; anti-communist rules are therefore unaffected. Secondly, the union must provide every candidate in the election with an opportunity of preparing an election address in his or her own words and submitting it to the union for distribution to voters together with the voting paper.[663] This provision is hedged about with extremely detailed requirements. Thirdly, before the election is held, the trade union must appoint a qualified independent person to supervise the election.[664] Finally, every union is required to compile and maintain a register of the

660. TULRCA 1992, s. 115.
661. Annual Report of the Certification Officer, 1991.
662. TULRCA 1992, s. 47.
663. TULRCA 1992, s. 48.
664. TULRCA 1992, s. 49.

names and proper addresses of its members.[665] Although this is subject to reasonable practicability, some unions may face considerable difficulties in fulfilling this requirement. This is particularly true for unions with a large and highly mobile membership.

Individual trade union members have the statutory right to apply to the Certification Officer, or to the court (but not to both in respect of the same complaint), for a declaration that their trade union failed to comply with these provisions. The CO must give reasons for his or her decision. From October 1999, the CO has been given the further power to make an enforcement order imposing on the union the obligation to hold the election or take such other steps to remedy the declared failure as specified in the order, or to abstain from specified acts with a view to ensuring that the failure does not occur in the future.[666] The first such order was issued in March 2000, requiring the Musicians Union to hold a fresh election for the post of general secretary after it had been conceded that one of the applicants had been unreasonably excluded from standing as a candidate in the election. The CO is now required to give both parties an opportunity to be heard. In certain circumstance, expenses incurred by applicants in attending hearings can be reimbursed. An appeal on a question of law lies to the EAT. In 1999–2000 there were 18 decisions issued by the Certification Officer concerning these provisions.[667]

514. Prior to the 1984 Act, about 61 per cent of trade unions who were affiliated to the TUC already elected their executives by votes of the whole membership.[668] However, very few used the precise method adopted by the statute, and many unions have had to make extensive rule changes in order to comply with the legislation. Moreover, views differ as to whether periodic direct elections do in fact promote internal democracy, or whether they lead to factionalism, more militant bargaining positions, or disruptive policy changes. Available evidence suggests that postal ballots in elections for executive members have not resulted in fundamental changes to the outcome.[669]

§12. Employers' Associations

515. The legal definition of an 'employers association' is identical to the definition of a 'trade union' except that the organization must consist 'wholly or mainly of employers or individual proprietors of one or more description'.[670] The legal status of employers' associations differs from that of trade unions (other than special register bodies), however, because such an association may be either a body corporate or an unincorporated association. If it is unincorporated it possesses the same quasi-corporate attribute as a trade union. An employers association may have its name listed by the Certification Officer (if it fulfils the statutory definition). Whether

665. TULRCA 1992, s. 24.
666. TULRCA 1992, ss. 54–56, as amended by ERA 1999, s. 29.
667. Annual Reports of the Certification Officer, 1999–2000.
668. R. Undy and R. Martin, *Ballots and Trade Union Democracy* (Oxford, 1984), pp. 105–106.
669. *Labour Research*, May 1990, p. 11. See generally S. Fredman, 'The New Rights', OJLS 24 (1992).
670. TULRCA 1992, s. 122.

or not listed, an employers' association is under the same duties as a trade union in respect of annual returns and accounting records. An employers association, like a trade union, is no longer immune from actions in tort, but there are no special rules regarding the vicarious liability of employers' associations.

516. No complete statistics are available regarding the number, size and membership of employers' associations. The Certification Officer reported that there were 100 listed and 100 unlisted associations to his knowledge in 2000.[671] Employers associations are, in any event, declining in importance, both in providing information and advice to employers, and in collective bargaining. Between 1984 and 1990, membership in employers' associations dropped from 22 per cent to 13 per cent of establishments, and later results show static or slightly falling membership between 1990 and 1998. In 1998, only about 8 per cent of respondents in the Workplace Industrial Relations Survey reported that the association negotiates with trade unions on behalf of its members.

517. The main national organization is the Confederation of British Industry (CBI) which was formed in 1965 by the merger of three earlier bodies. It claims to have direct corporate membership of companies employing over 4 million people and trade association membership representing companies employing over 6 million people, for a total of around 7 to 8 million. Since its most influential membership has traditionally been from the manufacturing sector, its capacity to speak for non-manufacturing establishments has been relatively limited. Moreover, the decline in manufacturing due to the recession of the 1980s has resulted in membership losses. The CBI, unlike the more right-wing Institute of Directors, tends to favour industrial relations based on collective bargaining.[672]

---

671. Annual Report of the Certification Officer, 1999–2000.
672. All figures have been obtained from the CBI. See P.B. Beaumont, *Change in Industrial Relations* (Routledge, 1990), p. 79.

Chapter 3. Workers' Participation in the Enterprise

§1. The Concept of 'Workers' Participation'

518. Corporate enterprises in the private sector are, in law, owned and controlled by their shareholders. The result of the 'managerial revolution' has been to concentrate power in the hands of boards of directors of companies, particularly the hands of executive directors. Major decisions are taken by the directors, and as enterprises have become larger and more complex, the effective decisions have been taken by directors of parent or holding companies, sometimes overseas, remote from the working environment.

An amendment to the Companies Act in 1980 required directors to have regard to the interests of employees as well as those of their shareholders when performing their duties,[673] but the employees as such cannot enforce this duty because it is owed to the company alone. It is unlikely that the company (acting through the board of directors or a majority of shareholders in general meeting) would seek to initiate legal action, and an employee or trade union with a minority shareholding would face almost insuperable barriers in proving that the directors had not acted '*bona fide* in the interests of the company'. A minor stimulus to directors was given by section 1 of the Employment Act 1982,[674] introduced by then Liberal and Social Democratic peers. This requires directors of companies with more than 250 employees to state in their annual reports what they have done over the year to promote employee involvement arrangements. Surveys by the then Department of Employment have shown that not all large companies fulfil this requirement; and the most recent survey concludes that about a quarter of companies appear not to be fully responding to the encouragement given by the legislation to review their existing practices.[675] However, there is also an increase in both the number and variety of employee involvement practices reported. In 1988, the most frequently reported practices were share schemes, incentive and bonus arrangements, management line communications and local consultative systems (formal and informal). It is noteworthy that trade unions and staff associations were mentioned as channels of communication or partners in joint decision-making in two-fifths of reports, despite the fact that the legislation envisages forms of participation which do *not* involve trade union channels or collective bargaining.

519. The notion that workers' representatives should be involved to a greater extent in the decision-making process has come to be described either as workers' participation or industrial democracy. The two essential characteristics of developments in this direction in Britain are, first that trade unions have traditionally regarded collective bargaining as the primary way to extend collective control by workers of their work situation, and, secondly, that participation has developed without institutional devices of the kind found in some other European countries, such as Works Councils. Before 1974, there had been no significant attempt to

673. Companies Act 1980, s. 46(1), now Companies Act 1985, s. 309.
674. Now Companies Act 1985, s. 235 and Sched. 7, Part V.
675. *Employment Gazette*, October 1988, 573 at p. 574.

establish forms of worker participation additional to collective bargaining in the private sector. But the participation of workers in the enterprise had grown primarily through the shop steward system and collective bargaining (see Ch. 4 below).

With the decline in the proportion of the workforce whose pay is determined by collective bargaining, the question arises whether the centrality of collective bargaining is being overtaken by other structures such as joint consultative committees. During the 1980s, such committees were to be found in 34 per cent. of all workplaces; throughout much of the 1990s, the percentage stood at 29.[676] Research has shown that consultation via consultative committees tends to complement rather than displace collective bargaining, with trade unions playing a positive role in those structures. Explanations for the fall in the number of consultative committees in the 1990s have focused primarily on 'the changing population of workplaces' in the public sector and changes in management policy, often arising out of a change of ownership.[677]

In recent years, there has been an increase in the number of 'higher level consultative committees', operating in multi-establishment organizations encouraged, it is said, by the European Works Council Directive. In 1990, 48 per cent. of workplaces belonging to a multi-establishment organization reported the existence of a higher-level committee in their organization. By 1998, that figure had risen to 56. However, throughout the period in question, only around two-fifths of such workplaces had a representative on the higher-level committee.[678] A CBI survey of 673 private sector employers in June 2001 found that almost half of them had introduced consultation arrangements for employees. Even among smaller companies, 40 per cent of those employing fewer than 40 employees had done so, with a further 11 per cent sating that they intended to do so soon.[679]

520. At the EU Council of Ministers meeting on 17 December 2001, the Council's Directive on Information and Consultation (Council Directive 2002/14/EC) was agreed. The Information and Consultation Directive is based upon the social partnership approach. That is, workers should have the basic right to consultation, but a mechanism for bargaining should be agreed between the parties and utilized accordingly. This new law requires companies with 50 or more employees to regularly inform on the enterprises' economic situation and to consult with workers on key decisions regarding the organization's future.[680] These include situations where jobs are threatened and where any anticipatory measures, such as training, skill development and other measures increasing the adaptability of employees, are planned. Consultation is also compulsory for decisions that are likely to lead to substantial changes in work organization or in contractual relations. National governments will enact their own implementing measures, with sanctions for breaches, and

676. N. Millward., A. Bryson, and J. Forth., *All Change at Work? British Employment Relations 1980–1998 as portrayed by the Workplace Industrial Relations Survey series* (Routledge, London, 2000), p. 109.
677. *Ibid.*, p. 110.
678. *Ibid.*
679. *Financial Times*, 15 June 2001; www.cbi.org.uk/employmenttrends2001.
680. S. Hardy, and N. Adnett, 'Breaking the ICE and democracy at work', *International Journal of Human Resource Management*, 17 (2006), pp. 1101–1123.

are free to extend further these minimal information and consultation rights. Since 2005, the directive has applied to those organizations with more than 50 workers.

This new directive was implemented in the UK by the Information and Consultation on Employees (ICE) Regulations 2004, which comply with the directive's provisions. In the UK, since 2005 this law will apply to those organizations with 150 or more workers, from 2007 for those businesses with over 100 workers and from 2008 for those with more than 50 workers.[681]

521. The UK government opposed this directive on the grounds of subsidiarity, in so far as it believes it to be an unnecessary measure. Under the new NIC Directive, consultation is required where an employer proposes to dismiss 20 or more workers as redundant at one establishment within 90 days or less. Where 100 or more redundancies are proposed, consultation must commence at least 90 days before the first dismissal. However, these rules duplicate existing legal arrangements required under the Collective Redundancy Directive. The information that must be disclosed is a statement of the proposed dismissals and reasons for such, the numbers affected and the proposed method of selection and what payments are available.

§2. Industrial Democracy

522. During the 1970s, a movement towards a wider notion of industrial democracy appeared to be gathering steam.[682] Developments during the 1970s made it clear that collective bargaining on its own could not cope with the ultimate power of management to close down an enterprise, to shift activities to other areas, or to introduce major changes; closer forms of participation were needed. This need was recognized by the TUC, which, in 1974, adopted a policy of pressing for legislative rights to board level representation for organized workers,[683] and given impetus by proposals by the EEC Commission for worker participation in certain contexts.

These developments led the then Labour government to appoint a committee of inquiry, under the chairmanship of Lord Bullock, which reported in January 1977.[684] The majority made wide ranging proposals for employee representation, proposals which were only partly accepted by the then Labour government. But the election in 1979 of the Conservative government effectively put an end to the debate about legislative change, that administration being implacably opposed to such legislation. A revival of the proposals made by the Bullock Committee is not envisaged.

Under the Labour government, 1997–2010, the approach which emerged in respect of labour relations policy can be characterized by the government as one of

681. M. Hall, 'Assessing the Information and Consultation of Employees Regulations', ILJ 34 (2005), pp. 103–126.

682. There is a vast literature on the subject. Special mention may be made of Otto Kahn-Freund, 'Industrial Democracy' ILJ, 6 (1977), 65; P. Davies, and Lord Wedderburn 'The Land of Industrial Democracy' ILJ, 6 (1977), 197, and J. Elliott, *Conflict or Cooperation?* (London, 1978).

683. TUC, *Industrial Democracy* (London 1974), revised 1976.

684. Cmnd 6706, January 1977.

'social partnership'. The centrepiece of the new measures was concerned with collective bargaining at enterprise level (see Ch. 4, below), accompanied by the adoption of EC-wide measures on European Works Councils and information and consultation with employee representatives.

523. Nevertheless, industrial democracy remains a live issue at European level, and has been so for the past three decades. During the 1970s and 1980s, at least three sets of proposals have emerged from the EEC. In 1975, the Commission of the EEC drafted proposals for harmonizing company law, the 'Draft Fifth Directive', including proposals for employee representation on the supervisory boards of all companies with over 500 employees in the EEC. The Draft Directive was renewed in 1983 in amended form. A second Draft Directive, the Vredeling draft,[685] contained proposals on procedures for informing and consulting employees of undertakings with complex structures. Consultation would be obligatory where a decision was taken which was liable to have 'serious consequences for the interests' of employees. Thirdly, a separate set of proposals were put forward for a 'European Company' or *societas europaea*, a new type of legal entity, which included workers' participation as an integral part. However, work on all these proposals was halted during the 1980s, largely because of the hostility of the UK, which was in a position to block all progress by relying on the requirement of unanimity. As a result, the only legislation to emerge on consultation or participation was in specific and limited areas, such as collective redundancies and transfers of undertakings.

524. Renewed impetus to worker participation was given by the Social Charter adopted in December 1989. The Charter states that the rights to information, consultation and participation should be developed along 'appropriate lines'. In particular, these rights should be implemented 'in due time', especially where changes have major implications for the work force. Examples of such circumstances include technological change, restructuring operations, collective redundancy procedures, and cases in which trans-frontier workers are affected by employment policies pursued by their undertaking.[686] In putting the Charter into operation, the Commission concentrated initially on the transnational element. It believed that the completion of the Single European Market in 1992 would increase the numbers of mergers, takeovers and joint ventures across borders, which in turn will mean that frequently the decision-making centre is not situated in the member state in which employees affected are employed. In order to facilitate the development of information and consultation procedures on a European level, the European Works Council Directive (EWCD) (Council Directive No. 94/45) was approved by the Council of Ministers on 22 September 1994 under the terms of the Agreement on Social Policy of the Maastricht Treaty (the so-called Social Chapter). The UK was not a party to

685. Official Journal of the European Communities, C217, 12 August 1983.

686. *Community Charter of the Fundamental Social Rights of Workers*, Articles 17–18; see generally Lord Wedderburn, *The Social Charter, European Company and Employment Rights* (Institute of Employment Rights, 1989).

the Social Chapter, the Conservative administration being wholly opposed to its terms.

However, following the signing of the Social Chapter by the new Labour government in 1997, the EWCD was implemented in the UK by the Transnational Information and Consultation of Employees Regulations (SI 1999/3323). The Regulations were introduced on 15 December 1999 and came into force on 15 January 2000.[687] The Directive and Regulations cover companies which have a total of at least 1,000 employees and at least two establishments in different member states with at least 150 employees each.[688]

525. Proposals for worker involvement were also contained in the draft directive accompanying the European Company Statute Directive, published in August 1989 and amended in 1991, on which a the Davignon group of experts reported in 1997.[689] In 1998, the Council issued a proposal for a directive to establish a general framework for informing and consulting employees at national level in Member States.[690] The Labour government, elected in 1997, was initially opposed to this measure but following their landslide victory in the general election in June 2001, they supported the Swedish Presidency's modified proposals for such a directive. In 2002 the EU thus introduced the Information and Consultation Directive. The Directive was to be fully implemented over a seven year period. The UK transposed the Directive in to national law throught the Information and Consultation Regulations 2004, which have been effective since 6 April 2005. . It is also to be noted that Article 27 of the EU Charter of Fundamental Rights adopted by European Council in December 2000 states that '[w]orkers or their representatives must, at the appropriate levels, be guaranteed information and consultation in good time ... in the cases and under the conditions provided for by Community law and national laws and practices'.

526. As an alternative to worker participation on a collective level, the Conservative government (1979–97) favoured employee involvement on an individualized level, in the form of profit-sharing or share-ownership schemes. Although some encouragement for share-ownership schemes were given during the 1970s, these were given greater impetus in the 1980s. In particular, tax concessions on profit-related pay were introduced in the Finance (No. 2) Act 1987. It was argued that such schemes would leads to a closer identification of employees with the companies in which they work. The extent to which such aims can or should be achieved is, however, highly controversial.[691] A survey of 1,063 employees found that 51 per cent

687. A critique of the Regulations is contained in B. Bercusson, 'A European agenda?' in K. Ewing, (ed.), *Employment Rights at Work: Reviewing the Employment Relations Act 1999* (Institute of Employment Rights, London, 2001), pp. 176–185.
688. For details see R. Blanpain, *European Labour Law* (7th edn), vol. 1 of this *Encyclopedia*, Part II, Ch. 2 (4).
689. Blanpain, *op. cit.*
690. COM/98/612 of 11 November 1998.
691. P.P. Beaumont, *Change in Industrial Relations*, pp. 244–246; C. Duncan, 'Why Profit related pay will fail'*Industrial Relations Journal*, 186 (1988) G.R. Smith, 'Profit Sharing and employee share ownership in Britain', *Employment Gazette*, September 1986, p. 380.

were more committed to the company, while as many as 45 per cent said shareholding made no difference.[692] By 1998, 46 per cent of workplaces operated a profit sharing scheme and 24 per cent operated an employee share ownership scheme.[693]

§3. Safety Representatives and Safety Committees

527. Before 1975 safety and health issues were generally not regarded as matters of active 'worker participation'. However, the Health and Safety at Work, etc. Act 1974, embodying the proposals of the Committee of Inquiry under the chairmanship of Lord Robens,[694] empowered the Secretary of State to make regulations for the election by employees of safety representatives from amongst the employees to represent employees in consultation with employers. The underlying philosophy was that employees and employers have a common interest in a self-regulating system of industrial accident prevention.

The Employment Protection Act 1975 amended the 1974 Act by limiting to recognized trade unions the power to appoint safety representatives, so clearly embodying the philosophy of collective bargaining, namely that health and safety should be a matter for negotiation between trade union representatives and management. At the same time, the dependence on recognized trade unions meant that employers who refused to recognize unions were permitted to sidestep their obligations under the Act.

Following a ruling by the European Court of Justice that the EU rules in respect of information and consultation with employee representatives in the case of collective redundancies and transfers of undertakings were not satisfied where consultation depended on the will of the employer whether or not to recognize a union,[695] the Health and Safety (Consultation with Employees) Regulations 1996 were made. These give the employers the choice of consulting employees directly or of consulting elected representatives of employee safety. As a result there are now two sets of regulations. The Safety Representatives and Safety Committees Regulations 1977, as amended, apply where the employer recognizes an independent union. These regulations empower a recognized trade union to appoint safety representatives from among employees in all cases where one or more employees are employed by an employer by whom it is recognized. The employer must be notified in writing of their appointment before they are entitled to exercise their statutory functions, and to make inspections of the workplace and to be provided with documents and information.

The Health and Safety (Consultation with Employees) Regulations 1996 apply only where groups of employees are not covered by union safety representatives appointed under the 1997 regulations. Safety representatives are entitled to time off with pay during working hours to perform their statutory functions and to undergo reasonable training. If at least two safety representatives request the employer in

692. *Industrial Relations Review and Report*, No. 483, p. 5.
693. Milward *et al.*, *op. cit.*, p. 214.
694. Cmnd 5034 (1972).
695. Cases C-383/93 and C-384/93, *Commission* v. *United Kingdom* [1994] IRLR 392, 412.

writing to establish a safety committee he or she must do so within three months, after consulting with those representatives and with representatives of recognized trade unions whose members work in any workplace in respect of which the committee is to function. The Health and Safety Commission has issued Codes of Practice giving guidance on the establishment and duties of representatives and committees. A breach of the Codes is relevant in any proceedings. A contravention of the regulations may result in the issuing of an improvement notice by the Health and Safety Executive, or criminal proceedings giving rise on conviction to a fine, or possibly to an action for civil remedies. In practice it is likely that disputes will usually be resolved through voluntary procedures. The UK provisions are augmented and strengthened by the EC Directive on workers' representatives' rights to information, consultation and participation about health and safety in the workplace, adopted on 12 June 1989.[696] The thrust of the directive is to require advance consultation on all safety issues, as well as 'balanced participation' in accordance with laws and practices of the Member States.

696. 89/391/EEC.

Chapter 4. Collective Bargaining

528. Collective bargaining was been a central feature of British industrial relations for much of the 20th century.[697] It stood out from most other collective bargaining systems because of the relative absence of legal regulation. Nevertheless, the State took a positive role in facilitating collective bargaining: from the end of the First World War until 1979: collective bargaining was actively encouraged by successive governments, both among state employees and in the private sector. Thus, in 1973, as many as 83.2 per cent of full-time manual men and 71.7 per cent of full-time manual women were covered by collective bargaining arrangements. By contrast, the salient feature of the 1980s and early 1990s was been the reversal by the Thatcher and Major Conservative governments of the supportive policy towards collective bargaining. Two striking examples were the dismantling in 1987 of well-established collective bargaining machinery for school teachers,[698] and the abolition in 1993 of Wages Councils which set minimum wages for workers in unorganized industries. The coverage of collective bargaining fell from 70 per cent in 1984 to 40 per cent in 1998.[699] This was accompanied by a fall in trade union density from 65 per cent in 1980 to 36 per cent in 1998,[700] and a decline in the incidence of trade union recognition from 64 per cent in 1980 to 42 per cent in 1998.[701] However, legislation introduced by the Labour government which came into force in 2000, promised to revive collective bargaining at enterprise level.

§1. Levels and Extent of Bargaining

529. A further feature of collective bargaining in Britain is its enormous diversity. Thus the extent to which pay is influenced by collective bargaining differs markedly from establishment to establishment and between the public and private sectors and the same is true for the levels at which it takes place. Such diversity makes it difficult to present any clear or comprehensive description, and only a few trends which have been of particular importance to legal and other institutional arrangements can be highlighted.

530. There are various ways in which levels of bargaining can be categorized. Traditionally, a distinction was drawn between industry-wide bargaining, regional or district level bargaining, and plant or workplace bargaining. Industry-wide bargaining developed largely after the First World War. It was given its major impetus by the influential Whitley Committee in 1919, which recommended that industry-wide negotiating agreements should be established on a voluntary basis in all major

697. Lord Wedderburn, 'Collective bargaining or legal enactment: the 1999 Act and union recognition', ILJ 29 (2000), pp. 1–42.
698. Teachers' Pay and Conditions Act 1987, School Teachers' Pay and Conditions Act 1991.
699. N. Millward, A. Bryson, and J. Forth, *All Change at Work? British Employment Relations 1986–1998*, as portrayed in the Workplace industrial relations survey series (Routledge, London, 2000), p. 197.
700. *Ibid.*, p. 87.
701. *Ibid.*, p. 97.

industries. By 1965, such agreements were widespread. But two and a half decades later a noticeable erosion of industry-wide bargaining had occurred in both public and private sectors, the proportion of workplaces covered by multi-employer agreements falling from 69 per cent in 1984 to 46 per cent in 1998.[702] Regional or district level bargaining was historically most important before the First World War, but is now of relatively small importance. Plant or company-level bargaining, by contrast, is increasingly significant. The most comprehensive evidence comes from ther workplace industrial relations surveys, which show that establishment-level bargaining in the private sector rose from 34 per cent in 1984 to 53 per cent in 1998.[703] Plant bargaining is likely to involve joint shop steward committees, possibly with the assistance of full-time union officials. Corporate bargaining is to be found among multi-establishment enterprises: here the negotiating committee is likely to involve convenors and senior shop stewards from individual establishments together with full-time trade union officials. Depending on the level of bargaining within the corporation, such bargaining could be either national or local.

531. The scope of collective bargaining has traditionally been relatively narrow, with the principal subjects being wages and working hours. During the 1970s, the subject range of collective bargaining widened considerably as a result of factors such as health and safety legislation, the increasing incidence of redundancies, the greater role of technology and the emphasis on the shorter working week. This trend was reversed in the 1980s: the 1984 workplace survey showed that the extent of negotiation over non-pay matters declined considerably for both manual and non-manual workers in the years 1980 to 1984.[704] This was particularly marked in the private services sector and for workplace level bargaining. Little change occurred in respect of the scope of bargaining between 1984 and 1998.[705] A further source of joint regulation of non-pay issues takes the form of 'custom and practice' at workplace level.

However, this remains largely un-codified and rarely leads to formal agreements, particularly in respect of matters such as discipline. Indeed, in respect of non-pay matters, not a great deal has changed in collective bargaining since the Donovan report. Sisson and Brown[706] comment that 'defining existing practices is often open to a great deal of argument. In these and other cases, then, one or other of the parties may refuse to enter into either a formal or an informal agreement or to recognize custom and practice. Usually, one of the parties seeks to impose a settlement on the other; it is left to the other party to react'. Managements have been reluctant to reach precise agreements on these matters for a variety of reasons including the

702. Millward and Forth, *op. cit.*, p. 186; see too, W. Brown, P. Marginson, and J. Walsh, 'Management, pay determination and collective bargaining' in P. Edwards (ed.), *Industrial Relations* (Oxford, Blackwell, 1995); C. Thornley, 'Contesting Local Pay: the Decentralization of Collective Bargaining in the NHS' *Brit. Jo. Ind. Rels.* 36 (1998), 413.
703. *Ibid.*, p. 188.
704. Millward and Stevens, *British Workplace Industrial Relations, 1980–1984* (1986), pp. 249–253.
705. Millward, Bryson and Forth, *op. cit.*, pp. 167–173.
706. Sisson and Brown, in Bain (ed.), *Industrial Relations in Britain* (1983), p. 151.

difficulty of withdrawing concessions, the danger of 'leapfrogging' to further formal concessions and the reduction of flexibility of local management. Formalization also tends to be opposed by shop stewards who believe it would restrict the scope of bargaining and limit their freedom of action, for example, to oppose managerial decisions over discipline and redundancy.

§2. The Role of Shop Stewards

532. Workplace bargaining is largely the responsibility of *shop stewards*. It is not easy to explain the essential character of the British shop steward. He or she is not the same, for example, as the French *délègue du personnel* or the German works council member. At one time it was unusual to describe him or her as an 'official' of the union. But since 1971, the legal definition of an 'official'[707] has included a person, elected or appointed as a representative of union members, who is an employee of the same employer as the members whom he represents. This includes a shop steward, who may go under other names such as (in the printing industry) 'father/mother of the chapel'. The steward is both an employee of the enterprise and also a representative of those other employees who hold union membership. He or she is usually elected by union members at the place of work, and is not appointed by the branch or executive committee of the union. However, in some unions the election must be ratified by a higher union authority than the members at the workplace. The courts have occasionally intervened to protect an elected shop steward whose credentials have not been issued by the union for reasons that are palpably bad, such as that the steward refuses to give an undertaking to follow all instructions of the union.[708] This highlights the 'dual authority' of the steward.[709] He or she is at one and the same time the representative of members at the workplace, which is the basis of the steward's power, and also the representative of the external union. The Conservative government's legislation of the 1980s displayed a similar ambivalence to the nature of the shop-stewards' role. The statutory provisions obliging unions to conduct secret ballots for the election of union officials, do not extend to shop stewards. However, the Employment Act 1990[710] introduced provisions by virtue of which a shop steward who calls on members to take industrial action can thereby make the union liable in tort, even if the union rules do not permit shop stewards to authorize such action. However, under the post-1997 Labour Government a more positive role for shop stewards was envisaged in the form of Sections 10–13 of the Employment Relations Act 1999 which grant to individual workers the right to be accompanied in disciplinary and grievance procedures by either a trade union official or another worker of the employer.

---

707. Now embodied in TULRCA, 1992, s. 119.
708. *Shotton* v. *Hammond*, *The Times*, 2 December 1976.
709. In *Heaton's Transport Ltd* v. *TGWU* [1972] ICR 308 (HL) this analysis was used to impose vicarious liability on the union for the acts of stewards.
710. Now embodied in TULRCA 1992, s. 20.

533. In most places of work there is likely to be more than one shop steward (the 'shop' is defined by custom and may cover one or more departments in a plant) and a shop stewards' committee with a 'chief steward' or 'convenor' (sometimes full-time) may then exist. Because of the structure of British trade unions (see Ch. 2, above) several unions are likely to have to work together in one office or factory. In these cases the stewards' committee will be multi-union. This has the important consequence that the committees are not easily made responsible to union authority outside the workplace. The shop steward organization at the workplace is also a far more important link between the member and the union than the trade union branch. In many unions the branch consists of small groups of members from a number of different factories and offices. The branch is therefore separate from the real business of the union at the workplace and it is left to the shop steward organization to conduct collective bargaining.

534. The number of shop stewards grew considerably in the 1960s and 1970s. This development was accompanied by the growing formalization of shop steward bargaining, partly as a result of legislative measures such as the encouragement of the closed shop by legislation of the Labour government (1974–9) and the establishment of health and safety committees and the election of shop stewards as safety representatives, as well as encouragement by managers who found stewards 'more of a lubricant than an irritant'[711] in the conduct of workplace relations. In the 1980s, the economic recession and the policies of the Conservative government put shop steward organization under great pressure. In some instances 'tough' managements moved from plant to corporate bargaining and severely undermined the shop steward movement. Nevertheless, the shop steward system has proved to be considerably more resilient than might have been predicted. While the proportion of unionized workplaces with on-site union representation fell from 82 per cent in 1984 to 71 per cent in 1990, no further fall was recorded in the 1990s.[712]

§3. Legal Support for Collective Bargaining

535. In the introduction an outline was given of the relatively few legal supports for the essentially voluntarist system of collective bargaining, and of the measures taken by the Conservative government between 1979 and 1993 to dismantle even those few statutory props for joint regulation. The repealed measures included: (1) the right to recognition for collective bargaining, first introduced in 1971, and renewed in 1975, removed by the Employment Act 1980; (2) the procedure for the extension of collective agreements, originating in war-time legislation, renewed and extended in Schedule 11 of the Employment Protection Act 1975, also removed by the Employment Act 1980; (3) the Fair Wages Resolution of the House of Commons of 1946, renewing and extending earlier Resolutions since 1891, obliging government contractors to observe terms and conditions not less favourable than

711. W.E.J. McCarthy, and S.R. Parker, *Shop Stewards and Workshop Relations*, Royal Commission Research Paper No. 10, London, 1968, p. 15.
712. Millward *et al.*, *op. cit.*, p. 152.

those established by collective bargaining, rescinded in 1983; (4) the Road Haulage Wages Act 1938, which established tripartite machinery to fix minimum wages in that industry, repealed by the Employment Act 1980; and (5) the provisions concering the Wages Councils (discussed in Part I, paras. 205–212, above), whose coverage had already been severely restricted in 1986, repealed by the Trade Union Reform and Employment Rights Act 1993. All that remained were: (1) Agricultural Wages Boards under the Agricultural Wages Act 1948, and the Agricultural Wages (Scotland) Act 1949; (2) the individual employment rights to protect those belonging to unions or participating in trade union activities at the 'appropriate time' (discussed in Ch. 1 above); (3) specific duties to consult workers' representatives over health and safety matters (Ch. 3, above), proposed redundancies (Part I) and over proposed transfers of undertakings (Part I); and (4) a duty to disclose information for bargaining purposes to recognized trade unions.

536. The only one of these items not so far discussed is the duty to disclose information. TULRCA, 1992, Sections 181–185 obliges the employer to disclose information to an independent trade union which he or she has already recognized for collective bargaining. The information must be such that without it the union would be impeded in collective bargaining to a 'material extent' and such that the employer should disclose it in accordance with good industrial relations practice. ACAS has issued a Code containing practical guidance, which suggests that subjects which are not listed in Section 178(2), TULRCA 1992 as subjects of collective bargaining can nevertheless be relevant so far as disclosure of information is concerned, such as the employer's investment plans, return for capital invested, sales and the state of the order book.

537. The enforcement procedure is complex. An independent trade union may complain to the Central Arbitration Committee (CAC) which must refer the matter to ACAS for conciliation. If this fails, the CAC must make a declaration stating whether it finds the complaint well-founded and setting out its reasons. The employer then has an opportunity to comply, and if he or she does not do so, a further complaint may be presented to the CAC. The CAC again makes a declaration stating whether the complaint is well-founded and giving its reasons. It may also determine a claim by the union regarding the terms and conditions of employment which should be observed by the employer. The award takes effect as a term of the contracts of employment of the individual employees affected. A number of statutory limitations on the duty to make disclosure are set out in Section 182 of TULRCA 1992. These include information disclosed to the employer in confidence, and information the disclosure of which would 'cause substantial injury to the employer's undertaking, for reasons other than its effect on collective bargaining'.

538. In view of the circumscribed nature of the duty to disclose, it is not surprising that relatively little use has been made of this right. Only a trickle of new complaints are brought to the CAC.[713] The CAC has always taken the view that the most useful avenue of approach has been to ascertain whether a complaint can be

713. CAC *Annual Reports*, 1997, 1998, 1999–2000 and 2012–13 (839 applications in total).

settled voluntarily. Such an approach, the Committee reports, has been very successful. Between the introduction of the disclosure provisions in 1977 and the end of 1999, the CAC had received 476 complaints, only 14 per cent of which had required a formal decision.[714] The vast majority of the remainder were withdrawn after a settlement had been reached.

§4. Union Recognition

539. One of the most significant supports for collective bargaining introduced by the then Labour government was the statutory recognition procedure, which originated in the government's promise to construct a labour relations regime which would be founded on the principles of fairness and social partnership.[715] It ought to be noted that the statutory recognition process is highly complex. The recognition procedure, the operation of which is overseen by the Central Arbitration Committee (CAC), is contained in Sched. A1 of the Trade Union and Labour Relations (Consolidation) Act 1992 (TULRCA), which was inserted by the Employment Relations Act 1999.[716] The quest for recognition by a trade union (or jointly by two or more trade unions) as the bargaining agent for 'a group or groups of workers' must begin with the lodging of a formal request for recognition with the employer.[717] The request will not be valid unless the union (or each of the unions) has obtained a certificate of independence and the employer employs at least 21 workers on the day it receives the request, or an average of at least 21 workers in the previous 13 weeks. Within 10 working days ('the first period') of receiving the union's (or unions') request for recognition, the employer can either accept the request and reach agreement with the union(s) in respect of the bargaining unit, in which case the remaining provisions in Schedule A1 will not apply, or it can reject the request but signal a willingness to enter into negotiations concerning a bargaining unit and the recognition of the applicant union(s). If the employer chooses to follow the latter route, the parties will then have a further 20 working days ('the second period') at the end of the first period – or a longer period, as agreed by the parties – in which to conclude a recognition agreement. The parties may call upon the Advisory Conciliation and Arbitration Service (ACAS) to assist in conducting the negotiations.

540. If the employer either fails to respond to the union's (or unions') request within the first period or rejects the request within that period, or if the parties fail to reach an agreement before the end of the second period, the union(s) may apply

---

714. CAC *Annual Report*, 1999/2000.
715. Former Department of Trade and Industry (DTI), *Fairness at Work*, Cmnd 3968 (1998), paras. 1.8, 1.9.
716. For analysis of the provisions, see S. Wood, and J. Godard, 'The Statutory Recognition Procedure in the Employment Relations Bill: A Comparative Analysis' BJIR 37 (1999) 203; W. McCarthy, *Fairness at Work and Trade Union Recognition: Past Comparisons and Future Problems* (Institute of Employment Rights, London, 1999); and B. Hepple, 'Supporting collective bargaining: some comparative reflections' in Towers and Brown (eds.), *Employment Relations in Britain* (Oxford, Blackwell, 2000), pp. 153–162.
717. B. Simpson, 'Trade union recognition and the law: a new approach', ILJ 29 (2000), pp. 193–222.

to the CAC to determine 'whether the proposed bargaining unit is appropriate or some other bargaining unit is appropriate' and 'whether the union has (or unions have) the support of a majority of the workers constituting the appropriate bargaining unit.' In the event of the parties reaching agreement in respect of a bargaining unit, but not in respect of the recognition of the union(s), the union(s) may call upon the CAC to determine the latter question. However, no such application may be made if within the period of 10 working days beginning with the day after that on which the employer signalled a willingness to negotiate, the employer proposed that ACAS be 'requested to assist in conducting the negotiations' and the union(s) either reject(s) the proposal or fail(s) to accept the proposal within 11 working days of the employer making it. Before the CAC can deal with an application for recognition, it must be satisfied that (1) the proposed bargaining unit is not already covered by a collective agreement in terms of which a union (or more than one union) is recognized as the bargaining agent of any workers falling within the bargaining unit, *unless* the recognized union(s) and the union(s) making the application are the same, or the matters in respect of which the union is (or unions are) recognized do not include pay, hours or holidays, or if the recognized union is not independent, was in the past recognized for the same or substantially the same bargaining unit, and had had its recognition withdrawn in the three years ending with the date of the existing recognition agreement; (2) at least 10 per cent of the workers in the relevant bargaining unit are members of the applicant union(s); (3) a majority of the workers in the bargaining unit would be likely to favour recognition of the applicant union(s); (4) the CAC has not processed an application for recognition submitted by the applicant union in relation to the same, or substantially the same, bargaining unit within the previous three years; (5) the CAC has not issued a declaration of de-recognition against the applicant union in relation to the same, or substantially the same, bargaining unit within the previous three years.

541. If the CAC is satisfied that a majority of the workers in the relevant bargaining unit are members of the applicant union(s), it is obliged to make a declaration of recognition, unless any of the following three 'qualifying conditions' is met: the CAC is of the opinion that a ballot should be held in the interests of good industrial relations; a significant number of the union's (or unions') members in the relevant bargaining unit inform the CAC that they do not wish the union(s) to conduct collective bargaining on their behalf; and evidence is produced concerning the circumstances in which the workers in question became union members, or the length of time for which they have been members, which leads the CAC to conclude that there are doubts as to whether a significant number of the union members in the relevant bargaining unit want the union(s) to conduct collective bargaining on their behalf. If any of the above conditions is fulfilled, or if the CAC is not satisfied that a majority of workers in the bargaining unit are members of the applicant union, it must furnish the parties with notice of its intention to hold a secret ballot to ascertain whether the workers in the relevant bargaining unit want the union(s) to conduct collective bargaining on their behalf. The ballot must be conducted by a qualified independent person appointed by the CAC, and must be held within 20 working days (or such longer period as the CAC may decide).

Chapter 5. Industrial Action

§1. Patterns of Industrial Action

542. The levels of industrial action in the United Kingdom since 1970 has markedly declined. In the 1970s, the annual average number of stoppages was 2,631, as contrasted with annual averages of 1,129 during the 1980s. Figures for the 1990s show an even more dramatic decline, with an average of 234 stoppages per year. A similar pattern emerges when we consider the number of working days lost through stoppages of work caused by industrial disputes. The annual average of 12.9 million for the 1970s fell to 7.2 million for the 1980s and then plummeted during the 1990s, within an average of less than a quarter of a million days lost in the years 1997–9. Although industrial action has traditionally been more prevalent in the public than the private sectors, by 1998 it was rare in all sectors. Notably, this was as true in unionized workplaces as in non-unionized workplaces, and the steep decline affected strong and weak unions alike. It is important to note that figures on strike activity are only partial indicators of industrial action, since increasing use is being made of action short of strikes.

A recent survey revealed that less than half of the establishments affected by any type of industrial action were affected by a strike which would have come within the definition used for official records. This is particularly so in local and national government.

543. The reasons for such fluctuations are complex, but an important factor has always been the level of unemployment.[718] Thus, the high levels of industrial action in the 1960s and 1970s were closely associated with a low incidence of unemployment and the rise of shop-floor bargaining. The most prominent characteristic of industrial action in the 1960s, in the manufacturing industries at least, was the high incidence of small unofficial strikes (i.e. strikes not ratified by the union executive). The lower levels of industrial action since 1980 reflect in part the steep increase in unemployment rates. The 1980s also saw a re-emergence of the large official strike, particularly in the public sector, involving hitherto strike-free groups such as civil servants, teachers, health service and local authority workers. During the 1990s, the picture changed again, with steadily increasing employment coinciding with an ever steeper decline in levels of industrial action. There are two possible explanations. First, it could be argued that the demise of industrial action is evidence of a more general decline in the strength of unions. Alternatively, it could be the case that legislative changes have prompted unions to threaten action to strengthen their bargaining position, often backed up by majority support in a ballot, without having to resort to actual industrial action.[719]

---

718. P.F. Edwards, in *Industrial Relations in Britain* (ed. G.S. Bain), (London, 1983), pp. 209–234.
719. Millward *et al.*, *op. cit.*, p. 179; Elgar and Simpson, 'The Impact of the Law on Industrial Disputes in the 1980s', in D. Metcalf and S. Milner (eds.), *New Perspectives on Industrial Relations* (Routledge, 1993).

§2. The Right to Strike[720]

544. The law regulating strike action in Britain is extremely complex, and can only be understood in the context of a century of overlapping and conflicting judicial and legislative developments. Although the 'right to strike' was described by a leading British judge in 1942 as being 'an essential element in the principle of collective bargaining',[721] there is no legally guaranteed 'right' of the individual citizen to withdraw his or her labour in combination with others; nor do trade unions have such positive rights. Nor is there a generally applicable legal definition of a 'strike' or 'lock-out' in British legislation: indeed, 'strike' is only defined for the purposes of one specific statutory provision.[722] Instead, industrial action is regulated by a series of common law wrongs, chiefly in tort and contract, limited and circumscribed by statutory immunities for action 'in contemplation or furtherance of a trade dispute'. The criminal law ceased to be a central regulating force in 1875, but it retains an important role in respect of ordinary criminal actions such as criminal damage or breach of the peace which may take place in the course of industrial action, particularly picketing. This chapter examines the common law liabilities, the scope of the statutory immunities and the law governing picketing.

545. It is useful to approach the question of whether industrial action is lawful in three stages:

1. Does the act in question give rise to civil liability at common law?
2. Is this liability removed by the immunities afforded by Section 219 of TULRCA? This in turn requires proof first that the tort in question is specifically protected by the statute (there are several torts which are not specified and are therefore out of the range of the immunity); and second that the act has been done in 'contemplation or furtherance of a trade dispute'.
3. Are these immunities in turn withdrawn because (a) the action amounts to unlawful 'secondary action'; (b) the balloting provisions have not been complied with; (c) the action has been taken in the course of unlawful picketing; (d) the purpose of the action is to enforce trade union membership; (e) it is a response to the dismissal of participants in unofficial industrial action; or (f) its purpose is to require the employer to pursue a 'union-only' or 'recognition only practice' in a supply contract? Immunity is also withdrawn in respect of an employer who has not been supplied with a pre-industrial action notice or the requisite information prior to and after a ballot.

It is crucial to note that the withdrawal of the relevant immunity gives rise to civil liability only if the original act is tortious. None of the provisions in (3) above give

720. See J. Bowers, M. Duggan, and D. Reade, *The Law on Industrial Action and Trade Union Recognition* (Oxford University Press, 2010), for detailed analysis; and K. Ewing, *The Right to Strike* (Clarendon Press, 1991).

721. *Crofter Hand Woven Harris Tweed Co.* v. *Veitch* [1942] AC 435 at p. 463.

722. TULRCA, 1992, s. 246 (ballot provisions).

rise to liability independently of the commission of a tort or other species of civil liability.

§3. Civil Liability

I. Contract and No-strike Agreements

546. An individual who takes part in industrial action almost certainly breaks his or her contract of employment. This is so even if strike notice has been given to the employer, since such notice is not generally construed as equivalent to notice to terminate the contract. At common law, this breach will usually be construed as a repudiation by the employee of the fundamental obligation to work, so entitling the employer summarily to dismiss him or her.[723] Although an attempt was made in one case to avoid this result by creating a legal right to suspend the contract by giving strike notice corresponding in length to the notice required to terminate the employee's contract,[724] this has subsequently been rejected.[725] The employer's remedies against an employee for breach of contract are, however, of limited value in this context. The courts will not grant specific performance of the employment contract, and the measure of damages has been held in the case of a non-production worker to be limited to the cost of finding a replacement for the absent worker.[726] A more effective strategy for employers is to make use of the 'self-help' remedy of withdrawal of wages. This is particularly powerful in cases of industrial action falling short of a total stoppage of work, a form of action which has become more frequent in recent years. Recent case law suggests that if a worker refuses to perform some of his or her contractual obligations, the employer may be entitled to deduct the full amount of pay, even if the worker has conscientiously performed most of his or her duties, provided the employer has made it clear that partial performance is not acceptable.[727]

547. It will be recalled that collective agreements are not legally binding unless the contrary is stated in writing.[728] Thus no action lies for breach of a peace (or 'no-strike') obligation in such an agreement unless the parties to the collective agreement expressly agree that this is to be the case and this is unusual. It is highly unusual for trade unions in Britain to conclude legally binding 'no-strike' agreements, although agreements restricting strikes have been on the increase in recent years, negotiated mainly by the Amalgamated Engineering and Electrical Union, and have led to fierce debate within the trade union movement. However, such

723. *Simmons* v. *Hoover Ltd* [1977] ICR 61 (EAT).
724. *Morgan* v. *Fry* [1968] 2 QB 710, CA *per* Lord Denning MR at p. 730.
725. *Simmons* v. *Hoover Ltd* [1977] ICR 61 at pp. 70–77.
726. *National Coal Board* v. *Galley* [1958] 1 WLR 16.
727. *Miles* v. *Wakefield* [1987] IRLR 193; *Wiluszynski* v. *London Borough of Tower Hamlets* [1989] ICR 493.
728. TULRCA, 1992, s. 179.

agreements very rarely have legal effect. A 'no-strike' clause in the collective agreement will be incorporated in individual contracts of employment only if five conditions are satisfied. These are laid down by TULRCA 1992, Section 180 as follows: (a) the collective agreement must be in writing; (b) it must contain a provision expressly stating that such terms shall or may be incorporated into the individual contracts; (c) it must be reasonably accessible at the workplace and available during working hours; (d) each trade union party to the collective agreement must be independent; and (e) the relevant individual contract must expressly or impliedly incorporate such terms into the contract. The fifth condition is particularly important because it means that the 'translation' problem must, in each case, be answered affirmatively before the term may be incorporated. The employer cannot contract out of these provisions either with the union or the individual worker. The provisions apply to any terms of a collective agreement which prohibit or restrict the right of workers to engage in a strike or other industrial action or have the effect of prohibiting or restricting that right.

II. Loss of Statutory Rights

548. Until very recently, workers dismissed while participating in industrial action could not in general complain of unfair dismissal. Initially, this was because policy-makers were reluctant to involve employment tribunals in the merits of industrial action, and preferred to leave both sides to make use of autonomous, non-legal sanctions. Only if the employer dismissed selectively could those dismissed complain of unfair dismissal.

However, during the neo-liberal period it was clear that this restriction operated unfairly, leaving workers vulnerable to mass dismissals. This was exacerbated by the modification introduced in 1990 permitting employers to dismiss workers selectively if they were participating in unofficial industrial action, and, in cases of official industrial action, allowing employers to re-employ workers selectively after three months. A central plank of the package of reforms introduced by the new Labour government was the introduction of protection against dismissal for striking employees. Thus a new provision was inserted making it automatically unfair to dismiss an employee taking part in 'protected' industrial action. In order to create an incentive for both sides to resolve the dispute, the legislation provides that this protection only lasts for the first eight weeks after the employee has commenced taking the industrial action, unless the employer has not taken reasonable procedural steps to resolve the dispute, or the employee has ceased to take action within the eight weeks.[729] Industrial action is only 'protected' for these purposes if it is immune from civil liability under TULRCA, 1992 and the protection against dismissal is confined to 'official' action, where action is only official if it has been authorized or endorsed by a trade union which has members participating.[730]

These limitations mean that in practice the protection against dismissal is based on a complex set of factors, which might well operate to restrict the right severely.

729. TULRCA, 1992, s. 238A
730. TULRCA, 1992, s. 237.

As will be seen below, industrial action may not be 'protected' in a wide range of situations, and it has been suggested that it will be sufficient if immunity is lost in relation to only one of a number of employees involved in the dispute. For example, if a union fails to give only one employer the statutory notice of the action to be taken, protection against dismissal will be lost by all participating employees. The linkage of the right of individuals not to be dismissed to the existence of immunity for trade unions against civil action also means that employment tribunals will have to decide very complex and wide-ranging issues relating to the scope of economic torts and the extent of statutory protection which they have not had to deal with in the past.[731] Claiming protection is also made more difficult by the fact that it is for the employe to show that the principal reason for the dismissal was that she or he was taking industrial action. In cases of unofficial industrial action, it remains automatically fair to dismiss striking workers, unless the dismissal was for a different, automatically unfair reason, such as that the employee was acting as a representative of the workforce, on the grounds of pregnancy or for specified health and safety reasons. Notably, it is not automatic-ally unfair to dismiss a worker taking unofficial industrial action on the grounds of trade union membership or participation in trade union activities. This means that the employer can use the opportunity presented by unofficial industrial action to 'weed out' union members perceived to be leaders or 'trouble-makers'.

549. Employees are not entitled to redundancy payments if dismissed while undertaking any industrial action which puts them in breach of their contracts of employment, unless redundancy notice was given before the industrial action began.[732] Nor are employees entitled to further pay during a notice period where their action amounts to a repudiatory breach of the contract of employment.[733] Similarly, an employee is not entitled to a guarantee payment if the failure to provide work is due to a strike, lockout or other industrial action involving any employee of his employer or an associated employer.[734] An employee will lose his right to statutory sick pay if there is a stoppage of work due to a trade dispute at his place of employment, unless he can show no 'direct interest' in the dispute.[735] Moreover, a dispute may disentitle workers to social security benefits.

III. Tort[736]

550. There are five main torts which have been developed by the judiciary with specific relevance to industrial action. Since each of these effectively removes the freedom of workers to withdraw their labour collectively, Parliament, in pursuit of the policy of tolerating industrial action has responded periodically by creating negative 'immunities' for those who commit certain specified torts 'in

731. G. Morris and T. Archer, *Collective Labour Law* (Hart, 2000), para. 6.98.
732. ERA 1996, s. 140.
733. ERA 1996, s. 91.
734. ERA 1996, s. 29(3).
735. Social Security Contributions and Benefits Act 1992, s. 153(3), Sched. 11.
736. See H. Carty, *Economic Torts* (2003), Oxford.

contemplation or furtherance of a trade dispute'. These immunities were narrowed significantly in the 1980s, thus exposing trade unions and their officers to civil liability. In particular there is the possibility of an injunction being obtained against the organizers of industrial action, including (since 1982) the trade union itself. Each of the main torts will be considered, followed by a description of the scope of the immunities, and the use of injunctions in disputes.

A. Civil Conspiracy to Injure

551. Conspiracy ceased to be of importance in trade disputes as a criminal offence after 1875 in situations where the act would not have been punishable if done by an individual,[737] and the common law crime of conspiracy was abolished (with a few exceptions not relevant here) in 1977.[738] However, civil conspiracy to injure (or 'simple' conspiracy) was developed as a major weapon against union organizers between 1901 and 1906. This tort consists of a combination of two or more persons whose predominant purpose is to inflict damage on the plaintiff rather than to serve their own *bona fide* and legitimate interests. In the early cases, trade union objectives, such as the closed shop, were not regarded as legitimate,[739] and this is why the Trade Disputes Act 1906 enacted an immunity in respect of 'simple' conspiracy in 'trade disputes'. However, by 1942 the House of Lords had come to recognize the legitimacy of at least some trade union objectives,[740] and later others, such as opposition to a colour bar, were also held to excuse combinations.[741] Accordingly, this tort ceased to have much practical relevance.[742] In 1981, the House of Lords recognized that the tort was 'highly anomalous' but felt that it was too well-established to be discarded.[743]

B. Civil Conspiracy to Commit an Unlawful Act or Use Unlawful Means

552. Where an act is itself a tort, then a combination by two or more persons to do that act is a tortious conspiracy. Some confusion over the scope of this tort was created in 1981, when the House of Lords appeared to have suggested that the tort

---

737. TULRCA, 1992, ss. 242–243.
738. Criminal Law Act 1977, s. 5. This Act created a new offence of conspiracy to commit an offence, but an agreement to commit a summary offence not punishable by imprisonment in contemplation or furtherance of a trade dispute is excluded from the scope of this offence. This overcomes the main criticism of the *Shrewsbury pickets* case (*R* v. *Jones* [1974] ICR 310) decided under the old law, in which sentences of up to three years' imprisonment were imposed on the organizers of 'flying pickets' for conspiracy to intimidate, a substantive offence with a maximum penalty of a fine of £20 or up to three months' imprisonment.
739. *Quinn* v. *Leathem* [1901] AC 495, HL.
740. *Crofter Hand Woven Harris Tweed Co.* v. *Veitch* [1942] AC 435, HL.
741. *Scala Ballroom (Wolverhampton) Ltd* v. *Ratcliffe* [1958] 3 All ER 220, CA.
742. But see *Huntley* v. *Thornton* [1957] 1 All ER 235, where district officers of a union were held liable for victimizing an individual who had failed to participate in an unofficial strike.
743. *Lonrho Ltd* v. *Shell Petroleum Co. Ltd* [1982] AC 173, 188–189.

was only committed if the combiners' predominant purpose was to injure the plaintiff, [744] thus equating this tort with its anomalous 'lawful means' counterpart. However, the House of Lords later clarified the situation by holding that, where unlawful means are used, it is sufficient for the conspirators to evince an intention to injure the plaintiff even if this is not the predominant propose.[745] The fact that the predominant purpose is to further the defendant's own legitimate self-interest is no defence where unlawful means are used. While this may be logical outside of industrial relations, for workers taking industrial action, it represents yet wider liability. In most industrial action, the predominant intention will be to further workers' interests, but this could not be achieved without intending to damage the interests of the employer. This is mitigated somewhat by the fact that the means will not be unlawful if protected by a statutory immunity. The allegation of conspiracy makes it possible to impose liability on a person who cannot personally commit the tort in question: for example, a union official who supports employees who threaten to break their contracts of employment.[746] The allegation may also make it easier to obtain exemplary and aggravated damages. What is unclear about this tort is whether it extends beyond combinations to commit a tort.[747] An unresolved issue is whether there can be an actionable conspiracy to break contracts, for example by two or more workers walking off the job.[748] As will be seen below, there is no immunity in respect of such a combination.

C. Inducing a Breach or Interfering with Performance of a Contract

553. If A (say a trade union official) intentionally induces B (say an employee) to breach a contract between B and C (the employer), A may be liable in tort to C.[749] This tort may take place *directly*, for example where A persuades B not to fulfil the contract, or indirectly, as where A persuades B's employees to prevent B from fulfilling the contract.[750] Direct inducement gives rise to liability in tort even if the act of inducement is itself lawful, whereas indirect inducement (or procurement) is tortious only if unlawful means are used. As we have seen, in most cases, employees who take part in industrial action are in breach of contract. Thus the organizers of such action will generally be liable for directly inducing breach of the contract of employment. Moreover, if the employer is thereby disabled from fulfilling commercial contracts, the organizers may be liable for indirectly procuring breach of the commercial contracts, provided unlawful means are used. This last criterion will be

744. *Lonrho Ltd* v. *Shell Petroleum Co. Ltd* [1982] AC 173 (HL), applied in *Metall und Rohstoff* v. *Donaldson* [1989] 3 All ER 14 (CA).
745. *Lonrho plc.* v. *Fayed* [1991] 3 All ER 303, HL.
746. As in *Rookes* v. *Barnard* [1964] AC 1129, HL.
747. In the *Lonrho* case, the House of Lords held that there cannot be liability to commit criminal acts which did not also constitute torts; *see too RCA Corpn.* v. *Pollard* [1983] Ch. 135.
748. A point left open in *Rookes* v. *Barnard.*
749. *Lumley* v. *Gye* [1853] 2 E&B 216; *South Wales Miners' Federation* v. *Glamorgan Coal Company Ltd* [1905] AC 239.
750. *D.C. Thomson* v. *Deakin* [1952] Ch. 646.

fulfilled in most cases, since the means of procuring the breach of commercial contracts will be the unlawful act of inducing breach of the employment contracts of individual workers. Thus, apart from the statutory immunities, the effect of this tort is to undermine the freedom to organize industrial action. This is further compounded by the more recent extension of the tort to include interference with a contract short of breach, for example, preventing performance in cases where a contract contains a *force majeure* clause, exempting a party in breach from liability to pay damages.[751] So it seems that there can be liability for direct or indirect interference even without any actual *breach* of contract.

D. Intimidation

554. This tort was developed by the House of Lords in 1964 to deal with a situation in which two shop stewards and a full-time union official threatened an employer with a strike, so causing the employer lawfully to terminate the contract of employment of a non-unionist who brought an action for damages against them.[752] It had been conceded, unusually, that a 'no-strike' clause in a collective agreement was incorporated as a term in the shop stewards' contracts of employment. It was the threat to break their own contracts which constituted the tort of intimidation. Generalizing, it appears that the tort is committed where A threatens B that he will use means which are unlawful as against B with the intention of causing B to do or refrain from doing something he is at liberty to do, so causing damage either to himself (two-party intimidation) or to C (three-party intimidation). There was some attempt after 1964 to cut down the tort to threats of breach of contract which were not minor ones (e.g. an incorporated no-strike clause),[753] but its potential as a weapon in the hands of employers or third parties against *threats* of strike action, an everyday part of the collective bargaining process, are obvious. In 1982, the House of Lords applied the related doctrine of economic duress to an industrial action situation.

Under this tort, money paid out under an agreement can be recovered on the basis that the agreement was entered into as a result of illegitimate pressure.[754] This is potentially a very wide cause of action, since most industrial action consists of coercive pressure. It enabled the owners of a ship flying a 'flag of convenience' to recover from the International Transport Workers' Federation payments which they had agreed, under threat of blacking, to make of back pay to the crew and a contribution to the ITWF's welfare fund. In deciding whether pressure is legitimate, the courts will be guided by the existing scope of industrial action immunities, even where these are not directly applicable. It is likely that facts which constitute intimidation may also amount to economic duress. Duress may be even wider than

751. *Torquay Hotel Co. Ltd* v. *Cousins* [1969] 2 Ch. 106, CA *per* Lord Denning, approved in *Merkur Island Shipping Co. Ltd* v. *Laughton* [1983] 2 AC 570, HL, which applies this as well to *indirect* interference. *See also Falconer* v. *ASLEF and NUR* [1986] IRLR 331.
752. *Rookes* v. *Barnard* [1964] AC 1127, HL.
753. *Morgan* v. *Fry* [1968] 2 QB 710 *per* Russell LJ.
754. *Universe Tankships Inc. of Monrovia* v. *ITWF* [1983] AC 366; *Dimskal Shipping Co. SA* v. *International Transport Workers Federation* [1992] IRLR 78 (HL).

intimidation covering a threat of coercive lawful action, or an implied threat not to perform a contract.

E. Interference with Trade by Unlawful Means

555. This tort is committed where A intentionally uses unlawful means with the purpose and effect of causing damage to B in his or her trade or business. This category of interference by unlawful means is a 'genus' tort wide enough to cover (iii) indirect interference with contract and (iv) intimidation above, but it is of wider and more uncertain scope. One of the main uncertainties is the meaning given to 'unlawful means' for purposes of this tort. It seems that breach of a criminal statute would be sufficient only if the breach in itself could give rise to liability in tort.[755] For example, breach of local byelaws regarding demonstrations would be insufficient.[756] However, the torts of nuisance (e.g. blocking the entrance to the employer's site) or defamation (e.g. by words on placards) would be unlawful means. A threat to induce employees to breach their contracts of employment by going on strike would be unlawful means.[757] It has also been held argued that a breach of contract of employment *per se* would be sufficient.[758] In such a case, liability would rest on striking employees themselves, even if the organizers of the action were protected by statute.[759] Equally important, particularly for public service workers, is the possibility that inducing breach of or interference with a statutory duty could amount to unlawful means for the purposes of this tort.[760] This may be limited somewhat by the requirement that the statutory duty in question be independently actionable by the plaintiff.[761] Nevertheless, the scope for judicial extension of liability under this 'genus' tort is seemingly endless. The tort has also been significantly widened by the finding that there is no need to show that the defendant's predominant purpose was to injure the plaintiff rather than to pursue his or her own legitimate self-interest.[762]

§4. THE 'TRADE DISPUTES' IMMUNITY

556. Until the beginning of the 1980s, the legislature responded to the judicial extensions of liability in tort for those who act in contemplation or furtherance of a trade dispute. The earliest was the Trade Disputes Act 1906 which gave immunity

755. *Lonrho Ltd* v. *Shell Petroleum Co. Ltd* [1982] AC 173, HL.
756. Cf. *Camellia Tanker Ltd* v. *ITF* [1976] ICR 274.
757. *Hadmor Productions Ltd* v. *Hamilton* [1983] 1 AC 191.
758. *Barratts & Baird* v. *IPCS* [1987] IRLR 3.
759. No injunction could, however, be granted, since this would amount to specific performance of a contract of employment.
760. *Meade* v. *Haringey London Borough Council* [1979] ICR 494; *Barratts & Baird* v. *IPCS* (above), *Associated British Ports* v. *TGWU* [1989] IRLR 305, 399.
761. *Lonrho* v. *Shell* (above); but this view was denied by the majority of the Court of Appeal in *Associated British Ports* (above).
762. *Lonhro plc* v. *Fayed* [1989] 2 All ER 65. Cf. *Barratts and Baird* v. *IPCS* (above).

from action for civil conspiracy to injure and inducing breach of the contract of employment. This was supplemented in 1965, in the wake of the decision in *Rookes* v. *Barnard*[763] establishing the tort of intimidation. The immunities were repealed during the currency of the 1971 Industrial Relations Act, and then reinstated and strengthened in the Trade Union and Labour Relations Act 1974 as amended in 1976. Since 1980, successive enactments have severely limited the applicability of the immunities.

557. The immunities are now contained in TULRCA 1992, s. 219 (formerly TULRA, 1974, s. 13) which reads:

1. An act done by a person in contemplation or furtherance of a trade dispute shall not be actionable in tort on the ground only (a) that it induces another person to break a contract or interferes or induces any other person to interfere with its performance or (b) that it consists in his threatening that a contract (whether one to which he is a party or not) will be broken or its performance interfered with, or that he will induce another person to break a contract or interfere with its performance.
2. An agreement by two or more persons to do or procure the doing of any act in contemplation or furtherance of a trade dispute shall not be actionable in tort if the act is one to which, if done without such agreement or combination, would not be actionable in tort.

It will be noted that the immunity does not extend to torts such as defamation or nuisance or breach of statutory duty.[764] Even more important is the fact that there is no immunity for the expanding tort of interference with business by unlawful means. This has allowed ingenious employers to begin proceedings for interlocutory injunctions on the basis of a wide variety of novel torts.[765] The scope of the tort is limited, however, by the principle that an act which is immune by virtue of Section 219 may not constitute 'unlawful means' for the tort of interference with business by unlawful means.[766]

558. he scope of the freedom to organize industrial action is thus delimited by what Wedderburn aptly labelled the 'golden formula'.[767] 'Trade dispute' is defined by TULRCA, 1992, Section 244. It is defined by reference to (i) the parties; (ii) the subject matter. In addition, Section 219 of the 1992 Act requires that the action be in 'contemplation or furtherance' of the trade dispute. The elements of this formula are examined below.

(1) The parties: the 'golden formula' only includes disputes 'between workers and their employer'. It thus excludes industrial action in protest against government

763. [1964] AC 1129, HL.
764. *Mersey Dock and Harbour Co.* v. *Verrinder* [1982] IRLR 152.
765. See for example *Falconer* v. *NUR and ASLEF*, *Baratts & Baird* v. *IPCS*, *Associated British Ports* v. *TGWU* [1989] IRLR 305 (CA), [1989] IRLR 399 (HL).
766. *Hadmor Productions Ltd* v. *Hamilton* [1982] ICR 114 (HL).
767. K.W. Wedderburn, *The Worker and the Law* (Harmondsworth, 1965), p. 222.

action, except where the government is the employer, or has a statutory power to control the settlement of the matters at issue, or is represented on the bargaining committee which is considering the issues.[768] However, in modern industrial society, governments are so closely involved in the economy that the line is often difficult to draw. As Kahn-Freund put it in 1954:

The level of wages depends today only partly and perhaps only to a minor extent on decisions of private employers. In all sorts of ways it depends on governmental policies ... How then can anyone ... determine how far any strike is intended primarily to induce the employers to pay wages of a certain amount or the government to change its policy?[769]

Since 1982 the formula has excluded disputes between workers and other workers, such as demarcation or inter-union disputes. Also excluded are cases where the employer's own workers are not in dispute, for example, where an employer is picketed or blacked for employing non-union labour or low-paid foreign workers, where the latter themselves are not parties to the dispute.[770] It should be noted that this does not exclude all action taken by one group of workers in support of another group ('secondary' action). Whether or not secondary action is lawful depends on separate provisions.

559. (2) The subject matter: Section 244(1) of TULRCA 1992 provides that the dispute should relate wholly or mainly to one of the subjects listed in that section. The phrase 'wholly or mainly' was inserted by the Employment Act 1982 in substitution for the phrase 'connected with'. The new phrase has been interpreted to mean 'predominantly about'[771] and will exclude disputes which, although connected with workers' fears for their jobs or their terms and conditions, are 'predominantly about' a subject not listed in Section 244(1).

560. Disputes which relate wholly or mainly to political or non-industrial subject-matter are thus excluded. For example, industrial action taken by a trade union in protest against apartheid in South Africa was held to be excluded from the definition.[772] Again, the line between a dispute about workers' terms and conditions and a political dispute is not always easy to draw. Thus a day of action taken by a trade union in protest against government economic policies[773] or industrial action taken by a trade union opposed to the government's plans to privatize their employer[774] have been held to fall outside the definition of a trade dispute. Since 1982, disputes concerning matters occurring outside the United Kingdom are only protected if the workers taking industrial action are likely to be affected in respect

768. TULRCA, 1992, s. 244(2).
769. O. Kahn-Freund, 'Legal Framework', in A. Flanders, and H.A. Clegg, (eds.), *The System of Industrial Relations in Great Britain* (Oxford, 1954), p. 127.
770. *Midland Cold Storage* v. *Turner* [1972] ICR 230; *Star Sea Transport Corporation of Monrovia* v. *Slater* [1978] IRLR 507; *NWL* v. *Woods* [1979] 1 WLR 1294, HL.
771. *Mercury Communications Ltd* v. *Scott Garner* (1984) ICR 74, CA.
772. *BBC* v. *Hearn* [1977] ICR 685, AC.
773. *Express Newspapers Ltd* v. *McShane* [1980] IRLR 247.
774. *Mercury Communications Ltd* v. *Scott-Garner* [1984] ICR 74, CA.

of one or more of the matters specified in Section 244(1) of the TULRCA, 1992 by the outcome of that dispute.[775]

561. (3) 'Contemplation or furtherance': since 1906, the test of whether an act was done 'in contemplation or furtherance' of a trade dispute has generally been regarded as a subjective one turning upon the *bona fide* purpose of the person doing the act. However, dislike of the consequences of the widening of the statutory immunities by the Trade Union and Labour Relations Acts 1974–6 led the Court of Appeal, between 1977 and 1979, to seek to add an objective element to this test in a variety of forms such as whether the act was too remote from the dispute to be protected, whether the act would help one side or another in a 'practical' way and whether the act was reasonably capable or had a reasonable prospect of achieving the honestly held objective of the person acting. These limitations were overruled by the House of Lords in a trilogy of cases[776] and the traditional subjective test was reasserted. Although the 'trade dispute' itself must exist or be imminent as an objective fact, 'contemplation' and 'furtherance' refer to states of mind and so long as the person acting honestly thought at the time that he or she might help one of the parties to a trade dispute to achieve their objectives and did it for that reason, he or she is protected. This subjective test was not altered by the Employment Acts of 1980 and 1982. Instead, its wider implications for the lawfulness of 'secondary' or 'tertiary' picketing or boycotts were limited by specific restrictions on such action.

§5. Restrictions on the Trade Disputes Immunity

I. Secondary Action

562. A central policy of the legislation since 1980 has been to restrict the extent to which industrial action is permitted to expand beyond the establishment concerned.[777] There is a long tradition in Britain of 'secondary action', or action taken by workers not employed by the employer in dispute (the 'primary' employer) in support of those who are directly affected. For example, workers not employed by the primary employer may refuse to deliver raw materials to or to handle goods produced by that employer. The aim of such action is to increase the pressure on the primary employer or, where that employer is being supported by the government, to disrupt economic life more generally in order to force government concessions.

The Conservative government was always hostile to secondary action, but in line with its step by step approach to restrictive labour legislation, it did not initially remove all protection from such action. Instead, secondary action was subject to a complex set of restrictions, leaving wide loopholes, which were exploited by employers. In 1990, the government legislated to remove even the limited remaining area of lawful secondary action, with a narrow exception for picketing. These

775. TULRCA, 1992, s. 244(3).
776. *NWL* v. *Woods* [1979] ICR 897; *Express Newspapers Ltd* v. *McShane* [1980] ICR 42; *Duport Steels Ltd* v. *Sirs* [1980] ICR 161.
777. Employment Act 1980, s. 17.

provisions, now found in TULRCA, 1992, remove immunity from liability in respect of some torts (inducing breach of contract and intimidation) whenever there has been unlawful secondary action.[778] Secondary action occurs where the employer party to the relevant contract of employment is not party to the dispute. For example, if employees of company A are in dispute with A, and their union induces employees of company B to break their contracts of employment with B, then unlawful secondary action has occurred and the union will lose its immunity from action in tort. There are three particularly restrictive aspects to these provisions. First, secondary action occurs even if the action by B's workers does not lead to a breach of or interference with a commercial contract to which B is party. This means that simple demonstrations of support, such as extended lunch hour meetings, are caught by the definition. Secondly, an employer may not be treated as party to a dispute between another employer and its workers; and where more than one employer is in dispute, the dispute between each employer and its workers is treated as a separate dispute. The effect of this is to make national industrial action impossible unless a dispute with each individual employer can be shown. It is no longer possible to take action against an employer who belongs to an employers' association merely because the association is in dispute with a union or confederation of unions.

However, if employees of B are genuinely in dispute with B, then the mere fact that the action assists those in dispute with A does not turn the action against B into unlawful secondary action. Thirdly, immunity is not only removed in respect of inducing breach of contracts of employment, but also from contracts personally to do work or perform services. This means that self-employed workers such as construction workers fall within the definition.

563. The above provisions mean that in effect almost no secondary action is protected. This is true even if A and B have identical shareholders and directors: in an earlier case, the court refused to lift the corporate veil to take into account real ownership and control.[779] Thus if A and B are two companies in a corporate group, workers employed by B cannot take action in support of workers in dispute with A even if they are indirectly affected, unless they can claim their own primary dispute with B. The union cannot call on B's workers even if A has diverted strike-bound work to B. Even more seriously, if A is a subsidiary company of B, and decisions on key industrial relations questions are in reality taken by directors of B rather than A, employees of A are restricted to ineffective industrial action against A. These provisions have particularly serious implications for the public sector, where Government policy has been to decentralize authority down to small units. For example, in education, teachers are now employed by the governors of individual schools rather than by the local education authority, and in the National Health Service, many hospitals are becoming autonomous employers. Employees in one school or hospital will not be able to call on colleagues at another school or hospital to support them in dispute unless the latter have their own primary dispute. In the private

778. TULRCA, 1992, s. 224. For commentary, see G.S. Morris, 'The Employment Act 1990', *Journal of Business Law* 46 (1991); B. Simpson, 'The Employment Act 1990 in context' [1991] 54 MLR 418.

779. *Dimbleby* v. *National Union of Journalists* [1984] 1 All ER 751.

sector, the new provisions give employers an incentive to restructure their employment units in such a way as to minimise the spread of industrial action. The extent of these restrictions on the right to strike means that Britain is now out of line with other Western European countries and is almost definitely in breach of its international obligations.[780] There is only one limited exception to the above provisions, occurring in the context of picketing. Immunity from liability in tort is retained if, in the course of picketing which is lawful under Section 220 of TULRCA, 1992, a picket or union official induces an employee of an employer not party to the dispute to breach a contract of employment.[781] For example, if a lawful picket peacefully persuades a truck driver employed by a supplier of the primary employer to refuse to cross the picket line and thereby induces him or her to breach a contract of employment, the picket will not lose whatever immunity he or she would otherwise have.

II. Union-only Practices

564. A second element of the restrictive strategy of the then Conservative government was to discourage 'union-only' or 'recognition-only' practices, whereby union members attempt to spread unionism by insisting that their employers require suppliers to employ union labour, or to recognize, negotiate with or consult union officials. By Section 222(3) of TULRCA, 1992, no statutory immunities are available to a person who induces or attempts to induce another to incorporate into a contract a term requiring work to be done by union or non-union members only, or requiring a party to recognize one or more trade unions, or to negotiate or consult with any trade union official. Nor is protection available to employees of one employer, A, who breach or threaten to breach or interfere with their contracts of employment, resulting in tortious interference with the supply of goods or services to B, because B uses or is likely to use union or non-union labour or refuses to recognize one or more trade unions, or to negotiate or consult with any trade union official. Protection is similarly withdrawn from the organizers of such action. It does, however, remain open to employees to put pressure on their own employer to achieve these ends.

III. Action Taken Because of Dismissal for Taking Unofficial Action

565. A third way in which action which is in contemplation and furtherance of a trade dispute may nevertheless lose its immunity arises in the cases in which a union or individual has taken industrial action, or threatened to do so, in support of employees dismissed in connection with unofficial industrial action. As will be recalled, employees dismissed in these circumstances have no right to complain of unfair dismissal; the current restrictions mean that they cannot be protected by

780. See Lord Wedderburn HL Deb Vol. 521, col. 172, 10 July 1990.
781. TULRCA, 1992, s. 224(3).

industrial action taken on their behalf by their fellow employees without being liable in tort.[782]

IV. Ballots Before Industrial Action

566. Even if a trade union has satisfied both Section 219 of TULRCA, 1992 and not lost the immunity by virtue of Section 224 of the 1992 Act the union and any individuals involved will lose their immunity from civil action in respect of certain torts if the balloting provisions in TULRCA, 1992 Sections 226–235, are not fulfilled. Notably, the remedy for breach of the provisions does not lie solely with members of the union, but with any person who suffered harm or threatened harm as a result of acts which constituted the relevant common law torts. This means that the balloting provisions place a significant tactical weapon in the hands of employers, suppliers or customers who are affected by the industrial action, belying the notion that their primary aim is to increase internal trade union democracy by increasing membership participation. Balloting has now become a routine part of the collective bargaining process; indeed, both ballots and the threat of legal action have been used as tactical weapons. Where, as is often the case, the ballot results in majority support for industrial action, the union is clearly in a stronger position.

However, as will be seen below, the statutory balloting provisions are so complex and technical that a positive result in a ballot by no means guarantees that industrial action will be lawful. This has per-mitted employers to resort to the court for interlocutory injunctions to prevent or delay action which has in fact been supported by a majority of those voting in a procedure that would pass as democratic by any measure. For example, an injunction has been issued to prevent a strike on which received majority support in a ballot because the pre-ballot strike notice did not give the names of all employees who were being balloted or who might be called upon to take strike action.[783] An injunction was granted when a union commenced the industrial action one day too late; and an injunction was granted when the employer showed that the union had inadvertently sent out ballot papers to 20 individuals who were no longer working for the company. This was despite the fact that there was no evidence that any of the 20 individuals had actually voted in the ballot, or had any impact on the result.[784]

Overall it seems clear that, far from facilitating real democracy, the government has made the requirements for balloting before industrial action so complex and technical as to minimize the extent to which unions can use the ballot to strengthen their position.[785]

567. Whenever a union is legally liable for organizing industrial action, a pre-strike ballot must be held. As was seen above, trade unions are liable for a wide

782. TULRCA, 1992, s. 223.

783. *Blackpool and the Fylde College* v. *NATFHE* [1994] IRLR 227, CA; *National Union of Rail, Maritime and Transport Workers* v. *London Underground* [2001] IRLR 229, CA.

784. *Labour Research*, October 1998, p. 15.

785. B. Simpson, 'Code of Practice on Industrial Action Ballots', *Industrial Law Journal*, 30 (2001), 194–198.

range of persons. The 1992 Act requires the union to specify in the ballot paper the person or description of persons who are authorized to call for industrial action if the ballot yields a majority in favour.[786] The Act also extends the ballot obligation to industrial action involving self-employed workers who personally do work or perform services.[787] A ballot is required even if the industrial action does not amount to a breach of contract. Although this will have little effect when an employer brings an action for inducing breach of contract, it may be significant if a union member complains that the ballot is unlawful. There must be no call by the union for participation in industrial action before the date of the ballot;[788] and the action must take place within four weeks of the date when the ballot is held. The rigidity of this requirement prompted the Labour government to introduce an amendment permitting the period to be extended to a total of eight weeks if this is the result of an agreement between the union and the members' employer.[789] This means that a union is not under pressure to commence industrial action within the four-week period rather than reach a settlement by further negotiation. If legal action by employers delays the commencement of industrial action, in that delay in authorization is due to a court order against the union which has subsequently been discharged, the union may apply to the court to extend the four week period to a maximum of 12 weeks.[790]

However, the court cannot make such an order if it considers that the result of the ballot no longer represents the views of those who voted, or if an event is likely to occur as a result of which those members would vote against industrial action if another ballot were to be held. This presumably refers to an offer of settlement by the employer; but the degree to which judicial speculation is required to predict voters' preferences makes this a highly uncertain provision.

568. The ballot has to be secret and postal. Entitlement to vote must be accorded equally to all members whom it is reasonable to believe at the time of the ballot will be called on to break or interfere with their contracts of employment, and to no others.[791] This has caused severe difficulties for unions: it needs only *one* relevant member to have been denied a vote or one irrelevant member to have been given one to invalidate the ballot as a whole. For unions whose members change employers frequently, for example lecturers on short-term contracts, this could make lawful industrial action impossible. This prompted a 1999 amendment which stated that if there is an accidental failure to comply with this requirement which is on a scale which is unlikely to affect the result of the ballot, that failure can be disregarded.[792] However, the ballot is invalidated if any union member whom it was reasonable for the union to believe would take part in the action was not accorded the right to vote

786. TULRCA 1992, s 229(3).
787. TULRCA 1992, s. 235.
788. TULRCA 1992, s. 233(3)(a).
789. TULRCA 1992, s. 234(1) as amended by ERA 1999.
790. TULRCA 1992, s. 234(2).
791. TULRCA 1992, s. 227.
792. TULRCA 1992, s. 232B. But see: *British Railways Board* v. *NUR* [1989] IRLR 348: An accidental failure to afford an opportunity to vote will not invalidate the ballot; but intentional failures will do so, even if the result would have been the same had the statute been fully complied.

in the ballot and was then induced to participate. This is the case even if the failure was accidental; but if individuals who take up employment or join the union after the ballot participate, the ballot remains valid.[793] This situation is made even more complex by the requirement that separate ballots be held at individual workplaces. Only in those workplaces at which a majority of workers has voted in favour of industrial action may a union call for action. This was justified by Conservative government's assertion that a union would draw its constituency boundaries in such a way that a more militant workplace could swamp a less militant one. However, no evidence was produced to support this assertion, leading the Labour government in 1999 to introduce exceptions to the workplace rule. It is now permissible to aggregate ballots across different workplaces, if those participating have a 'common interest' in the subject-matter of the dispute, if they share a common occupation, or where entitlement to vote is accorded all the members of the union employed by a particular employer, or set of employers with whom the union is in dispute. For common occupation or common employers, the union is not entitled to be selective but must ballot all relevant employees: meaning that the union must intend to call out all of them. Only under the common interest test, can a union wishing to aggregate workplace ballots be selective.[794] Every voter must be allowed to vote without 'interference' or 'constraint' from the union and any of its members, officials or employees. Employer interference and interference by another union than that conducting the ballot does not invalidate the ballot. An independent scrutineer must be appointed. She or he must be required to make a report within four weeks of the ballot stating whether he or she is satisfied of the compliance of the ballot with the statutory provisions and whether satisfactory security arrangements have been put in place to minimise unfairness or malpractice.[795]

569. The content of the ballot paper is subject to detailed statutory regulation. First, the ballot paper must pose at least one of two separate questions, asking whether the person is prepared to take part or continue to take part in a strike or asking the same question in relation to action short of a strike. The courts have taken a particularly stringent view of this requirement. A union cannot assume that approval of a strike is also approval of action short of an all-out strike: it is thus crucial to decide on which side of the dividing line an action falls. Thus in response to a Court of Appeal decision that an overtime ban was a 'strike' and therefore had not been mandated by the ballot, legislation now specifies that for the purposes of this provision, an overtime ban constitutes industrial action short of a strike.[796] A 'rolled up' question posing both issues in the same question has been held to be invalid.[797] The High Court has made this provision even more stringent, by linking the content of the ballot-paper to the legal definition of 'trade dispute'. On this view, it is not permissible to ask members to vote on an issue which is not in law a trade dispute, nor to roll up some trade dispute questions with others in the same

793. TULRCA 1992, s. 232A
794. TULRCA 1992, s. 228A.
795. TULRCA 1992, ss. 226A and 226B.
796. TULRCA 1992, s. 229(2A), responding to *Connex* v. *South Eastern* v. *RMT* [1999] IRLR 249, CA.
797. *Post Office* v. *UPW* [1990] IRLR 143, CA.

paper.[798] Even a minor and innocent transgression of these principles will lead to loss of immunity.[799] As well as these two questions, the ballot paper must contain the the words: 'If you take part in a strike or other industrial action you may be in breach of your contract of employment.' This statement cannot be qualified or commented on by anything else on the voting paper and is required even if the industrial action will involve no breach of contract. This requirement, introduced by the Conservatives in a clear attempt to deter would-be yes voters, has now been softened somewhat to reflect the recent introduction of protection for strikers against dismissal. Thus in addition to the above statement, the ballot paper must also include the following words: 'However, if you are dismissed for taking part in strike or other industrial action which is called officially and is otherwise lawful, the dismissal will be unfair if it takes place fewer than eight weeks after you started taking part in the action, and depending on the circumstances may be unfair if it takes place later.' A union may not include other material such as a statement of the merits of the action.

570. As well as the detailed requirements above, successive statutes have introduced increasingly onerous requirements of information and notice which the union is required to give to the employers. There are three notices which must be given. First, notice of the ballot and a sample voting paper must be given to all employers of persons entitled to vote in the ballot. This notice must be received at least seven days before the opening day of the ballot[800] and should specify both the intended date of the ballot and such information which would help the employer make plans and bring information to those of his employees whom the union to ballot. The sample voting paper must be received by no later than the third day before the opening day of the ballot. Secondly, as soon as is reasonably practicable after the holding of the ballot, the union must ensure that the results are communicated to these employers. This information must include the number of votes cast in the ballot, the number voting yes to each question; the number voting no and the number of spoiled votes.[801] Thirdly, due notice must be given to employers that industrial action will commence.

This notice must include information which helps the employer make plans and bring information to those of his employees whom the union intends to call out on strike (the 'affected employees'). The notice must also state whether industrial action is intended to be continuous or discontinuous and in each case specify when any of the affected employees will take part.[802] It is the extent to which the pre-ballot and pre-strike notices are required to name individual employees that has proved most controversial about these provisions. Prior to the Employment Relations Act 1999, the union was required to describe those employees who it was reasonable to believe would be entitled to vote in the ballot so that the employer could 'readily ascertain them'. This was held by the Court of Appeal to constitute a

798. TULRCA 1992, s. 229(2); *London Underground* v. *NUR* [1989] IRLR 341, 343.
799. *Post Office* v. *Union of Communication Workers* [1990] IRLR 143 (CA); contrast *British Railways Board* v. *NUR above*.
800. TULRCA 1992, s. 226A.
801. TULRCA 1992, s. 231A.
802. TULRCA 1992, s. 234A.

requirement that the union provided the employer with names of individual members.[803] Unsurprisingly, this was perceived as so great a breach of the relationship of trust between the union and its members as to make lawful industrial action almost impossible. It might also in some cases simply be impossible to provide such a list, if the union could not be sure that the information in its current possession was still accurate. This requirement was amended in 1999 so that the union is required to give 'such information as in the union's possession as would help the employer to make plans'. It was certainly the intention of the legislators that this would be a less onerous provision.

However, the Court of Appeal ruled in 2001 that although the union was no longer required to provide a list of names of members affected, the underlying legislative purpose had not changed. This meant that the union had to give the employer any information in its possession which would enable an employer to know which parts of its workforce were to be called out, so that the employer could try to dissuade them, and if unsuccessful, make plans to avoid or minimize disruption. It was therefore held that a union which stated in its notice that the industrial action would be of all members employed in all categories at all workplaces failed to comply with the amended requirements because the notice did not provide any details of the separate categories or workplaces of the members involved. This meant that although a majority of the union had voted in favour of the action, an injunction was granted preventing the strike.[804]

The current Conservative Government has introduced changes to the balloting system through the Trade Union Act 2016. It introduces a need for at least 50 per cent of those entitled to vote in the ballot to do so,[805] alongside the need for a majority of those that did vote in the ballot answered in support of the industrial action proposed.[806] This is further increased to a need for at least 40 per cent of all eligible voters to answer in the affirmative (irrespective of the proportion that did actually vote) where industrial action involves important public services, such as health and education. This makes it much more difficult for a lawful strike to take place, and thus makes it more difficult for industrial action to attract the necessary immunities.

571. A trade union which fails to comply with the balloting requirements loses its immunity under Section 219 of TULRCA. This means that the employer or other affected party may bring an action in tort. Union members have also given the right by Section 62 of TULRCA, 1992 to complain to the court about breach of the balloting provisions. This is available to any member who was induced or was likely to be induced to take part in industrial action, even if he or she refused to comply. Application lies to the High Court, which has wide powers to make such orders as it considers appropriate to require the union to ensure that there is no further inducement of members to take part in action which was not authorized by a ballot. The

803. *Blackpool and Fylde College* v. *NAFTHE* [1994] IRLR 227 CA.
804. *National Union of Rail, Maritime, and Transport Workers* v. *London Underground* [2001] IRLR 228, CA.
805. This was introduced by s.2(1) of the Trade Union Act 2016, which inserted a new s.226(2)(a)(iia) into the TULRCA 1992.
806. TULRCA 1992, s. 236(2)(a)(iii)

Court cannot, however, directly order the union to hold a ballot, nor require that those taking industrial action return to work.

§6. PICKETING

572. Picketing has been a traditional feature of industrial action in Britain. Striking workers gather at the gates of the workplace in order to persuade non-strikers or substitute workers not to undermine the strike by continuing to work. Picketing may also take the form of secondary action, with employees in the primary dispute picketing other places of work in an attempt to gain support from other workers, or other workers picketing their own places of work in support of the primary strikers. Large scale picketing was a favoured tactic of the National Union of Mineworkers (NUM) and was widely used in the protracted miners' strike of 1984–5. Picketing is one area of industrial conflict in which the criminal law plays a central role. Indeed, in the 1984–5 miners' strike, the criminal law was far more extensively used than the civil law regulating industrial action. A range of criminal laws are applicable to picketing, especially where violence takes place or is apprehended. These include: (a) conduct likely or intended to cause a breach of the peace; (b) obstructing the police; (c) criminal damage; (d) obstructing the highway.

One criminal offence which relates specifically to picketing is contained in Section 241 of the TULRCA 1992, which outlaws actions such as 'watching or besetting' a person's house or place of business, with a view to compelling that person to do or abstain from doing any 'act which such other person has a legal right to do or abstain from doing'. Despite its anachronistic flavour, this offence was brought back into use during the miners' strike when almost 650 such charges were laid, particularly in cases of picketing of working miners' homes.[807] During the same strike, the police made use of traffic control powers and general preventative powers to stop pickets massing at working pits, often by turning back pickets hundreds of miles from their intended destinations.[808] Subsequent legislation has given the police even more extensive powers to control public assemblies and processions. Under the Public Order Act 1986, police have wide powers to impose conditions on public assemblies and public processions, breach of which constitute criminal offence. Thus a senior police officer may impose conditions in advance or on the spot, if he or she reasonably believes that the gathering may result in serious public disorder, serious damage to property, or serious disruption to the life of the community. Similarly, conditions may be imposed if the police officer considers that the purpose of the organizers is to intimidate others with a view to compelling them to do an act which they have a right not to do, or vice versa.[809] This last provision could be used in cases where pickets are attempting to prevent workers from going to work. In such circumstances, the police officer may place such conditions on the place, size and maximum duration of the assembly or procession as he or she considers necessary.

807. (1985) 14 *Industrial Law Journal* 145 at 151.
808. *Moss* v. *McLachlan* [1985] IRLR 76.
809. Public Order Act 1986, ss. 11–16.

The attitude of police to pickets has been significantly influenced by the Code of Practice on Picketing, issued by the Secretary of State in 1980 and revised in 1992. Although the Code is no more than a guide, its suggestion that the number of pickets be limited to six has frequently been used as a working rule for controlling pickets. However, the Human Rights Act 1998, guaranteeing the rights to freedom of expression and of peaceful assembly, may require this approach to be revised. In addition, the Act introduced five new statutory offences which may be relevant to the conduct of picketing. These are: riot, violent disorder, affray, causing fear of violence or provoking it, and (particularly relevant in the context of picketing) causing harassment, alarm or distress.[810] All may be committed in a public or private place, and all, apart from the last, carry a power of arrest. Finally, the Protection from Harassment Act 1997 provides for a new offence where a course of conduct amounts to harassment or where a reasonable person would think such course of conduct would cause another to fear violence.[811]

573. Picketing may also lead to civil liability. Thus the 'economic torts' described above may be applicable. For example, pickets who dissuade a fellow worker from continuing to work may well commit the tort of inducing breach of contract of employment.[812] Other relevant torts include public[813] and private nuisance. In addition, it has been held in one case that it is a tort unreasonably to harass others in the exercise of their right to use the highway for the purposes of going to work.[814] Finally, there may be liability for a course of conduct amounting to harassment of another under the Protection from Harassment Act 1997.[815]

574. The freedom to picket peacefully is delimited by Section 220 of TULRCA, 1992. Section 220 states that 'it shall be lawful for a person in contemplation or furtherance of a trade dispute to attend (a) at or near his own place of work or (b) if he is an official of a trade union, at or near the place of work of the member of the union whom he is accompanying and whom he represents for the purpose only of peacefully obtaining information or persuading any person to work or to abstain from work'. This section differs from section 219 of the 1992 Act in that it is not limited to specific torts, but applies to all criminal and civil liability, provided the statutory conditions are observed. However, the extent of the immunity afforded for criminal liability has been limited by highly restrictive judicial interpretation, which held that the section protects only the 'attendance' at or near the workplace, and not the detention of persons or invitations to them to stop and listen to the pickets' arguments.[816] Above all, pickets generally have to follow police instructions.

---

810. Public Order Act 1986, ss. 1–5.
811. Protection from Harassment Act 1997, ss. 1, 4.
812. *Union Traffic Ltd* v. *TGWU* [1989] IRLR 127.
813. *News Group Newspapers* v. *SOGAT 82* [1986] IRLR 337.
814. *Thomas* v. *NUM* [1985] 2 All ER 1, Ch. D.; but *see Hunter* v. *Canary Wharf Ltd* [1997] 2 All ER 426, HL, restricting private nuisance, used in *Thomas*, to cases where the claimant has an interest in the land affected.
815. Protection from Harassment Act 1997, s. 3.
816. *Broome* v. *DPP* [1974] ICR 84, HL.

575. The scope of the immunity afforded by Section 220 was substantially narrowed by the requirement introduced by the Employment Act 1980 that picketing should take place at or near the person's own place of work. Where Section 220 does not apply, neither does the usual immunity afforded by Section 219 of the TULRCA, 1992.[817] Immunity is thus withdrawn not only from employees who picket premises of other employers but also from those who picket other premises of their own employer in a multi-plant group. There are only three exceptions: (i) a trade union official may accompany a member to the latter's place of work; (ii) an employee who has been dismissed in connection with the industrial action may attend at his or her former place of work; (iii) where a person does not normally work at any one place or the location of the place (e.g. an oil rig) makes it impracticable to picket that place, he or she may picket any premises from which he or she works or from which his or her work is administered. Picketing may be conducted 'near' the workers' place of work, even if this is a short distance away.[818] But the statute makes no provision for workers whose former place of work has been closed down, and who therefore wish to picket another establishment of their employer.[819]

576. Employees picketing their own workplace may well find that they have committed secondary action. For example, if pickets induce a truck driver to breach his or her contract of employment by refusing to cross a picket line to deliver supplies to the employer in dispute, they would fall within the definition of secondary action. However, this is the only situation in which immunity from tort is specifically retained. If this were not the case, the right to picket granted by section 220 of the 1992 Act would be rendered nugatory.[820]

§7. LABOUR (INDUSTRIAL) INJUNCTIONS

577. The most important intervention of the law in collective labour disputes is through the power of the High Court to issue injunctions before, during or after the trial of an action. The most common form of injunction in such disputes is interlocutory, that is pending trial of the action. This may be negative, for example restraining the union and organizers from acts of interference with trade by unlawful means, or mandatory, requiring the union executive to withdraw instructions which are alleged to constitute some tort. The interlocutory injunction is a particularly powerful tactical weapon in the hands of the employer or third party. Frequently the action is started for the sole purpose of restraining a strike or boycott, and the employer or third party has no intention of proceeding to a full trial. As a result, the substantive issues, whether torts were in fact committed, are never decided. At the interlocutory stage, the court cannot assess the evidence fully. Thus a two-stage test has been evolved to assist in deciding whether or not an injunction

817. TULRCA 1992, s. 219(3).
818. *Rayware Ltd* v. *TGWU* [1989] IRLR 134.
819. *Union Traffic Ltd* v. *TGWU* [1989] IRLR 127.
820. TULRCA 1992, ss. 224(1) and (3).

should be granted pending the full trial of the issue.[821] First, the applicant must show that there is a serious issue to be tried. This has proved to be a relatively easy hurdle for employers to surmount: the courts have tended to accept an 'arguable case' as sufficient, and in the fluid area of economic torts, this is not difficult to show. Secondly, the courts will determine where the 'balance of convenience' lies. This again almost always favours the employer or third party, whose tangible business interests are being threatened, in contrast to the union and its officials, who can merely point to intangible industrial objectives.

An attempt is made to mitigate this in cases concerning industrial disputes by Section 221 of TULRCA 1992. Section 221(1) requires reasonable steps to be taken to give notice of the application and an opportunity to be heard to a party likely to claim a 'trade dispute' offence, but this has not allayed trade union criticisms that excessive speed is usual in granting such injunctions, giving the union defendants little time to prepare their evidence and denying them the opportunity to cross-examine those on whose allegations the application is based. Section 221(2) requires the court to have regard to the likelihood of the defendant establishing the 'trade dispute' defence, but despite this the courts have insisted on retaining their residual discretion to grant the injunctions where this factor is outweighed by the 'disastrous' consequences of the industrial action to the employer or the public.[822] Recent years have seen an increased willingness on the part of the courts to develop and adapt procedures which facilitate the granting of injunctions. For example, in the seafarers dispute of 1988, an injunction was granted restraining the National Union of Seamen from conducting a ballot on industrial action, even though there was nothing unlawful about conducting a ballot.[823] In addition, the court was willing to 'transfer' a sequestration order issued in contempt proceedings initiated by one company, to a different company, P&O.[824]

578. Traditionally, many British employers were reluctant to use judicial remedies, preferring to resolve matters through the bargaining process. However, during the 1980s, this attitude changed and injunctions were sought in an increasing number of cases. This change was particularly marked since 1982, when unions were first liable as defendants. A survey by *Labour Research* shows that between 1983 and 1990, a total of 117 injunctions were sought.[825] The vast majority of such injunctions were granted: in the two year period 1989–91, 18 out of 24 injunctions sought were granted unconditionally, and several others were initially granted and later withdrawn.

During the 1990s, however, the number of employers seeking injunctions has declined, so that only 9 injunctions were served on unions in 1997– 8, compared to about 20 per year in the mid-1980s. But it is still highly likely that an injunction

821. *American Cyanamid Co.* v. *Ethicon Ltd* [1975] AC 396.
822. *NWL Ltd* v. *Woods* [1979] 3 All ER 614; *Express Newspapers Ltd* v. *McShane* [1980] 1 All ER 65; *Duport Steels Ltd* v. *Sirs* [1980] 1 All ER, 529, HL.
823. *P & O European Ferries* v. *NUS*, *The Independent*, 28 March 1988.
824. See S. Auerbach 'Injunction Procedure in the Seafarers' Dispute' (1988) ILJ 227.
825. The figures in this section are taken from *Labour Research*, October 1991, pp. 19–21; and *Labour Research*, October 1998, p. 15.

sought will be granted: 8 out of 9 injunctions sought in 1997–8 were granted. A total of 218 injunctions were granted between 1983 and 1998.

579. Technical breaches of the complex statutory balloting provisions remain by far the most common reason for an injunction. In the early years, several injunctions were ignored by Defendant unions, but successful contempt of court proceedings followed by sequestration of assets in some highly publicized cases led to a greater degree of compliance with injunctions. At the same time, it is clear that the threat of legal action is a significant deterrent to unions contemplating industrial action. Even if the injunction is refused, legal proceedings are costly to trade unions.

Selected Bibliography

Employment Court Practice 2008, Sweet & Maxwell, Editors – Chapman, C.; and Swift, J. QC

Harvey's *Industrial Relations and Employment Law*, London, 1971 with supplements (5 vols.) (texts of selected legislation and commentary), General Editor – Smith, I.

Sweet and Maxwell's Encyclopedia of Employment Law, London, 1972, with supplements (4 vols.) (comprehensive texts and digests of all relevant case law, legislation, rules and orders, awards, reports and inquiries, precedents and EC and international law with commentaries), General Editor - Hardy, S.

Specialist Law Reports

Industrial Cases Reports, London, 1975–

Industrial Court Reports, London, 1972–1974

Industrial Relations Law Reports, London, 1972–Periodicals

British Journal of Industrial Relations, London, 1963–

Equal Opportunities Review, London, 1985–

Equality Law Reports, 2009-

European Industrial Relations Review, London, 1974–

Incomes Data Service Ltd, *Incomes Data Reports, Incomes Data Brief* and *Incomes Data Studies*, and *International Report*, London, 1971–

Industrial Law Journal, London, 1972–

Industrial Relations Journal, London, 1972–

Industrial Relations Review and Report, London, 1972– (including *Industrial Relations Legal Information Bulletin*)

Official Reports etc. Published by Her Majesty's Stationery Office (HMSO)

Advisory, Conciliation and Arbitration Service, Annual Reports (1975–)

Central Arbitration Committee, Annual Reports (1975–)

Certification Officer, Annual Reports (1976–)

Commission for Racial Equality, Annual Reports (1977–07)

Equal Opportunities Commission, Annual Reports (1976–07)

Report of the Royal Commission on Trade Unions and Employers' Associations 1965–1968. Chairman: The Rt. Hon. Lord Donovan, Cmnd 3623, and 11 research papers published by the Commission.

Report of the Committee on Safety and Health at Work. Chairman: Lord Robens, 1972, Cmnd 5034.

Report of the Committee of Inquiry on Industrial Democracy. Chairman: Lord Bullock, Cmnd 6706.

Selected Bibliography

GENERAL BOOKS

Anderman, S.D., *Labour Law: Management Decisions and Workers' Rights* (3rd edn, London, 1998).
Bain, G.S. (ed.), *Industrial Relations in Britain* (Oxford, 1983).
Blackstones Employment Law Practice 2012 (eds. Bowers, J. et al.).
Deakin, S. and Morris, G., *Labour Law* (6th edn, Hart Publishing, 2012).
Kahn-Freund, O., *Labour and the Law* (3rd edn) by P.L. Davies and M.R. Freedland (London, 1983) (also available in German and Italian translations).
Kahn-Freund, O., *Labour Relations: Heritage and Adjustment* (London, 1979).
Kahn-Freund, O., *Selected Writings* (London, 1978).
Morris, G. and Archer, T.J., *Collective Labour Law* (London, 2000).
Smith, I.T. and Baker, A., *Smith & Wood's Employment Law* (11th edn, London, 2013).
Upex, R., Benny, R. and Hardy, S., *Labour Law* (3rd edn, Oxford 2008).

SPECIALIST BOOKS

Auerbach, S., *Legislating for Conflict* (Oxford, 1991).
Barnard, C., *E.C. Employment Law* (3rd edn, London, 2006).
[the late] Bercusson, B., *European Labour Law* (London).
Bowers, J., Duggan, M. & Reade, D., *The Law on Industrial Action and Trade Union Recognition* (Oxford, 2004).
Collins, H., *Justice in Dismissal* (Oxford, 1992).
Davies, P.L. and Freedland, M.R., *Labour Legislation and Public Policy* (Oxford).
Dickens, L., Jones, M., Weekes, B. and Hart, M., *A Study of Unfair Dismissal and the Industrial Tribunal System* (Oxford, 1985).
Doyle, B., *Disability Discrimination* (Bristol, 2008).
Dunn, S. and Gennard, J., *The Closed Shop in British Industry* (London, 1984).
Elias, P. and Ewing, K.D., *Trade Unions, Democracy, Members' Rights and the Law* (London, 1987).
Ewing, K.D., *The Right to Strike* (Oxford, 1990).
Ewing, K.D., *Trade Unions, the Labour Party and the Law* (Edinburgh, 1982).
Fredman, S. and Morris, G.S., *The State as Employer: Labour Law in the Public Services* (London, 1986).
Freedland, M.R. *The Contract of Employment* (London, 1976).
Hepple, B., Jacobs, A., Ramm, T., Veneziani, B. and Vogel-Polsky, E., *The Making of Labour Law in Europe: a Comparative Study of Nine Countries to 1945* (London, 1986).
Lord Wedderburn, *The Worker and the Law* (3rd edn, London, 1986).
Lord Wedderburn, *Employment Rights in Britain and Europe* (London, 1991).
Lord Wedderburn, *"Labour law: 40 years on"[2007]* Industrial Law Journal, vol. 36, pp. 397–424.
McMullen QC, (HHJ) J., Tuck, R., and Criddle, B. *Employment Tribunal Procedure* (London, 3 ed. 2004, LAG).
McMullen, J., *Business Transfers and Employee Rights* (London, 1998 updated).

Monaghan, K., *Equality Law* (Oxford, 2007)
Morris, G.S., *Strikes in Essential Services* (London, 1986).
Peston, R., *Brown's Britain* (London, 2005).
Upex, R., and Hardy, S. *Termination of Employment* (8th edn, Bristol, 2012).

Table of Cases

References are to paragraph numbers

Table of Statutes

References are to paragraph numbers.

Table of Statutory Instruments

References are to paragraph numbers.

Index

References are to paragraph numbers.

Index

Index

Index

www.ingramcontent.com/pod-product-compliance
Lightning Source LLC
Chambersburg PA
CBHW071422230926
51846CB00001B/112
* 9 7 8 9 0 4 1 1 9 9 6 3 8 *